D1283444

Brazil and the Great Powers, 1930–1939

The Politics of Trade Rivalry

LATIN AMERICAN MONOGRAPHS, No. 38

Sponsored by the Institute of Latin American Studies

The University of Texas at Austin

Brazil and the
Great Powers, 1930–1939

The Politics of Trade Rivalry

by Stanley E. Hilton

Foreword by José Honório Rodrigues

University of Texas Press   Austin & London

Library of Congress Cataloging in Publication Data

Hilton, Stanley E   1940–
    Brazil and the great powers, 1930–1939.
    (Latin American monographs; no. 38)
    Bibliography: p.
    Includes index.
    1. Brazil—Commercial policy. 2. Brazil—Commerce.
3. International economic relations. I. Title.
II. Series: Latin American monographs (Austin, Tex.);
no. 38.
HF1513.H54   382′.3′0981   75-17747
ISBN 0-292-70713-4

Contents

Tables

Foreword

This book began in a seminar on Brazilian history that I offered in 1963 at the University of Texas (Austin), where the author was a beginning graduate student. He quickly distinguished himself by his capacity for argumentation and his keen sense of criticism. During that semester he worked on the theme that would continue later to absorb him and he produced the embryo of this book in the form of a research paper, "Brazil and the German-American Schism, 1936–1942." He subsequently wrote a master's thesis (1964) and a doctoral dissertation (1969) on the same general topic. This subject, great-power rivalries in South America, has thus held Professor Hilton's interest for several years. During that time he has meticulously investigated the myriad aspects of the subject and consulted the relevant source materials. This unprecedented multiarchival research; the author's domination and assimilation of a vast array of documents; his capacity for interpretation and objectivity, which allowed him to overcome his own political leanings; and his organizational skills all combine to make this study a model of scholarship.

Hilton's book describes and interprets the absorbing subject of the struggle waged by the great powers—the United States, Germany, and Great Britain—for commercial supremacy in Brazil during the 1930s, a struggle highlighted by the conflict between the bilateralism of Nazi Germany and the liberal trade program defended by the government of Franklin D. Roosevelt. The United States, which by 1930 had replaced Great Britain as the dominant foreign power in Latin America, looked suspiciously on Nazi economic activity in the region, particularly in Brazil, where the Germans were most successful. This study analyzes the clashing interests of the three powers and the impact of their rivalry on Brazilian policy. One of the major contributions of this analysis is to reveal the decisive role played by the Brazilian military in the formulation of that policy.

This is the first full-scale treatment of the subject of German-American trade competition in a South American country during the 1930s. Alton Frye's *Nazi Germany and the American Hemisphere* (1967) touches only briefly on the issue, and his information is not always correct. Hans-Jürgen Schröder's *Deutschland und die Vereinigten Staaten, 1933–1939* (1970) is a solid study that discusses, in a general sense, German-American rivalry in South America. His major concern, however, is relations between Berlin and Washington, and his research, accordingly, was restricted to Germany and the United States. John D. Wirth's *The Politics of Brazilian Development, 1930–1954* (1969) was the first attempt, based on limited Brazilian and German materials, to explore the Brazilian side of the story. The reader will want to compare his study with Hilton's convincingly revisionist arguments. The account of the trade dispute in Frank D. McCann's recent *The Brazilian-American Alliance, 1937–1945* (1973) is based essentially on American documents and is hence unidimensional.

One of the most valuable documentary sources for recent international history is the voluminous collection of microfilmed German diplomatic records deposited in the National Archives in Washington, D.C. A small portion of these documents has been published in French, German, and English. Those relating to Latin America that appeared in the English-language volumes—a minute fraction of the total available—were translated into Portuguese under the title *O Brasil e o Terceiro Reich* (1968). The German archives, therefore, are practically unknown in Brazil and, indeed, in the field of Brazilian studies, a fact that greatly adds to the value of Hilton's book. On the two occasions that I had the pleasure of serving as visiting professor at the University of Texas, I was able to peruse a good deal of the German materials relating to Brazil and I can testify to his skillful handling of those materials. Hilton traveled to Germany to complement his research in the microfilmed records, and he utilized extensively American, British, and Brazilian archives as well. Among the latter were those of men like Getúlio Vargas and Oswaldo Aranha, who played decisive roles in national politics. It is this multiarchival character that makes this book the great lesson that the historiography of modern Brazil has been waiting for.

It is not only because of its unique documentary foundation, however, that this book is of great value to Brazilian studies. It is unique also because of the author's control and use of those sources in reconstructing the past. Hilton has brought an uncommon critical capacity to bear on the analysis of motives, policy options, and bargaining power. One may disagree with some of his views. He is reluctant, for example, to label a spade a spade, for he leaves aside the recent arguments of British historians who see in economic liberalism an instrument of imperialist penetration and does not, as I think he should, read imperialism into the trade struggle among the great powers. Be that as it may, I know of no book on Brazil by an American that compares with this one in its exhaustive examination of the most varied documentary sources and its new and original contributions to our understanding of modern Brazilian history. His capacity for work, his analytical skills, and his ability to reconstruct have permitted Professor Hilton to make what is to date the most important contribution of his generation to Brazilian studies.

José Honório Rodrigues

NOTE: José Honório Rodrigues is widely recognized as Brazil's leading contemporary historian. Former director of the Arquivo Nacional and the Instituto Brasileiro de Relações Internacionais in Rio de Janeiro, Professor Rodrigues has written numerous books, two of which—*Brazil and Africa* (1965) and *The Brazilians: Their Character and Aspirations* (1967)—have been published in English translations by the University of California Press and the University of Texas Press, respectively.

Acknowledgments

Research for this book was undertaken during several trips to Brazil and two to Europe, between 1966 and 1971. Generous grants from the National Defense Foreign Language Fellowship Program (1966), the Foreign Area Fellowship Program of the Social Science Research Council (1966–1969), and the Fulbright-Hays Faculty Research Program (1971) made this field work possible.

Professor Thomas F. McGann of the University of Texas at Austin offered encouragement and judicious guidance at every stage in the development of this book, and it is a pleasure to acknowledge my indebtedness to him for his aid and friendship. Robert A. Divine, also of the University of Texas at Austin, was likewise a valuable teacher and critic. José Honório Rodrigues stimulated my interest in Brazilian history, followed my work closely, and has been a source of constant encouragement. Francisco de Assis Barbosa provided assistance in countless ways, and I am indebted to Thomas E. Skidmore, Eul-Soo Pang, Robert Laurenty, Leslie Bethell, and Richard Graham for instructive critiques and helpful suggestions. My former colleagues at Williams College allowed me a semester's leave in 1971 to continue my research and I am grateful to them, especially Russell Bastert, who gave me the benefit of his perceptive criticism, and Robert G. L. Waite.

This study is based overwhelmingly on unpublished documents, many of them in private hands, and my debt to those many Brazilians who gave so generously of time and resources to assist me is profound. Alzira Vargas do Amaral Peixoto heads the list. She opened her father's papers to me, as she has done for several scholars, and tolerated my intrusion into her Praia do Flamengo home almost daily for the better part of a year. Ever willing to discuss her father or Brazilian politics, Dona Alzira in many enlightening conversations added new dimensions to the evidence available in the Vargas "archive." Another person who made a major contribution to this study is Dr. Euclydes Aranha Neto, son of former Foreign Minister Oswaldo Aranha. In addition to permitting me the use of his father's personal files, Dr. Euclydes kept the door of his office open and was a receptive listener to ideas and problems. Both he and Dona Alzira were most helpful in steering me to other people with information about either the period in general or the specific subject of foreign economic policy. General Pantaleão da Silva Pessôa, former head of the presidential Casa Militar and army chief of staff, spent countless hours in conversation with me over lunch, tea, or dinner illuminating many aspects of Brazilian history during his period of government service in the 1930s. Drawing upon an elephantine memory, this spry octogenarian provided an inquisitive interrogator with details that invariably proved correct when checked against other sources. He not only allowed me to consult his personal files, which had not been used previously, but also insisted that I take them to my apartment to peruse at my convenience. Ambassadors Afonso Arinos de Melo Franco and Afrânio de Melo Franco Filho gave me access to their papers, and their sister, Sra. Maria do Carmo Nabuco, graciously permitted me to examine the correspondence of two other brothers, Caio and Virgílio. In each case, they made a gratifying gesture of confidence in handing papers over to my possession for return at an uncertain date. Ambassador Maurício Nabuco was of great assistance in gaining permission for me to consult the personal papers of Ambassador Hildebrando Acioly. Sra. Olga Acioly, the latter's widow, upset her daily routine over a period of two months to enable me to use her husband's papers. For authorization to consult the files of Otávio Mangabeira, I am indebted to Sra. Edyla Mangabeira Unger and Dr. and Sra. Ival Távora Gama. The Bouças family— Drs. Vítor, Jorge, and D. Marinete—kindly opened the papers of their father, Valentim Bouças, and D. Marinete took time out from a busy schedule to accompany me to Ilha do Governador, where the papers are stored. Sra. Leda Collor Arnon de Mello generously allowed me to peruse the the files of her father, Lindolfo Collor, Brazil's first labor minister, and the family of Bertholdo Klinger kindly permitted me to consult the general's papers.

The enlightened attitude of Dr. Raul do Rêgo Lima, director of the Arquivo Nacional, made research in the Arquivo a profitable and pleasant experience. José Gabriel da Costa Pinto, the assistant director, and Margarida Diniz Câmara, head of the Seção Presidência da República, were particularly helpful. A special note of thanks must go to Marita España Iglesias, librarian at the Arquivo, who on occasion served with great efficiency as a research assistant and typist. Professor Pedro Calmon, president of the Instituto Histórico e Geográfico Brasileiro, kindly permitted me to consult the uncatalogued papers of José Carlos de Macedo Soares. Professor Calmon's capable assistant, Adelaide Alba, greatly facilitated my work at the Instituto. The many afternoons spent in the Arquivo Histórico at Itamaraty Palace, former home of the Ministry of Foreign Affairs, were made pleasant by the cheerful attentiveness of Constança Wright and her staff and by the extraordinary professional zeal of Miss Wright's successor, Martha Gonçalves. I am also deeply appreciative of the friendly assistance rendered by the staffs of the Arquivo da Marinha, the Fifth Section of the Estado-Maior do Exército, and the Seção de Manuscritos of the Biblioteca Nacional in Rio de Janeiro.

Deserving of praise for their efficiency and courtesy are the staffs of the Public Records Office in London, the Archiv des Auswärtigen Amts in Bonn, and the Bundesarchiv in Koblenz. In the United States the staffs of the Roosevelt Library at Hyde Park, the Library of Congress, Hoover Institute at Stanford University, and the Southwestern Archive and Manuscripts Collection at the University of Southwestern Louisiana were most helpful. All researchers of recent American foreign policy owe an immeasurable debt to Patricia Dowling, who supervises the State Department records in the National Archives. Robert Wolfe, head of the Modern Military Branch of the Archives, on numerous occasions gave me the benefit of his unparalleled knowledge of the captured German records collection.

My wife, Linda, rendered the invaluable service of reminding me from time to time that I was not living in the 1930s. Her faith and optimism added seasoning to whatever it is that I have brewed here.

S.E.H.

Introduction

The student of foreign policy and its formulation has traditionally faced special research problems in dealing with Latin American countries. Archival materials have simply not been available, particularly for more recent periods. Typically, the American scholar has relied almost solely on United States diplomatic records, and interpretations therefore have suffered inevitable distortion. The availability of untapped German official records, the recent decision of the British government to release its files for the World War II era, and, especially, the enlightened attitude of diverse Brazilian authorities and private individuals have now provided an opportunity for a fully documented case study in the recent foreign policy of a major Latin American nation. This book is the story of how Brazilian policy makers responded to the challenge—and opportunity—of trade rivalry among the great powers during the decade preceding World War II and why they responded as they did.

The history of Latin America as an arena of competition, if not for land then for commercial profit, among various extracontinental powers dates back, of course, to the early days of Spanish conquest, when French privateers seized two of the first treasure ships dispatched by Cortés from New Spain. The Caribbean throughout the sixteenth and seventeenth centuries was a major battleground among the Spanish, English, French, and Dutch, and the Dutch also seized and held part of Brazil for a quarter-century. Imperial rivalries in the New World came to a head in the eighteenth century, a period that saw the emergence of a new competitor in North America.

The contest in the nineteenth century was largely for markets and sources of raw materials. Except for Louis Napoleon's short-lived Mexican adventure, there was no serious undertaking by any extracontinental power to gain further territories in the New World. In Brazil, Great Britain enjoyed definite commercial supremacy until the latter part of the century. A longstanding special politico-commercial relationship with Lisbon greatly facilitated British penetration of Brazil after the flight to Rio de Janeiro of the Portuguese monarch, João VI, who escaped aboard a British man-of-war as Napoleon's troops over-ran the Iberian kingdom. Under tariff privileges conceded in 1810 by the Imperial government in Rio de Janeiro, British manufacturers dominated Brazil's import trade and British shipping companies figured prominently in the carrying of trade to and from Brazil. British capitalists invested heavily in Brazilian railroads, often built by British engineers; British investors purchased Brazilian bonds; and London banking houses periodically extended substantial loans to Brazilian government entities. Indeed, throughout the Empire—that is, until 1889—Brazil's only foreign loans were processed in London. After establishment of the republic that year, British financiers continued to play a dominant role in Brazilian financial life. By World War I the face value of total British investment in Brazil had risen to £224 million, British merchants were supplying nearly one-quarter of Brazil's imports, and they were purchasing about 13 percent of its exports.[1]

Late in the nineteenth century a formidable rival appeared in the form of Imperial Germany. Rapid industrialization in the service of a policy of national aggrandizement turned German attention to the promising markets and raw materials of South America. An expansion of trade with the region became, in the eyes of the devotees of *Weltpolitik*, a "necessity of life." The fact that German states had sent, and continued to send, colonists to Brazil, something that neither Great Britain nor the United States did on any significant scale, aided Germany's cause. The estimated 50,000 German settlers who emigrated to Brazil during the Empire had created by 1890 a German-speaking community of around 200,000, many members of which were engaged in import-export and banking activities. The low price of German goods and the capacity of the German manufacturer to adapt his product to local market conditions and tastes were additional factors in the growth of German commerce with Brazil. By the mid-1880s the Reich had become Brazil's second most important buyer, had surpassed France as a supplier of goods to Brazil, and ranked second only to Great Britain in exports to the South American nation. Hamburg became the leading coffee market in Europe, taking 20 percent of Brazil's production by the end of the century. German leather manufacturers purchased one-third of Brazil's offerings, and the Reich was by far the best market for Brazilian tobacco. During the decade preceding the world war, Germany's share of Brazil's import trade rose from 11.4 to 17.5 percent, and the Central European power purchased a steady average of around 15 percent of Brazil's exports.[2]

The United States since early in the nineteenth century had eyed British involvement in the Brazilian economy with misgiving, but it was unable to compete effectively until after mid-century. A rapid expansion of coffee cultivation in Brazil, the result of an opening up of new lands, coupled with a rising demand for coffee in the United States, which was experiencing a post–Civil War industrial boom, placed the United States in a position to challenge British interests in Brazil. After it abolished import duties on coffee in 1870, the United States consumed annually more than half of Brazil's coffee exports, and by World War I it was purchasing over half its rubber imports and most of its cacao from Brazil. In terms of value, American purchases of Brazilian products far exceeded those made by Great Britain and Germany, and in 1913 they constituted one-third of Brazil's overseas sales.[3] This trade relationship was not, however, a balanced one. American exports to Brazil lagged distantly behind imports from Brazil, a function of "Yankee thirst for Brazilian coffee and Brazilian predilection for European manufactured goods."[4] The American merchant not only fought against established tastes; he also lacked the credit and shipping facilities enjoyed by his British and German competitors. The result was that when the war began the United States was third on the list of suppliers to Brazil, with 15.7 percent of the latter's imports.[5]

The world war had a drastic effect on the trade relationships of the three powers with Brazil, providing the American merchant with an unparalleled opportunity. Brazil's trade with Germany was nonexistent by the war's end, and political relations between the two countries deteriorated to the point of Brazil's declaring war on Germany. Great Britain's purchases of Brazilian raw materials and foodstuffs declined only slightly, but, since it was forced to concentrate on the production of war items, its share of Brazil's import trade dropped to about 18 percent of the latter's total imports. The United States, on the other hand, made tremendous comparative gains. By 1918 it was supplying 47 percent of Brazil's imports, a threefold increase since 1913. American consumption of Brazilian products rose by one-third, from 33 to 46 percent of Brazil's total exports.[6]

The decade following the end of the war witnessed a revival of the intense prewar rivalry, as Great Britain and Germany endeavored to recapture their prewar positions and the United States maneuvered to consolidate its gains. American exporters managed to hold an average of 26 percent of Brazil's imports during the 1920s, which represented a striking advance over the prewar share but also reflected an inability to retain completely the ground won during the abnormal wartime situation. Purchases of Brazilian products by the United States remained fairly steady, at an annual average of 43 percent, during the decade preceding the Great Depression. Indicative of the rapidly growing American interest in Brazil was the increase in the investment of American capital there from $50 million in 1913 to over $550 million by 1930.[7]

Great Britain, the major source of Brazil's imports up to World War I, succeeded in surpassing the United States in the Brazil import trade only twice in the postwar years (1922 and 1923). The British share of the Brazilian market did rise—from 13 percent in 1921 to 21 percent in 1928—but Great Britain had to content itself with second place. As the Depression opened, British investments in Brazil stood at £287.3 million, an increase of nearly one-third since the beginning of the war. German interests showed a surprising resiliency. In 1918 the Reich had provided none of Brazil's imports; by 1929 it had risen to third on the list of Brazil's suppliers, furnishing 12 percent of that country's imports. Purchasing 11 percent of Brazil's exports in 1928, Germany was again the second leading market for the South American nation.[8]

The onset of the Great Depression inaugurated a new era in world politics. The rules of international political and economic intercourse were bent—or broken—with alarming ease in an era whose dominant attitude seemed to be that of beggar-thy-neighbor. Leaders of some countries sought radical solutions to national problems and adopted forceful means to satisfy national aspirations. Germany, of course, headed the list of unsatisfied states. The directors of the new Reich dreamed of German hegemony in Europe, but to attain that supremacy the nation had to develop its military capacity. To that end—the rearmament of Germany—various phases of national life were subordinated, including its economic activity. Industrial expansion and the acquisition of raw materials and foodstuffs became twin necessities of the Nazi program, and therefore an integral part of German foreign policy during the 1930s was an aggressive commercial policy aimed at finding new markets—or reconquering old ones.

A major feature of the international economy of the Depression decade was the clash between the bilateralism exploited by Nazi Germany—a "cut throat trouble-breeding method of trade," Secretary of State Cordell Hull once branded it—and the liberal system of trade championed by the Franklin Roosevelt administration. South America was the chief battlefield of this commercial struggle and Brazil the outstanding example of the success of German efforts, as Reich merchants doubled their sales to Brazil within a few short years. The remarkable expansion of trade between Brazil and the Third Reich was largely a result of methods and practices inimical to Washington's reciprocal trade agreements program, to which Brazil adhered, at least in principle, and which lay at the heart of the New Deal blueprint for international understanding. Because of the conflicting policies of the two major commercial partners, Brazilian decision makers faced serious problems in relations with both powers. The growth of Brazilian-German commerce also had important political connotations in an era of Nazi aggressiveness and became an active ingredient in the embitterment of relations between the United States and Germany, especially in the latter years of the decade when the United States became alarmed about alleged Nazi political penetration of South America. Great Britain, moreover, took a keen interest in the commercial resurgence of Germany in South America, since British sales to Brazil felt most keenly the pinch of German competition.

The resultant debate in Brazil over the nation's trade program, together with the Getúlio Vargas government's efforts to resolve the problems arising from the divergent demands of national and international clients, provides a revealing case study of decision making on a foreign policy issue vital to a country whose economy was largely dependent upon trade. The emphasis of this book is on the politics of the issue: the interests involved, alternatives perceived, sources of power, and bargaining techniques. Insights are offered into the influence of individuals and organizations on national policy during a period generally acknowledged as a watershed in modern Brazilian history. I have endeavored to go beyond the common level of analysis involving gross categorization and to "humanize" policy formulation by identifying personalities and probing their attitudes and motivation. One aspect of decision making that receives strong emphasis in this book is the policy maker's image of external reality, an image that determines his political action. This study also pays special attention to the impact of military demands on Brazil's economic policy, and the analysis here differs radically from previous interpretation. To place Vargas's trade program in proper context, a lengthy discussion of his government's attitude toward industrialization, which has likewise been misinterpreted, is included in chapter 1.

Although this book focuses on the formulation of Brazilian policy and diplomatic "style," it also provides revisionist insights into the nature and effectiveness of German, British, and, particularly, American diplomacy in South America during the critical era of the 1930s. In a sense, this book is a study in the failure of Good Neighbor diplomacy in an area of foreign relations dear to New Deal strategists.

Brazil and the Great Powers, 1930–1939

The Politics of Trade Rivalry

Chapter 1

Brazil's View of the World Crisis

Time has dulled the ominous character of the insistent warnings during the 1930s of impending international disaster, but to perceptive and concerned contemporaries such places and events as Manchuria, the Gran Chaco, Abyssinia, the Rhineland, Spanish Civil War, Anschluss, and Munich had grave significance. At the heart of the international political instability, many believed, lay the financial and commercial upheaval that ushered in the decade and whose reverberations touched all nations. As the Brazilian foreign policy elite— government leaders, diplomats, senior army and naval officers, business spokesmen, intellectuals—attentively surveyed this general unrest, vital questions came to mind: Where was the world heading? What was the essence of the crisis and what made states behave as they did toward other states? How did Brazil fit into the international scheme of things and what policies would best serve the national interest?

The men responsible for national strategies in the 1930s took little comfort from the Brazil they examined. A former foreign minister, writing on the eve of the Depression, had put it bluntly: ". . . Brazil," he bitterly acknowledged, "without a navy, without an army, and divided to the marrow, is worth next to nothing in international life."[1] The great bulk of the approximately 35 million inhabitants in 1930 were concentrated in urban clusters along an irregular coastline that would connect Maine to California, which meant that the country's huge interior was largely uninhabited. Indeed, there was less than one inhabitant per square mile in the great Amazon basin and adjacent areas. The country's transportation network was markedly inadequate for its size, a fact constantly lamented by geopolitically conscious military planners. At the time of the Revolution of 1930, Brazil had a total of slightly more than 76,000 miles of roads, mostly unpaved. Railway mileage in 1934 was less than 21,000. Communications with the hinterland were adequately developed only in the Southeast, and thus the North and drought-ridden Northeast could be reached from the nation's political and industrial center only by ship or plane. The quality of human resources was adversely affected by severe problems of health and nutrition. The infant mortality rate, even in urban areas, was strikingly high. In the northeastern city of Recife, for example, 27 percent of babies born did not live a full year. As late as 1940 over 40 percent of army recruits were being rejected for physical reasons. Roughly half the population, moreover, was illiterate.[2]

The nation's economy was unbalanced and no integrated national market existed. Industry in 1930 was still in its adolescent stage, and Brazil's traditional dependence upon the exportation of primary products—coffee constituted over 61 percent of total exports during the period 1889–1933—subjected national finances to the fluctuations of the international market. The impact of the Depression was marked, as coffee prices fell by 1931 to one-third of those prevailing during the five years preceding the crisis. Coupled to financial instability was a military capacity regarded by Brazilian and foreign professionals alike as deficient in all respects, particularly in terms of matériel and transportation.[3]

The nation's political experience during the early and middle years of the decade seemed to justify the most pessimistic of evaluations. The revolutionary coalition that took up arms against the federal government in October 1930 was a motley assortment of radical nationalists, liberal reformers, and disgruntled old-guard politicians. Some revolutionaries had vague notions of sweeping socioeconomic modifications; others wanted mainly to correct political abuse by instituting electoral reforms; still others took sides against the incumbent out of rancor over his obstinate insistence that the governor of his native state of São Paulo be selected as "official" candidate to succeed him as president. The opposition elements, led by the state political machines in Minas Gerais, Paraíba, and Rio Grande do Sul, campaigned under the banner of the Liberal Alliance and hoped to put Getúlio Vargas, the forty-two–year–old governor of Rio Grande do Sul, in presidential Catete Palace. Defeated at the polls, younger, more radical *aliancistas* led by Oswaldo Aranha, a small-town lawyer who had become a state secretary under Vargas, refused to accept the electoral verdict and engineered the revolt that in October drove the incumbent into exile.

Once the fighting was over, the revolutionary coalition disintegrated rapidly. The first two years of Vargas's dictatorial rule were characterized by constant political turmoil, as he maneuvered delicately between those who demanded a return to constitutional government and the radical elements headed by men like Aranha, his lifelong friend, who served the Revolution first as minister of justice and then as minister of finance; General Pedro de Góes Monteiro, who had commanded the rebel armies; and João Alberto, who became federal interventor in São Paulo. Regional jealousies compounded the situation, as *paulista* leaders resented the sudden political ascendency of the *gaúchos* from the South. The agitation of the first two years of the Provisional Government was capped by a three-month civil war that found the state of São Paulo, supported by a handful of old-guard malcontents from Minas Gerais and Rio Grande do Sul, pitted against the rest of Brazil.

Following suppression of the *paulista* rebellion, the political energies of the administration were drained by the tasks of pacifying São Paulo, weathering a severe political crisis in Minas Gerais late in 1933 that led to cabinet-level resignations, and organizing and supervising a constitutional convention. With Vargas's election by the convention in mid-1934 as president for a four-year term and promulgation of a new constitution, the political system opened up again. Politics, however, became even more turbulent and radical, with both military dissidents and Communists plotting against the government. The Left found organized expression in the Brazilian Communist party and its short-lived offspring, the National Liberation Alliance, whose supporters took to the streets for sporadic clashes with Plinio Salgado's right-wing Integralists, who sported green shirts and vociferously proclaimed the virtues of God, Family, and Country. The abortive Communist-led revolt in November 1935 came after months of tension, and it set in motion a train of events that ultimately led army chiefs to back Vargas in dissolving congress and establishing a discretionary regime known as the Estado Novo that would last from November 1937 to October 1945.[4]

If the national scene offered small cause for complacency, the international presented even less. Indeed, a major component of the foreign policy elite's image of the international environment in the 1930s was that an upheaval of unprecedented proportions was in the making. Fueling that conviction were repeated warnings of deep-rooted national antagonisms and ill-disguised hegemonic aspirations from observation posts around the globe.

Carlos Martins, later wartime ambassador to Washington, was deeply impressed by conditions in Europe during the early years of the decade, and in private letters to Foreign Minister Afrânio de Melo Franco (1930–1934) he voiced his concern. Depressed about the "collective insanity" he saw spreading across the continent, Martins warned of the imminent "change or end of European civilization." Europe, agreed Minister Mario Pimentel Brandão from Ankara, was heading toward a "gigantic *sauve qui peut!*" To be sure, said a leading Rio de Janeiro daily, "Europe was never so near to war as today." All countries, General Góes Monteiro cautioned Vargas early in 1934, "are actively preparing themselves for the new conflagration." Aboard the liner carrying him later that year to his new post as ambassador to the United States, Aranha recorded impressions of the European scene gathered during a brief stopover in Italy. "War industries are engaged in unprecedented activity," he informed Vargas. "Instincts are bristling, like those of threatened or aggressive beasts."[5]

Spain in 1934 reminded a Brazilian official of Ernest Renan's France: "It seems always to be threatened with rupture of an aneurysm." One day, he remarked prophetically, there would be a "spewing of blood and *adiós República en España* . . . [sic]" Painfully obvious were the instability and indecisiveness of France, so dear to the more tradition-steeped members of the elite, particularly the "old-guard" at Itamaraty, who chafed at Gallic impotence. "France, *our* France, is like a woman going through menopause!" cried the minister in Berlin with poignant irritation in 1933. When he visited the French capital the following year, the counselor of the London embassy encountered a "general anarchy" that revived memories of the "troubled days that preceded Fascism in Rome." The Paris embassy was a sad witness to French internal divisions and the ominous challenge from across the Rhine. France was experiencing "one of the worst crises in its history . . . ," an embassy official privately wrote in 1935. "People are talking openly of war . . . ." Official reports supported that view. "In the present state of things . . . ," reported the chargé d'affaires, "the slightest thing may launch the catastrophe."[6]

As Europe stumbled from crisis to crisis, the probability of a general conflict occupied an increasingly prominent place in the political commentaries of Brazilian observers. Confirming previous forecasts, the Ethiopian embroglio came to a head in 1935, laying bare the "real situation" in Europe, according to a diplomat in Geneva, who saw the continent divided into "satisfied and unsatisfied" states. "3,500,000 men in arms and 9,000 planes are ready for battle at any moment and tempers are ripe for the fight," noted General Staff analysts. "The struggle," Aranha generalized, "is one of life and death among nations."[7]

Germany was accurately described by Brazilian envoys in Berlin as the real storm center, and policy makers in Rio de Janeiro could by the middle of the decade leaf through stacks of dispatches and telegrams from the mission at 25 Tiergartenstrasse assessing the Nazi military buildup, the impotency of the League of Nations, and turmoil across the continent.[8] Ratification of the Franco-Soviet pact and Hitler's daring march into the Rhineland in 1936 launched, in the words of the Berlin legation, a "more agitated and grave" phase in the unfolding of the international drama. "The four horsemen of the Apocalypse are again on the move," cried one publicist. To officers on the General Staff, Hitler's bold move meant that for all practical purposes the conflict had begun. The navy minister, too, privately worried that the "international political situation is becoming daily more grave," a theme that his army colleague sounded in an official report to Vargas.[9]

The outbreak of civil strife in Spain a few months later provided additional reinforcement of Brazilian perceptions. Bolstering what government leaders read in official reports and newspapers were private letters from Berlin, Rome, Paris, Tokyo, and other points signaling the inevitable: "War!"[10] On vacation in southern France, a member of the Paris embassy listened to Nationalist cannon bombarding Irún and San Sebastián across the Bay of Gascony and brooded over the European situation. "The fact is that one speaks only of war and thinks only of war," he gloomily advised the director of the Political Section of the Ministry of Foreign Affairs. After spending several days in Germany, Itamaraty's press officer called the attention of Foreign Minister José Carlos de Macedo Soares (1934–1937) to the "intense and formidable" rearmament there, where "everything is done militarily and the country lives and develops with weapons in hand." Luis Simões Lopes, the administrative expert and confidant of Vargas who subsequently organized Brazil's civil service, was also in Europe at the time and wrote the president that he was caught by the "violent and absorbing" feeling of being on the "eve of catastrophe." The whole continent, agreed the minister at the Hague, stood at the brink of a "great bloodbath."[11]

Although understandably less inclined to discuss them publicly, Brazilian leaders were also deeply concerned about developments on the South American continent. The Leticia territorial dispute between Peru and Colombia (1932–1933) and particularly the bitter and bloody

Chaco War (1932–1935) between Bolivia and Paraguay greatly reinforced the image of general international instability that formed in the minds of policy makers in Rio de Janeiro. A high-ranking diplomat summed up widespread feeling when he remarked that Bolivia and Paraguay might prove to be the "Balkans of our America."[12] Cessation of hostilities in neither case changed that image. Brazilian leaders in 1934 still were keeping an uneasy eye on the disgruntled neighbors to the northwest, since their duel for Leticia might "at any moment" be rekindled, and after well more than a year of Chaco peace talks that situation remained cause for "grave apprehension" in Rio de Janeiro, especially in high military circles.[13]

The focal point of uncertainty and instability in South America, in terms of Brazilian strategic planning, was traditional rival Argentina. Brazilian observers watched uneasily in the 1930s as Argentine military preparations reached unprecedented heights and the machinations of the Argentine Foreign Office strengthened the already grave suspicion in Rio de Janeiro, where policy makers viewed that southern antagonist as an expansionist, potentially aggressive power. Argentina's poorly concealed support of Paraguay in the Chaco War and her own alleged designs on Bolivian territory were proof sufficient, in Brazilian eyes, that "constant vigilance" was needed.[14] General Góes Monteiro, now minister of war, suggested early in 1934 that "Argentina . . . has real interests in the continuation of that conflict, since this is a step toward the hegemony she has always desired." A general recently returned from the Mato Grosso frontier reached the same conclusion. "The war may continue for a long time," he recorded, "given the well-known fact that Paraguay has a rich uncle (Argentina) who favors it with credit and officers . . ." Vargas himself privately noted at the end of the year that Argentina was openly providing Paraguay "with all resources," while at the same time she massed troops on the Bolivian border and advocated the "reabsorption of Bolivia as a former part of the vice-royalty of La Plata." A naval officer voiced the general anxiety of Brazilian policy makers when he commented that the goal of Argentina's foreign policy was to "establish solidly its political, military, and economic hegemony on the continent."[15]

The idea of the precariousness of peace and likelihood of a major war thus formed an important ingredient in the foreign policy elite's perception of the international environment. That image was made even more ominous by a conviction that power and naked self-interest were the only determinants of international behavior. "The truth of the moment is nationalism," Minister of Education Gustavo Capanema put it. Brazilian officials like General Eurico Dutra saw the world as divided into two classes of nations: "the large and the small, . . . those who have great interests at stake and those who have minor ones . . ." One publicist likened the international arena to a "gaming board where five or six are the players. . . . The other nations are second-class figures," he concluded.[16]

That smaller powers lived in the shadow of the stronger was a typical comment in policy-making circles. As head of the delegation to the Geneva Disarmament Conference, Macedo Soares on one occasion admonished his compatriots to "stick to reality" and expect no consideration from the great powers that Brazil could not impose. "International relations," he reminded them, "are not yet regulated in the slightest by the principle of the juridical equality of sovereign states. The great powers for certain will make the decisions . . ." Indeed, a nation's voice, wrote the minister of navy in mid-1932, was listened to "in accordance with the cannon that it represents, whether this please or displease the theorists of pacifism." The difficulties often encountered by weaker countries in international confrontations became irritatingly clear to Valentim Bouças, a prominent businessman-official representing Brazil at the London Monetary Conference. Exasperated, Bouças dispatched a letter to Aranha, then minister of finance, saying that he was convinced of the need first to develop "a great army and navy and then come over here and strut about."[17]

These beliefs gained strength as the decade progressed. Aranha in mid-1934 spoke of his concern that "right and protection" were rapidly disappearing from the world arena, while a naval captain alerted O Jornal readers to the fact that not reason or justice but the "law of the strongest" prevailed in international politics. History and current trends certainly vindicated the view, noted Góes Monteiro, that "no diplomacy, however brilliant and astute, can succeed without the decisive support of arms."[18] German scorn for the Versailles Treaty, coupled with Italy's scorn for Ethiopian sovereignty in 1935 and the response that Italy's military onslaught on the African country elicited from the great powers, was in Brazilian eyes further confirmation of the lawless, selfish character of world society. Evaluating the policies of European states in the Ethiopian crisis, one Itamaraty analyst depicted them as designed only to further national interests under the guise of law and principles of justice. Hitler's unopposed advance into the Rhineland early in 1936, in violation of the Locarno agreements, merely showed Brazilian observers once again that "right is always on the side of the stronger and that a battery of cannon is worth as much as an entire treatise on international law."[19] The failure of the League of Nations to meet the challenges and the accommodating attitude of its principal members were studied carefully by Brazilian officials, one of whom typically dismissed the League as a reflection of "human capacity for simulation and perfidy." The Spanish conflict was only the latest in a chain of examples that by 1937 had convinced Brazilian diplomats that no country "plays a clean game and each one pursues only its own interests."[20]

If realism and self-interest guided international behavior in a world heading for catastrophe, the essence of that realism, the *Zeitgeist*, appeared to be economic in nature. "Diplomacy," remarked Vargas in his platform speech in 1930, "is increasingly orienting itself in the direction of economic problems." To defend Brazilian interests in the "stiff economic competition characteristic of these times" was the major objective of administrative reforms undertaken by Foreign Minister Melo Franco after the successful October revolt. Bouças's missions to London and New York left him convinced that the era was one of "struggle [for] financial domination among the major countries," a conclusion that became common currency within government and diplomatic councils. The minister of agriculture, for example, in a closed session of the CFCE late in 1934, was unequivocal: "All courtesy, all diplomacy serve only to conceal one fact—the commercial battle among nations," he exclaimed. Surveying the European situation, a consul in Brussels predicted that the "wars of tomorrow will be world, instead of continental, ones because of the economic question, which is increasingly urgent." The experience of a special financial mission to Europe early in 1935 seemingly justified such pessimism. "We encountered in Europe a policy of commercial aggression that cannot be gauged from afar," a member of the delegation subsequently informed the CFCE. To one prominent figure on the Conselho, it was clear that Brazil found itself "in a period of economic war in time of peace."[21]

A wild scramble for overseas markets and sources of raw materials was seen as the essence of the economic conflict. In order to conquer markets, "all civilized nations have become gladiators," observed Vargas in 1931. The politics of the Far East certainly seemed to support that judgment. Tokyo proved to be a thoroughly disagreeable assignment for Carlos Martins—". . . we have already set a record in six months: diphtheria, typhoid and scarlet fever, pleurisy" and "a dozen earthquakes, some really terrifying,"[22]—but it permitted the ambulatory diplomat to observe at close hand that "frightful chaos" spreading across Asia that he had distantly glimpsed from his post in Europe three years earlier. Japan was being swept by an "insatiable and restless nationalism," and imperial expansion was the common goal of both military and civilian leaders, he privately warned Macedo Soares in 1934. Japanese authorities, according to Martins, saw salvation from economic woes in "an intense commercial policy," and in a long letter to Vargas at the end of that year he noted that the "leitmotif" of his conversations with government and business representatives had been Japan's need for Brazilian cotton, wool, manganese, nickel, and other products. So intense was Japanese interest that it was alarming him, Martins exaggeratedly claimed, to speak of business deals. "Get me out of here before they propose to buy Sugar Loaf," he exclaimed. Martin's successor shared his perception of the expansionist thrust of Japanese trade policy, arguing in 1936 that Tokyo's interest in Brazil was not so much political as it was "commercial and directed toward our raw materials."[23]

The Good Neighbor policy of the new Roosevelt administration had essentially commercial objectives, in the eyes of responsible Brazilian officials. The United States was seeking to emulate "Japan in Asia, who is excluding by all methods the Europeans from trade with China . . . ," wrote the head of the delegation to the Montevideo Conference in 1933. "Given the impossibility of employing the means that Japan is using in the Orient, the Americans want to intensify the process of peaceful approximation." In surveying the South American scene, Brazilian observers perceived the same forces at work. A desire for Bolivian petroleum, for example, was the dominant theme in diplomatic and military documents explaining Argentina's policy in the Chaco embroglio, and Vargas privately expressed the belief that the aim of Argentina's continental policy was to carve out an enlarged sphere of influence in central South America and transform Buenos Aires into a "great emporium of raw materials."[24]

The thrust of European politics left Aranha convinced that a "new era of colonial ambitions, determined more by economic factors than strictly political ones, is going to take charge of universal destinies." Reflecting on the response of the powers to the Italo-Ethiopian crisis, Melo Franco sardonically commented that "what they all want is to take over Ethiopia's natural resources, each one trying for the greatest share." João Alberto, future wartime coordinator of economic mobilization, likewise viewed Mussolini's venture as an "objective demonstration of Europe's colonial demonstration."[25]

Given Brazil's lack of military strength and its political and economic stability, a feeling of being endangered, not only economically but politically as well, of being vulnerable or exploitable, was a logical and inevitable result of the perceived ruthlessness of international competition, the imperialistic bent of stronger states, and the apparent willingness of other powers to accommodate such urges.

The level of threat perception was logically high within military circles. The Letícia dispute gave rise to a series of incidents on Brazilian borders and raised in the collective mind of the high command serious doubts about Brazil's being able to remain neutral and assert its sovereignty without resort to arms. The General Staff was sufficiently uneasy to urge a strenghthening of defenses in the Northwest and recommend that plans be formulated to meet a possible attack on Brazil.[26] The Chaco War was a source of even deeper anxiety to military planners, who kept an attentive eye focused on frontier defenses in the West and South. Border incidents during the conflict were frequent, and Brazilian shipping on the Paraguayan River was harassed and on at least one occasion subjected to an air attack. The main fear of the General Staff was that the war might spread and Brazil might find itself pitted against a militarily superior Argentina.[27]

If the danger at home seemed more urgent, the implications of extracontinental trends were not to be ignored. In the midst of "worldwide agitation," remarked General Pantaleão da Silva Pessôa, head of the presidential Casa Militar, in 1934, "this Brazilian corner of the earth heightens curiosity and awakens greed." A renowned literary figure and prominent official in the fascistic Integralist party, Gustavo Barroso, published a book that year entitled *Brasil: Colônia de Banqueiros* [Brazil: colony of bankers], in which he argued that the "fundamental problem of our country is its century-long enslavement to international capitalism," a theme oft heard in Brazil during the 1930s. The book struck a responsive chord in the Brazilian reading public and quickly became a best seller by local standards. By 1937 it had gone through six editions. One general, the commandant of the Military Academy, recommended the book to cadets in 1935 because it was "a protest and cry of alarm for our economically enslaved Fatherland . . ."[28]

Could economic dependency become political subordination? This was a question many Brazilians asked themselves, and the times suggested an ominous answer. The argument that European interest in tapping the economic potential of Africa was a decided threat to Brazil's export sector was a common one;[29] translation of that interest into military action turned the attention of policy makers to Brazil's own unpopulated interior, and the similarity was disquieting. Army intelligence officers, taking uneasy note of the "new imperialist thrust" that seemed to be seeking the "line of least resistance," reminded the high command in 1935 of Brazil's weak military posture and its geographic handicaps. In its annual report for the following year, the General Staff again underscored the fear that the "ambitions and claims of Germany, Italy, and Japan, propagandists of a new division of lands, constitute a latent danger for Brazil." General Waldomiro Lima, after returning in 1937 from a tour of observation with the Italian army, openly cautioned fellow officers that Brazil was arousing the "greed of the desperate." Indeed, because of its geography and military weakness, Brazil was "a magnetic field that excites the greed of stronger powers," declared Góes Monteiro on assuming the post of chief of staff, an idea he reiterated in a subsequent secret report to the minister of war.[30]

The conviction that international political trends boded ill for Brazil was not one imposed by military men, whose very profession might make them overly sensitive in that regard. Civilian policy makers shared fully the high command's uneasiness over international developments. If the subjugation of Ethiopia were allowed, wrote one diplomat in Europe, "it would be difficult to limit that expansionist tendency, and tomorrow one might discover that the Amazon is a vast propitious field for Italy to pour her surplus population into." João Alberto expressed his anxiety when he admonished Vargas early in 1936 that "to cross our arms before the spectacle of abandonment of more than 60 percent of our territory is to justify Italy's performance in Abyssinia." Foreign Minister Macedo Soares (1934–1937) was sufficiently concerned to propose during the planning stages of the Buenos Aires Peace Conference that year that nations of the Western Hemisphere make a strong declaration against the notion that industrialized nations deficient in raw materials "have the right to take possession of lands where they exist in abundance." Aranha also underscored the problem, since "more than any other country" Brazil was the "natural and easy" target for imperialist ambitions. In 1937 the secretary general of Itamaraty privately spelled out the sources of danger: not only Russia, but also Germany, Italy, and Japan, the "three great powers of prey, hungry for land and raw materials," were casting "greedy glances" at Brazil. The nation, in view of its "natural riches so coveted by others," had never faced a greater challenge, agreed industry spokesman Roberto Simonsen.[31]

An image of national isolation in South America, where Brazilian policy makers saw their country surrounded by latently hostile Spanish American neighbors, reinforced the Brazilian sense of threat. The theme of Brazil as a Portuguese American island in a Spanish American archipelago was a traditional one in Brazilian thought, but in the turbulence of the 1930s it gained new dimensions. In case of general war on the continent, Brazil must reckon with the opposition of all border countries, a naval strategist warned in 1932. "Racial hatred, difference in language, smallness of territory . . . all conspire against us." An army planner voiced the same preoccupation. The "harsh reality" was that Brazil was "isolated in the concert of nations," he wrote, especially in South America, where the "enmity" of Spanish American countries was "traditional." From his vantage point in Santiago, Ambassador José P. de Rodrigues Alves saw the situation in the same light. Brazil was the only country in South America that did not speak Spanish and this fact, combined with its size, made it an object of "jealousy," he reminded Itamaraty in 1934. Commercial Attaché Paulo Hasslocher in Washington went so far as to argue that "all the Spanish American countries" would already have turned on Brazil had it not been for its "firm friendship" with the United States. Aranha sought to reinforce the warning. "The Indo-Spanish countries are our natural enemies; they cannot inspire confidence and even today . . . they retain suspicions toward us inherited from Iberian struggles and heightened by continental rivalries," he privately cautioned Vargas. During the preparatory stages of the Buenos Aires Peace Conference, Itamaraty planners opposed the idea of creating an inter-American court, because Brazil "not only cannot count on the sympathies of the majority of the Spanish American countries, but even more" their "natural tendency" would be to favor Brazil's adversary in any litigation. That tendency could have serious consequences, Góes Monteiro concluded early in 1938. Should Brazil find itself forced into war in South America the nonbelligerent Spanish American states would not remain neutral very long, he told Minister of War Dutra. "On the contrary," he explained, "all of them consider themselves despoiled of territories by Brazil" and would "not lose the opportunity, if they were not already set for invasion."[32]

It was the Western Hemisphere, and more specifically the South American continent, that Brazilian policy makers regarded as their country's arena of active international political activity, one that constituted a subsystem in which Brazil sought the status of great power. With no colonies or territorial ambitions, Brazil—its leaders believed— had but slight stake in the politics of the European crisis. Government officials were well aware of national capabilities and needs, and they were alive to the challenges and special demands of the decade. The conclusion to which their self-image and their perception of international conditions led them was that Brazil should avoid involvement in political quarrels beyond its borders, especially in Europe, and should concentrate instead on a strategy designed to reduce national economic dependence upon external clients as a means of cushioning the nation against the economic and political shifts of international life, as well as a means of equipping the country for its longed-for role of arbiter of South America's future. The strategy adopted by the men of 1930 consisted of two major elements: industrialization and its necessary complement, expanded foreign trade. And only increased state intervention and supervision, Vargas and his counselors reasoned, would make execution of that strategy possible.

The historians' judgment of Vargas and his attitude and achievements in the area of industrialization and planning has not done justice to the enigmatic and reluctant revolutionary of 1930. He has been depicted as a man devoted to the pre–World War I international division of labor, with consequently no interest in economic planning or industrialization, at least prior to establishment of the Estado Novo in 1937.[33] The record shows, however, that Vargas was strongly committed to a policy of balanced economic development, and that industrialization therefore ranked high on his list of national objectives from the very beginning of his long period of rule. Examination of this question is necessary in order to place Brazilian trade policy in proper perspective.

The international crisis had a profound impact on the economic ideas of the revolutionary leaders, who strongly questioned the wisdom and suitability of an export-dominated economy. Not only the country's "industrial development," declared Vargas in 1930, but also its "very national security" required that it develop its own steel industry in order to gain greater independence from foreign suppliers. The same theme he emphasized in a speech four months after taking over the government. "Our epoch marks in the history of the world a grave moment of serious social transformations . . . ," he said, urging his listeners to adopt as a "civil postulate a commitment to increase our agriculture and perfect our industries, so that feeding and clothing ourselves with imported foods and clothes will be considered a lapse of patriotism." But the "maximum problem" of the economy, he reiterated, was the development of steel-making capacity.[34]

The conviction that industrialization was necessary for national self-preservation hardened in ensuing years. Valentim Bouças, one of Vargas's intimate counselors, on more than one occasion stressed the necessity of industrialization. International economic life, he wrote early in 1935, was "intransigently dominated by an intolerant economic and financial nationalism of fatal consequences for nations unable to transform the basic products of the land." Brazil must continue to work toward creating "an efficient and orderly agro-manufacturing system," he admonished. "Countries that neglect their industries will play only the role of colonies," he reminded government planners on another occasion. "That is the spectacle we see today in Africa. Ethiopia was an agrarian country, rich in unexplored mineral resources. . . . An industrial power absorbed it. Agrarian China is crumbling . . . Agrarian Manchuko and Korea are dependencies of industrial Japan."[35]

The lesson of world trends was not lost on other influential presidential advisers. Aranha in Washington took anxious note of the impending holocaust and warned of the need to prepare for its "grave" consequences. Brazil had to develop its industries in order to free itself from "countries that are carrying out a colonial policy," he asserted. "We are in this instant seeing the colonial expansion of Europe threatening our economy . . . ," agreed a member of the Conselho Federal de Comércio Exterior. "Let's organize our domestic market through development of our industrial potential . . ." Reflecting on the current international "economic war," even the agricultural representative on the Conselho campaigned on behalf of manufacturing. It was a question, he explained, of "making redoubled efforts to develop a policy for defense of . . . our very national existence."[36]

The steel question, as his speeches indicated, was an issue dear to Vargas's heart. On numerous occasions he spoke of his dream of Brazil as a steel-producing nation to General Pessôa, his chief military counselor during 1933–1935. The problem, of course, was complex and required careful planning. Consequently, Vargas set up special committees to study related aspects, such as transportation facilities, mineral resources, and internal steel needs and consumption.[37] Establishment of a large-scale industry also required capital, which the Brazilians did not have and which European and American investors were unable or reluctant to invest.

Political stability was clearly necessary for execution of a program requiring coordinated planning and considerable governmental resources, and such stability was lacking prior to May 1938. Vargas also was confronted by a lack of consensus on the steel issue. A National Steel Commission set up in the Ministry of War in 1931 concluded that the "important problem at hand" was acquiring coal by exporting iron ore. "The development of metallurgy, in the Commission's view, depended on a number of other factors, such as the growth of the domestic market and the improvement of technical skills in Brazil."[38] The scheme of Percival Farquhar, an American promoter who wanted to set up a modern steel works and run it with coal obtained by shipments of iron ore, initially caught Vargas's sympathy, but open discussion of the plan inevitably provoked unproductive ultranationalist attacks.[39] After 1935, when Vargas submitted Farquhar's plan to congress as a government-sponsored proposal, debates "dragged on inconclusively" until the closing of the political system in 1937.[40] After that, with a stable internal situation and the American government now disposed—because of fear of German penetration of South America—to assist in development projects in Brazil, Vargas moved relatively quickly to carry out his long-sought objective of providing his country with a modern steel complex.

Textile manufacturers, given Vargas's strong commitment to industry, enjoyed particularly "harmonious" relations with the revolutionary regime. They lobbied effectively with the central government to obtain various favors, including a ban (1931) for three years on machinery imports to combat alleged overproduction. Spokesmen for plant owners, at Vargas's express instructions, were consulted on tariff matters and sat on various government councils.[41] A multitude of interstate taxes hindered the internal circulation of products, thus discouraging entrepreneurial activity. Vargas, decrying this situation, signed a decree in 1931 providing for the gradual elimination of interstate duties, a step hailed with "lively enthusiasm" and "gratitude" by the Centro de Indústrias in São Paulo.[42] Although the government did not systematically utilize exchange control as a mechanism for promoting industrialization, it did favor industry in its allocation of scarce foreign exchange, classifying "essential imports" as second in importance to government expenditures. American exporters having difficulty placing industrial products in the Brazilian market discovered that "essential imports" meant items needed by Brazilian manufacturers, who received "highly preferential" exchange treatment. Manufacturers of some items, such as tobacco products, interested in foreign sales also received special privileges when exchanging foreign currencies for milreis.[43]

The tariff was a weapon consciously used by the Vargas government to encourage industrialization by shaping the composition of imports. The tremendous growth of cement manufacturing, for example, was a result in part of the elimination in 1932 of import duties on plant equipment. Entrepreneurs interested in industrializing the meat industry were at the same time given reductions of 30 percent in the duties on imported machinery, tools, and vehicles needed to operate canning plants. In response to inquiries from anxious state officials and manufacturers, Vargas made a point of assuring them that he would continue his protectionist policies, and early in 1934 his government moved to fulfill that pledge. Exemptions or reductions of tariffs were granted to importers of equipment used by producers of glass, tires and other rubber items, alcohol, cellulose, and similar light manufactures. While encouraging vital imports, the government kept the duties on imported articles, cement for example, at levels sufficient to enable domestic industry to compete effectively.[44] The plight of American exporters of paper drinking items provides a graphic illustration of the protection extended to Brazilian manufacturers under the tariff revisions of 1932. Bemoaning a 300 percent ad valorem duty levied on paper cups that year, a New York firm complained two years later that its previous "considerable" trade in Brazil had been "almost completely eliminated" as a result. British observers likewise noted that a "good deal" of the market for paper products was being seized by the expanding domestic industry, and that imports were also dropping rapidly "in every department and branch of the cotton and wool industries" because of the "deliberate policy of . . . increasing the protection given to the national industries."[45]

The new tariff of 1934 was, as Finance Minister Oswaldo Aranha assured Vargas, a protectionist one. Some rates were maintained, those on foreign goods similar to domestically produced ones were raised "in just terms," and semifinished items and equipment for domestic industries continued to receive "really impressive" concessions.[46] Not only the government, which one might suspect of political motives, but interested commercial observers as well, foreign and Brazilian, also hailed—or denounced—the tariff as a shield for domestic manufacturers. The new scale, said an American spokesman, was "frankly a protective one," a judgment that a French analyst ("nettement protectioniste") shared. Most conclusive of all, however, was the reaction of the Brazilian Industrial Confederation (BIC): ". . . the new customs tariff, in general, left the best of impressions in industrial circles," wrote the president of the Confederation to the new finance minister. Of the "relatively small number" of revisions sought by the Confederation, the duties in most cases were judged too high. The fact that the BIC drew up its request for modification only on August 24, one week before the new duties went into effect, when the tariff had been published early in June, further suggests the Confederation's overwhelming satisfaction with the tariff.[47] When it was politically convenient, of course, manufacturing interests criticized the tariff, but they never succeeded in demonstrating that it damaged their production.

The tariff during the 1930s was not erected indiscriminately around all forms of manufacturing activity. Because of the severe exchange crisis of the early Depression years, those manufacturers dependent upon imported raw materials suffered most. To attenuate that problem, one of the campaigns-within-a-campaign undertaken by the Vargas government was to prod industry into using domestic raw materials. "Industrial exploitation of this country's raw materials is without doubt a factor decisive to our economic progress," Vargas declared after one year in office. The idea of independence from foreign suppliers underlay, of course, the importance that he attached to a domestic steel industry based as much as possible on domestic fuels. With regard to the tariff revisions sought by the Brazilian Industrial Confederation in 1934, the government in several cases—oils for soap, for example—justified the higher rates on the grounds that similar domestic ingredients were available. It was thus primarily to those manufacturers who collaborated in the drive to heighten Brazil's self-sufficiency, without imposing huge sacrifices on the consumer, that the Vargas administration directed tariff favors. Graphic evidence of the extent to which tariff—and foreign exchange—privileges attended manufacturing needs was revealed by industry itself in a postwar study that showed that *bens de produção*—raw materials, fuels, equipment, and machinery—constituted an average of 95 percent of Brazil's imports during the triennium 1935–1937, that is, roughly the period between the Tariff of 1934 and launching of the Estado Novo.[48]

A major conceptual weakness of the argument that Vargas was opposed to industry lies in its neglect of a question crucial to an evaluation of his economic program: the relationship between economic policies and development, on the one hand, and human resources and social environment, on the other. The process of industrialization involves more than capital and entrepreneurship, and the conception and implementation of policies does not occur in a vacuum. By ignoring the importance of human capital for industrial growth and divorcing policy formulation and execution from its political and bureaucratic milieu, previous writers have overlooked not only major hurdles confronting the Vargas administration, but also other contributions that it made to the development process prior to 1937.

Vargas's approach to economic development was not conventional in the sense that he perceived only the "modern" sector as the proper focus of government attention. More appropriately, he would belong in the camp of what Charles Anderson has called the "democratic reformers," whose emphasis is on the whole spectrum of interests and needs. Vargas's public statements reflect, indeed, a keen awareness of the necessity for social overhead and infrastructural improvements before sound development could occur. The general message contained in the Liberal Alliance platform that he read to a *carioca* audience in January 1930 was that he favored a government dedicated to the interests of all Brazilians. He spoke of a renovation of political and administrative practices, promising such electoral reforms as the secret ballot, which was instituted in 1933 along with female suffrage. The "social question" demanded attention, he said, stressing that workers needed "tutelary" laws covering education, hygiene, housing, factory conditions, and old age and disability protection.[49]

Education, economists agree, is an area of social investment vital to industrial growth in underdeveloped regions.[50] Vargas realized the significance of education for national development when, in his platform speech, he labeled it an "urgent" problem and said that the creation of a federal ministry in that field was "indeferrable." Within months of assuming dictatorial powers, he issued a decree establishing the country's first Ministry of Health and Education, and the code that he promulgated in September 1931 to govern the administration of the interventors he appointed in the various states stipulated that they spend at least 10 percent of local revenues on public education. Efforts of the central government during the prewar decade were severely hampered by budgetary difficulties, but progress was nonetheless significant. The number of students per 1,000 inhabitants rose from 50 in 1929 to 80 ten years later. The Revolution found 28,000 primary schools throughout Brazil; by 1940 it had provided an additional 14,000. The elementary school population was 75 percent greater when the war broke out than it had been in 1931, and the number of students enrolled in secondary schools increased from 90,000 to 227,000, a doubling of the number per 1,000 inhabitants.[51]

Federal activities in the field of labor and social welfare legislation, as well as education, show that the concept of human capital, that is, that the quality of human resources is a key ingredient in the development mix, was not alien to government leaders. Vargas is known as the father of Brazilian labor laws. It was he who decreed the establishment of Brazil's first Ministry of Labor, Industry, and Commerce only weeks after taking control of the government. Over the next few years his administration decreed laws limiting working hours and providing for paid vacations, old-age and disability compensation, and, subsequently, minimum wages.[52]

Politics undoubtedly played a role in Vargas's labor policy, but without question he perceived the developmental implications of improving the worker's situation. In January 1930 he explained that the goal of the social welfare measures he advocated was a "valorization of human capital, since the gauge of man's social utility is his productive capacity." Four years later he reminded the Constitutional Assembly that the common man could not achieve "social efficiency" as long as he was physically unsound or worked in an unhealthy environment. Ministry of Labor technicians, in discussing the advantages of a minimum wage, emphasized the favorable repercussions that amelioration of working-class conditions would have on industrial production, and Vargas himself unequivocally made the point. Referring to the labor laws enacted since 1930 and to steps taken toward a minimum wage, he noted in 1938 that such achievements not only heightened the worker's "social dignity," but also enabled him to "increase consumption, acquire more from the producers, and, consequently, better the conditions of the internal market."[53]

The administration's opposition to the pronounced rural exodus during the 1930s has been attributed to agrarian preferences on

Vargas's part.[54] Such opposition, however, had a solid grounding in economic common sense. Analysts today argue that overurbanization in developing countries can be uneconomical since it forces governments to divert funds to social overhead projects that could be invested more profitably elsewhere. Migrants to cities in Latin America, furthermore, have tended to be "pushed" by unfavorable rural conditions rather than "pulled" by industrial job opportunities.[55] In the early 1930s the flight of workers from the countryside reached dimensions that often handicapped rural productivity. Private remarks by the minister of Labor in 1934 reveal that the administration was amply aware of the developmental repercussions of premature urban growth caused by the influx of rural migrants. It was better, he wrote, to improve rural conditions and hold workers in the countryside, "where they may find productive work and consume what industry produces."[56]

These efforts in the area of social investments were hindered, as was Vargas's general economic program, by political and administrative instability. The problem of devising and executing economic policies in an environment of social and political unrest has long plagued Latin American policy makers. Not only does political turmoil divert attention and resources from planning and execution, but it also creates an atmosphere in which the political consequences of economic measures become a "constant, day-to-day concern" to government leaders. In Brazil, particularly, attempts to elaborate and carry out development programs have historically been "enormously hindered" by social and political turmoil.[57]

Vargas longed for internal stability, since, as he pointed out two months after seizing power, it was vital to the country's "financial restoration and economic development." But it was not until the suppression of the desperate putsch by hapless Fascist-led opponents in mid-1938 that the government enjoyed domestic calm. A major cost of this political effervescence was personnel instability at policy-making levels. During the seven years that separated the Revolution from the Estado Novo, Vargas had seven ministers of justice; five of war; four each of labor, foreign relations, navy, agriculture, and transportation; and three of education and of finance, for an average of over five cabinet changes a year. Between 1934 and 1937 there were five army chiefs of staff and the Conselho Federal do Comércio Exterior had two directors. At the state government level the instability was equally striking. Between November 1930 and November 1935—the period

stretching from Vargas's assumption of power to the Communist revolt—the twenty states had sixty interventors or governors. Including
the interventors or prefects of the Federal District and interventors in
the territory of Acre, that total would rise to ninety-eight by the end of
November 1937.[58] Empirical evidence is lacking, but one may safely
assume that, in accordance with the traditional rules of the Brazilian
political game, political and administrative turnovers at the top state
level resulted in even more numerous displacements in state port-
folios, just as each federal cabinet change was undoubtedly a stone
tossed in the administrative pool. At any rate, it is clear that would-be
government planners operated in an environment of marked politico-
bureaucratic fluidity.

Quality of personnel was another major ingredient in the general
"administrative lag" and a weakness that the Vargas government
made the first serious effort to correct. In 1936, after lengthy discussions in politico-administrative circles, Vargas approved the creation
of a central personnel agency. He appointed as director of the new
Civil Service Council his friend and former secretary, Luis Simões
Lopes. "We found a heavy and very complicated administrative ap-
paratus that functioned irregularly, whose characteristic feature was
poor adaptation to the material and economic needs of the country,"
Simões Lopes reported to Vargas after eighteen months in office. "To
the organic defects of such a mechanism was added the incurable
qualitative deficiency of the personnel . . ." One key prong in the
Council's attack on administrative inefficiency was the competitive
civil service entrance examination, which was first administered in
1937.[59] Although no miracles were worked in the field of administrative reform, the Vargas government did succeed in establishing "a semblance of order in the federal civil service."[60]

In addition to a lack of trained personnel, federal planners faced
another severe handicap: an absence of reliable statistical data. After
the will, the most important requisite for formulating development
policies is factual information on the various factors involved in economic growth. But reliable statistics were simply unavailable to the
government during the 1930s. The country's first statistical almanac
had been published in 1916 and covered skimpily the years 1908–1912.
A special commission set up in 1931 to study the foreign debt struggled
in the face of statistical "disorder, waste, and irresponsibility" to arrive
at some notion of the extent of state indebtedness. Some local governments did not even have copies of their loan contracts with foreign

bankers. Data on interstate trade was unobtainable, as Finance Minister Aranha learned early in 1932. Indeed, "the states themselves do not have those statistics," reported the Departamento Nacional de Estatística, "since they only collate them for exports, and not all [states] discriminate them according to their respective destinations." Lack of trustworthy data on the balance of payments was an embarrassing handicap to Valentim Bouças during his official negotiations with Brazil's foreign creditors in 1933. "You can't imagine the terrible impression that the lack of this information causes here . . . ," he privately complained from New York. In mid-1934 Aranha began preparing a report for his successor, and he again ran into stumbling blocks. The data for "several [agricultural] products, many of great importance," were unavailable. The American commercial attaché late that year discovered an "almost total absence of statistical or descriptive material" for a report on the state of Brazilian manufactures. Because no up-to-date demographic profiles existed, when army intelligence officers late in the decade sought information on foreign nationals residing in Brazil, they had to consult a census of 1920.[61]

Vargas was well aware of the necessity of grounding his economic policies in social reality. As he once put it succinctly, "Nobody can govern without good statistics." After assuming power, his government endeavored constantly to improve, or create, adequate statistical services. During 1931 his administration promoted an interstate accord on educational statistics and also established the special committee to measure the extent of state and municipal indebtedness. Early in 1932 he ordered the fusion of the separate statistical departments of the Ministries of Agriculture and Finance into a new Departamento Nacional de Estatística subordinated to the recently created Ministry of Labor, Industry, and Commerce. The DNE hoped to impose some uniformity on local statistical compilation, and it established offices in the various states, encouraging federal-state agreements in commercial statistics.[62]

Such measures were nonetheless piecemeal, and in mid-1933 Vargas established an interministerial committee to study a general reorganization of statistical gathering and processing. The deliberations of the committee led to a Vargas decree in July 1934 creating an Instituto Nacional de Estatística, whose major goal was the standardization and perfection of data compilation at all governmental levels. For technical, bureaucratic, and political reasons the INE began functioning only in 1936, but the installation of its headquarters in Catete

Palace, next door to the Secretariat of the Presidency, was symbolic of Vargas's personal interest in obtaining statistical bases for his economic program. Under a National Statistics Convention of August 1936, the states were obligated to supply statistics on various economic and social matters to the central government. That same year the INE published a 435-page *Anuário Estatístico*, the second in Brazil's history and the first since 1916. By early 1937, INE offices were functioning in an estimated one-third of Brazilian communities, and later that year the INE issued another *Anuário*, a hefty volume twice the size of the preceding one. The gap between signing and complete execution of the Convention was great, however, and the INE continued to struggle against the same forces that had long prevented development of reliable statistical services: poor communications, bureaucratic inertia and disorganization, and, particularly, a lack of cooperation from local authorities. The state of São Paulo, for example, was widely considered the best organized in Brazil; yet, despite repeated requests from 1936 on, authorities did not submit the desired statistical data until 1939. By late 1940 the Federal District itself had still not delivered its report to the INE.[63]

The efforts and not inconsiderable achievements in the area of statistics gathering during the 1930s were a function of a noticeably strong commitment on Vargas's part to government supervision and planning of national economic activity. A belief in the need for sectoral planning permeates his presidential platform speech of January 1930, which also stamped Vargas a devotee of overall planning. "In order to determine the path to follow," he said, "we need a careful examination of the general environment of our [economic] activity, based on a weighing of national possibilities and calculation of the obstacles to overcome." Following the Revolution, Vargas repeatedly stressed the need for planning. Looking back on his first fifteen months in office, he privately labeled the steps already taken as valuable but "fragmentary conquests" and spoke of the necessity of "a great overall plan" of development, something he hoped to achieve before the drafting of a new constitution. The invitation extended to Sir Otto Niemeyer to make recommendations on Brazil's general financial predicament, which he had done in a report published in 1931, and the establishment of the special committee on state finances were practical evidence of Vargas's desire for more careful planning of economic programs. Between 1933 and 1935 his government also moved to encourage rationalization of transportation expansion, agriculture, and foreign trade. Since previous transportation growth had not obeyed a "technical and economic orientation," Vargas appointed a special commission in 1933 to draft a "general transportation plan," one that was concluded in 1934 and contributed to a doubling of the national highway mileage by the end of the decade. In 1935 the minister of agriculture, with Vargas's authorization, announced plans for increased federal intervention in agricultural activities, a step toward the "planned systematization of production and distribution, in accordance with the norms of a prudent directed economy."[64]

The creation and activities of the Conselho Federal de Comércio Exterior demonstrated perhaps more clearly than anything else Vargas's early commitment to governmental supervision of the economy. Launched in mid-1934, the CFCE was an independent agency subordinated directly to Vargas and empowered to study and make recommendations on all matters relating to domestic and foreign commerce. The Conselho functioned as a sort of extended cabinet, including as members the various ministers of state (except war), and representatives of banking, industrial, and agricultural groups. Vargas, in the first months of the CFCE's existence, frequently presided over what were often confidential sessions at its headquarters in Itamaraty Palace. By providing for the representation of private interests, Vargas sought to ensure broad support for his decisions. The interest and investigations of the CFCE ranged far beyond such matters as tariffs, export diversification, and commercial propaganda to include finances, transportation, and industrialization. It was the CFCE that undertook late in 1936, on Vargas's personal instructions, the first great national industrial survey. That project, intended to analyze obstacles to industrial expansion in both domestic and foreign markets, was a logical consequence of Vargas's previous economic policy and his vision of Brazil's future role in the greater South American economy.

The development of an industrial export capacity depended, of course, on domestic growth, which was striking in the post-Revolution period. Brazil pulled out of the Depression in 1933, and it might have sooner had not the São Paulo revolt interrupted business activity. ". . . employment was good and industry booming under the shelter of the tariff and the rate of exchange," Foreign Minister Melo Franco had noted on the eve of the civil war. Spurred on perhaps in part by government revolt-related expenditures, manufacturing intensified after the rebellion was suppressed. During 1933 British embassy experts found that "industrialisation proceeded steadily, existing factories developing and increasing their output and new factories and industries being established all over the country." Indeed, factories had hired additional workers, restored full workweeks, and, reported a Brazilian official in 1934, "even then they cannot keep up with the orders." As the nation entered what it futilely hoped would be a constitutional respite from the political turmoil of the dictatorial period, Vargas himself privately surveyed general industrial trends. "The economic rebirth is palpable," he wrote to Aranha. "The factories are working intensely."[65]

Industrial progress continued throughout the decade, giving Brazil an annual industrial growth rate of 11.2 percent for the period 1933–1939. The textile industry increased its output at the same rate, while the manufacture of paper products increased by 22 percent annually. In some sectors of São Paulo industry, the expansion was higher than the national average. The *paulista* pharmaceutical, metallurgical, and cement industries, for example, grew at annual rates of 30, 24, and 16 percent respectively.[66] Domestic industry by 1938 was accounting for approximately 85 percent of the supply of manufactured articles, and it was "mainly as a result of growth during the middle and late 1930's" that Brazil's capital goods industry was supplying well over half the total equipment purchases by the late 1940s.[67]

In view of this progress, government leaders devoted increasing attention to Brazil's potential role as a supplier of industrial goods for the rest of South America. The corollary of industrial expansion, Vargas had stated early in 1931, was the conquest of markets, and it was naturally contiguous countries that drew the attention of government leaders. The necessity of improving communications with neighboring countries, particularly Bolivia and Paraguay, in order to open up those markets to Brazilian manufacturers—in large part as a means of checking Argentine influence—was a recurrent theme in Brazilian diplomatic and military communications. The minister in La Paz, for example, sent a series of dispatches to Rio de Janeiro in 1931 calling attention to the future possibilities. At the end of 1933, Foreign Minister Melo Franco took advantage of the Pan-American conference at Montevideo to urge his Paraguayan colleague to end the Chaco War and undertake, along with Bolivia, a program of economic cooperation with Brazil. The relationship that Brazil envisioned for itself with its neighbors was precisely that enjoyed by industrial North America and Europe with Latin America in general. Railroads could be built to Brazil, read the memorandum that Melo Franco gave the Paraguayan foreign minister, where they would "pass through São Paulo, which today is undeniably the greatest industrial center of South America, thus making it possible for Bolivia and Paraguay to supply themselves there with an enormous series of industrial products already manufactured, . . . at the same time that Bolivian and Paraguayan producers of raw materials would have before them a new great consuming market for their products."[68]

As fighting in the Chaco entered its final phase in late 1934 and early 1935, Brazilian diplomats talked increasingly of expanding Brazilian influence in the belligerent countries through closer economic ties. "It is urgent," wrote a member of the Asunción embassy in October 1934, ". . . that our powerful industries conquer those markets, so naturally suitable for their expansion." Brazil should indeed act quickly, reported the new envoy to La Paz. "The moment is evidently extremely important for the future life of Brazil." Argentina was active, explained the General Staff, so it was necessary that Brazilian products "penetrate and capture" neighboring markets. Aranha, in urging intensified import substitution in 1935, did not refer to the development of an export trade in manufactures in South America, but his concomitant expressions of concern about Brazil's "preeminence in South America" suggest the linkage he undoubtedly made between industrial expansion and international power. With the end of the war and beginning of peace talks, Itamaraty invited Paraguay to send a special mission to Rio de Janeiro, where talks were held in September 1935 on various means of collaboration between the two countries. Brazil had in middle South America "a real and growing interest that is to open markets in those countries for our industry," Itamaraty analysts repeated.[69]

Vargas himself strongly supported the idea of Brazil as the industrial heartland of South America. When producers of textiles, furniture, hats, shoes, paints, and other light items suggested in mid-1931 that depreciation of the milreis presented a good opportunity for an "attempt to conquer South American markets," Vargas reacted with the "greatest of interest" and authorized an industrial exposition in Buenos Aires. That glimpse of the future for certain lay behind the provision in the tariff, which his counselors elaborated in 1934, for a "drawback," or temporary exemption or reduction of duties on imported raw materials to be used in the manufacture of a product destined for exportation. The president, of course, accompanied and approved of Itamaraty's efforts to draw Bolivia and Paraguay closer to Brazil, and, when he in mid-1935 underscored the necessity of building an economic foundation for Pan-Americanism, he was more than likely in part thinking of greater efforts to develop markets for Brazilian manufacturers. His businessmen-advisers vigorously endorsed and shared in the development of a policy of industrial expansion on the continent. Bouças in CFCE councils in 1935 urged greater efforts on behalf of industrialization, describing the future Brazil as "a kind of industrial entrepôt for the consumer markets of South America." The president of the Brazilian Rural Society and representative of that association on the CFCE, Artur Torres Filho, became a forceful advocate of industrialization and, as head of a special advisory mission to Paraguay late in 1935, an equally strong proponent of Brazil's industrial expansion in the heartland of South America. Euvaldo Lodi, a leading spokesman for manufacturing interests and, like Bouças and Torres Filho, a member of the CFCE, also championed greater exports of goods and even capital to neighboring countries.[70]

One important recommendation that Torres Filho made that year when declaring himself in favor of intensified industrialization, and one that struck a responsive chord in planning-oriented higher spheres, was that systematic study of the industrial sector and internal market be undertaken. The CFCE readily approved the idea and invited comment by other governmental agencies. Political turmoil centering around the Communist revolt in November delayed action on the proposal, but the CFCE did not lose interest, particularly in view of a marked expansion of industrial activity during 1936. Cement production, for example, rose 36 percent, while production of pig iron and rolled iron was respectively 15 and 20 percent higher than it had been for 1935. The textile industry continued to expand with an output 54 percent greater than it had been in 1927, a situation that delighted the administration. "We are no longer an exclusively agrarian country . . . crushed by the weight of acquisitions of industrial goods [abroad]," Vargas exulted in September 1936.[71] It was now possible, he thought, to launch a systematic, nationwide survey of industry's needs in order to determine where the country had gone and where it might be able to go as an industrial power in South America.

In his instructions to the director of the CFCE in November 1936, Vargas opined that Brazilian industry had emerged from its "initial phase of consolidation" and could expand production not only for domestic consumption but for export as well. Impediments to Brazil's industrial expansion, he believed, could be overcome through a "uniform method of combined action" between industry and government. Among the products that the government judged capable of sale abroad Vargas included cotton and woolen goods, beer, canned foods, cigarettes and cigars, pharmaceuticals, furniture, and tires and other rubber articles. It was on South American markets, said the president, that Brazilian manufacturers should focus their attention. Recalling his various pronouncements on the advisability of strengthening Pan-American ties, Vargas concluded that "to Brazilian industry belongs the principal role in this task of continental expansion," since the other South American countries were producers of raw materials.[72]

The CFCE circularized the major industrial associations, state governments, and chambers of commerce, requesting information on local industrial conditions. Many state authorities thereupon appointed special study groups to prepare the necessary reports. Replies ultimately came from various parts of the country, but the information received was often incomplete and out-of-date. The Industrial and Commercial Association of Ceará, for example, forwarded a *cahier de doléance* drawn up seven years earlier. Many recommendations were so broad—"stable monetary system," "balanced budgets"—as to render them useless. A firm in Sergipe replied that it was overburdened with taxes and that political turmoil hurt its sales. The important Industrial Federation of Rio de Janeiro, which had welcomed the survey with "real enthusiasm," limited itself to urging greater official consumption of domestic equipment and supplies. According to a Ministry of Labor, Industry, and Commerce representative, the ministry distributed 20,644 questionnaires and received only 3,624 replies, of which only 800 were usable. Eleven months later, in October 1937, Roberto Simonsen, president of the Brazilian Industrial Confederation and member of the CFCE, summarized the findings of the survey in a memorandum calling for, among other things, a nationalistic trade policy, agricultural and export credits, greater tariff benefits, improvement of transportation services, and government support for industrial missions to neighboring countries. The CFCE endorsed this report and then sent it to the various ministries in November 1937, soliciting suggestions and comments.[73]

Some of the information and experience gathered during 1936–1937 helped in the elaboration of the five-year Special Plan for Public Works and National Defense of January 1939, and some of the recommendations of the survey were taken up later. The government, for example, in 1940 dispatched an industrial mission to several Latin American countries in the hope of encouraging exports of manufactured goods. In general, the fact that private associations and firms tended to advocate policies that the government was already attempting to implement only reinforced its conviction that it was following the proper path. The industrial survey and the assumptions upon which it was based constituted striking evidence of Vargas's commitment to industrialization. Viewed in this context, his government's emphasis on foreign trade takes on new meaning.

The argument that Vargas was opposed to industry before 1937 draws heavily on the fact that his administration gave strong support to exports, particularly coffee.[74] But Vargas clearly had no ideological commitment to an agrarian economy; a better explanation for the emphasis on exports is that it was a function, in large part, of a realization that export earnings determined the nation's capacity to import, a factor vital to the development of manufacturing. The Vargas government, in other words, perceived what contemporary economists regard as an axiom of development.[75] Even Roberto Simonsen, the major spokesman for manufacturing interests, acknowledged at the time that coffee, which accounted for approximately two-thirds of Brazil's export earnings, was the "backbone of our economic organism."[76] The collapse of international markets for raw materials and foodstuffs "nearly paralyzed" industries in São Paulo, the country's industrial heartland. Coffee sales in 1930 were worth "almost 40 percent" less than in 1929, and the decline in rural demand resulted in a widespread shutdown of factories. The abrupt decline in foreign trade was the cause of an exchange crisis in Brazil that made it "almost impossible" for plants relying on imported raw materials to continue operation.[77] In those "calamitous" circumstances, Vargas later recalled, it was simply impossible to "abandon once and for all our former ways, delivering agriculture over to its own fate and throwing the entire country into economic chaos." The government's price-support program for coffee launched in the early weeks of the new regime was consequently a measure intended to have a general impact. As Vargas's first finance minister privately wrote to his successor, "In going to the aid of coffee, the government did what was most urgent: reestablish the normal rhythm of life in the coffee-growing states, allowing them, especially São Paulo, to resume work in the fields, business, and factories."[78] The pump-priming effects of coffee stockpiling may have been attenuated by new taxes, but the program did help to maintain rural employment levels and in so doing guarantee some market for textiles and other manufactures.[79]

Foreign trade thus assumed great importance for Brazilian policy makers, who saw it as perhaps the main responsibility of the government in its relations with other countries. Diplomats trained in the "realistic school" of commercial competition were what Melo Franco had hoped to turn out during his tenure at Itamaraty, and Vargas by 1934 was convinced of the "urgent need to adapt our diplomacy to a modern, constructive program of commercial expansion and economic policy." Three years of experience as minister of finance and a few months at the Washington embassy were sufficient to persuade Aranha. "The political era proper of Brazilian diplomacy has passed and will return only when we become a great power . . . ," he argued with conviction. In the meantime, "everything indicates that the content of our diplomatic activity should be economic and commercial matters."[80]

The Vargas government formulated two major, interrelated foreign trade goals. It wanted to revive and increase sales of raw materials and foodstuffs, and, at the same time, it sought to stimulate a greater variety of exports in order to reduce dependence upon coffee. Attainment of these objectives would require energetic efforts to discover new markets. Brazil began its drive to diversify and expand exports in what its leaders rightly perceived as an international environment that demanded "constant vigilance" to protect national interests vis-à-vis aggressive competitors.[81] The attitude of national spokesmen toward the special conditions of international life was ambivalent. The political dangers inherent in the perceived colonial thrust of stronger countries and the probability of war produced anxieties reflected in restrictive immigration laws, a series of measures late in the decade to force the assimilation of immigrants and hyphenates, and efforts to improve governmental efficiency and national military capabilities. On the other hand, the competition among industrial nations also afforded opportunities for commercial profit, and advocates of seizing such opportunities were not lacking.

The world "commercial struggle" made it obvious, said industrialist Simonsen, that "there is no longer any room for out-of-place sentimentalism or for a visionary and complacent policy." All opportunities, in other words, should be tested. When Japan sounded the Brazilian authorities in 1935 on the possibility of sending a trade mission to Brazil, Macedo Soares had no doubts. The Asian nation's reasons for wanting the raw materials were of no consequence to Brazil, nor, in his judgment, should possible resentment on the part of the United States prevent Brazil from responding to trade overtures from Tokyo. Given Brazil's financial difficulties, it would be folly not to encourage an "opportune meeting of interests" with a country needing Brazilian products.[82]

If the politics of the European crisis were none of Brazil's concern, the trade opportunities were. Mussolini's drive for African conquests created for Brazil "an exceptional situation," said Itamaraty, which recommended that the government endeavor "at all costs" to increase sales of primary products to Italy. "Entering into war, the Europeans will need foodstuffs and raw materials with which to manufacture the implements of war," wrote one publicist three days after German troops entered the Rhineland. "We possess them in large scale and we can furnish them in limitless quantities." Indeed, a general European war would "bring only benefits to a country in our condition," agreed the minister to the Netherlands late in 1936. Adding his voice to the chorus, another diplomat remarked that "countries like ours rich in raw materials stand, by force of circumstances, to gain most" from the impending conflict. England and other belligerents, he predicted, "inevitably will have to come knocking at our door." Suggestive of the attitude prevailing in military circles was the confidential statement by army planners in 1939 that Brazil had to strengthen its military capacity in order to "protect and ensure its natural commercial and economic expansion" during the war. The national slogan, suggested Chief of Staff Góes Monteiro, should be "maximum commercial relations and minimum political relations with Europe."[83] There was, of course, no incompatibility between the "exploited and exploitable" mentality characteristic of the foreign policy elite and the desire to take advantage of all occasions that might arise to realize financial profit, since clearly an improved economic situation would better enable the country to meet the perceived threats to national security.

One huge market of seemingly vast possibilities that appealed to Brazilian export interests was the Russian. Brazil had no diplomatic ties with the Soviet Union, and there were consequently no shipping services between the two countries. What little trade that took place had been indirect, and it had ceased altogether with the Depression. Faced with slumping exports and falling prices, Brazilian exporters thought new efforts should be made to overcome those barriers. As early as December 1930, the Agrarian League of São Paulo voted to urge the government to establish direct trade relations with Russia, and the Institute of Coffee not long after solicited official support for attempts by Lloyd Brasileiro to establish a shipping run to that country. Federal authorities, imbued with strong anti-Communist sentiment, were wary of Russian political intentions and responded cautiously. Debate over the question was intensified in 1934 when the state government of Rio Grande do Sul pressed for similar action. Following talks between Governor Flores da Cunha and a director of the Soviet state trade organization for South America, IUYAMTORG, *riograndense* spokesmen were enthusiastic about the possibilities. Russia would constitute "an immense market of unlimited possibilities," declared the official organ of the governor's party, at the same time that it warned that competitor nations were actively seeking Russian trade favors. The recently created CFCE thereupon undertook a full-scale review of Brazil's relations with Russia and concluded, with the blessings of Vargas and his new foreign minister, Macedo Soares, a dedicated anti-Communist, that the political dangers of allowing Soviet "commercial" delegates to set up official operations on Brazilian soil outweighed the unlikely advantages of trying to encourage the Russian masses to alter their drinking habits.[84] The Russian case is interesting, however, precisely because it was the exception to the rule. In no other instance did the Vargas government let political scruples stand in the way of possible commercial gain.

As a corollary to the need to seize all commercial opportunities, Brazilian leaders accepted the idea that the times demanded a flexibility of response, an abandonment when necessary of traditional procedure, a relaxation of principle in favor of a practical adjustment to the requirements of the moment. As in romantic rivalry, all seemed fair in economic warfare. With Melo Franco in charge of Itamaraty, until 1934, Brazil's commercial policy rested in principle on most-favored-nation treatment and opposed, again in principle, more primitive measures, such as barter and clearing agreements. The "Chancellor of the Revolution" enjoyed sufficient personal prestige and influence to assert himself vis-à-vis other departments and had, moreover, the weight of tradition behind him. Negotiation of a spate of most-favored-nation agreements in 1931 was one of his first achievements as foreign minister.[85] But younger leaders were skeptical. Melo Franco himself later recalled that he had experienced considerable difficulty in convincing the younger, impassioned Aranha, his colleague at the Ministry of Finance, that the government should endeavor to "soften the hostile and exalted nationalism that had led the world to the universal crisis." As for Vargas, he was a thoroughgoing pragmatist, and his orientation was a lead for subordinates to follow. To increase exports, he once said candidly, "all means" should be used, even, "in many cases," direct barter of goods. Although the most-favored-nation principle was the foundation of Brazilian policy, it was, Vargas argued, "not incompatible with certain reciprocal or conditional formulae or with special treatment . . . in certain cases."[86]

The pragmatic orientation of Brazilian authorities was strengthened by the results of the London Monetary Conference in mid-1933. To Brazilian experts, this international gathering represented "a desperate, perhaps final, effort" to restore, through international cooperation, some stability and prosperity to the world economy.[87] When the new Roosevelt administration invited Brazil to send a delegation to Washington for preliminary talks, Vargas complied, but his counselors were skeptical. What could a nation like Brazil, with no gold reserves, hope for from the forthcoming conference? a member of the delegation asked American negotiator Herbert Feis. Improved international conditions, replied Feis.[88] This was true but not very specific, and how to bring about that improvement remained a dilemma.

In London the powers wrangled for more than six weeks over monetary problems and then ended the Conference without an agreement, largely because Washington insisted on devaluation of the dollar. "The disillusion . . . was great," wrote Ambassador Regis de Oliveira from London.[89] Prime Minister Neville Chamberlain declared at the last plenary session his "profound deception" over the results of the Conference, and German delegate Hjalmar Schacht and others echoed Chamberlain's lament. Ambassador Regis could, for appearance's sake, suggest that something had been accomplished in that each country had made its position clear,[90] but the negotiations had obviously been in vain. Observers in Brazil followed closely what *A Nação* labeled the "most crashing failure that pessimists could foresee." Why did the Conference fail? The "large States sought . . . to attain objectives that were purely and simply national ones." Indeed, the London fiasco served only "to demonstrate the irreducibility of the interests of the great powers," concluded a *paulista* daily. Joaquim Eulalio de Nascimento e Silva, the Itamaraty trade expert who accompanied the delegation to London, more fairly pointed out

that at the Conference there had been "no fewer than sixty-six countries with interests and points of view absolutely divergent,"[91] but he
made essentially the same point: the principle of each-nation-for-
itself-and-with-any-means was more firmly entrenched than ever as
the key to international relations.

It is interesting to speculate that not only their image of world trends
and national needs but their cultural background as well encouraged
Brazilian leaders to behave opportunistically and regard as acceptable
certain kinds of decisions and procedures. As Feliks Gross has noted,
"Foreign policy . . . sooner or later becomes a social process. Patterns
of political behavior, or of general cultural patterns, are thus paramount." If a direct causal linkage between the "psycho-social" environment and policy decisions is impossible to establish, students of
foreign policy are nonetheless generally agreed on the importance of
cultural norms as determinants of the behavior of national leaders,
who internalize what other experts call "patterned responses" characteristic of a particular society.[92] Even "men of diverse backgrounds
are socialized to a common way of thinking as they move up the
ladder of politics, business and other key aspects of social life."[93] In
Brazil's case, a strong correlation seems to exist between the approach
of the foreign policy elite to trade problems and commonly recognized
features of the sociopolitical system and national character.

Native and foreign observers alike have stressed the primacy of
personal relationships in Brazilian social and political intercourse. "To
place emphasis on direct relationships and personal liking rather than
on relationships of an impersonal, indirect, unqualified nature was a
basic feature of Portuguese character," according to José Honório
Rodrigues, "and despite all variations, this trait is still strongly evident in Brazilian character." It is not institutions or legal authority
that the Brazilian respects but the individuals occupying positions of
power. One reflection of this personalism throughout most of Brazil's
history was an absence of political parties with well-defined programs.
In a seminal essay written in 1936, Sérgio Buarque de Holanda pointed
out that in vain did politicians "imagine they are interested more in
principle than in individuals: their very acts are a flagrant denial of
that pretension." One insightful analysis of Brazilian career patterns
underscored the fact that even in recent times what is most important
to the typical Brazilian politician is personal projection and he will
pragmatically adopt an expedient, such as embracing a radical doctrine, in order to achieve that objective.[94]

A logical correlate of this emphasis on personal relationships is a lack of regard for formal institutions and legal procedures or, as the above comments suggest, for any sharply defined, impersonal program of thought or action. The "domination of the senses" was too great in Brazil, remarked a French diplomat early in the nineteenth century, to permit "obedience to the laws" or orderly public administration. "A regime that will assure an effective legal order here," he said, "is therefore as desirable as it is difficult to establish . . ."[95] The Brazilian customarily seeks a practical way, a *jeito*, of circumventing legal hindrances to attainment of his goals. "Perhaps the most important characteristic of the *jeito*," one observer aptly perceived, "is the subtle bypassing of the system through the mechanism of mere 'formal' satisfaction of rules and regulations."[96]

Some writers have sought the roots of Brazilian pragmatism in the colonizing experience of the Portuguese settlers: "In Brazil man would have to conquer Nature by temporizing, detouring, distrusting, wriggling, tucking, biding his time, waiting for opportunities."[97] Adaptation—"malleability in the face of whatever gods are more efficacious" —to the New World environment produced linguistic changes that expressed those same qualities. As an American scholar has noted, "human communication became more functional, more responsive to needs of the moment, more cautious of conclusive assertions." Modifications of Portuguese included a softening of nasal endings, a slurring of diphthongs, superfluous negatives that "act less to point up than attenuate a denial," and the quite frequent prefacing of assertions with a *they say*, "signifying the vagueness of a rumor or the wily provisions of a loophole."[98]

A prominent Brazilian intellectual historian saw the Brazilian's lack of ideological commitment as an outgrowth of the Portuguese tradition. "From earliest times Portuguese thought had a practical end in view," he wrote. "It gravitated around realistic problems, with limited, precise, and concrete objectives. The sense of the useful, the immediate, is what by preference appears in his thought."[99] The traits and attitudes in question have historically been reinforced by the gap between social reality and the legal or constitutional framework of society. Laws in Brazil tend to anticipate, rather than reflect, social patterns. This discord between legal norms and social reality has encouraged a tendency to observe form but not substance. Within the Brazilian context, subterfuge and evasion are socially acceptable, and Brazilians are adept at rationalizing any conflict of values.[100]

Foreign diplomats often called attention to what they considered the special conditions in Brazil. Not long after independence, a French envoy in Rio de Janeiro referred not without disdain to the "system of delay and temporization so invariably followed in this country."[101] Comments by representatives of the powers contending for the Brazilian market in the 1930s reflected an encounter with administrative and political behavior based, in part, on different cultural premises. Typical was the remark by a State Department agent that the "American training" of Valentim Bouças made it "possible to lay a proposition before him in a straightforward manner." British diplomats also ran into divergences from what they regarded as a more sporting standard of conduct. Sir William Seeds, London's ambassador until 1935, once alluded with resignation and fatigue to "Brazilian gifts of shilly-shally and obstruction"; and in 1935 the chargé d'affaires believed that a default on the foreign debt was "less probable than increasing dilatoriness in payment, a much more Brazilian method of accomplishing the same end." Berlin's envoy on one occasion explained to the Wilhelmstrasse that "in this country governmental methods are different from those in Europe. Elasticity, evasion, and dilatory handling are traditional here," he declared.[102]

Albert O. Hirschman has questioned the general applicability of the "slippery concept of style." The technique of problem solving, he suggests, probably hinges "as much on the nature of the problem as on the historical and cultural background of the community which is confronting the problem."[103] One of the greatest challenges—and opportunities—facing Brazil during the 1930s was the trade rivalry among the great powers in South America. Because of the clashing commercial programs of the major antagonists, that rivalry presented Brazil with a foreign policy problem. The nature of the dilemma posed by conflicting international demands was made to order for Brazilian policy makers and called into play all the skills of pragmatic, opportunistic problem solving they had acquired in the process of socialization, skills sharpened by a view of the international arena as one in which only the resourceful would survive.

Chapter 2

Between Washington and Berlin (1934)

The opening salvo in the commercial battle between the great powers in the Brazilian market was fired in mid-1934, when Berlin dispatched a special trade delegation to South America and the American Congress passed the Reciprocal Trade Agreements Act. Brazil immediately found itself caught between the clashing commercial systems of these two major trading partners, each of which reserved a major role for Brazil in its trade program. Compelled to make a decision in an environment of conflicting external pressures that struck responsive domestic chords, Getúlio Vargas typically avoided a definitive commitment. Instead he expediently charted an ad hoc course designed to placate all parties concerned, postponing the necessity of a clear and open choice until circumstances demanded it. The content of that initial decision, what determined it, and how it was reached form the subject of this chapter.

The unorthodox German commercial techniques so irritating to American and British traders—and so competitively effective—originated in the sharply adverse effects of the Depression on German finances. Prior to the economic crisis the Reich had maintained a high export surplus in trade with industrial nations that served to balance the import surplus characteristic of its commerce with countries exporting raw materials and foodstuffs. With the Depression came a general decline in the demand for imported goods, higher tariff rates, and widespread financial disequilibrium. Devaluation of the pound also visibly affected Germany's sales abroad.[1]

Languishing exports forced the German government to draw increasingly on gold reserves to cover import requirements. To halt the nation's downward economic plunge, and in pursuit of what the Brazilian minister in Berlin scorned as the "harebrained ideas" of autarchy,[2] authorities there resorted to import embargoes, tariff and import quotas, direct barter, and clearing or compensation agreements. Foreign exchange, furthermore, was gradually restricted to imports of industrial raw materials. A Raw Materials Act of March 1934, for example, established special boards to control imports of primary products, including cotton, wool, rubber, tobacco, hides and skins, and nonprecious metals.[3]

Despite such measures, which spelled abandonment of the most-favored-nation principle, the drain on foreign exchange reserves continued. Between 1931 and 1934 the country suffered a net outflow of over 5 million reichsmarks in gold and foreign currencies,[4] and by the spring of 1934 Reichsbankdirektor and soon-to-be Reichswirtschaftsminister Hjalmar Schacht had "practically exhausted all of the resources which his cleverness could lay hold of."[5] A few weeks later the Reichsbank warned the Ministry of Economic Affairs that "in no circumstances" should a further decrease of exchange holdings be permitted.[6] German importers now found themselves forced to secure exchange on a daily basis, and allocations were made only in amounts equal to the currencies received by the Reichsbank.[7]

The financial crisis led to a thorough review of trade policy and national requirements. The problem as German planners viewed it involved not only economic considerations but also, and more importantly, defense needs, which were regarded as "decisive and urgent." Faced with the necessity of promoting exports and the inability to pay cash for imports, they looked more and more to countries that could accept industrial products in return for badly needed raw materials. Britain and France were increasingly monopolizing trade with their dependencies in Africa and elsewhere through preferential agreements, so German policy would have to be "territorially turned around." Karl Ritter, the head of the Economic Policy Department in the Auswärtiges Amt and future ambassador to Brazil, coined an expression that synthesized the anticipated directional shift in trade channels: "Away from Africa and the commonwealth, toward South America, the Balkans, and the Far East."[8]

The Wilhelmstrasse confidentially apprised its missions abroad of this decision in June 1934. Under growing pressure for barter arrangements, it said, Berlin's general goal was now to transfer purchases "from Africa and from the British overseas territories . . . to countries that offer future possibilities to German exports, such as, for instance, South America and the Dutch Indies." Particularly significant for the subsequent development of trade with Brazil was the intention to import coffee "preferably from coffee-growing countries that are themselves prepared to take German goods in exchange."[9]

Adoption weeks later of Schacht's so-called New Plan for foreign trade was a major step in the Reich's campaign to intensify commercial relations with South America. The scheme was, in the words of one Wilhelmstrasse expert, "a revolutionary reform of our whole foreign trade policy."[10] Designed to ensure a balance between imports and available foreign exchange, it called for careful scrutiny of purchases abroad by some twenty-five control boards. The system enabled the government not only to protect its meager reserves of foreign currencies, but also to designate the nature and source of commodities entering the country. Since raw materials and other items indispensable to industry received priority in the allocation of exchange permits, the plan rapidly opened up new markets in Central and South America.[11]

The introduction of special blocked marks for payment of imports also served to boost sales in South America. This restricted currency, known usually as *Aski*, or compensation marks, could be used only to buy German products, so its employment stimulated exports at the same time that it reduced pressure on foreign exchange holdings.[12] Increased purchases by German importers automatically led to greater accumulation of compensation marks in countries trading with the Reich on this basis, and, because of the limited negotiability of the currency, preferential treatment of German exporters in placing orders for manufactures was the inevitable result.[13] As a British observer once complained, the expansion of German-Brazilian trade was like "a plant of exotic growth . . . forced by the hot-house atmosphere of the compensation mark."[14]

Export bounties and other forms of subsidization helped to offset the advantage that rival nations gained through currency devaluation and aided considerably in winning new markets. After the foreign exchange reserves declined to a crisis point in mid-1934, Reich authorities raised funds for export promotion by means of a direct levy on industry itself.[15] Price supervision boards granted subsidies varying between 10 and 90 percent of the production cost, allowing German manufacturers to undersell in many lines their American and British counterparts.[16] Official subsidization covered about 60 percent of German exports by the spring of 1936.[17]

The Nazi trade thrust in Brazil was not entirely a "plant of exotic growth," since it had firm underpinnings in business and commercial relationships dating back decades.[18] The world war had temporarily checked this intercourse, and the two countries even found themselves at war with one another. But the clash had been only a "platonic" quarrel, one German businessman explained in 1922 as he urged his colleagues to "reconquer" lost ground.[19] The admonition was well received and mutual interest quickly rekindled after the conflict ended. Suggestive of the latent strength of the ties between the two nations was the experience of one Brazilian official who visited Europe on the eve of the Depression and encountered a general ignorance of his homeland everywhere but in Germany. "For the Germans," he happily discovered, "a Brazilian was not in those days part of the mysterious *là-bas* to which the French took so much pleasure in relegating us."[20] Regular German air service to South America, inaugurated in 1933, meant that Reich exporters could place offers with Brazilian firms a full day earlier than American competitors, and it stimulated even greater interest in Brazil.[21] Does the German exist "who does not know the geographic position of Brazil and who does not seek to inform himself about our way of life?" was the exaggerated reaction of one surprised Brazilian visitor to Berlin.[22]

Banking and credit facilities were more readily available to Brazilian tradesmen active in the European market, since over twenty-five European houses operated in Brazil. The Banco Alemão Transatlântico, one of the two German banking concerns in the country, had branches in six major cities.[23] Contrasting this situation with the fact that only one American bank maintained an office in Brazil, Bouças warned Cordell Hull on one occasion that, "while American exporters are trying to get cash payment for their goods, the exporters from other countries, especially Germany, are offering to sell their merchandise on from one to five years' time." Aranha, too, called attention to this contrast: "Americans do not relate themselves to Brazil in a permanent way," he once told Secretary of Commerce Dan Roper. "They do not extend credits upon the annual basis as does Germany. They usually interest themselves in 'quick turnover' transactions and send the profits back to Wall Street."[24]

Endorsing this argument, a Wilhelmstrasse expert noted that the individual or family-owned firm with deep local roots typical of the German business community in South America played "an important role" in the advantageous position it enjoyed in comparison with British and American competitors, who favored the corporative form. The large numbers of German immigrants and their descendants living in Brazil—Reichsdeutsche, or German nationals, numbered about 100,000 in the mid-1930s while German-Brazilians totaled around 800,000—formed an "active outpost" for the Reich in South America and constituted another key link in the commercial bond between the two countries, a fact that did not escape the New Germany.[25]

The strength of German nationals and *teuto-brasileiros* in the import and retail trade, as well as in local manufacturing, in the southern states and, to a lesser extent, in São Paulo and Rio de Janeiro lay behind much of the preference traditionally shown for goods from Germany. Firms in Brazil recommended to businessmen by Reich authorities included such names as Stoltz, Wille, Lohner, Berndt, Müller, Schmeling, Engel, Becker, Hauer, Zimmermann, Hoffman, and a host of others of German origin.[26] The consul in Curitiba, Paraná, noted proudly in 1933 that it appeared to be "economically supported almost solely by its German factories and German businesses," a fact grudgingly acknowledged by a Brazilian nationalist of Portuguese descent.[27]

Germany's long-standing interest in the Brazilian market and excellent business connections there thus formed a major component in the rapid expansion of trade with Brazil after 1934, a fact usually overlooked by alarmists in other countries who tended to associate the bulging commercial statistics with alleged Nazi designs for territorial conquest.[28]

The underlying purpose of the innovations in German trade policy was to establish a balance between imports and exports while at the same time stimulating industrial recovery. The methods adopted meant that the Reich would be most likely to expand its trade with a country that produced abundant raw materials and foodstuffs and depended mainly on imports to satisfy its demand for manufactured goods. A desirable trade partner would also rely to a considerable extent on export proceeds to cover government expenditures and, like Germany, possess limited reserves of foreign exchange. In the mid-1930s Brazil met every one of these criteria.

The series of most-favored-nation agreements negotiated by Itamaraty in 1931 had not brought any improvement in Brazil's financial situation, as agricultural prices continued to straddle the declining end of the commercial seesaw with tariff barriers astride the other end. The 1932 drought in the Northeast and the São Paulo revolt were additional drains on the national treasury, and in mid-1933 Vargas ordered government departments to follow the "most rigorous economy" in drafting new budget proposals.[29] Servicing the foreign debt, which amounted to around L250 million in 1933, was another burden, and in 1934 the so-called Aranha Plan perforce reduced and consolidated payments.[30] Strident outcries by American exporters about unpaid bills acted as a barometer for Brazil's financial plight.[31] German sellers likewise had cause for complaint: by the fall of 1934 they had credits worth nearly 50 million reichsmarks frozen in Brazil.[32] The financial squeeze was so tight by that year that it became "more or less normal" for Brazilian importers, provided they had an influential contact, to pay a high premium in order to obtain "a bit of money" for inventory renewal.[33] Contributing to Brazil's predicament was the fact that export duties were vital sources of revenue for many state governments, particularly in the North.[34]

Export prospects seemed dim. In the case of Germany, warning signals from the legation in Berlin early in 1933 had unhappily proven well founded: a favorable commercial balance with the Reich of well over a million pounds sterling in 1932 plummeted to an adverse one of less than half a million the next year.[35] But informed observers quickly perceived new possibilities after the *Machtergreifung.* Hitler's manifest determination to rebuild the German economy could mean an "enormous advantage" for Brazil, one consul recently returned from the Central European country pointed out to Melo Franco. The commercial attaché in Berlin echoed this in painting the New Germany as a future "radiating center of consumption" for Brazilian products.[36]

Heavy German purchases during the first half of 1934 substantiated those predictions. Cotton shipments, especially, showed an enormous increase: during the first six months of 1934 the Reich bought ten times the amount from Brazil that it had during the entire preceding year.[37] Berlin's decision to establish quotas for coffee imports and to manipulate exchange permits for these quotas as a "first step" in making import demands serve as a *"direct* means of extending German export possibilities" offered Brazil even greater opportunities for expanded sales. The Nazi government made this clear to authorities in Rio de Janeiro, indicating that, if they were willing to accept German products in payment, coffee orders previously placed in Central America could be transferred to Brazilian shippers.[38]

As part of the effort to realign trade patterns, the Commercial Policy Committee recommended in May 1934 that a special delegation be sent to South America to negotiate with the governments of Brazil, Argentina, and other countries.[39] A former consul general in New York and counselor of embassy in Washington, Dr. Otto Kiep, was asked to conduct this *Bewährungsprobe* ("trial run") for the new trade policies.[40] Kiep's main goal was to find a way to vault the exchange barriers standing in the way of a rapid increase in commerce with South America. Arranging for payment of frozen German credits with raw materials was a related objective.[41]

The nearly 50 million Reichsmarks being held in Brazil, when added to that country's general commercial potential, explain why Ministerialdirektor Ritter attached "special importance" to the negotiations in Rio de Janeiro and why Berlin promised, "in case of reciprocity, a favorable treatment [of Brazil] in the projected reorganization of coffee importation."[42] Aware of the appeal that the prospect of definite markets would have, German authorities also dangled before Brazilian eyes the possibility of "fixed and even greater" quotas for Brazilian products, provided the Vargas administration made "practical and not theoretical" concessions in return.[43] For policy makers in Brazil, who were painfully conscious of the surplus raw materials on hand and of the lack of foreign currencies to pay for imports, the sudden attention from abroad seemed a godsend.

Otto Kiep and his colleagues sailed aboard the *Cap Arcona* in July, heading first for Argentina, at that time the Reich's leading trade associate in South America. The delegation, the first to be sent to the region, was a formidable one. It included Ritter's "right hand," Dr. Hans Kroll, as well as representatives of the Ministries of Economic Affairs and Food and Agriculture and the director of the Reichsbank. A short stopover in Rio de Janeiro afforded occasion for a preliminary conference with Brazilian authorities, whom the Germans found averse to the idea of direct barter or compensation of goods. The task in Brazil, Kiep quickly realized, would be to "enlighten" the Brazilians about Germany's situation and "convince them of the advantages of our proposals, with simultaneous reference to the otherwise unavoidable alternative [of being cut off from the German market]."[44]

The necessary conditions in Brazil for trading with the Central European power on some bilateral basis were, however, rapidly taking shape. Kiep's allusions to recent sales Brazil had lost to a "neighboring country" that had agreed to Berlin's terms and his reaffirmation of the possibility of guaranteed quotas undoubtedly fired Brazil's competitive imagination.[45] The sizeable German purchases during the first part of the year had considerably stimulated interest in that market, and new or enlivened traditional dependence upon such sales prompted anxious pleas from Brazilian exporters for protection of that outlet. Increasing this pressure for an agreement was the fact that at that very moment of "rising expectations" new German exchange measures and import licensing procedures temporarily halted imports from Brazil.[46]

Growing concern about slumping exports and the resultant financial hardships, especially the embarrassing problem of daily-mounting commercial arrears, heightened the receptivity of Brazilian policy makers to the idea of bilateral accords, a question then claiming the attention of the newly created CFCE. This body was an offspring of the union of economic difficulty and a spirit of administrative reform and central planning given impetus by the Revolution. Economic councils were popular with the statist-minded revolutionaries of 1930. While still head of the Ministry of Finance, Aranha months prior to establishment of the CFCE had impressed upon Vargas the "urgency" of providing for supervised coordination among the various departments connected with foreign trade. An Itamaraty official had also emphasized the need for a central organ, "a kind of Foreign Trade Council."[47]

The response of Catete Palace was a decree of June 1934 creating the CFCE, an agency that represented an effort to meet the nation's trade difficulties rationally and with the best possible information. The attendance at its meetings of various cabinet officials, as well, many times, of the president himself, reflected the initial importance of the Council in decision making on issues linked to international trade.

Highlighting its opening sessions in August 1934 was debate over a proposal to adopt clearing agreements as a general solution to the financial crisis. Principal author of the plan was Marcos de Souza Dantas, exchange director of the Banco do Brasil. A former secretary of finance in his native state of São Paulo and director of the National Coffee Department, Dantas was one of the new breed of young *técnicos* emerging in the Brazil of the 1930s. During the initial decision-making period he played a prominent role in the formulation of trade policy. Indeed, Macedo Soares thought the youthful financial specialist exercised too much influence. Dantas, he complained, enjoyed the "most complete freedom of action," a judgment shared by the British ambassador, who likewise attributed a decisive voice in financial affairs to this "expert with all the statistics at his fingers' ends."[48]

Accounting for Dantas's status were not only his technical expertise and ability to articulate forcefully a point of view, but also his close personal relations with Aranha and other leaders of 1930,[49] as well as a considerable amount of administrative laxity and confusion born of tradition and, more immediately, the absorption of the administration in domestic political problems. The fact that he was a technician rather than a politician probably contributed to Vargas's tendency to allow Dantas substantial latitude.[50] Intellectually Dantas was predisposed to favor active governmental intervention in trade relations, and his authoritarian propensities—a few months later he would resign from office, announce his disenchantment with liberalism, and declare his adherence to the Integralist party—undoubtedly led to personal sympathy with the Nazi experiment. Above all, Dantas was intensely nationalistic and thoroughly practical. As he once candidly confessed to a British diplomat, his position on economic questions was determined by "sheer expediency."[51]

In a lengthy memorandum of August 10, Dantas argued the necessity of an urgent attack on the problem of overdue import payments, which was giving rise to interminable complaints and "even threats." Clearing agreements in which payments for imports from a particular country would be debited in a special account against the proceeds of exports to that nation would be the most practical solution, he contended. Pragmatically admonishing Council members to bow to requirements of the moment, Dantas predicted that Brazil would "irresistibly" adopt bilateralism, either of its own accord or because other nations imposed it.[52]

Artur Souza Costa, the newly appointed finance minister who was to remain at his post until 1945 and whose influence on economic policy was often decisive, viewed the proposal with distaste. Eminently conservative—"Desist from this nonsense of revolution!" he had advised a young plotter on the eve of the October uprising[53]—the largely self-educated former president of the Bank of Rio Grande do Sul and, until recently, the Banco do Brasil was steeped in the doctrines of economic liberalism. "Balance the Budget!" became his battle cry throughout the decade, provoking the opposition of those who regarded his loyalty to what he called the "old and salutary classical principles" as a sign of imperviousness to new ideas.[54] Vargas, also from Rio Grande do Sul, trusted and listened to the counsel of this long-time friend, relying on him to keep a close watch on the national coffers. "Financially, Costa is the prop, the mainstay, 'miser emeritus' who closes the purse strings and cuts avoidable expenses," the president confided.[55]

But if nature and study inclined Souza Costa to oppose the interference with natural market mechanisms inherent in the clearing proposal, orthodoxy did not render him so doctrinaire that he was blind to the imposing gravity of the financial crisis. To be sure, one of the traits that Vargas most admired in the corpulent, forty-one–year–old *gaúcho* banker—and one that largely explains the affinity between the two men—was his "plastic and practical spirit," his readiness to accept the dictates of logic and facts. As Souza Costa himself once acknowledged, in reference to Aranha's observations on the futility of appealing to friendship in commercial negotiations, by inclination he harbored "no illusions" in that regard. With marked reluctance Souza Costa now told the CFCE at its second meeting that he approved Dantas's proposal only as an "imposition of circumstances and not as useful to our interests." The administration had successfully resisted previous pressure for special agreements, but compensation now seemed to be a "fatality" from which there was no escape.[56]

During the next few days events materially strengthened Dantas's hand, as Berlin's manipulation of coffee import licenses began to work, not unintentionally, to Brazil's advantage. Approached by exporters with tempting offers from German importers, Dantas seized the opportunity to set up private clearing accounts, and the result was a boom in coffee shipments. At a session of the CFCE on August 27, he reported that a half-million sacks had been ordered in just ten days. This, he argued, indicated what the country could expect from trade on a bilateral basis with the Reich. Failure of the government's London creditors to respond to an appeal from Souza Costa for assistance and his announcement that Brazil could therefore "without scruples" adopt a clearing scheme further bolstered the arguments of the Bank of Brazil expert.[57]

Appointed head of an ad hoc committee established to study the German suggestion, Dantas presented a counterproposal calling for the opening in the Reichsbank of a special account to handle all transactions between German and Brazilian traders. With the endorsement of its subcommittee on trade agreements, the CFCE ratified the plan at its next meeting.[58] Once the idea of a bilateral accord with the Reich had been approved, it remained to be seen how far the Brazilian government would go in implementing this resolution in the face of strong opposition from the United States.

The State Department had been trying to get Brazil seated at the bargaining table since the middle of the previous year, and the recent passage of the Reciprocal Trade Agreements Act sharpened Hull's eagerness to launch his crusade. As he watched Roosevelt sign the bill into law, "each stroke of the pen seemed to write a message of gladness on my heart," the secretary of state later wrote.[59] As a major exporter of raw materials and importer of manufactured articles, Brazil appeared to be an ideal place to begin the liberalization of world commerce, and Hull and his colleagues were anxious to conclude what they hoped would be a model treaty for negotiations with other countries. Hull also thought that, by making the initial agreement under the new Act with a country like Brazil, he could parry domestic thrusts at his program.

Within the administration itself the secretary was encountering serious criticism of his views on the need to eliminate restrictions on international trade. Heading the opposition was George N. Peek, former head of the Agricultural Adjustment Administration and champion of what the president called a "very hard-headed practical angle of trade." Peek had been designated special foreign trade adviser the previous March. "If Mr. Roosevelt had hit me between the eyes with a sledge hammer," Hull recalled, "he could not have stunned me more than by this appointment."[60]

Peek saw in unconditional most-favored-nation accords "one more sacrifice the American farmer would be called upon to make for the industrialist." He advocated instead an aggressive, nationalistic policy, including such practices as dumping and direct barter, to protect the American economy from what he regarded as an increasing challenge from rapidly industrializing countries. "Coffee has taught the Brazilians the great lesson that nations which depend upon the export of raw materials can never be free," he once remarked.[61]

The government had also been under heavy pressure during the preceding two years from exporters upset by Brazil's continual delay in paying for imports from the United States. Early in 1934 the State Department received a deluge of such protests. Typical was the colorful lament of a representative of fruit shippers that Brazil had "our apples and pears and money as well." One export managing firm angrily charged that the American exporter was "left to his own devices" in South America, where he was "practically a man without a country," while governments of competitor nations "vigorously" protected the interests of their nationals. As the best customer for Brazilian coffee, the United States held both the "cheese and knife," so "what are we waiting for?" the firm demanded to know.[62]

Despite such pressure, the State Department, under "standing instructions" from Roosevelt, had refrained from intervention in the wrangling over funds between the Vargas administration and American holders of Brazilian bonds and exporters or companies with unpaid bills and frozen credits.[63] Ambassador Hugh Gibson, in Rio de Janeiro, expressed prevailing opinion in the department in 1934 when he reproved a subordinate who found Banco do Brasil authorities "shamelessly impervious to appeals for ethical action" and thought more forceful measures should be taken to ensure better handling of American claims. "I told the Consul General that if securing exchange cover was our only problem with Brazil we might well enough send the fleet, land marines, and get what we wanted," said Gibson, "but that we must not forget that this is only one phase of the relations between the two countries and that we will go on having relations even if the exchange problem is settled or not settled."[64]

Rio de Janeiro was the first South American assignment for Gibson, a career official with a long tenure of service in Europe. He had arrived the previous year feeling "a good deal like a cat in a strange garret," but life in Rio had proven delightful and the people surprised him.[65] "If anybody had told me a year ago that I'd find the Brazilian congenial," he confided, "I should have winked the other eye, but strange to say, such is the case."[66] The ambassador soon developed an image of the country and its leaders as dedicated, unwavering allies. Indeed, Brazilian friendliness, after his experiences in Europe, was "almost too much to bear," he told a diplomat-friend. "These strange people really seem to like us . . ."[67] This image became fixed over the next two years as Itamaraty officials collaborated closely with the embassy on the Chaco question. But on other issues, such as trade policy, Brazilian authorities saw their interests as divergent from those of the United States, and Gibson's perceptions of Itamaraty would later prevent him from accurately assessing Brazilian maneuvers.

Ironically, America's competitors viewed Gibson in a different light. Because of Brazil's dependence on coffee sales, British officials regarded her as "a conquered country," and they suspected Gibson of being "by temperament perfectly at home when using an iron hand, if necessary without the velvet glove." Yet firsthand observation of New Deal diplomacy in action puzzled tough-minded Sir William Seeds, who headed the embassy in Rio de Janeiro. In a personal letter to the head of the American Department of the Foreign Office in June 1934, Seeds candidly remarked that if he possessed Washington's leverage he would force Brazil to use coffee earnings to pay its debts to American citizens. "Of course the Americans may not wish to go the whole hog: they have so, unaccountably to me, delayed in doing anything serious in that line hitherto," he observed, "that one feels they think it more politic to let Brazil gradually realize her position vis-à-vis the States than to impress it on her *vi et armis*."[68]

Convinced that the reciprocal trade agreements program held greater promise for general economic improvement, the State Department had indeed even declined an offer in July by Aranha and Dantas of a clearing agreement that would have permitted American exporters to "offer prices and conditions more advantageous than their competitors [could]." What Hull wanted instead was a new liberal treaty, and, when Aranha presented his credentials to Roosevelt on October 2, the president was "very expressive" in telling him that "like two good friends" their countries needed to conclude a trade pact.[69]

Aranha's arrival in Washington opened the decisive phase of the negotiations both there and in Brazil. The world of diplomacy was alien to the impulsive, forty-year-old former revolutionary leader, but he brought to his new duties an "unusual intelligence and a readiness to learn," a keen sense of humor, and a dedication to public interest, as well as considerable personal ambition. Physically and temperamentally, the tall, handsome, volatile Aranha was a study in contrast when placed beside the short, slightly heavy, seemingly imperturbable Vargas. "He was brought up and still belongs in Rio Grande do Sul, the Brazilian Wild West," Gibson noted, "where men are quick on the draw and devote an adequate amount of time and attention to racing, cock-fighting, and other red-blooded sports." In the American envoy's opinion, Aranha was "not altogether house-broke, but makes up for this by quickness, resourcefulness and anxiety to play ball with us."[70]

One thing the fledgling diplomat shared with Vargas was a nationalistic concern for Brazil's welfare. As former finance minister, Aranha was intimately acquainted with his country's economic plight and was convinced that the road to salvation ran through Washington. "So far as I can judge, he is the initiator of the present definite movement in Brazil to draw away from Europe and throw Brazil's lot in with the United States," Gibson advised Roosevelt. "He has done this on realistic grounds, which is the best assurance that he will stand hitched." British business interests in Rio de Janeiro had a similar opinion of Aranha, but they placed a different value judgment on his orientation. Before the Brazilian politician-diplomat departed for his new post, they complained, he had been "saturated with the American point of view."[71]

What might be termed his "American experience"—his contact with

American society—made an indelible impression on Aranha, as his personal correspondence showed. Such phrases and words as "land without equal," "spectacle of grandeur and beauty," "seething with activity," "majesty that exceeds the most audacious and fertile imagination," "incredible," and "colossal" were abundant in his early private descriptions of the United States. "Don't think that I am exaggerating or that I am hallucinated," he told Vargas. "I am seeing and noting facts. And I do so with the sole aim of helping to acquaint you with the reality of this country, so distorted in Brazil."[72]

Aranha's favorable image of the United States, which remained more or less constant throughout the decade and was strengthened by personal regard for Roosevelt and Sumner Welles, thus reinforced earlier inclinations born of the statistics of foreign trade and became a major determinant of his foreign policy attitudes. A fortuitous merger of political ambition—an ambassadorship successful in terms of expanded trade and perhaps other economic benefits would boost his political stock when the next presidential campaign took place at home —and solicitude for Brazil's national interest, as he perceived it, made him a sedulous champion of cooperation in Hull's program.

American concern about German competition became immediately apparent to Aranha in his initial discussions with Assistant Secretary of State Sumner Welles and his staff early in October. News reports a month earlier of forthcoming German-Brazilian negotiations had spread consternation among business and governmental interests. The American Exporters' and Importers' Association was moved to appeal to the State Department, warning that "unless we are on our guard" Berlin and Rio would sign an agreement "and the exchange which rightfully belongs to us will go elsewhere." Germany's demarche and the resultant hue and cry from American exporters in fact prompted a reassessment of policy by a special State Department committee. But the result of this reexamination was a recommendation against imposing any preferential accord on Brazil. Such a step, explained economic adviser Herbert Feis, would weaken the general stand against bilateralism advocated by Hull.[73]

Department officials recognized, of course, that a compensation or special payments agreement between Brazil and the Reich would be an "unfortunate development,"[74] and concern about that possibility dominated Brazilian-American talks. The Brazilian government was not particularly keen on a new treaty with the United States—the problem, said Aranha, was not high tariffs but inadequate banking, shipping, and credit facilities—and the ambassador's remark that Brazil had no choice but to negotiate with the Germans was disquieting. American officials urged that Brazil make no decision regarding German overtures until the possibilities of credits from the United States had been examined, and privately department planners discussed the need to do "everything we can" to persuade Brazil not to strengthen the "barrier of special exchange-grabbing agreements." There was, however, a marked reluctance within the State Department to consider any means of bringing decisive pressure on Brazil. One official spoke of making it clear to Aranha that if his country acquiesced in German trading methods the American government might "be forced" to protect itself, and another spoke of taking what steps the department "properly" could to prevent Rio de Janeiro from making a bilateral pact with Berlin. But the latter official, conscious of the still-unresolved struggle between Peek and Hull, admitted that the department could not require an "iron clad" assurance from Brazil, since it could not itself guarantee the permanence of American policy.[75]

Aranha duly reported to Itamaraty the frame of mind in Washington, warning that a "hasty" accord with the Germans would bolster the forces of economic nationalism in the United States, with "harmful" consequences for Brazilian interests. Both he and Commercial Attaché Paulo Hasslocher also sent private assessments directly to Vargas. Noting the State Department's "mistrust" of the German-Brazilian discussions underway in Rio de Janeiro, Hasslocher reminded Vargas that foreign policy should rest "exclusively on self-interest" and argued that cooperation with the United States was essential for Brazil. Aranha agreed "on all points" with Hasslocher. The State Department, he reiterated, had insisted that a bilateral agreement with Berlin would be economic suicide for Brazil. "I used all the arguments to show that nowadays nations lived by expedients while awaiting the era of *equality* and *liberty*," said Aranha, "and that when the great powers reached the [point of] suicide they were talking about, we would already be dead." Department spokesmen had "found this very funny" but remained firm in rejecting bilateralism, he concluded.[76] Unhappily for Aranha and his American allies, two men especially eager to do business with the Germans were in charge of the negotiations in Rio de Janeiro.

A former consul general in New York, where he had known Otto Kiep, fifty-year-old Sebastião Sampaio was chief of Itamaraty's Commercial and Economic Section and executive director of the CFCE. A "nervous, energetic" man, he had been managing editor of the prestigious *Jornal do Commércio* during the war and had opposed Brazil's participation. After the war he had entered diplomatic service and found advancement relatively easy. An archconservative, Sampaio sympathized with many of the aims delineated by architects of the New Order in Europe—in 1938 he would extol the "very able" anti-Communist front erected by Rome and Berlin. Anxious now for promotion to minister and his own mission abroad, he was also deeply impressed by the Reich's potential economic hegemony in Europe, and he saw the German market for raw materials as a ripe plum waiting to be picked.[77] A profitable agreement with Berlin would both please his superiors and, in his eyes, benefit Brazil, so Sampaio was a responsive negotiator—the "Rasputin of this compensation problem," Gibson later put it—in talks with Kiep, whom he regarded as "very practical" and "inspired by the best disposition" toward Brazil.[78]

As a career official, Sampaio had no particular political influence to lend weight to his opinion, although perhaps by that very fact he was allowed, as Dantas was, more freedom to maneuver. By virtue of his position, Sampaio received the assignment to handle negotiations on commercial matters—"He is the one who determines everything," complained Bouças, a technical consultant to the CFCE[79]—while Dantas conducted discussions on the financial aspects of German-Brazilian trade. This enhanced significantly the influence of both men, since their reports formed to a considerable degree the informational basis of subsequent policy decisions.

Sampaio was backed up in Itamaraty by Macedo Soares, a religious, conservative businessman-politician from São Paulo who had received the portfolio of foreign affairs in July as a reward for his prominent role in the reconciliation of his native state with the central government after the 1932 civil war. Macedo Soares had only a modicum of diplomatic experience, his first responsibility in this field having been chairmanship of the delegation to the Geneva Disarmament Convention two years earlier. He was first and foremost a politician, one with deep regional loyalties and increasingly manifest presidential aspirations.[80]

The British embassy appraised Macedo Soares as an "undoubtedly clever" man "strongly imbued with State patriotism," but one who lacked Melo Franco's "personal charm" and whose "reputation for trustworthiness is not high." However, a leading spokesman for nationalist solutions for Brazil's problems, Afonso Arinos de Melo

Franco, a son of the former foreign minister, served under Macedo Soares at Geneva and thought him "morally a man of highest quality," if ambitious and a bit vain. And Gibson, who also had worked with Macedo Soares at the disarmament convention, was captivated by his "real friendliness" toward the United States and held him in high esteem. "He is one of the Brazilians who is convinced that the real future of this country lies in drawing away from Europe in order to follow the closest cooperation with the United States . . . ," the ambassador believed.[81]

On the wider diplomatic front Macedo Soares did advocate such a policy, but, as a man new to his post and lacking an exceptionally strong state or national political base, he was little inclined to risk his cabinet position and potential springboard into Catete Palace by making a determined stand one way or another on the trade issue. For political and emotional reasons he was sensitive to the requirements of the *paulista* economy, which meant that he would favor exploring all market possibilities. Macedo Soares was also actively involved during this period in the diplomatic wrangling over the Chaco question that would lead enthusiastic publicists to bestow on him the title of "Chancellor of Peace," and this left even greater initiative in the trade negotiations to Sampaio.

The alarm signals from Washington, coupled with an easing of exchange controls to permit all but coffee exporters to sell drafts on the open market, led to a reconsideration of the decision to enter into a formal clearing agreement with Germany. Sampaio read Aranha's messages to the CFCE on October 8, and Dantas concluded that any direct compensation of goods under official auspices, as Kiep had proposed, would "expose us to reprisals and demands, especially on the part of the United States." Anyway, the new exchange policy would permit private compensation transactions, so there was no longer any reason for an official commitment, said Dantas. Although he had never opposed close relations with the United States, he did not think Brazil should "carry this to the point of exaggeration." Itamaraty, he suggested, should point out to Aranha that any dislocation of Brazilian purchases from North America to Europe was a result not of Brazilian initiative but of the greater advantages offered by the Europeans.[82]

To allay Aranha's misgivings, Sampaio and Dantas drafted a telegram informing him that all Brazil sought now was a "simple understanding" with the Reich that would guarantee fixed quotas for

Brazilian products. The government would take "no measures what-soever that may create a special, privileged, or advantageous situation for Germany," they assured the ambassador. Brazil would acquiesce in the German practice of paying for imports in compensation marks, but this "*de facto* conformity" was not to be contractual. The "only" blocked marks that the Banco do Brasil would control under the envisioned setup would be those derived from coffee sales.[83]

Otto Kiep received a different explanation of what the Brazilian negotiators intended. Sampaio candidly told him that Brazil could not jeopardize its large trade surplus with the United States by signing a formal pact with Germany. But the two countries could forego a treaty and merely continue the recently begun commerce in compensation marks, extending it through a "purely technical" agreement between the Reichsbank and the Banco do Brasil to all trade between them. As a "concession" for Brazil's acquiescence in bilateral practices, the Reich could grant attractive quotas for Brazilian exports. Requesting "strictly confidential" handling of the proposal, Sampaio aptly observed that it represented "considerable favoritism" toward Germany.[84]

The quota figures suggested by the CFCE director, which included fifty thousand tons for cotton, were, in Kiep's judgment, an expression of Brazil's desire to move into the German market "to the greatest possible extent." Sampaio also wanted guaranteed percentages of the Reich's imports of raw materials, mainly "for publicity reasons, since [the] secret quota figures probably will not be published," Kiep reported. These percentages included 70 for coffee, 30 for hides, skins, cacao, and tobacco, 25 for rubber, and 20 for wool and rice.[85]

During the next two weeks the negotiating teams "informally" reached a "practical" understanding. The ultimate agreement, Sampaio informed the CFCE on October 22, could take the form of "vague notes" stating mutual desire to continue trade and specifying quotas for Brazilian exports, which could assume, he stressed, "much greater" proportions under Germany's new policies. He acknowledged that the compensation system would require Brazil to buy more from the Central European power, but the latter was a better market for Brazil's general economic interests than the United States, which serviced mainly the coffee-producing states.[86]

Dantas reminded Council members that existing most-favored-nation treaties meant that the projected concession of "certain advantages" to Germany would elicit protests from other countries. To make an official commitment would therefore be "dangerous," he pointed out. But Brazil could use "an intermediate formula" to accomplish its aim, without running the risk of being charged with "irregular" conduct by third countries. The Reichsbank could simply offer to open a special account for the Banco do Brasil, a service the latter would agree to accept "whenever opportunity should arise." Dantas, knowing that German exporters would, in effect, be guaranteed prompt payment for their goods while British or American shippers would continue to wait weeks and even months for payment, admitted that the arrangement "naturally will place Germany in an advantageous position in Brazil in relation to other countries." But the alternative, he argued, was a trade war with Berlin, which would benefit only Brazil's competitors.[87]

Insistent messages from Aranha led to sober reflection in Rio de Janeiro. The talks with the Germans, he remonstrated, had caused a halt in his negotiations with the State Department. Before signing a treaty, the ambassador hoped to arrange guarantees for Brazil's present surplus in trade with the United States and to obtain financing for liquidation of frozen commercial balances. Feis, "a technician in credit matters and superman of the New Deal," had promised him a memorandum on credit possibilities but had not produced the document, since the State Department, Aranha thought, was awaiting Brazil's decision about Germany.[88]

What actually accounted for the State Department's delay in getting a written statement of policy into Aranha's hands was lingering indecision within the administration about trade policy. When Welles began his conversations with Aranha, he had presumed, "somewhat naively perhaps," that opinion in government councils was now agreed on a liberal orientation. He soon discovered that he was wrong and that it would be necessary to deal with "George Peek and his cohorts." Peek, in fact, on October 19 in committee argued strongly against the State Department's attitude and then dispatched a letter to Assistant Secretary Francis Sayre emphasizing anew his opposition to the elimination of special bilateral agreements. The rest of the month was taken up in discussions of the text of an aide-mémoire to be delivered to Aranha.[89]

Welles, in the meantime, again appealed to Aranha to persuade his government not to make a decision until it had considered the promised American memorandum. Unless there was a reaction to German policy, the assistant secretary emphasized, all other countries would be forced to adopt bilateralism. Unimpressed by the "touch of messianism" in the American attitude, Aranha nonetheless agreed with Hasslocher that a "wholehearted alignment" with the United States was the wisest course for Brazil, and he urged Itamaraty to heed Welles's advice. The Americans regarded Brazil's cooperation as "fundamental" to the success of their program, he said, and they were ready to aid Brazil in return. If the latter entered into bilateral arrangements, however, Washington would refuse any assistance, he warned.[90]

The memorandum that Welles finally handed him on October 30 confirmed, in Aranha's mind, his earlier appraisals of the alternatives. The memorandum, a politely phrased reminder of the need for a new deal in Brazil's commercial policies toward the United States, pointed out that Brazilian sales to the United States yielded dollars "far in excess" of the amount needed to cover debts to American citizens, and it hinted at restrictions should the two countries not be able to reach an understanding. Back in his office, Aranha penned a lengthy dispatch to Macedo Soares. The "capital point" in the American trade blueprint was to bind Brazil to its system, he noted. The choice offered by the State Department seemed clear: "Either we follow a liberal policy or it will be forced to apply to us the antiliberal one."[91]

Vargas, in a letter written that same day, before he learned of the memorandum, had already concluded that Brazil had reached a "crossroads" of sorts. Communications over the past month from Washington and recent telegrams from Aranha, whose importance was dramatized by the heavily underlined copies that Sampaio had sent the chief executive, caused him to weigh carefully the alternatives. He had called Souza Costa, Dantas, Sampaio, and Macedo Soares to Guanabara Palace the previous evening for a thorough review of the problem. This informal council discussed the American reaction, and Dantas pressed the case for an understanding with Germany.[92] It was undoubtedly at this conference that the plan to enter into a noncontractual arrangement with the Reich was ratified. The warning inherent in the State Department memorandum, details of which reached policy makers in Rio de Janeiro the day after the Guanabara meeting, served possibly to postpone for a few days the implementation of that decision, but it did not alter its substance.

By the end of the first week in November, the negotiators had finished their bargaining—Berlin rejected any percentage guarantees and insisted on some quota reductions—and had worked out the texts of the notes. The Brazilians urged that they be kept secret since publicity would evoke protests from third countries. Alleging that Souza Costa's preoccupation with budgetary matters would delay for a few weeks a formal agreement, they suggested that the notes be at first only "provisionally" signed but that they take effect immediately, pending definitive signature. At least this way, Kiep was told, the government could tell other countries that no treaty had been signed with Germany.[93]

The exchange took place on November 8, with Sampaio and Dantas acknowledging in writing only the receipt of the German communications and reiterating their lack of authority to undertake any formal commitment. The note on quotas pledged Germany to import fixed amounts of various products, including 25,000 tons of cacao and 20,000 of rice, and unlimited quantities against compensation marks of wool, cotton, hides and skins, tobacco, rubber, "and other raw materials for industry." Also included was an intricate schedule making any increase in coffee imports dependent upon greater imports of raw materials. The letter dealing with the banking arrangement stated that the proceeds obtained from the sale of coffee to Germany would be deposited by the Reichsbank in an *Aski* account for the Banco do Brasil, which in turn would provide credits to Brazilian importers of German goods.[94] This informal understanding governed trade relations between Germany and Brazil for the next eighteen months. A close analysis of the roots of the decision leading to that settlement reveals clearly the pragmatic, consciously opportunistic nature of the response of Brazilian policy makers to domestic pressure and conflicting external demands.

Otto Kiep offered a number of reasons for the fact that Brazilian leaders, unlike their Argentine counterparts, had from the beginning wanted to establish the "closest possible" economic relations with the Reich. For one thing, he suggested, Argentina seemed content with its strong dependency upon Great Britain, the major consumer of pampas-grown beef, whereas Brazil appeared eager to find other clients abroad in order to lessen its economic dependence upon the United States, the country's biggest coffee market. "They openly fear the Americans more than they like them," said Kiep, "and regard the strong position of the United States as Brazil's creditor and source of investments apparently with a certain resentment tinged with nationalism."[95] But Brazil's present economic ties with the United States were foreign policy realities impossible to ignore, and the potential reaction from Washington weighed heavily on Brazilian policy makers. Everything, Vargas had cautioned the CFCE late in August, counseled maintenance of friendly ties with the United States, "a vast market for our products," and Vargas realized, as he sanctioned the informal arrangement with the Germans, that the possibility of an estrangement from Washington was a matter to be weighed "with greatest care."[96] But did the understanding with Berlin necessarily imply such an estrangement?

The State Department, according to reports from the embassy in Washington, threatened to invoke sanctions—a clearing agreement that would force Brazil to pay promptly its various debts to American citizens—if Brazil signed an agreement with Germany. Welles's memorandum of October 30 at least implied this. For that threat to be completely effective two conditions were necessary. First, the sanction would have to be regarded by the Brazilians as a severe enough deprivation to outweigh the potential advantages of noncompliance with American wishes. And, second, Brazilian policy makers would have to be persuaded that the United States government would actually carry out the threat if Brazil refused to cooperate.[97] Vargas, in the face of American opposition, declined a formal agreement with the Germans, but he found a *jeito* of clearing that hurdle and in practice proceeding as Brazil's interests seemed to indicate. As Kiep noted, the Brazilians were actually not hindered by American pressure, having insisted on "camouflage" of the agreement "purely out of practical considerations."[98] Washington's attitude was a constraint on Brazilian authorities, but it affected the form rather than the content of Brazil's relationship with Berlin. Why was this?

The answer, in part, is probably that a clearing agreement with the United States did not represent for decision makers in Rio de Janeiro the dire consequence that the State Department thought it did. So intense was their own commitment to "free" trade that Hull, Welles, and their associates apparently assumed that Brazilian authorities would likewise regard such a bilateral accord as unpalatable. Brazilian assurances of at least theoretical dedication to the most-favored-nation principle no doubt encouraged this assumption. But Aranha and Dantas had, after all, offered to set up a clearing account with the United States in July, its realization contingent upon a long-term loan. Dantas certainly was not averse to the idea. His original proposal to the CFCE in August had called for a general use of clearing agreements, which were acceptable to him because they seemed reasonable.

He admitted that a country like the United States could with justification view as "absurd" the fact that Brazil failed to pay for American
goods, or made payment only after lengthy delay, when American
importers paid "on demand and without restriction" their debts to
Brazilian shippers.[99]

Vargas and Itamaraty also viewed a clearing agreement with the
United States as a distinct possibility and had learned to live with the
idea. Macedo Soares recognized that Washington "logically" might
insist on it, and he advised Aranha two weeks after Kiep departed
that Brazil would agree. In normal circumstances Brazil should even
take the initiative in proposing such an arrangement, he said, since it
would mean "only that we are going to pay what we should pay."[100]
So the weapon that the State Department regarded as the ultimate
horror was contemplated with some equanimity by officials in Rio de
Janeiro. When coupled with signs that Washington's "hard line" was
razor thin, that anticipation made a paper sword of the department's
threatened sanction. American officials seemed to be projecting their
own values onto the other side and they failed to perceive the error of
their assumptions.

Policy makers in Brazil had received ample signals that the good-
neighborliness of the Roosevelt administration opened up permissive
cracks in the wall of resistance to bilateralism that Cordell Hull was
feverishly trying to erect. A potential weapon of considerable weight
in the hands of the American government was the threat of a tax on
coffee imports, a possibility that had given Brazilian authorities an
"unpleasant shock" several months before.[101] Rumors late in August
of a revival of the idea set the Rio de Janeiro–Washington cable lines
humming. Itamaraty anxiously wanted to know, Was there anything
to this? With considerable relief, Chargé Freitas-Valle replied after
investigation that the rumors were "entirely devoid of serious foundation." When a representative of the National Coffee Department
brought the matter up at the next session of the CFCE, a pleased
Macedo Soares announced that there was no cause for alarm.[102]

The observations of Sir William Seeds suggest ample awareness in
diplomatic circles of Washington's soft tread—and perhaps widespread puzzlement about it—which could not have escaped government officials endeavoring to determine how much credibility to place
in alleged American intentions. Numerous reports came to Vargas that
the new administration was eager to cultivate Brazilian friendship.
"Simply extraordinary" was how Bouças in March had described

Brazil's resulting position. "In my opinion, they will do everything possible to get our cooperation for their policy" was a typical comment by Aranha, who unwittingly contributed to the suspicion in Rio de Janeiro that there was more bark than bite to State Department expostulations by this constant tendency to juxtapose remarks about beckoning opportunities with warnings of likely reprisals should Brazil go along with Germany. "This country wants our solidarity for its international figurations," he reported. "We are sought after. This position makes us strong and valuable. Let's make the most of it," he admonished Vargas. Hugh Gibson probably helped to weaken the force of the department's pleas by assuring Macedo Soares that it would act to dilute the demands of private business circles for payment guarantees in the projected American-Brazilian treaty.[103]

Vargas and Dantas were quite aware that Washington's desire to enlist Brazilian support in the war on bilateralism enhanced their maneuverability. When the question arose in the CFCE of whether or not to await Aranha's arrival in the American capital before beginning negotiations there, Vargas opted to wait, since the United States was more anxious to conclude a new treaty than he was. Dantas made the same point when he observed, in connection with the possibility of a duty on coffee, that the United States was unlikely to levy one, since it was eager to get Brazil's signature on a new commercial pact. In a skillful attempt to screen over the divergence in trade orientation, Macedo Soares made repeated references during the negotiations to Brazil's cooperative attitude in other areas of foreign affairs. The "perfect synchronization" of Brazil's foreign policy with that of the United States should, he argued, merit sympathetic understanding from Washington of Brazil's trade problems.[104]

Rio de Janeiro's response to the State Department memorandum of October 30, a telegram drafted by Souza Costa and cleared with Vargas before it went to Itamaraty for transmission,[105] was essentially a probing of the American perimeter. What officials in Brazil wanted to know was "how far" the Americans actually intended the campaign against compensation trade to go. The memorandum was "imprecise," noted Souza Costa, and seemed to indicate that understandings like that contemplated with Germany might be "tolerated." Clarifying messages from Aranha in mid-November referring to the department's desire to make "energetic declarations and undertake effective action" were sufficiently vague to cause no basic reevaluation of policy in Rio de Janeiro. Indeed, the ambassador's reiteration of the strong wish of the department to make Brazil its first major recruit for the crusade against bilateralism[106] only reinforced his government's perception of the atmosphere in the American camp as one of fluidity and, ultimately, permissiveness.

Kiep correctly alluded to an eagerness to increase exports of various products as a consideration of major importance to Brazilian policy makers. Satisfaction of regional interests and export diversification were related goals that, although they had immediate political and financial significance, also stemmed from a painful realization of the disadvantages inherent in substantial dependence on a single export commodity. Vargas consequently had his negotiators seek guaranteed quotas to encourage production of such items as cotton, rubber, and cacao. And he remonstrated with his ambassador-friend in Washington that Germany was a market for products that had no sale in the United States and that were of special interest to Rio Grande do Sul, "such as hides, wool, lard, meats, and tobacco." Even military leaders wanted to see reduced financial reliance on one export commodity.[107]

Interest-group pressure played a significant part in decision making. Kiep pointed to the German community in Brazil (*Kolonialistentum*), producers of wool, tobacco, and beef and active in the import business, as effective lobbyists on behalf of an understanding with Berlin.[108] And Vargas's reference to the benefits that his home state would derive from trade with Germany suggests that appeals from producers in that state, as well as in others, had not been without effect. When news of the Kiep mission first reached Brazil, *gaúcho* livestock spokesmen had wired the central government anxiously requesting that it arrange the sale to Germany of surplus stocks of some 165,000 hides. During CFCE sessions in October, a delegation of representatives of *riograndense* cattle and agricultural associations traveled to the federal capital, where they met with Sampaio almost daily for a week to press for protection or opening up of the German market.[109]

Other important local groups, such as Bahian tobacco growers and cacao producers, closely followed the talks with Kiep. Germany was a vital market for tobacco farmers in that state, absorbing about 70 percent of their production. The commercial director of the Bahian Cacao Institute flew to Rio de Janeiro for special conferences with Sampaio, while Governor Juracy Magalhães, then a mainstay of the regime, added a personal entreaty. The state's economic health, he told Vargas, depended "exclusively" on an understanding with Berlin. From Minas Gerais, Amazonas, and São Paulo came similar pleas.[110]

Brazil's cotton potential was particularly seductive to German importers and dealers in textiles, who were deeply preoccupied in mid-1934 with the damaging effects of foreign exchange shortage on their supply of raw material.[111] *Burgermeister* from Bremen took their troubles to Nazi "philosopher" and foreign policy "expert" Alfred Rosenberg early in June. They told him that, unless cotton could be acquired from Brazil through compensation trade, one-fourth of their textile workers would soon have to be laid off.[112] Later that month some importers went directly to the Brazilian embassy in Berlin with offers to trade manufactured goods for cotton, and reports from the Brazilian Commercial Bureau there indicated that the Ministry of Economic Affairs "not only endorses such an exchange but insists on its realization . . ." During a top-level conference in mid-October, Schacht warned Hitler and other Nazi leaders that the textile industry was running dangerously low on cotton supplies, with some factories having enough for only a fortnight.[113]

Heavy buying by German importers earlier in the year and the recent tempting barter proposals awakened Brazilian authorities to the opportunities for diversifying the composition of overseas sales. One member of the CFCE found "most encouraging" the statement by German agents that Brazilian fibers could replace American cotton in their factories. A special committee set up to study the question of cotton production recommended to the CFCE, in view of the present "voluminous" crop and an anticipated heavier one in 1935, that the administration seek through the Kiep delegation to "ensure and possibly extend" sales to the Reich, a recommendation approved by a plenary session at the end of August and forwarded to Catete. Vargas endorsed both the suggestion and its implicit goal, hailing the "possibility of a new market for cotton" in his letter to Aranha outlining the necessity of an accord with the Germans.[114]

Continuation of the financial crisis weighed heavily on the minds of policy makers. Vargas had called a cabinet meeting in August at which, in view of serious budgetary difficulties, he once more admonished each ministry to adopt the "most rigorous" economy measures. A few weeks later an opposition deputy urged that the "slogan of Brazilians must be—war on the deficit!" A sharp decline in coffee earnings during this initial decisional period further weakened the milreis, and commercial arrears mounted rapidly, as Dantas constantly reminded the CFCE. Early in November the government leader in the Chamber of Deputies informed Aranha that the administration's greatest concern stemmed not from electoral problems "but rather from the financial difficulties threatening the Union."[115]

Within government councils, in fact, a debate was in progress over the feasibility of continuing service on the foreign debt under the Aranha Plan. Dantas favored suspension of debt payments, and he announced to a concerned member of the British embassy that it had become impossible to satisfy foreign bondholders and at the same time satisfy commercial obligations. As he prepared to leave for a short stay in Rio Grande do Sul in November, Vargas discussed the financial situation with Souza Costa. The president concluded that they would continue a policy of putting off all but "absolutely indispensable" expenditures.[116] It was only by a "supreme effort" that the finance minister scraped together sufficient funds to meet the December 1 payments to creditors in Paris, London, and New York, and he was convinced that it would be impossible to make the next ones.[117] The decision early that month to distribute the available foreign exchange to foreign exporters on the basis of the amount of coffee purchased by their countries—a step "conceived in deliberate sin," a prominent tea-drinker fumed[118]—reflected the urgency of the financial bind confronting Brazilian leaders in the latter part of 1934, one that helped to nudge them along the path of bilateralism. Import demand had to be met, and payment indirectly in goods was at least one way of acquiring some of the necessary manufactured items.

But gratifying internal economic needs was not the sole positive reason for the readiness of Brazilian policy formulators to cooperate in Germany's New Plan. Kiep pointed to another motive, not yet so strong as others but gaining rapidly in relative importance as the decade wore on, when he reported that Rio de Janeiro was interested in the possibility of using compensation transactions to place government orders for various items, especially equipment for the army and navy.[119] The question of military influence on economic policy during this period is discussed in detail in chapter 4, but it is pertinent to note here that a ground swell of military disgruntlement over deficiencies of matériel had been building up since the Revolution, and senior officers made no secret of their dissatisfaction. In such circumstances and, in part, because they shared the military's misgivings about the international situation, civilian leaders began in 1934 to look increasingly upon compensation trade as a means of acquiring new equipment for the armed forces. Unquestionably, pressure from the military high command heightened civilian receptiveness to bilateralism with Germany, the country's traditional source of armaments.

Brazilian perceptions of alternative responses were essentially realistic. There was substance to the apparent inevitability of trade along lines desired by the Reich, whose financial crisis militated against payments in foreign currencies for imports. By October, monthly receipts by the Reichsbank of foreign exchange were amounting to but slightly more than 70 percent of requirements.[120] This fact justified previous somber reports by the Brazilian legation in Berlin, which had also been substantiated by the introduction of the New Plan in September. Another event had reinforced the no-alternative character of the incoming signals: Hitler's smashing victory at the polls in August meant, as Macedo Soares informed the CFCE, that the Nazi regime was firmly in the saddle and that there was consequently small likelihood of a loosening of the reins on trade policy.[121]

Despite the objective situation prevailing in Germany, Brazilian officials clearly rationalized their opportunism, to a certain extent, in terms of the "imposition" of external forces. After all, upon receipt in June of the German memorandum on import licensing, Sampaio had exulted that the German initiative "meets our wishes exactly,"[122] and subsequent manipulation by Berlin of import permits showed that the Reich was willing to grant preferential treatment to Brazilian shippers —providing, granted, that imports spelled exports. Remarks by Sampaio and Dantas in meetings of the CFCE and Kiep's reports of their eagerness during the negotiations belie the alleged helplessness of Brazil's position. The fact that Brazilian quota requests exceeded even Berlin's willingness to expand trade is also suggestive.[123] Brazil, furthermore, had an unfavorable trade balance with the Reich, so a clearing or compensation agreement, whether signed or unsigned, was as much in its interest as Germany's, as Itamaraty acknowledged.[124]

The opportunism of Brazilian leaders emerged in sharp focus during policy debates. In his memorandum of August 10, Dantas had underscored the necessity of a general solution to the trade and financial crisis that would avoid giving rise to "misunderstandings and protests because of unequal treatment or privileged situations." The fact that two months later he was advocating an arrangement that "naturally will place Germany in an advantageous position in Brazil in relation to other countries" is striking proof of his flexibility in reacting to new opportunities.[125] A suggestion by one member of the CFCE that a "liberal" treaty with the United States would be only fair, given the decades of "disorder" in Brazil's treatment of American creditors, prompted Souza Costa to emphasize tersely that Brazil's policy was "not to do justice. What we need," he said bluntly, "is to obtain advantages." After all, the minister of agriculture later added, "we are verifying every day that, where international trade is concerned, nations conduct themselves with complete cold-bloodedness, each one defending its own interests." A clear inference may be drawn from Sampaio's satisfied pronouncement, a week after reaching agreement with Kiep, that Brazil "continues with her hands free": to be unencumbered by formal restraints in order to be able to respond flexibly to unforeseen situations was a positive value for Brazilian leaders.[126]

The personal intervention of Vargas in the negotiations was, in Kiep's opinion, a key ingredient in Germany's success. The president, he reported, took a *"starke Interesse"* in economic questions, as the CFCE, his "personal creation," indicated. Vargas's attitude during the period when the decision was formulated unquestionably did create a "climate of opinion" conducive to the type of arrangement that resulted.[127] His remarks revealed a thoroughgoing pragmatism. At one point, when the relative values of England and the United States to Brazil's commercial interests were being considered, he reminded the Conselho that trade opportunities, not "sentimental motives," should determine Brazil's policy. He replied in the same vein to a letter from Hasslocher in which the attaché urged full collaboration with the United States. The matter, said Vargas, would be resolved "in accordance with the interests of Brazil, without precipitation or sentimental motives."[128] During CFCE sessions the president customarily remained a passive but attentive participant, opting characteristically for further study and examination when others pressed for decisions. His occasional suggestions and admonitions reinforced similar tendencies in his subordinates, who could from his attitude anticipate approval of certain kinds of suggestions.[129]

The German-Brazilian discussions laid bare personal rivalries within the government that affected the conduct of subsequent negotiations and the structure of decision making. It was inevitable that the friction would remove the glow from the experiment in formulating policy by council. In his eagerness to work things out with the Germans, Sampaio even wanted to guard the content of his talks with Kiep from the embassy in Washington, and he therefore opposed sending copies of CFCE minutes to Aranha. The ambassador relied on a special confidant, Bouças, to supplement his official reports from Itamaraty.

Valentim Bouças was the Brazilian representative of International Business Machines and also director of the CFCE's Technical Section. A specialist in financial affairs, he had easy access to Vargas and enjoyed good personal relations with the president. Later he would become one of Vargas's steady golfing partners on the links at Gávea Country Club. Bouças frequently handled negotiations for the government with its creditors abroad. He had been a delegate to the London Monetary Conference the previous year and had then undertaken a mission to the United States. Because of his prominent role in matters pertaining to the foreign debt—he had served as secretary of the special committee set up after the Revolution to gather data on the foreign debts of the states and *municípios*—he had worked closely with the new American ambassador, who felt "great appreciation" for the Brazilian expert's assistance in smoothing the ruffled feathers of American bondholders. "Bouças has been in to see me every day lately," Gibson had written in June, "because we've had all sorts of headaches in different parts of the country."[130]

Bouças believed strongly with Aranha that Brazil's future lay in a firm alignment with Washington, rather than with London or Berlin. "He is 100% pro-American and, like many other intelligent Brazilians," said Gibson, "is completely sold to the idea that Brazil's fundamental policy should be to go along with us in all things; he not only preaches it, but has practised it consistently."[131] The American business community in Brazil viewed Bouças as a definite asset to the cause of American-Brazilian relations, and in 1936 the American Chamber of Commerce authorized him to act as its spokesman before the National Foreign Trade Council in the United States.[132] The embassy also came to value highly his cooperative attitude—"It's a pity that unlike other nations we have no nice red ribbon we can pin on him," Gibson once remarked.[133]

Bouças, of course, had a personal stake in good business relationships with the Americans, but he liked to think of himself as an enlightened nationalist. If he was well disposed toward the United States, he said, it was because he wanted to protect the nation's interests. His frequent public service, Gibson aptly noted, was ample evidence of the government's realization that he was not grinding a personal ax. According to the American envoy, Bouças "steadfastly refused to touch a penny of remuneration" for his official work, explaining that he had sufficient money of his own and placed "more importance in keeping his independence and being able to disagree with anybody in Brazil, from the President down."[134]

Bouças was expectedly the most outspoken opponent in Brazil of compensation trade. Later, in 1936, he founded a highly respected monthly, *O Observador Econômico e Financeiro*, to serve as a forum for debate on national economic problems. The fact that bilateralism became one of his chief targets was, he remarked to Gibson, a "clear demonstration" of his dedication to a sound program of financial recovery. During the CFCE debates in 1934 he consistently urged a strengthening of ties with Washington and argued against any special arrangement with Germany. "We, who are trying to get rid of financial (exchange) control, are heading for economic control," he wrote in exasperation to Aranha.[135]

When the ambassador at one point complained to Itamaraty of an information leak to the American embassy, Sampaio pointedly directed Bouças to conduct an investigation of his staff, which handled the mimeographing of the minutes of Conselho meetings. When Bouças explained that he had transmitted documents to Aranha because he thought the Washington post should be kept abreast of all developments, "everyone became silent." The CFCE secretariat immediately stopped sending records to the Technical Section for duplication, and Bouças began using a private code provided by Aranha to keep the ambassador informed about proceedings in Rio de Janeiro.[136]

A previous indiscretion on someone's part had already made Itamaraty representatives uneasy about the CFCE's potential for inconvenient publicity on sensitive issues,[137] and the protests from Aranha made them even more wary. Vargas also resolved to take precautions.[138] Late in November, Sampaio informed the CFCE's members that the president had decided that the minutes of meetings would no longer be mimeographed and distributed.[139] It was not long before the CFCE ceased to be a party to the confidential aspects of official negotiations.

Ill feeling between Aranha and Sampaio grew apace in succeeding weeks. But this friction was merely part of the rift between the ambassador and Macedo Soares that began to take shape during this period. The upshot of the whole episode was an intensification of dissension and rivalry within the government and a decline in the influence of both the CFCE and Itamaraty on foreign economic policy.

The response of the Vargas administration to its two insistent foreign suitors in 1934 was an opportunistic one, designed to keep both options open. The German market was a tempting prize and it seemed to suit Brazil's export interests. A consensus of objectives between the federal authorities and regional associational interest groups substantially reinforced the direction of Vargas's resolve. The convergence of military demands and commercial requirements contributed to his decision not to shun German overtures. But the debate on trade policy had shown that government leaders felt a constant necessity to weigh the possible effects of their commercial alignment with Berlin on relations with Washington. Vargas had arranged a working formula for trade with the Reich, but he had not committed himself irrevocably. The task now was to make secure Brazilian interests in the American camp and, at the same time, determine how much latitude Brazil could obtain in order to protect expanding ties with the European power.

Chapter 3

Between Washington and Berlin

(1935–1936)

In the period from November 1934 to June 1936 Brazilian policy makers reexamined their decision on the German trade issue, worked out some of the problems arising from bilateralism, and then, under the influence of overwhelmingly positive feedback from interested domestic groups, strengthened Brazil's ties with Germany by reaching a secret gentlemen's agreement with Berlin that controlled their trade relations and significantly influenced their political relations until the outbreak of war in 1939. Brazil's trade decision in 1936 has been interpreted as a setback for Germany's economic program in South America.[1] The reverse is true. The Berlin-Rio understanding that year not only consolidated and extended German gains in the Brazilian market, but also was negotiated despite Brazil's ostensible commercial partnership with Washington, symbolized by the Brazilian-American Reciprocal Trade Agreement of 1935. Brazil's response to American-German rivalry in this period was indeed a triumph for Berlin and a solid defeat for Good Neighbor diplomacy.

The new treaty with Washington was one that Vargas contemplated unenthusiastically. Brazil was selling more to the United States than it was buying from her, and Vargas was reasonably satisfied with the status quo. The treaty was therefore largely the personal project of Oswaldo Aranha, undertaken in response to insistent American overtures. The CFCE was not an active party to decision making, nor was there widespread manifestation of opinion by interest groups. The absence of both debate during negotiation of the treaty and vigorous support within government councils in Rio led to unexpected delay in securing ratification by the Brazilian congress. That delay was highlighted by press debates between supporters of the treaty and spokesmen for São Paulo manufacturing interests, a debate resolved only after intense diplomatic pressure from an exasperated State Department.

Sumner Welles, whom Aranha found to be an "intransigent partisan" of closer Brazilian-American relations, stressed in talks with the Brazilian agents in the latter weeks of 1934 that the general goal of American policy was a reaction "against economic nationalism." Herbert Feis summed up American aims more concisely as most-favored-nation treatment, some tariff reductions, and a joint pronouncement against bilateralism. The unresolved German problem was indeed constantly on the minds of State Department spokesmen, who repeatedly emphasized the importance they placed on Brazilian cooperation and remonstrated about Rio de Janeiro's flirtation with the Reich. Both Welles and Feis on November 12 separately indicated that Washington regarded Brazil as a model for the reciprocal treaties program. At a subsequent meeting Welles cautioned embassy counselor Cyro Freitas-Valle, the ambassador's cousin, that any bilateral accord with Germany would be the "first link of a chain that could later strangle" Brazil. The United States, he once again affirmed, counted heavily on Brazil in the "struggle" against bilateralism.[2]

Aranha mistakenly assured Welles on November 15 that Dantas was the only influential figure in the Brazilian government backing a deal with Berlin and said he expected to convince Dantas that an agreement with the Reich was not in Brazil's long-range interests. Aranha was overly optimistic, for Sampaio had confidentially informed the CFCE three days earlier that the arrangement with Berlin was "already being adopted in desirable fashion and without provoking alarm" from other countries. Brazil, he had proudly noted, "continues with her hands free and [yet] the accord is already practically in effect."[3] That Aranha's arguments did not change the decision of his government is evident from Macedo Soares's response on November 23 to his handling of the negotiations. Brazil could join Washington in a formal statement against bilateralism, said the foreign minister, but "in practice we cannot sacrifice the freedom or maintenance of our commerce with important customers like Germany to that theory." Not only did Brazil need to increase exports, but also its collaboration now in Hull's campaign might be interpreted as a "gesture of vassalage," since other nations had accepted bilateralism with the Reich. The best that Brazil could do, Macedo Soares indicated, was to refrain from signing formal treaties with bilateralists and let the status quo be regulated through informal interbank arrangements that could be terminated whenever convenient.[4] The pragmatism displayed by Brazilian leaders was measurably strengthened in December by interesting developments in Washington that revealed grave confusion and indecision within American government circles over trade policy. When the Rio de Janeiro press at the beginning of December picked up an item in a London newspaper on a projected compensation deal between Germany and the United States, Itamaraty's cryptographer was put to work on a telegraphic inquiry to Washington.[5] The German government had, in fact, proposed to American authorities a transaction involving 800,000 bales of cotton to be paid for mostly in blocked currency. This gambit from Berlin highlighted the debate between Cordell Hull and George Peek over commercial policy.

Aranha had the "worst impression" of Peek, who headed a "terrible current" of nationalist opinion favorable to a less flexible position on the question of Brazil's delayed payments to American exporters and creditors.[6] The special presidential adviser understood the leverage inherent in the threat of a coffee tax, urged seizure of coffee payments to service Brazilian indebtedness, and opposed the recent drafts of the Brazilian-American treaty because they did not include what he considered effective guarantees for American shippers.[7] Peek endorsed the German offer, and his arguments initially impressed Roosevelt, whose hesitancy over trade policy caused considerable embarrassment to Hull and his colleagues.

In a meeting at the State Department on December 5, Aranha learned of the possibility that the White House would approve the proposal. The Brazilian envoy noted "great confusion and discrepancy" in government spheres, an impression hardened by subsequent sessions with State Department spokesmen, who reluctantly acknowledged that the cotton scheme contradicted the underlying principles of the projected pact with Brazil. When one of Aranha's aides told them that Brazil was deferring a decision on the agreement with Germany pending the results of the talks in Washington, chagrined department officials lamely defended the president's anticipated approval of the deal on the grounds that "there might have to be a few actions in the opposite direction from the [liberal] policy which might still be maintained as a main principle."[8]

Nothing showed better than this affair, the aide later remarked to Aranha, the "essentially doctrinaire" nature of Hull's policy, which "ill accords with present economic reality." Authorities in Rio de Janeiro skeptically viewed the debate in Washington as further proof of the uncertainty of the economic times. "Imagine if we had rejected completely the negotiations with Germany and . . . adhered to the liberal program!" exclaimed Souza Costa.[9]

A frantic phone call from the State Department delayed what looked like imminent endorsement of the scheme by Roosevelt, following a long session with Peek on December 12. The president promised Assistant Secretary William Phillips that he would not make a final decision until Hull had returned from Nashville, where he had gone to deliver a speech. The next day Phillips sent Hull's personal aide, Harry McBride, to intercept the secretary, who was en route back to Washington. McBride met his chief in Charlottesville and delivered a message from Phillips about the "distressing" turn of events. "I pointed out that it was not merely this particular deal with Germany that was of importance," wrote Phillips about his call to the White House, "but that the new policy ran counter to your whole trade program and that it would be upsetting to the Brazilian trade agreement."[10]

Only after energetic intervention was Hull able to persuade the president to decline the Reich's proposal and check this final challenge from his archopponent. Importers of German goods, Hull protested, would obtain them at lower prices than they paid for the same articles from other nations because the blocked marks were to be sold at a discount. This, he said, would constitute inequality of treatment. He also urged the president to consider the impact of his decision on the Brazilian negotiations.[11] Aranha was as relieved as the State Department when he was summoned on December 15 and told of Roosevelt's second thoughts and of his instructions to inform the ambassador before releasing the news. Having made the choice because of Rio de Janeiro's cooperation, alleged a department spokesman, the president wanted the treaty with Brazil to be structured as that country desired, without its "coming to suffer in its trade with other countries."[12]

Roosevelt's alleged remarks implicitly sanctioned Brazil's "simple understanding" with Germany and undoubtedly reduced Brazilian anxieties about possible retaliation from the United States. American hesitation in the face of the German cotton proposal was merely one additional signal that ensured that the Brazilian government would not dismantle its new machinery of trade with the Reich. Indeed, the fact of Washington's temptation was as damning, or convincing, as actual acceptance of the German offer would have been to Brazilian policy makers conditioned by *Weltanschauung*, their own recent decision about Germany, and national trade requirements to seek justification for their actions in the behavior of other nations.

Since Brazil's expectations in the negotiations with the United States were limited, Rio de Janeiro had few suggestions and no great enthusiasm for a new treaty. Either it would entail an improvement in economic relations with the United States, "or we will leave everything as it is, which isn't bad," Vargas had counseled. Macedo Soares left tariff to Aranha's discretion, since "almost all" of Brazil's main exports paid no duties in the American market. The indispensable objective, said Macedo Soares, was a guaranty that coffee and other products currently on the free list would remain there. Aranha, of course, knew that the treaty itself presented no problems, since Brazil in fact had "little to ask and little to give." Over 97 percent of Brazil's exports to the United States entered duty-free. As for the American products on which Washington wanted lower Brazilian duties, their sale price in Brazil, Aranha discovered, was higher than competitors', and concessions on Brazil's part would therefore not bring any special advantage to American manufacturers.[13]

Aranha was mainly interested in securing concrete, immediate aid— countries like Brazil, he told Welles, had first to "think about living and only later could they philosophize"—in the form of a long-term loan that would permit abandonment of exchange control and in that way improve trade and restore confidence in Brazilian conditions. According to his reports in mid-November, Welles assured him that various New York banks would be willing to extend credits to Brazil. The ambassador's recommendations, however, once again met with an unenthusiastic reception in Rio de Janeiro. The financial crisis and ensuing debate over the foreign debt had in fact now led Souza Costa to the conclusion that a modification of the Aranha Plan for payment of that debt might be necessary. Dantas favored suspension of service on the debt as well as a policy of compensation in foreign trade, while Vargas and Souza Costa were more cautious. But concern about the problem made Souza Costa question the wisdom of contracting new obligations through bank loans to clear up the backlog of import debts, as his friend in Washington advocated. It was better, advised the finance minister, to "await the course of events."[14]

The draft of the Brazilian-American treaty reached Rio de Janeiro in the middle of December, and over the next month the mutual tariff concessions were debated, adjusted, and finally agreed upon. In granting an average reduction of some 23 percent on automobiles, tires, radios, and related articles the Brazilian government cut in half the original American requests. Even with the lower rates the American vehicles would pay ad valorem duties of 28 to 36 percent, auto accessories over 40 percent, and tires and radios between 20 and 60 percent. Brazil agreed also not to raise rates on agricultural machinery, refrigerators, sewing machines, and office equipment. Washington in return guaranteed the continued free entry of over nine-tenths of Brazilian products, including coffee, as well as a tariff reduction of 50 percent on other items, including manganese and *castanha* nuts.[15]

The major bone of contention proved to be a clause on equitable exchange treatment, which the State Department insisted on. Itamaraty wanted one that would allow Brazil the freedom to negotiate with other countries "in whatever way possible," especially since it hoped to acquire military equipment through compensation trade.[16] Initially there was little difficulty, and the article as drafted merely committed both countries to grant the other unconditional most-favored-nation treatment in the event either should establish exchange control.[17] But the unexpected announcement in January that a special mission headed by Souza Costa and including Dantas and Sampaio would arrive in Washington later that month for discussions of Brazil's financial crisis led to a more exacting attitude on the part of the Department of State.

Vargas's decision to dispatch the team of trade and financial experts, who would also go to England and the continent, was a heavy blow to Aranha. Personally wounded by what he saw as a diminution of his own prestige and authority, the ambassador was equally dismayed at the reflection on his country of an abrupt, unexpected move, a "demoralizing spectacle" that gave rise to rumor and speculation about Brazil's economic position.[18] "These people here are tolerant and affable and friends of Brazil," he wrote to his old comrade Melo Franco. "Brazilians are the only enemies of Brazil that I have met in my life."[19]

Sampaio's inclusion in the delegation reminded the ambassador and, according to the latter, the State Department, too, of the still formally unresolved question of the German-Brazilian agreement. His pride hurt, Aranha turned his wrath on the supporters of bilateralism and renewed his warnings against such trade. He wrote caustically to Vargas that Brazil's "slick dealings" with Germany were "positively senseless." State Department officials adopted the same line of argument in talks with Souza Costa, who wired Vargas that any formal agreement with Germany or Italy "would evidently compromise in an irrevocable way the success of the negotiations with the United States."[20]

Revelation of the serious financial muddle in Brazil prompted a re-evaluation by the State Department of its treaty requests and led it to insist on minimum guarantees of fair exchange treatment. There was general agreement that a relaxation of exchange controls would best meet the problem of commercial arrears. American officials also urged Brazil to maintain service on the foreign debt, even if this adversely affected the interests of private American capital invested in Brazil.[21] If financial stringency forced Brazil to make a choice, they insisted, then preference should be shown to exporters and bondholders. Welles told Souza Costa and his colleagues on January 30 that, even though the greater part of the debt payments went to England, the good credit of Brazil was of "such importance to the United States, in all aspects," that he felt no hesitation in urging continuation of the Aranha Plan. The Brazilians accepted the American arguments and recommended to Vargas a new exchange policy, which he approved, requiring Brazilian exporters to turn over a percentage of their exchange to the Banco do Brasil at a fixed "official" rate and allowing them freely to negotiate the balance.[22]

The delay in the negotiations caused by the visit of the special mission proved to be only temporary. Washington was still eager to enlist an important ally in its crusade. "We need to march together—our reserve is but a reserve of friendship; and that is our desire," remarked Aranha in the language "good neighbor" enthusiasts liked to hear. "And our history," Roosevelt added as he beamed at his White House guests.[23] The signing of the treaty took place at the president's desk amid popping flashbulbs on the afternoon of February 2. Hull, Welles, Feis, and other State Department officers joined Aranha and Souza Costa for the widely publicized ceremony at the White House, an "unprecedented distinction" for Brazil, the finance minister wired Vargas. Hull afterward enthusiastically hailed the pact as the "first break in the log-jam of international trade" and a move away from "medieval mercantilism." Using the Brazilian-American accord as a springboard for the reciprocal agreements program, the secretary hoped to cast "a broad beam of light and hope into the existing economic darkness."[24]

Aranha initialed a separate note the same day promising that the Banco do Brasil would grant sufficient exchange to pay for future imports from the United States and for the "gradual liquidation" of the backlog of unpaid commercial debts. The Brazilian envoy assured "most-favored-company" treatment for American firms with regard to the transfer of profits and dividends, and he also declared that if his government succeeded in obtaining credits from American banks it would meet payments to American bondholders under the Aranha Plan.[25] With this clarification of Brazil's commitment to the most-favored-nation principle underlying the treaty, Hull's victory seemed complete.

Aranha exulted over the conclusion of the treaty, which he considered eminently satisfactory to the "vital interests" of Brazil. "It marks an important event for the world economy," he wrote officially.[26] In a personal note to Macedo Soares he affirmed his conviction that the understanding with the United States was "highly favorable to our interests and to our international position."[27] Privately, the ambassador confessed to mental and physical exhaustion from the long weeks of negotiation and the strain of bargaining "with Itamaraty more than with the Department of State."[28] The government's dealing with the United States and Germany at the same time was "madness and lack of integrity," he complained to a friend. "I don't know why this government didn't lose its patience and plunge the knife in!" Rio de Janeiro's negotiations with Berlin, Rome, and others continued to preoccupy Aranha, and in following weeks he warned Vargas that a strengthening of ties with Berlin would be a "disaster." Brazil must avoid the "nonsense and foolishness" of bilateral trade, he urged, and fulfill its commitment to the United States.[29]

The major concern of Ambassador Aranha and of the State Department was to see that the treaty and exchange agreement worked effectively, and the first step was obviously to secure ratification of the documents by the Brazilian legislature. Analysis by Itamaraty confirmed that, despite Brazil's tariff concessions, imports from the United States would still face what were protective duties in appropriate cases, while Brazilian exports would be encouraged.[30] Confident that ratification would be a fairly automatic and speedy process, the chief executive sent the treaty to the legislature late in April with nothing more than a perfunctory note accompanying a general statement by the foreign minister. Macedo Soares arranged with the American embassy for release of the treaty to the press on April 24 and secured from the president of the Chamber of Deputies a promise to do everything possible to push the treaty through within a month.[31]

The treaty in fact was not ratified for seven months. The administration, convinced that it held winning cards, underplayed its hand by making no effort to line up decisive congressional backing for the treaty. Furthermore, the departure in May of both Vargas and Macedo

Soares for Buenos Aires—the foreign minister returned only on June 19—where they helped to open the Chaco Peace Conference, left the initiative to opponents of the treaty, who mounted a concerted offensive against it late in May. Spokesmen for São Paulo rubber, paint, and metal industries sent telegrams to congress warning that the agreement would hurt some three hundred plants using domestic raw materials.[32] Euvaldo Lodi, a deputy from Minas Gerais, president of the Industrial Federation and member of the CFCE, bluntly told the American chargé that, unless some tariff provisions were revised, he and other deputies would block ratification. Before the CFCE, Lodi argued that the concessions granted to the United States created a "menacing" situation for Brazil's economy. The powerful Simonsens of São Paulo joined the opposition because of reduced rates on American radios, and Assis Chateaubriand's *O Jornal* led press criticism with a series of articles by "An Industrial Observer" challenging the wisdom of the agreement. That these articles, which were picked up by other newspapers, including Rio de Janeiro's *Diário da Noite*, were inspired by *paulista* manufacturers, several of whom were shareholders in Chateaubriand's newspaper chain, was common knowledge.[33]

The "Industrial Observer" called attention to the spirit of "intransigent protection" that the United States had allegedly displayed on its road to industrial power, and he recommended that country as a model for Latin America.[34] It was actually fear of Brazil's industrialization, he argued, that led industrial nations to demand tariff reductions from Brazil.[35] With the favors it would obtain in the treaty, the United States would make a "satellite" of Brazil, the anonymous industry spokesman charged.[36] Washington's "offensive" against Brazilian tariffs would, he warned, have a "tremendous repercussion" on the economy, reducing "extraordinarily" the value of its manufactures and affecting nearly six hundred factories and eight thousand workers in São Paulo state alone.[37]

Government analysis of industry's complaints confirmed the previous conclusion that Brazil's manufacturers had little to fear. Only thirty-three tariff reductions were being made, and most of the new rates were at least as high as the protective duties prevailing before the September 1934 tariff. For the eleven items—including paints, tires, and rubber tubes—on which lower rates were actually to be granted, the industrialists could present no evidence to show that domestic producers would be affected.[38]

To offset the attacks from what he labeled the "Captains of Industry," Valentim Bouças undertook a personal campaign to arouse public support for the treaty.[39] Beginning on June 25 the important Rio daily *Correio da Manhã* carried a run of articles authored by Bouças under the pseudonym "A Brazilian Observer," in which he excoriated the "Industrial Observer." The only industries that might suffer from American competition, he argued in his lead-off article, were those "parasitic manufactures encysted in our economic system" and, by implication, dependent upon lofty tariff walls. Bouças sounded the same theme in other articles, five thousand multilithed copies of which he daily mailed to congressmen "and all those who can influence public opinion." Vargas, he wrote privately, was "really delighted" with his efforts.[40]

If the president, in fact, was pleased with Bouças's campaign, he did not himself come out actively in favor of the treaty. Bouças complained to Aranha of an "absolute lack of cooperation and coordination" among government forces, a conclusion that jibed with the American chargé's observation that the treaty was making little progress in the Chamber simply because nobody was "actively interesting himself in avoiding such delay."[41]

The chargé suggested implicitly that Macedo Soares's preoccupation with the Chaco peace discussions was an important reason for his reluctance to take energetic steps in the treaty debates. The foreign minister was also in an awkward position because of the unforeseen outcry from São Paulo. Hoping to succeed Vargas in 1938 and therefore anxious to build up popularity in his home state, he wanted to avoid alienating any influential sector of opinion there. Vargas and Souza Costa were by nature inclined to approach problems cautiously. As Aranha noted unhappily when urging a more activist stance by the government, "Getúlio doesn't like this tactic . . ."[42] The case of the American-Brazilian agreement was a good example of Vargas's legendary tendency summed up in the phrase *deixar como está para ver como fica* ("leave as it is to see how it comes out"). What seemed to ardent supporters of the treaty as indecisiveness or apathy within administration circles was probably, in part, the decision makers' natural momentary withdrawal to reconsider an original decision in the face of unanticipated criticism. Also serving to explain the apparent lack of concern, or certainly the milder anxiety, of high officials in Rio de Janeiro was the smaller degree of commitment they felt toward the treaty than either the Washington embassy or the State Department.[43] Vargas, of course, had never displayed much enthusiasm for a new commercial pact.

As weeks went by pressure from Washington mounted. Aranha late in May warned of the "very disagreeable" atmosphere developing there, an appraisal confirmed a few days later by a resolution introduced in the House of Representatives calling on Hull for information about Brazil's failure to approve the February trade pact.[44] Itamaraty at the end of May promised ratification "before the latter part of June," but July came with the treaty still in committee. Aranha fired off a blunt message on July 3 asking whether or not the agreement was going to be ratified, and he was assured that it would be ratified "in the next thirty days," a forecast changed on August 3 to "by the end of August."[45]

Prodding Vargas, the ambassador wrote angrily that, if the government was more interested in the "Indians"—the Chaco question— than in ties with the United States, then "send me my ticket home, Getúlio, because I am not here to play the imbecile and even less the clown of Itamaraty." Additional personal letters in July to Vargas and Souza Costa reminded them of his resentment and American discontentment over the situation. "Between a market like this and a little radio plant the government and the country cannot choose," he commented disgustedly to Bouças. "It's incredible!"[46]

The American chargé had been doing what he could to stimulate action, but ambassadorial prestige was needed and Gibson had been away in Buenos Aires, where he represented the United States in the Chaco peace talks. On his return late in August, the ambassador immediately began pressing Macedo Soares about the trade treaty.[47] Gibson deliberately composed a "rather ominous little telegram" to Hull, hoping to elicit a dramatic and forceful reply that would spark action in Rio de Janeiro.[48] He warned Hull that, unless Brazilian authorities took prompt and strong measures, Washington faced "a definite possibility" that the Chamber would reject the treaty. This gloomy assessment produced the desired result, Gibson gleefully confided to a friend, "in the form of a telegram from the secretary saying that liberty, justice and humanity were sunk if this thing didn't go through in a hurry."[49]

Hull, who had expected long before now to see the "log-jam" of international commerce breaking up, was indeed despondent. His telegram to Gibson told how "very much disturbed" he was by Brazil's placing his whole program in jeopardy. Domestic opponents were daily becoming more emboldened, he complained, and Gibson should make this clear to Macedo Soares and even Vargas if necessary. To reinforce the embassy's action, State Department officials called in Chargé Freitas-Valle and hinted at "an inevitable change of policy up here." Hull himself told Freitas-Valle that it appeared that only "very resolute and aggressive action" would save the treaty. Irate American citizens holding defaulted securities and frozen credits in Brazil were planning "a sort of uprising" against Brazil, said Hull, by raising anew the specter of an import duty on coffee. It was impossible to resist these attacks much longer, and, he warned, "serious developments might arise very soon."[50] Although Hull's lecture had borne a "seal of cordiality," Freitas-Valle realized the depth of the secretary's anxiety and he immediately wired Macedo Soares, reminding him of Hull's personal political investment in the reciprocal agreements program. "At bottom, the affair is one of domestic politics," Freitas-Valle suggested to another Itamaraty official, "with Hull wanting something to show Peek."[51]

Under heightened pressure from Washington, Brazilian leaders began a more concerted drive to roll back the opposition. Macedo Soares "rose up like an old warhorse" and "went forth to battle with greatest good-will and enthusiasm."[52] He met several times with key legislators, one of whom later remarked that Macedo Soares had "read the riot act to them."[53] He attended Chamber committee meetings and "urged and cajoled and threatened" until he split the opposition.[54] Vargas reportedly was also deeply impressed by Hull's gloomy forecast and determined to take "all possible measures" to push the treaty through the Chamber.[55] As Macedo Soares reported it, the president summoned Lodi and told him that further obstruction would result in a public confrontation between them. Vargas also called in Raul Fernandes, majority leader in the Chamber, and instructed him to make every effort to secure a speedy ratification.[56]

On September 4 Fernandes called the Chamber's attention to the "powerful" opposition forming in the United States and vigorously urged his colleagues to make a gesture of "good faith" to the American government by approving the treaty. A fellow deputy on September 9 pointed to the danger of a tax on coffee imports into the United States and argued that inflation had weakened the tariff concessions extended to the Americans.[57] Three days later the determined campaign by the administration paid off, over four months after the treaty had gone to the Brazilian legislature.

The Chamber's endorsement of the agreement by a "rather eloquent" vote of 127 to 51 did not mean that it was "out of the woods yet," Gibson cautioned Hull, "but it is the first and probably the hardest hurdle, and I am distinctly more hopeful."[58] Since success had been "in no small measure" a result of Macedo Soares's initiative, Gibson suggested that the secretary of state send to his Brazilian counterpart an autographed photograph in appreciation. Bouças, too, should get one, Gibson thought, because he had "worked like a Trojan and wore down opposition which we had no way of getting at."[59]

Hull was pleased to follow up on the ambassador's recommendation,[60] while he prayed for smoother sledding in the Brazilian Senate to relieve the domestic pressure on his department. The president of the influential National Foreign Trade Council, E. P. Thomas, had recently written to Welles about the "continued protests" of American exporters about Brazil's failure to refund frozen commercial balances and about German competition. It was to be hoped, said Thomas, that activation of the treaty would "automatically" stop compensation trade, "so highly discriminating" against American sellers.[61] After the treaty had been in the Brazilian Senate two weeks, American export interests launched an obviously coordinated appeal to the State Department to take all possible steps to secure ratification.[62] The American Chamber of Commerce for Brazil also began laying plans to finance a lobby in Washington to push for an import tax on coffee in the event Brazil failed to ratify the treaty before the next session of the United States Congress.[63]

The deliberations of the Senate proved embarrassingly slower than Brazilian leaders had calculated, although the delay was more bureaucratic than anything else. "Things are turning sour," a dejected, hapless Aranha confided to Bouças after six weeks of delay. "Posthumous decay would be more like it, I should say," remarked Theodore Xanthaky, a former vice-consul with fourteen years of experience in Brazil who served Gibson as a special "free-lance" assistant, to whom Bouças showed Aranha's letter.[64] Xanthaky was right. The final approval of the treaty by the Senate on November 14 and the formal exchange of ratification on December 2—coming as they did nearly a year after a beaming, confident Cordell Hull, flanked by other smiling State Department officials, had watched Aranha lean over Roosevelt's desk to place his signature on the agreement—could not rehone the secretary of state's initial enthusiasm. Indeed, the months-long battle over ratification was a keen disappointment to Hull and his colleagues, particularly as they had watched an alarming growth in Brazil's trade with the archopponent of his program.

The German trade delegation had sailed home early that year, delighted with the results of their *Südamerikatournee* and assured of Berlin's gratitude.[65] Hans Kroll, the Wilhelmstrasse's expert on South American economic affairs and a member of Kiep's troupe, later recalled that the "great success" of the trip in terms of expanded commerce with South America so fired the hopes of his government that it promptly dispatched a similar, but unhappily not so fruitful, mission to the Far East.[66] The response of the South American countries to Berlin's initiative also seemed to offer interesting possibilities for Germany's rearmament program, and, after Kroll's return, Hermann Göring personally plied him with questions on the likelihood of increased imports of strategic raw materials from Brazil and its neighbors.[67]

Reich authorities sent out word that the prospects for sales on the Brazilian market were now "really favorable," and businessmen on both sides of the Atlantic heard the call.[68] Trade between the two countries boomed, and by late 1935 Brazil had replaced Argentina as Germany's leading partner in Latin America and become the tenth most important in the Reich's overall foreign commerce.[69] The harbors of Santos, Rio de Janeiro, Bahia, and Recife were crowded with vessels sporting German pennants, including the now popular *Hakenkreuz*. Amid these fluttering swastikas and other flags of the Reich appeared the ensigns of Dutch carriers that served German ports.

The number of German ships entering Brazilian ports rose from 868 in 1934 to 1,057 in 1935, a difference of over 20 percent. The carrying capacity of these vessels showed an increase of more than a half-million tons.[70] Rubber, fruits, and nuts from the Amazon and Northeast, tobacco from Bahia and Rio Grande do Sul, along with the latter's meats and hides, *paulista* citrus fruits, coffee from the Center-South, and cotton from São Paulo and the North filled the holds of the Europe-bound ships after they had unloaded their coal, machinery, drug supplies, electrical equipment, iron and steel products, and a variety of finished goods. Compared with 1934, German manufacturers expanded sales of various kinds of machinery to São Paulo more than 100 percent in both volume and value in 1935. Exports of such items as chemical fertilizers, insecticides, and typewriters showed extraordinary increases.[71] A report from the German consul there in midyear also indicated a "strong competition" among radio distributors, with German brands making significant gains, "especially in recent times."[72]

The course of this trade expansion was an unpaved one. Brazilian exchange regulations created one temporarily serious problem. Under prodding from Washington, Brazilian authorities decided in February 1935 to permit the sale of all exchange drafts on the free market, requiring only that 35 percent of the proceeds be delivered in free exchange to the Banco do Brasil at the reduced "official" rate to enable the government to satisfy its obligations.[73] Artur Schmidt-Elskop, the German minister, quickly complained to Itamaraty that the measure violated the compensation arrangement and that, by causing an artificial demand for free currencies and inflating the cost of Brazilian products, it would very seriously hamper trade between the two countries. In a subsequent note he warned that the new regulation jeopardized further expansion of Brazilian exports to Germany.[74]

To lessen the impact of the ruling and to avoid a "sudden paralysis" in trade with Germany, the Banco do Brasil permitted exporters to negotiate without restriction the compensation marks they held as of February 11, denying this privilege to holders of other blocked currencies.[75] The effect of the new measures was nonetheless negative from the point of view of Brazilian exporters, who loudly voiced their dissatisfaction. Appeals from Rio Grande do Sul were particularly insistent, and Governor Flores da Cunha personally wired Vargas on at least two occasions calling attention to the "enormous damage" wrought upon the state's economy by the regulation.[76]

But certain drawbacks of compensation trading were becoming evident. There was a trend toward excessive dependence of some sectors, notably cotton, upon German buyers, and stocks of compensation marks tended to accumulate rapidly as German purchases outstripped Brazilian demand for German goods.[77] The shortage of freely negotiable foreign exchange was also growing more acute: by May, in the words of one German observer, Souza Costa was grasping "at every straw" in order to get exchange.[78] One method of doing so, the Brazilians thought, would be to suspend sales in restricted currencies, a step announced that month.

The sudden curtailment of orders from Germany brought inevitable protests from regional interests: the Commercial Association of Belém bemoaned the threatened loss of an indispensable outlet for rubber and *castanha* nuts; a *gaúcho* deputy foresaw "ruinous" times ahead for producers of lard, hides, and wool in his state, while a colleague from Maranhão predicted "collective bankruptcy" for the North; Governor Magalhães underscored the "grievous" position of Bahian tobacco growers; and the Commercial Association of Santos warned that the torch was the only alternative to selling coffee to the Reich.[79]

As American officials forecast, the Germans immediately put to the test Brazil's ability to "stick to her guns." The Auswärtiges Amt quickly objected that the new decree amounted to an embargo on imports from Brazil and would oblige Germany to transfer business to that nation's competitors. After consultation with the Wilhelmstrasse, the Ministry of Economic Affairs had major import firms notify their Brazilian associates that orders would now have to be placed with Colombia and other countries. In Brazil both the legation and private business actively set about the task of securing a resumption of compensation trade. Recognizing that the most effective means of changing the Brazilian government's attitude was domestic pressure, Schmidt-Elskop advised Berlin that it was "absolutely necessary" to halt for the time being all purchases of Brazilian products.[80]

The German envoy also wired Berlin for additional funds for commercial propaganda, a request endorsed by the Economic Department of the Auswärtiges Amt because of the "extraordinary importance of our economic relations with Brazil."[81] With financial backing from the Deutsche-Brasilianische Handelskammer, German businessmen in Rio de Janeiro established a special committee that began subsidizing press articles favorable to the compensation system. The group placed its propaganda items in Brazilian newspapers through a *Verbindungsmann*, a "go-between," and hoped to achieve a "permanent influence" on the Brazilian press. Its campaign was later hailed by one German representative as a "substantial success."[82]

Anxious to avoid any permanent damage to trade relations with Germany, both Vargas and Souza Costa sought to reassure Berlin. The finance minister, in a typical frame of mind, went so far as to remark that an "exclusion from the general rule" would have to be found for Germany. A letter to Macedo Soares from a friend in São Paulo indicates that the foreign minister, through private channels, also worked to retain the good will of German importers.[83]

After a month had passed, it became clear that the prohibition was untenable, although Souza Costa was reluctant to sanction the sale of cotton, a good exchange earner, for blocked currency.[84] At a meeting of the CFCE on June 17, after noting that the ruling of May 13 had "completely paralyzed" exports to the Reich, he proposed that compensation trade in all products except cotton be permitted. After "lively debate" the Council approved the recommendation.[85]

The cry from northern cotton interests against the decision was loud and insistent. State governors and commercial associations wired their displeasure, charging the federal government with discriminatory treatment to the advantage of the South, and in Rio de Janeiro northern deputies denounced the administration's move on the same grounds to their colleagues in the Chamber.[86] Refusing to give way in the face of this criticism, Souza Costa told a special gathering of cotton producers that the United States would demand a compensation agreement of its own, thus depriving Brazil of a vital trade surplus, if Brazil wholeheartedly went along with Germany's restrictive program.[87]

The exclusion of cotton from the compensation list appeared to be a decided setback for Germany's plans, since that product was the one most eagerly sought by its importers. Cotton exports to the Reich had expanded so rapidly following the initiation of compensation trade that Liverpool merchants, until then Brazil's best customers, found themselves "competing wildly" to get supplies.[88] Brazilian sales to Great Britain had amounted to nearly twenty thousand tons during the first five months of 1934; now they dropped to less than half that figure for the same period in 1935. By midyear over forty thousand tons had gone to Germany, approximately twice the total amount that nation had purchased from Brazil during the preceding year.[89]

The gains in the German market were made largely at the expense of American shippers, justifying the fears of one dealer who had noted at the end of 1934, just after Roosevelt had turned down the barter proposal from Germany and as Brazilian cotton was hastily being loaded into ships bound for Hamburg and Bremen, that German mills seemed disposed to rework their spindles to accommodate non-American cotton. This would be very costly, he told a member of the embassy in Berlin, "but I have reason to believe that the Germans are getting ready to spend that money, and once that expenditure is made it would seem to me that our cotton planters will have definitely lost the German market."[90]

Statistics bore out his pessimism: American sales to Germany declined sharply from 1,364,000 tons in 1933–1934 to only 384,000 in 1934–1935.[91] Whereas in 1932–1933 American shipments had made up an average of nearly 78 percent of Germany's total cotton imports, the figure dropped to less than 60 percent in 1934 and to about 24 percent in 1935. On the other hand, Brazil's share of German consumption, negligible until 1935—an average of less than 1 percent a year during 1932–1934—leaped to nearly 27 percent in 1935.[92]

The quality, as well as the quantity, of the product was an important element in the growth of Brazilian exportation to Germany, since the cotton consisted to a considerable extent of low-grade fibers from Paraíba, Alagoas, Pernambuco, and Ceará. Speculation in Rio de Janeiro was that the shorter staples were being used not only for ersatz fabrics but also, more significantly, in the manufacture of high explosives, as part of the Nazi rearmament program.[93] The expanding German market gave strong impetus to the cultivation of inferior grades in the Northeast. From an estimated yield of around 260,000 bales from the 1932–1933 crop, production in that region more than tripled with the 1935–1936 harvest.[94]

"With the resources that cotton has given me, I am year by year increasing the planting of that precious Malvaceae," wrote a Cearense *fazendeiro* in July 1935. "Last year I earned $574; the year before, when I began cultivation, my profit was a little less than $246; this year I expect to make some $800," he exulted.[95] Even a bit farther to the south, in Bahia, not normally a cotton-producing area of any significance, the emergence of the German buyer started a local boom: of the 354 bales produced by Bahian planters in 1934, 15 had gone to Germany; in 1935, however, production rose to 5,248 bales, of which over 4,700 were shipped to the new consumer.[96]

The regional impact of German purchases was evident in the different reactions of northern and *paulista* growers to the increased sales to the Reich. The former welcomed this development because German importers were not only willing to accept the poorer grades but also able to pay prices 10 to 20 percent higher than other importers because of the discounted blocked marks.[97] The state of Paraíba, for example, realized a profit of some $1.6 million on its 1934–1935 crop by such price advantages.[98]

But São Paulo interests feared the trend toward almost exclusive reliance on German consumption. Noting that the Reich had purchased nearly 85 percent of Brazil's cotton exports during the first four months of the year, spokesmen for São Paulo producers cautioned the government in May that a healthy expansion of production was contingent upon diversified outlets. The *paulistas* were especially concerned about the stimulus being given to the planting of low-quality fibers.[99] Their support for restrictions on compensation trade was a natural consequence of this viewpoint, whereas northern interests bitterly protested the government's decision. Even if Germany should agree to pay in free currency, complained northern growers, they would still suffer the loss of the price advantages of compensation marks.[100]

The question of securing cotton for blocked marks was the fundamental issue in commercial relations between Brazil and Germany during the remainder of the year and was closely allied to the problem of negotiating a formal agreement between them. Berlin had warned Brazilian authorities in May that a decision to sell cotton only for free exchange would deprive a treaty of any foundation and markedly reduce the current "strong German interest" in Brazil.[101] Noting Brazil's replacement of the United States as the Reich's principal source of cotton, Kroll observed in a confidential review of Germany's trade situation in South America, in June 1935, that the solution of the problem would largely determine "the significance of South America for the supply of raw materials to Germany in one of the most important spheres." In his opinion, it was of "considerable importance" that the Reich continue to outbid other buyers of Brazilian cotton, in order to make Brazilian planters firmly dependent on the German market.[102]

When Souza Costa secretly agreed to permit German banks to deliver compensation marks instead of free currency to the Banco do Brasil in satisfaction of the 35 percent free exchange requirement, Berlin accepted the limited victory of June 17, undertook to resume purchases from Brazil, and agreed in principle to recognize Brazilian tariff and quota requests in the projected formal pact. But the Auswärtiges Amt instructed Schmidt-Elskop to press "on every occasion" for an understanding on the cotton question, which was of "decisive importance for future development of our economic relations with Brazil."[103]

To make the point, German authorities limited the value of renewed imports so as to permit an immediate embargo should talks on the cotton problem prove inconclusive, and they arranged to resume purchases of only those goods in which they had "an especially urgent interest."[104] Brazilian exporters of such items as tobacco and fruits thus learned in ensuing weeks that import licenses for their products would be granted only when cotton was reincluded in compensation trade.[105] The Vargas government was reluctant to take that step, however, and it delayed settlement of that issue as well as treaty negotiations throughout the balance of the year, arguing mainly the necessity of first reaching an agreement on commercial and exchange matters with the Americans.[106]

Germany declined to force Brazil's hand, essentially for three reasons. In the first place, the importance of trade relations was a mutual one, as Brazil was rapidly climbing higher in the list of the Reich's principal customers. Berlin's "very urgent" need to obtain meat supplies from Brazil in October was one specific indication of the latter's significance as a source of supply.[107] And considerably enhancing its status in German eyes was the continued refusal of the American government to sanction the special accord repeatedly offered it by the Germans. Berlin's perception of Brazil as a victim of American coercion was also an ingredient in its response to Brazilian hesitation on the cotton question. Indeed, the German records show that Reich officials habitually attributed a more coercive policy to Washington than it in fact was willing to adopt toward Brazil, a situation that Brazilian policy makers exploited to the hilt.[108]

The third and principal reason for Germany's reluctance to force the issue was the fact that the defeat on the cotton question was more apparent than real. Indeed, a memorandum drawn up by Kroll more than two months after the ban on compensation trade revealed that Hamburg and Bremen traders continued "briskly" to receive Brazilian cotton in "really considerable amounts," because of a "broadly sympathetic interpretation and application" of the ruling that contracts concluded prior to May 13 could still be sold for compensation marks.[109] By October, exports to the Reich reached a level six times greater than the total for 1934, and sales for the year amounted to more than eighty thousand tons. Shipments during the second half of 1935 were thus roughly equivalent to those made during the first semester.[110]

That cotton continued to be sold for blocked marks was an open secret, and responsible voices denounced clandestine predating of contracts, falsification of documents, and other forms of bureaucratic malfeasance as largely responsible for the continued traffic.[111] Paulista merchants had apparently also contracted for large orders—exceeding even existing or anticipated stocks—by international telephone the very day the CFCE approved the cessation of compensation transactions. Northern exporters, lacking the means of communication available to their southern counterparts, were cut off from the German market and compelled to sell to southern firms, who then used the cotton to satisfy their recently undertaken speculative commitments.[112] J. A.

Kulenkampff, a German businessman who served the Wilhelmstrasse in a semiofficial capacity as an economic counselor to its missions in South America, even predicted in November that if the 1935–1936 crop was as large as expected the Brazilian government would "close its eyes" and allow continued shipments to Germany under the guise of old contracts, or ones closed prior to May 13.[113]

In the absence of a formal agreement on the cotton question, official negotiations during the year for a trade treaty were likewise unproductive. Kulenkampff, however, saw possibilities for further expansion of trade under the existing noncontractual arrangement. Pressure from exporters was intense, and the federal authorities, he recognized, would have to consider their demands. In regard to the threat of action from Washington, Kulenkampff told the Auswärtiges Amt that "even then Brazil, assuming that the present government is still at the helm, will meet North American wishes only temporarily and will find an unofficial way that is suited for evasion [*zur Umgehung geeignet*], so that its own interests are not damaged."[114]

The evident concern of Brazilian leaders for national welfare in what they perceived as a ruthlessly competitive international environment was a tender spot that German agents skillfully probed in an effort to secure raw materials. Brazil's infant but expanding export trade in cotton provided a particularly sensitive target, and German spokesmen hammered on the theme of Brazil's need to make secure the German market in the face of the potential threat represented by American surpluses.[115]

After determining that some American firms were privately selling cotton on an *Aski* mark basis, the legation in Rio de Janeiro drew Brazilian attention to this as evidence of the harm the resolutions of May 13 and June 17 were causing to Brazilian interests.[116] Observing that Brazil had become the largest single supplier to the Reich, a Bremen firm warned a Brazilian exporter that under the present Brazilian policy the Americans seemed likely to recapture their former position.[117] This argument was not without effect. Reporting on a conversation late in November with Souza Costa and Alberto Boavista, Dantas's replacement as exchange director of the Banco do Brasil, Kulenkampff observed that the information about the American-German transactions had made "a quite visible impression" on Boavista and that the finance minister had received it with "quite remarkable" interest.[118] Sampaio relayed this news to the CFCE at its first meeting after these talks, and subsequent word from the embassy in Berlin seemed to confirm it.[119] With a large crop of low-grade cotton expected, Kulenkampff assured Berlin that "with calm waiting our time must automatically come."[120]

The fundamental willingness of the Vargas administration to continue its cooperation in the trade program of the New Germany found symbolic expression at the end of November, when, certain of the approval of the American treaty and "considering the increasing importance of relations between Brazil and Germany," it agreed to raise its legation in Berlin to an embassy.[121] Months earlier the news of France's intention to establish an embassy in Chile had concerned Wilhelmstrasse officials, who feared that further delay in raising Germany's legations in the ABC countries to embassy status would make that "inevitable" act appear to be a "reluctant, clumsy imitation" of the other *Grossmächte*, rather than a "friendly gesture." But the step, it was authoritatively suggested, should be linked to economic negotiations, since it could then appear as a concession on the Reich's part. The Brazilian chargé in Berlin thus accurately interpreted the move as one connected to progress in commercial matters.[122]

The understanding that Brazil and Germany now reached can be read only as a sign of a mutual commitment to closer economic ties. The short-lived Communist revolt in Brazil at this very time and the resultant absorption of the legislature in domestic political affairs delayed the necessary legislation, so the new Brazilian envoy, José Joaquim Moniz de Aragão, sailed for Germany in mid-December bearing two sets of credentials: those of minister plenipotentiary and, for later use, those of ambassador. The forty-eight–year–old career diplomat also carried with him verbal instructions from Vargas to dedicate himself to the task of strengthening commercial bonds with the Reich.[123] When Moniz de Aragão subsequently presented his credentials, the Führer expressed his own "particular interest" in intensifying trade with Brazil.[124]

The year closed with no formal agreement between the two countries, but both were basically satisfied with the results of their understanding. A formal solution to the cotton question remained to be found, but the Brazilian authorities had shown in practical fashion their desire to cut as large a slice as possible of the German market for Brazilian planters. All indications were that the statistics of trade between Brazil and the Reich would continue to multiply.

A Vargas decree in December ordering a revision of commercial treaties signed during the Provisional Government (1930–1934) gave immediacy to the problem of placing trade relations with Germany on a statutory footing. The president's action was taken in response to the restrictive policies of other countries and the resultant continuing decline in Brazil's export revenues. Sampaio, designated to negotiate new agreements in Europe, privately explained that the government sought greater export guarantees and wanted to stop generalization of the most-favored-nation clause.[125]

The conduct of Brazilian officials during the ensuing negotiations with Berlin leading to the modus vivendi, or gentlemen's agreement, of June 1936, their statements to representatives of the major powers, and the form of the understanding reached with Germany showed clearly that Brazilian leaders were willing to risk a sacrifice of international prestige or credibility in order to protect domestic economic interests and, increasingly, the demand of the Brazilian military for armaments.

The negotiations also reveal a narrowing of the decisive policy-making unit, as the CFCE ceased to be an authoritative participant in ultimate decisions. Itamaraty, moreover, assumed a role clearly subordinate to that of the Ministry of Finance. During 1935 Souza Costa had gradually become the forceful voice in economic matters, especially since Dantas no longer spoke for the Banco do Brasil. The decision in mid-1935 secretly to recognize compensation marks as valid currency for satisfaction of the "free exchange" requirement, for example, had been arrived at directly between the German embassy and Souza Costa. According to Schmidt-Elskop, the finance minister had declared that he "wanted to know nothing of notes and Itamaraty."[126] If Itamaraty was a party to the details of the arrangement of 1936, it is difficult to escape the impression that this was primarily because Macedo Soares endorsed compensation.

The proposals that led to the German-Brazilian modus vivendi were formulated largely outside official channels by private businessmen from both countries, headed on the Brazilian side by Olavo Egídio de Souza Aranha. Scion of one of São Paulo's leading families and a cousin of the ambassador in Washington, Souza Aranha was a partner in the firm of Monteiro and Aranha, the Brazilian representative of the Schroeder Banking Corporation. Prominent in the construction field, the firm had varied interests and was well connected in Brazilian banking circles. Financing of cotton and coffee shipments brought Souza Aranha and his colleagues into close contact with *paulista* planters and exporters. Personal acquaintance with Dantas, Macedo Soares, Souza

Costa, and Vargas further enhanced the influence of the São Paulo financier.[127]

Souza Aranha was particularly interested in the great market potential of the Third Reich, and he welcomed the flourishing trade that developed after Otto Kiep's visit. Politically conservative, he had previously lived in Germany for three years, spoke German, and was "very well-disposed" toward the renascent Central European power.[128] His business operations over the years had led to close relationships with members of German financial circles, especially in Hamburg.[129] Among his influential associates in Berlin was a prominent lawyer-businessman named Wilhelm Beutner, who had excellent personal contacts in both the Wilhelmstrasse and the Ministry of Economic Affairs.

In October 1934 Beutner had led a commission representing a number of German industrial and import firms to Brazil to explore the possibility of a large-scale exchange of raw materials for industrial equipment. Together with Souza Aranha, the German agent discussed his plans with Brazilian officials, and upon his return to Berlin he sought to enlist the cooperation of authorities there. In June 1935 he and Souza Aranha presented to the Auswärtiges Amt a proposal calling for a government-to-government exchange of coffee for industrial items. Another scheme they promoted in ensuing weeks was liquidation of the frozen German credits in Brazil, worth over £500,000 sterling by the end of 1935, with extra cotton shipments.[130]

By the beginning of 1936 the two enterprising partners were ready to bring their governments officially together. With Berlin's endorsement they formed a consortium, later registered in Rio de Janeiro as an import-export firm with the name Sociedade Internacional de Comércio (SOINC), and presented their proposal to Moniz de Aragão for transmission to the Brazilian government. SOINC would act as a middleman, handling the shipping, storage, and sale of the additional coffee quota, which would come from surplus stocks held by the Departamento Nacional de Café, and would likewise act as intermediary in the compensating purchases of German industrial goods by the Brazilian government. Berlin also subsequently informed the Brazilian government that it had authorized SOINC to negotiate with the Banco do Brasil and appropriate agencies in Rio de Janeiro for the liquidation of German frozen credits in foreign currencies.[131]

Mounting pressure from domestic agricultural interests aided Souza Aranha and Beutner considerably by helping to create a receptive atmosphere in Rio de Janeiro for adoption of their plans and greater expansion of trade with the Reich. Bahian tobacco producers had for months been concerned about surplus stocks, and a projected heavy crop for 1936 led to appeals to both state and federal authorities for protection of the German market, whose share of Bahian exports had risen from less than 35 percent at the start of the decade to nearly 60 percent in 1935.[132] *Paulista* citrus farmers urged the CFCE to secure from Germany a larger quota for their oranges, since overproduction seemed imminent, and both the state government and major commercial organizations in Santa Catharina pointed out to the CFCE that exports of pine wood to the Reich were of growing importance to the local economy, especially since the new market lessened dependence upon the La Plata buyers.[133]

The most insistent pressure came from northern cotton producers, who, like the tobacco and citrus fruit growers, were holding large stocks—Paraíba alone had an estimated thirty thousand tons awaiting a buyer[134]—and anticipating a superabundant crop. Early in the year cotton interests in the North mounted an intensive, concerted campaign to persuade the government to reconsider the ban on sales in compensation marks. In January and February the CFCE and the presidential desk were flooded with multisignature telegrams from individual firms containing the same text, clearly a result of coordinated movement: the Northeast, said the wires, was "squeezed" by the "most terrible crisis" and had before it a "painful perspective," but renewal of exports to Germany would be the "salvation" of the region's economy.[135] The Commercial Association of João Pessôa complained that the Northeast was "choking" in "mountains" of low-grade cotton with no possible market other than the German, a judgment shared by similar groups in other states.[136] Governor Menezes Pimentel of Ceará appealed personally to federal legislators, the CFCE, and Vargas for assistance.[137] The president also received a petition from several federal deputies requesting reestablishment of compensation trade in cotton.[138]

Northern grievances occupied a prominent place in CFCE discussions during February and March. Macedo Soares and Alberto Boavista reaffirmed their support for the viewpoint of southern planters, and Souza Costa also reiterated his basic opposition to bilateralism. The Banco do Brasil had over 14.5 million compensation marks, an amount equivalent to 80 percent of its capital, said the finance minister, and permitting the sale of cotton in such currency would only aggravate the situation.[139] But some way of disposing of northern cotton had to be found, since, as one member of the CFCE wrote on March 18, the conditions causing the "impasse" would only worsen as the new harvest period approached. Adding his personal entreaty to the now legion appeals, a northern deputy stressed the reliance of state treasuries in the North on export taxes, and Souza Aranha helped his own cause by having "interested circles in São Paulo" manifest support for the northern position.[140]

Against this background of domestic pressure and in the knowledge that Germany had begun negotiations with other coffee producers when Rio de Janeiro failed to reply immediately to SOINC's bid,[141] Brazilian policy makers weakened in their opposition to cotton sales in blocked marks. They also knew that the Wilhelmstrasse had recently underscored the linkage between trade expansion and the acquisition of cotton. "If we focus our whole trade policy so strongly on Brazil (and the rest of South America) as we have in the past two years," Karl Ritter had stated, "then Brazil must not expect to export only goods that it chooses . . ."[142] Too, there were the usual indications that cooperation with the Reich would pay handsome dividends.[143]

Souza Costa reluctantly recommended to Vargas early in April that, in view of the cotton surpluses, Brazil release cotton for compensation trade, provided Berlin raised the coffee quota. If Vargas approved, said the finance minister, he would proceed with the negotiations through diplomatic channels, informing the CFCE of only the "general lines of the matter, without making known our decisions." To avoid difficulties with third nations, said Souza Costa, a "maximum reserve" was necessary. Vargas did approve the idea, and on April 16 the CFCE, having concluded its study of the cotton question, likewise recommended that the government "at once" reach an understanding with Germany. The principle of selling cotton for compensation marks was now "definitely established," exulted Souza Aranha, who had returned to Brazil to lobby on behalf of the SOINC proposals.[144]

Commercial talks with Berlin over the next six weeks were based on a merger of the SOINC transactions and general trade aims. Both sides agreed on a coffee quota of 1.6 million sacks, of which 500,000 would be handled by SOINC in return for Brazilian government orders from Germany, and they eventually concurred on a cotton quota of 62,000 tons, plus an additional 10,000 tons as payment, also via SOINC, for frozen German credits. Because of the European situation, Brazilian leaders balked at the idea of signing a formal treaty; it was agreed that, in addition to approval of the SOINC schemes, Berlin would establish one-year quotas for all Brazilian products, and that a provisional treaty would be worked out during that year. One new requirement put forward by the Brazilians in mid-May was a limitation on imports of German automobiles, typewriters, office and sewing machines, gasoline, and oil. But Itamaraty suggested curious limits: a quota equivalent to a 10 percent increase in Brazil's imports of those products during 1935.[145]

The reason given for this request was "repeated inquiries" from the American government. Since the announcement of the CFCE's resolution of April 16, the State Department and the embassy in Brazil had kept a watchful eye on the progress of German-Brazilian relations. Souza Aranha in fact complained that Gibson's assistant, Xanthaky, went about "spying on me everywhere" and making inquiries about the financier's relationships with various Germans. The final straw for Souza Aranha was a telegram from the Schroeder agent in New York informing him that the State Department had learned of an alleged barter deal involving an exchange of railway equipment for "five hundred thousand bags" of coffee, and that the American government was carefully following the matter because of its possible effects on the American-Brazilian treaty. "Would appreciate your informing State Department that Brazil is not United States colony and that I am not a citizen of the United States," read the irate cable that Souza Aranha fired off in reply.[146]

Because of his uncritical acceptance of information supplied by Itamaraty, Hugh Gibson was a mine of misinformation about Brazil's intentions and objectives in the trade negotiations with Germany. His image of the Vargas government as a dedicated partner of the United States had in recent months become even more positive and firmly rooted. True, the Brazilians were dealing in compensation marks, but Gibson tended to regard this as a foolish move by an inexperienced junior colleague, as it were. He had remonstrated with his friends at Itamaraty over this and, according to his trusted and devoted assistant, had done so successfully. "As a result of our efforts," Xanthaky had written the previous November, "I don't think that any more trick agreements will be concluded prior to your return."[147]

Gibson was deeply impressed by Macedo Soares's cooperative attitude in the Chaco matter and other questions, and he found "something very comforting in the clear desire of these people to play ball with us . . ."[148] Gibson unofficially acknowledged to Sumner Welles in February 1936 that he had been "rather tiresomely repetitious" in describing Brazil's desire to "collaborate with us politically and otherwise." The ambassador was convinced by Rio de Janeiro's policy in other spheres that it "wants to play the game with us 100%."[149] Gibson obviously believed that his personal association with Macedo Soares, and Washington's good-neighborliness, precluded anything but complete candor between the two governments.

The ambassador correctly interpreted the CFCE decision of April 16 as evidence that the government would have to give "some satisfaction" to northern cotton producers, but he advised Washington that Brazil actually intended to reduce its trade with the Reich by imposing quotas for both exports and imports based on 1933–1934 averages. The agreement Brazil envisioned was designed, Gibson erroneously reported, "expressly to favor the English and American exporters to this market and this is, in fact, its primary purpose."[150]

Brazilian decision makers, of course, had no intention of reducing trade with Germany but rather wanted to exploit the situation described for Vargas by the director of the Brazilian Commercial Bureau in Berlin as "right down the line favorable to our exportation."[151] The Brazilians had requested and obtained a doubling of the coffee quota in comparison to sales to the Reich in 1935, and they had agreed to a cotton quota that was more than twice the amount that had gone to Germany in 1934. Furthermore, when Karl Ritter proposed that, instead of using 1935 as a base year for calculating the 10 percent increase to be allowed German exports, the two countries use the twelve months preceding the date of the new agreement, Itamaraty readily assented, and in so doing it sanctioned a further increase of German shipments to Brazil.[152]

Both countries were anxious to get the agreement signed, Berlin "immediately" in view of its need for cotton, and Brazil "with all possible urgency" in order to avoid "complications" that might adversely affect the negotiations.[153] Macedo Soares no doubt had in mind the difficulties that could arise should Washington get wind of the projected accord. A sensational report in a leading *carioca* daily on May 24 that Aranha had threatened to resign because of the negotiations with Germany led to the complications the foreign minister feared.[154]

On learning of the press allegations, Hull immediately queried Aranha, who denied them and said they must be based on letters he had written to Vargas in 1935. The secretary then cabled Gibson, instructing him to impress upon Macedo Soares that press accounts indicated that the proposed agreement contravened the "spirit if not the letter" of the American-Brazilian treaty. "These people are very alarmed," Aranha added in a report to Vargas that expressed his own "serious fears."[155] Macedo Soares was caught off guard when Gibson politely confronted him, but he led the ambassador to believe that he was "greatly troubled" about possible violations of the American treaty and, apparently to gain time, told Gibson that he would have a copy of the draft German accord ready for his perusal the next morning.[156]

In Berlin that same day Moniz de Aragão placed in the mail a dispatch summing up recent telegrams and confirming Germany's acceptance of the "restrictions" on its exports. When Gibson returned to Itamaraty the following day, however, Macedo Soares had concocted a story that the negotiations had been interrupted by last-minute requests by Berlin for quota modifications. He now revealed, to the American envoy's surprise, that the base year for calculating imports from Germany would be 1935, but, to make it appear as though he had struggled against German demands, he alleged that Berlin was "pressing for 25%." Puzzled but confident, Gibson left the meeting convinced that Aranha's appeals and his own friendly intervention had "slowed up the entire negotiations" and that Washington would have "ample opportunity" to plead its case.[157] The next day telegraphic instructions went out to Moniz de Aragão from Itamaraty on the texts and handling of the secret and public notes. Wilhelm Beutner also received a cable from Rio that day. The English text bore the telegraphic signature of his partner and read: "Foreign minister wishes to sign both on the first June in order place USA in front of an accomplished fact thus avoiding further interference of USA rulers politicians and newspapers still dangerously active."[158]

To thicken the smoke screen for the dealings with Berlin, Macedo Soares on May 30 handed Gibson a note purportedly outlining the intended understanding with Germany. The document mentioned the various quotas granted by the Reich, including the 1.6 million sacks of coffee and the change of the base year for German imports from 1935 to the twelve months preceding "entry into force" of the agreement. No mention was made of the SOINC transactions. Macedo Soares asked Gibson to let Hull know that he had made a "decided stand" against demands for an arrangement that would have left German exporters "practically unrestricted" in their battle against

American competitors. Embellishing the story, the foreign minister told Gibson that Berlin had been "truculent and threatening," with Hitler himself leading "a strong fight" to exclude automobiles from the restricted list. The American envoy found it "rather curious" that Brazil seemed eager to conclude the agreement, but he saw no purposeful evasion on the part of the foreign minister.[159]

In going over the Brazilian note later, however, Gibson realized the meaning of the agreement the Brazilians were seeking. They not only intended to sell more to the Reich, but they had also "failed to realize," he thought, that they would be allowing Germany to consolidate or expand its export gains by taking German goods in quantities impossible to "calculate accurately until some time after the signature." As far as the ambassador could tell, Brazilian leaders had been "dazzled" by the chance to increase exports and had not pondered the effects of their action on the "broader principles of international trade to which they profess their devotion." Grave consequences for American commerce would ensue, he predicted, if the agreement were effected.[160]

Gibson was disconcerted and a bit irate, telling Hugh Gurney, Seed's replacement as British ambassador, that "he had been let down" by Macedo Soares, since it looked as though the Brazilian government, despite the foreign minister's assurances, had attempted to conclude the agreement without allowing him to examine it. He complained unfairly that Aranha had misled the State Department, having recently informed it that Brazil and Germany were only in the preliminary stages of negotiations. "Gibson went so far as to say . . . that he felt that the affair might mean the death knell of both Macedo Soares and Oswaldo Aranha," reported Gurney. "I imagine that in neither case will his prognostication be fulfilled, but it shows how far he has worked himself up over the affair."[161]

Concern within the State Department about the developments in Brazil led Sumner Welles to give Aranha a lengthy homily in the form of an *aide-mémoire* setting forth familiar arguments. Brazil's previous "invaluable support" for liberal trade practices made the United States confident, Welles admonished in conclusion, that Brazil would avoid agreements "in any sense compromising the position which it has so helpfully and resolutely maintained." Returning to the Brazilian chancellery, Aranha drafted two cables to Rio de Janeiro. A personal one to Vargas urged him not to sanction the arrangement with the Reich, because it would have a "terrible repercussion" in the United States.

The second wire, an official one to Itamaraty asking the reasons for the government's action, was marked by ill-concealed acerbity.[162]

Policy makers in Rio de Janeiro, confronted with a situation similar to that obtaining during the first decisional period in 1934, once again paused to reevaluate the form—but not the substance—of their decision. On that same evening of June 1, after Aranha's cables had been decoded, a trans-Atlantic phone call and later a telegram of confirmation advised Moniz de Aragão in Berlin that Souza Costa no longer wanted to sign both the confidential and the public notes, but wanted to rearrange them. The next day Macedo Soares sent more explicit instructions. "Everything that was negotiated continues in effect," the foreign minister explained. "We need now to find a practical formula for putting into practice what was agreed upon." He suggested a series of communications, public ones by Itamaraty on cotton and by the Wilhelmstrasse on import quotas and secret ones on the provisions of the accord.[163]

German authorities agreed to the rearrangement of the notes, but they insisted that the two SOINC transactions constituted a commitment and had to be carried out, especially since it was around them that negotiations had developed. To bolster what appeared to be a weakening of nerve in Rio de Janeiro, German spokesmen alleged in conversation with Moniz de Aragão that Brazil's competitors, including American cotton producers, were engaged in "great activity," trying to impede the negotiations with Brazil.[164]

The establishment of complete censorship on news of the talks with Germany hinted at last-minute behind-the-scenes maneuvering.[165] Bouças, who had sponsored several articles against the impending agreement in various leading newspapers, saw the enforced curtailment of publicity as the result of a "muffled and subterranean campaign" in favor of the accord. Gibson redoubled his efforts. He sent Macedo Soares a copy of Welles's *aide-mémoire* on June 2 and called on Souza Costa at home the next day. To his great relief, he learned from the finance minister that the agreement "could be considered as abandoned in its present form." Macedo Soares, said the finance minister, now agreed with him and favored "some other method" of resolving the dilemma.[166]

That "other method," arranged the previous day with the German government, underwent one final modification on June 5, when Souza Costa insisted that the "restrictions" on German exports not be put into writing. Macedo Soares advised Moniz de Aragão that the "limitation" would still be maintained and instructed him to make a verbal statement to that effect to the Wilhelmstrasse, with a request that the latter not make public that declaration.[167]

On June 6 the secret exchange of notes occurred in Berlin. That same day in Rio de Janeiro the Brazilian foreign minister told Gibson everything the latter wanted to hear. Macedo Soares said that it had proved impossible to devise "any method for reconciling in the form of even a temporary agreement" the divergent policies of Brazil and Germany. Brazil therefore merely intended to declare that it would permit the sale of 62,000 tons of cotton in compensation marks and require free currency for purchases above that amount. Berlin would announce quotas for imports from Brazil, said Macedo Soares, and the two governments would also grant each other most-favored-nation treatment pending negotiation of a formal treaty. In an official memorandum that he handed Gibson in reply to Welles's *aide-mémoire*, the foreign minister expounded at length on Brazil's "unalterable conviction" that Hull's program was indeed the answer to international commercial woes. In Germany's case, Brazil had sought a "provisional formula" that would not violate Brazil's liberal policy, "from which it does not propose to deviate," and yet would satisfy immediate economic needs.[168]

Believing that he had triumphed, Gibson was inclined to be generous. He told Hull that Macedo Soares originally had been overwhelmed by German and domestic pressure but now saw things "in their true light" and, as a result, had dropped the idea of an agreement with Berlin. This had placed the Brazilian official in an uncomfortable position, yet one that he was accepting "with good grace." Gibson thought that, in order to show that Washington did not want to "rub it in," Hull might send Macedo Soares a friendly note of thanks for his response to American representations. The secretary of state was pleased to have Macedo Soares informed how "deeply appreciative" he was of Brazil's attitude. "The action of a great trading nation like Brazil in standing forth resolutely for a liberal trade policy," proclaimed Hull, "immeasurably enhances the possibilities of general adoption of these broader principles."[169]

Macedo Soares, like Brazilian officials on both sides of the policy dispute, acted in accordance with his perception of national interests. But for the foreign minister, as for many civil servants, the line between patriotic service and personal political ambition was finely drawn. And now, having parried the thrusts from Washington, he turned to domestic politics. The presidential elections were scheduled for January 1938 and it was time to begin preparing a campaign. The foreign minister invited various congressmen to Itamaraty on the day of the secret exchange of notes and proudly assured them that the arrangement with Germany would completely satisfy Brazilian interests.[170] His brother's newspaper, the *Diário Carioca*, carried a five-line headline the next day congratulating him, along with Vargas and Souza Costa, on the success of the negotiations.[171] The Brazilian press hailed the "trade agreement" with the Reich, an interpretation Macedo Soares encouraged. In a clear effort to boost his political stock in his home state, he sent a telegram to the governor of São Paulo stating that a "provisional commercial accord" had been signed.[172]

From state officials and commercial and agricultural groups throughout the country the foreign minister received commendatory messages.[173] São Paulo agricultural interests were pleased. Even cotton producers had finally come out in favor of a resumption of sales in compensation marks,[174] which explains the volte-face of Macedo Soares, who in February had argued before the CFCE that it would be "more fair" not to sell cotton to Germany for blocked marks, in order to protect São Paulo.[175] The *Folha da Manhã* of the *paulista* capital, directed by a wealthy planter with extensive coffee and cotton holdings, praised the "treaty" and candidly remarked that whether cotton was sold for international currency or compensation marks was "of absolute indifference to us." In an interview with a *carioca* daily, the *Folha* director suggested that traditional trading methods were no longer valid anyway.[176]

Berlin was likewise satisfied with the outcome of the talks. Ritter sent Souza Aranha a personal letter expressing gratitude for the "great service" rendered and a desire to be able to "work together in a similar way in the future." Although "only" about one-fifth of the Reich's cotton needs were satisfied by the arrangement, German experts were pleased that Brazil had pledged itself to heavier importation of German manufactured goods.[177]

The elevation of their legations to embassies on June 17 was a timely symbol of the approximation between the two countries. The ceremonial presentation of credentials by Moniz de Aragão in Berlin was marked by "greatest solemnity," and in his brief official discourse the Führer expressed satisfaction not only that general relations with Brazil were good, but also that German-Brazilian commerce had increased over the past year. In private conversation with Moniz de Aragão later, both Hitler and Foreign Minister von Neurath were "extremely cordial." The Nazi leader again referred to trade relations with Brazil—"to which, he emphasized, he attributes special interest"—and congratulated the minister-finally-ambassador on the felicitous results of the recent negotiations.[178]

Reich authorities carefully guarded against any public discussion of the full contents of the agreement. On June 9, following the publicized mutual extension of most-favored-nation treatment and unilateral declarations on quotas, the Ministry of Propaganda instructed the German press not to mention any figures in commenting on the arrangement. The Reichsstelle für den Aussenhandel sent out greater details to its subsidiaries for their "strictly confidential" information, and other official agencies warned subordinate departments not to inform individual firms of the quota figures. Any commentary in the press or trade journals was "under all circumstances" forbidden.[179]

The satisfied pronouncements of Brazilian officials and politicians and the accounts of both the Brazilian and the American press caused doubt and concern to American observers. Gibson assured the State Department that his reports had contained the "facts," but other embassy officers disagreed. The ambassador's messages to Washington had been "unduly optimistic and pro-Brazilian," in the opinion of the commercial attaché and counselor. "The fact is that the Brazilians put through the German agreement precisely as planned except that instead of signing it they left it an oral 'gentlemen's agreement,'" the counselor wrote to a friend in the department. "The length to which Macedo [Soares] went in preparing the agreement behind our backs," he observed, "is significant in relation to Embassy standing with him."[180] As additional information leaked out, it gradually became clear that this was in fact the correct version of what had occurred, and even Gibson was plagued by the unpleasant thought that he had been duped. Reporting a chance encounter with him, Schmidt-Elskop noted that his "irritation was clearly perceptible, whereas before the agreement he always wore a superior smile."[181]

Bouças was thoroughly exasperated by the "hoodwinking" of Brazil's most important client. "It's positively the killing of the goose that lays the golden egg!" he cried.[182] At a meeting of the CFCE on June 22, the Brazilian businessman criticized the understanding with Germany, only to be attacked "in a violent manner" by Macedo Soares, who exclaimed that, "happily for us, Brazil is not a colony of the United

States to bow to the impositions of the Americans, who are only trying to hinder the sale of our cotton to Germany." There seemed to be no fear of German expansion in Brazil, retorted Bouças, but, when Washington made a "completely justified" defense of its interests, the move was labeled "Yankee imperialism." The July issue of Bouças' *O Observador Econômico e Financeiro* sharply questioned the discrepancy between official declarations of commercial principles and acquiescence in bilateralism with Germany.[183]

Aranha was incensed at the "absurdity" of his government's action. "Imagine that the proposal was not German but ours, conceived, drawn up, and presented by us!" he raged.[184] Since press reports had differed from what Macedo Soares had told him by telephone, Aranha had requested the terms of the notes, and the foreign minister had sent him those on quotas but said nothing about SOINC.[185] It was only through Vargas that Aranha received the texts of the notes on credits and SOINC's share in the coffee quota. This attempt to conceal information from him hastened the unraveling of what few threads of confidence remained between the Washington embassy and Itamaraty, and it heightened Aranha's suspicions about the modus vivendi. "Don't you think there is something fishy about all this?" he asked, calling Vargas's attention to SOINC's role in the coffee arrangement and to the fact that the German government had singled out an individual firm. Broader policy considerations also bothered Aranha, and he pleaded with the president to proceed cautiously in dealing with Berlin: "I am increasingly convinced that we must be especially careful with present-day Germany," he warned, "because the expansion of that country is inevitable, and the only people who don't see it are those who don't want to."[186] Itamaraty, of course, had good reason for wanting to conceal the fact that it planned to dispose of sizeable frozen German credits, since the very existence of such debts weakened the argument, oft-used in defending Brazil's participation in compensation trade, that the Reich held all the aces in the commercial game.[187]

Subsequent messages from Aranha to Vargas and Itamaraty, saying that the State Department had made bitter representations and saw no alternative but to impose a bilateral payments agreement on Brazil, caused no great anxiety in Rio de Janeiro, where experience told policy makers that the bite of the barking American dog was innocuous. Souza Costa replied for the administration and matter-of-factly justified the SOINC transactions. Paying for frozen credits in compensation marks was obviously to Brazil's advantage, he said, and the extra coffee quota could not hurt American interests and would only become effective if the government placed orders in Germany. "None of the stipulations," he concluded, "affects the direction of our foreign policy." Vargas added a reassuring note for his younger friend, saying that some details of the modus vivendi had "surprised me also" and that he had taken steps to see that Aranha was kept informed of all developments.[188]

Sumner Welles denied having made such harsh statements to Aranha. His record of the last talk with the Brazilian envoy showed that he had merely repeated mild admonitions against "further" compensation pacts.[189] Welles believed that Aranha had deliberately sent the "alarmist" telegrams in order to startle his government and shake its conviction that Washington would remain passive. The assistant secretary also saw domestic politics in Aranha's gambit, since the ambassador was concerned about Macedo Soares's rival political ambitions. Welles feared that Aranha, for political purposes, might take public issue with Macedo Soares over commercial policy; yet at the same time he considered Aranha's action "decidedly helpful" for American interests.[190] Gibson shared Welles's anxiety about the possibility of an open political feud between the two Brazilian officials. "The danger is real and the results might be extremely distasteful for everybody concerned," he wrote, "and for some time I have been increasingly apprehensive lest the flying brick-bats strike some of us innocent bystanders."[191] Gibson was also concerned that the Brazilian government might think that threats had been made but not carried out. It would be best, he thought, simply to inform Macedo Soares that, while no threats had been articulated, Washington was distressed by the fact that Brazil was countenancing bilateral practices.[192]

With Washington's approval, Gibson called at Itamaraty on July 29. Following Hull's instructions, he not only made clear to Macedo Soares that the State Department was not menacing Brazil, but he also weakened what force his representation might have had by qualifying American concern as directed at a possible "series" of compensation agreements.[193] What the State Department in effect did, through Gibson, was to tell Macedo Soares that it would sanction the German agreement but hoped that agreement would be the last. Once again reassured that Washington would not retaliate, the foreign minister, who some two weeks earlier had told the German chargé to consider him the "representative of German industry for the sale of German products to the federal government,"[194] indulged in the rhetoric so treasured in Washington. Brazil's policy, he declared, was "definitely" aimed at meeting American desires by "reducing to a minimum" its imports from Germany.[195]

Gibson now was not so easily convinced. Indeed, Macedo Soares's "somewhat devious methods" had "shaken" his faith in the foreign minister and destroyed the previous bond of cordial, almost fraternal warmth between them. Macedo Soares's political aspirations were a major complication, Gibson realized. Subordinate officials at Itamaraty were even overcome with "scarcely concealed irritation and disgust," he reported to Welles, "as they feel this whole thing has now ceased to be an official matter and has become a sort of political football." Macedo Soares had become "so secretive and shifty" that it would be difficult to gain accurate information on the government's proceedings, so Gibson recommended that Aranha be encouraged to continue his vigilance and to make his views known to his government—"not necessarily in the same exotic way as the last time"—so that Vargas would not take "his eye off the ball. That is the only way," Gibson concluded, "we can be sure to avert a fresh upset."[196]

Some details of the June "upset," including the general outline of SOINC's role, had quickly become public currency. Souza Aranha was being singled out as the "great defender" of the agreement because he was to negotiate the sale of coffee for "railroad material," wrote Bouças less than a week after the exchange of notes.[197] Resentment in Brazilian exporting circles over the increasingly apparent preferential treatment given to SOINC grew apace as weeks passed.[198] Early in August a sensationalist newspaper in Rio de Janeiro carried two articles on successive days by an anonymous author revealing SOINC's share in the government-backed operations. The official German note on the coffee transaction was even printed verbatim.[199] The abrupt halt to this press coverage suggests the censor's hand: it was probably censorship that kept the scandal expected by Schmidt-Elskop from developing.[200]

Ritter informed the embassy in Brazil that SOINC did not have a monopoly position, as was rumored, but enjoyed certain privileges because of its efforts on behalf of an agreement between the two countries. "I don't think it too much to say . . . that without the cooperation of [Souza] Aranha an understanding would not have come about," said Ritter. "Certainly, at least, it would not have turned out so relatively advantageous for us." Weeks later the German official moved quickly to quash rumors that SOINC had fallen into disfavor with the Reich government. These were "completely false," he told Moniz de Aragão, and Souza Aranha continued to enjoy Berlin's "full confidence."[201]

Trade between the two nations progressed rapidly under the June modus vivendi, which Macedo Soares labeled "a completely new act, with none of the juridical characteristics of the acts of international law, a true gentlemen's agreement."[202] For the year, Germany provided around 23 percent of Brazil's total imports while purchasing about 13 percent of her exports.[203] For some states the importance of the German market continued to grow. Nearly 40 percent of Rio Grande do Sul's foreign exports, for example, went to the Reich. This was a 20 percent increase over 1935; state imports from Germany went up 40 percent.[204]

Cotton exporters were only partially satisfied with the arrangement, which stipulated that the quota would be divided equally between the North and the South. Immediately following announcement of resumption of compensation trade in cotton, a Pernambuco deputy branded the quota restriction an "iniquitous imposition" and a "draconian" measure. Berlin quickly sent word to Itamaraty that Germany was ready at any time to increase purchases in compensation marks. Brazil could easily sell 150,000 tons of cotton a year, Moniz de Aragão was informed. Macedo Soares cited this possibility in his attack on critics of compensation trading during the CFCE meeting on June 22.[205]

Out of "imperious necessity" northern producers launched a drive in August to persuade federal authorities to permit extraquota shipments of low-grade fibers to the Reich.[206] The CFCE finally bowed to the pressure late in September, and a week later Vargas approved its resolution authorizing the sale of an additional ten thousand tons to German importers for compensation marks.[207] The foreign minister's assurance to Gibson on June 6 that the agreement with Berlin "makes it clear" that purchases beyond the quota would have to be made in free currency thus proved to be merely one more in a long series of assertions without substance.[208]

The decision on trade in 1936 has been interpreted as a sudden shift in Brazil's orientation, as abandonment of a "new liberal trade policy" decided upon in December 1935,[209] which in turn then would have to be viewed as a departure from the decision made in 1934 to trade bilaterally with Germany. In 1934 Brazilian leaders had responded to promising opportunities for expanding, diversifying, and, through quotas, to a degree stabilizing Brazil's exports. But Vargas's resolution in December 1935 to denounce the most-favored-nation agreements signed in 1931–1932 was likewise designed to give the government more freedom of action in trade matters and to allow it to find firmer guarantees for Brazil's exports. Ensuing negotiations with Germany were in harmony with these previous decisions and reflect a continuity, rather than dramatic shifting, of policy since 1934. What that policy understandably boiled down to, of course, was seizing all opportunities in order to get the best commercial deal for Brazil.

The insistent demands from regional politicians, planters, and exporters had heightened the urgency with which government leaders approached national financial and economic problems and had strongly influenced policy decisions. Another factor of pressing nature also decisively conditioned the response of the government to the trade policy challenge: the patriotic desire—and political necessity—of doing something about the material needs of the armed forces.

Chapter 4

Military Influence on Economic Policy (1934–1937)

An assessment of the relationship between the high command and economic policy in the 1930s requires the posing of the following fundamental question: What did military leaders want? And, therefore, in what areas of economic policy were they actively interested? Were they then, as they are in many underdeveloped countries today, "bearers of modernity as represented by industrialization"?[1] Were they, as has been suggested, inactive insofar as trade policy was concerned but vigorous and decisive lobbyists on behalf of large-scale industrial projects who pushed the government into undertaking the construction of a huge, modern steel complex?[2] Or did the sense of urgency with which the high command evaluated national needs channel military pressure into other directions?

The Brazilian military wielded tremendous, often decisive, political influence throughout the 1930s. Following the army's overthrow of the monarchy in 1889, the armed forces had taken an increasingly active part in national political life. The army and navy had been called upon to suppress revolts during the first two decades of the century, and the political confusion surrounding the army's five-year pursuit of a large, elusive rebel column during the 1920s had resulted in the politicization of a significant part of the officer corps, particularly at the junior levels. The Revolution of 1930 gave strong impetus to that process. The fact that the Vargas government was installed through the use of violence seemed to stir up a general spirit of indiscipline in the barracks. Military-politicos made no secret of their disdain for politicians; many younger officers, especially the so-called *tenentes*, many of whom as cadets had participated in the revolts of the 1920s and had been reinstated after the Revolution, did not mask their contempt for some senior officers; and within the upper echelons of the officer corps there were deep-running personal rivalries and antagonisms. The São Paulo revolt in 1932 was partially a result of schisms within the officer class, and high-ranking officers who led that uprising plotted again in 1934–1935 to oust Vargas. The radicalization of politics after 1934 heightened the restlessness of the high command, and in order to ensure some degree of stability—perhaps even to remain in power—civilian leaders had to heed military demands in all areas of national activity.[3]

A crucial aspect of policy formulation must be borne in mind in order to understand the extent and direction of military demands on national resources in the post-1930 period: the military image of the external environment. Whether or not that image coincided with reality is immaterial—how military leaders perceived international conditions determined their objectives, which in turn shaped their political action. The cardinal fact to bear in mind when sorting out the priorities set up by military planners in that turbulent decade is that they were convinced from the beginning that another major international war was in the making. Given a generalized perception of threat within the high command, the vital factor then becomes the military's self-image, that is, its view of its own defensive capabilities.

Military strategists looked primarily southward, and Argentina, the traditional rival and strongest power on the continent, served as the yardstick by which they measured Brazilian capacity. An army study in 1932 estimated that the La Plata nation could mobilize a well-equipped force of 300,000 men in two weeks and have them massed on Brazil's southern frontier a month later. Brazil, on the other hand, would be "extremely slower" in mobilizing and deploying half that number of troops bearing "old and worn-out" arms in insufficient quantities. The author of the study calculated that the government would have to provide the army with an annual credit of $3.5 million over a fifteen-year period to permit it to counter with an equivalent force the army Argentina could initially raise.[4]

The brief civil war that broke out in July 1932 laid painfully bare the inadequacies of the armed services. Typical was the complaint of one local commander who had only "two old and also slow-firing 75 [millimeter] cannon, without breeching and with little ammunition" and lacked even the rope necessary for tents.[5] A month in the field was enough to lead Góes Monteiro, head of the main federal army, to caution Vargas to prepare himself for a "persevering and drawn-out war," because of deficient supplies and equipment. His advance on rebellious São Paulo bogged down in the Paraíba Valley under a paulista counterattack and the Minas Gerais front was almost paralyzed, "all as a result of the lack of troops and material," the general complained. Clearly a complete reorganization of the army was necessary, he said, including the acquisition of planes, modern artillery, and ample stocks of ammunition, as well as an increase in the number of troops.[6]

Shortly after the conflict ended, Minister of War Augusto Espírito Santo Cardoso, nonplussed by Finance Minister Aranha's recommendation that the army's budget proposal be slashed, penned a lengthy letter to Aranha recalling the recent unhappy battlefield performance. The document illustrates both the deep frustration that pervaded the high command and the implications of its attitude for the subsequent allocation of the country's sparse monetary resources. The army, Cardoso reminded Aranha, had found itself on the outbreak of war "without troops, without armaments, without munitions, without matériel." The bitter consequence was that most of the hastily organized battalions demonstrated "total inefficiency" and suffered "fantastic casualties." Logistic problems had been staggering: ". . . on the combat front 265,000 rounds were used per day and we were producing in the [federal] factory 75,000; they would ask for more artillery ammunition and the Depot would be empty; they would ask for gas masks and we would not reply to avoid having to say there were none; they would ask for air support and *one* plane would be sent . . ." Actually, the government should increase his budget, Cardoso argued, so that he could reorganize air services and send attachés to neighboring countries. From a military standpoint, the "humiliating" lack of such observers constituted "deplorable neglect," he charged, particularly when adjoining states were at war and "for that very reason compromising our border."[7]

Victory over the rebels did not remove the sources of internal political unrest, and, as Cardoso's remark suggested, the recent renewal of hostilities between Bolivia and Paraguay and the continuing Leticia imbroglio heightened the already deep anxiety of army chiefs, who protested with undisguised concern the paucity of the tools of war at their disposal. Góes Monteiro, ever sensitive to real or imagined threats to the central authority, alerted Vargas early in 1933 to new plots in the wind, counseling him to "deal urgently with the good moral and material organization of the armed forces." Vigilance must not slacken, said the general, who was then commander of the First Military Region: "It is preferable to spend more on the army and prepare it well [now] than to risk spending a hundred times more in the face of greater attempts against national security." Later that year Góes Monteiro publicly labeled existing military facilities "really ridiculous" and declared that despite previous budgetary sacrifices Brazil's defense requirements necessitated "increased and costly" supplies and equipment.[8]

A general newly arrived at his Pernambuco post found the Seventh Region at "rock bottom" as far as physical facilities and equipment were concerned, and he made "bitter complaints" to Vargas when the president visited the area in 1933.[9] "There are no quarters, there is no matériel, there are . . . no officers," moaned the regional commander in São Paulo. The widespread sociopolitical instability made necessary the "immediate restoration" of Brazil's military power, he privately wrote Góes Monteiro. Underscoring once again the need for a "strong army," the commander in a subsequent letter urged Góes Monteiro to intercede with Aranha in order to secure funds. The head of the Mato Grosso district, General Pedro Cavalcanti, also implored the government to remedy the "precarious" conditions of frontier garrisons. Pointing to the "grave aspect" of international events, Cavalcanti was blunt. "If you had seen what I saw, I am certain [this] district would immediately receive matériel," he informed Góes Monteiro after an inspection tour. The lack of armaments became one of the "constant preoccupations" of General Pessôa, whom Vargas appointed head of the Casa Militar in 1933.[10]

The navy, too, lived "eternally in hope of better days."[11] At the time of the *paulista* revolt the only ships in the fleet worth mentioning were three battleships, two cruisers, nine destroyers, and one submarine. Except for the sub, which had been acquired from Italy in 1927, all those ships were at least twenty years old, the battleship *Floriano* being over thirty. Discontent was serious in naval circles, especially since both Chile and Argentina possessed larger fleets, the latter having more than twice the total tonnage of the Brazilian navy. "The Brazilian ships are the oldest, least swift, and have the weakest armament," groused one admiral after comparing the strength of the three countries shortly after the Revolution. Both the army and navy opposed a League of Nations proposal in 1931 for a one-year truce in naval acquisitions. Although the nation's financial situation was "disheartening," said a navy spokesman, acquiescence in the moratorium would only keep the fleet in its present "sad situation of patent inferiority."[12]

A detailed analysis of the individual units of the fleet at the beginning of 1932 led the chief of naval operations to the despairing conclusion that it consisted of nothing but a "heap of aged vessels" with "no appreciable value." Navy Minister Protógenes Guimarães realized this. If a crisis should occur beyond the vicinity of Rio's harbor, he candidly admitted to Vargas on the eve of the civil war, the navy would not be able to meet the challenge. Preparations for fleet maneuvers three years later bore out the admiral's pessimism. The General Staff had to warn ship commanders to proceed at only "moderate" speed because of the age of the vessels, while a report on the destroyers found them to be in "very bad" shape and warned that even firing the heavier guns was "absolutely inadvisable" because of the ships' doubtful structural resistance. The submarine *Humaytá* was in such "precarious" condition that it had to withdraw from the maneuvers.[13] "We are becoming discouraged with promises," remarked the captain of the destroyer *Santa Catharina*, bluntly summing up naval opinion. "We need ships."[14]

The administration was not insensitive to the plight of the armed forces. Vargas had prudently included in his 1930 presidential platform a pledge to satisfy their matériel requirements insofar as finances permitted, and he reiterated this promise after the Revolution. Then in 1932 he authorized an annual credit of $2.8 million over a twelve-year period for fleet renewal, and, after the dismal showing of the federal forces during the São Paulo revolt that year, he issued a new decree raising the annual credit to $4.7 million and reducing its time span to eight years.[15]

The civil war indeed left Vargas, in General Pessôa's words, "profoundly impressed" by the material inadequacies of the services, particularly the army, which was both militarily and politically the more crucial. On receipt of Góes Monteiro's dismal battlefield reports, the chief executive had assured him that "nobody suffers more than I do in face of the deficiencies and slowness of our defense services." Aranha was also swayed by the logic of the army's arguments, and he reversed his position on the budget slash. He even sent Vargas a secret note advising him to sanction greater military expenditures. Such outlays during a period of worldwide upheaval, the finance minister was now convinced, were "a nondeferrable sacrifice."[16] The army budget approved for 1933 was approximately 16 percent higher than the previous one, and the number of troops was raised from the pre–civil war level of less than thirty thousand to nearly sixty thousand. The government also authorized a secret credit of some £6 million for the acquisition of equipment abroad by a special purchasing commission.[17]

During a serious cabinet crisis at the end of 1933, Vargas committed himself even more fully to the difficult task of placating the disgruntled army leaders when he invited Góes Monteiro to take over the war ministry. In a confidential memorandum setting forth his conditions for acceptance, the general emphasized that the lack of arms and equipment was one major problem the administration would have to resolve. And all acquisitions, he stipulated, should be "absolutely secret." On January 18, 1934, the day of his appointment, Góes Monteiro made public some of the ideas contained in the memorandum and indirectly warned the nation to expect greater financial sacrifice. That same day he sent a private reminder to Vargas that his assumption of ministerial duties was based on the condition that the army be given extrabudgetary "special credits and allocations indispensable for its progressive outfitting within a predetermined time limit."[18] With the matter so clearly defined, the signing of the decree of Góes Monteiro's appointment represented, in effect, a pact between Catete Palace and the high command for rehabilitating the services. And the general was insistent on the government's fulfilling its commitment. Two weeks after assuming office, he sent a memorandum to Aranha asking him "urgently" to indicate "how and on what terms" the Ministry of War could expect additional credits.[19]

The question was whether or not the administration could meet its pledge by utilizing traditional commercial methods. Since Vargas's promises of aid at the beginning of the decade, the government had been plagued by empty national coffers. To mollify military leaders, Vargas had decreed credits for projects that would take time to complete, hoping that the necessary funds could be found before the bills had to be paid. The financial picture, however, remained bleak: prices of raw materials continued to decline, exports were falling off, and commercial arrears were piling up. There was simply no foreign exchange to spend on armaments. When the two military ministries presented new budget proposals calling for substantial increases over current appropriations, the Ministry of Finance felt compelled to recommend heavy cuts.[20] Because of an anticipated deficit for 1934–1935, Aranha during his last weeks in Brazil opposed several requests from both branches for special credits.[21] When the government did agree, under pressure from Góes Monteiro, to provide $16.8 million over the next four years for army reorganization, Aranha was careful to insist on a payments schedule that would give free play to the manipulative talents required of Finance overseers.[22]

To hasten execution of the military remodeling program, General

Pessôa, an ardent champion of modernization and professionalization of the armed forces, elaborated what became a joint army-navy plan to institute through higher consumer taxes on tobacco and luxury items a special fund for renovation of military equipment.[23] Aranha's classification as a "political error" and successful shelving of the proposal through modifications inacceptable to military leaders was an irritating bluff. General Pessôa retorted that the real political mistake would be to leave the Brazilian people "delivered over to a complete lack of foresight, dependent on chance, deceived about their security, and exposed to the risk of humiliation."[24]

A remark by the authoritative *Revista Militar e Naval* that Brazil's power had been reduced to "almost nothing" by the "criminal negligence" of previous administrations may have been public evidence of a hardening of the military position and a veiled warning to civilian administrators to change old habits. Following the return to constitutional government in July, both Góes Monteiro and Admiral Guimarães again stressed in written communications to Vargas the needs of their respective services. Within days of the promulgation of the new constitution, the war minister advised the president to spare no opportunity "or sacrifice whatsoever" to strengthen the armed forces, since the national situation caused the "greatest concern" to responsible authorities. The admiral, in his annual report, underlined the "unexceedable deficiency" of the fleet and complained that "insuperable budgetary difficulties" were forcing the navy to continue with a "material situation that yearly grows more risky."[25]

Friction between civilian and military administrators became common knowledge in diplomatic circles. Ambassador Gibson recognized that some money would have to be spent for naval equipment "to keep politically-minded naval officers from going off the reservation," and the British chargé agreed that there might be "danger in trying the patience of the navy too far." Vargas, predicted the latter, would need "all his adroitness to steer a smooth course" between the requirements of the treasury and those of the navy.[26] The response of the administration to bilateral overtures from Europe showed that civilian leaders were now wondering whether that "smooth course" was not paved with compensation marks—and lire.

In 1934 satisfaction of regional economic interests was probably a more important consideration than military needs to the Brazilian government. But the possibility of acquiring equipment for the navy and army, with payment not in scarce foreign exchange but in blocked currency earned by the sale of surplus raw materials, was an effective goad to policy makers as they set off on the path of bilateralism. By the fall of 1934, naval planners, in fact, were already thinking of bilateral commercial agreements involving an exchange of raw materials for ships. Admiral Guimarães instructed a naval supervisory committee to study this possibility, and the chief of naval staff subsequently informed representatives of foreign firms that the "pressing conditions of the exchange market in no way whatsoever" would permit cash payments, but that Brazil would have "*grande satisfação*" in receiving compensation proposals. Although British embassy observers suspected Souza Costa of having simply "maneuvered for time" in going along with these plans, there was more serious intent behind them.[27]

Under prodding from the Ministry of Navy, Macedo Soares had endorsed and now actively promoted the navy's scheme. He had headed Brazil's delegation to the Geneva Disarmament Conference two years before, and he shared the high command's sensitivity about Brazil's military weakness. Cautioning Aranha to make certain that nothing in the projected treaty with the United States would hinder the "exchange or compensation of credits indispensable for the purchase of the future squadron," Macedo Soares set his staff to work with representatives of the Banco do Brasil and the Ministries of Finance and Navy on a general plan to link naval contracts to trade agreements. The navy wanted to order submarines and possibly destroyers from Italian builders, who had already indicated a willingness to accept raw materials in payment. "Happily for our commercial interest," read a confidential memorandum on the subject, "the navy does not insist on buying the destroyers from England."[28]

Ensuing commercial and naval negotiations with Italy centered around the concept of compensation. Brazilian negotiators, in fact, at one point early in 1935 deliberately delayed talks on a new trade agreement to await the results of bargaining for naval contracts. The "greater advantages" that the government anticipated from joint conclusion of the two agreements had as their core the forcing of the Italian market for several products, not solely the cotton that Mussolini, despite his "notorious sympathy" for Brazil, initially insisted upon. A meeting of naval minds was not difficult: on January 29 the Ministry of Navy announced that it had decided to begin renewal of the fleet with construction of submarines in Italy, a declaration that Rome's disconcerted London competitors found "particularly infuriating."[29]

Despite interest on both sides—". . . the Duce is eager for Brazil to have ships built here in order to combat the ever-increasing unemployment of this kingdom," Macedo Soares learned from his brother, a member of the Rome embassy[30]—reaching agreement on details of payment for the submarines took time, and securing formal signature of the contracts turned out to be an even more elusive goal. Brazilian desire to link the contracts to a trade agreement was one stumbling block, as Italian exchange modifications later that year necessitated similar revisions in the agreement drafts. Souza Costa was also reluctant to definitively sanction payment terms of 60 percent in cotton, as the Italians wanted.[31] But the worsening Italo-Ethiopian crisis was the major cause of Brazilian hesitation, and ultimately the war delayed signature of a commercial modus vivendi with Rome until August 1936.

That agreement, which came less than a month after Macedo Soares assured Ambassador Gibson that Brazil would reach no understanding with Italy that would contravene the American-Brazilian treaty, was in fact a clearing agreement between the Banco do Brasil and the Instituto Nazionale di Cambi. As Souza Costa subsequently acknowledged privately, what Brazilian policy makers had in mind when they negotiated this accord was buying submarines with the compensation lire earned from exports to Italy. Within three weeks of the modus vivendi, a contract for three submarines was signed, and early in 1938 Italy made delivery.[32]

For the Brazilian army, on the other hand, the commercial lanes to Germany proved to be the most promising route to modern equipment. Even before Otto Kiep and his colleagues arrived in Rio de Janeiro in 1934, Brazilian authorities had put out feelers to Krupp about an exchange of raw materials for armaments. One of Krupp's foremost agents, Fritz von Bülow, had sought diplomatic support in June 1934 for negotiations between his employer and the Brazilian government for the sale of artillery, tanks, warships, torpedoes, and other matériel. Payment difficulties were a major problem, he told a Wilhelmstrasse official, so discussions were proceeding on the basis of Brazil's meeting from 10 to 15 percent of the cost "im Kompensationswege," with cotton the projected item of exchange.[33]

In talks with the German trade delegation later that year, Brazilian negotiators expressed interest on "repeated occasions" in purchasing military hardware with part of the compensation marks to be earned from increased exports to Germany under the envisioned informal banking agreement. Early in 1935 both Macedo Soares and Secretary General Pimentel Brandão discussed the possibility with Schmidt-Elskop, who learned that the Brazilian government was interested in "great quantities" of cannon. The foreign minister wondered if it would be possible to work out a triangular deal among Rio de Janeiro, Berlin, and Stockholm. The Swedish armaments firm Bofors could deliver artillery to Brazil for payment in agricultural products, and then Swedish authorities could, if necessary, exchange them with the Reich for manufactured goods.[34]

Bofors, with Krupp's encouragement, had been in earnest negotiations with the Brazilian government since the end of the *paulista* revolt. Krupp was Brazil's traditional supplier of armaments, having sold "more than eight hundred cannon" to the Brazilian army prior to the war, but the Versailles settlement had disrupted this relationship. To circumvent treaty restrictions, Krupp had reached a long-term financial and technical agreement with Bofors that had "practically assured" it the management of the Swedish enterprise.[35]

An army committee that included Góes Monteiro and Pessôa, who by training was an artillery officer, had tentatively approved the Bofors bid, and one task of the purchasing commission sent to Europe in 1933 had been to conduct on-the-spot tests. By the end of 1934 army technicians had decided that the Bofors product met Brazilian requirements.[36] A special secret credit of £6 million existed, but only on paper. Finding a feasible method of payment was still the major hurdle, which is why Macedo Soares was interested in a triangular exchange.

Berlin had no objection in principle to an understanding with Sweden and, anxious to boost domestic rearmament and industrial recovery, readily accepted the idea of supplying cannon for raw materials.[37] This notion was actively promoted by Souza Aranha and Beutner. Armaments figured prominently among the compensating orders included in the proposal they presented to Karl Ritter in mid-1935.[38] The director of the Brazilian Commercial Bureau in Berlin, a German Brazilian and strong advocate of close economic relations with the Reich, also campaigned on behalf of the plan, and in October he wrote to both General Pessôa, now chief of staff, and Vargas describing the opportunities for meeting the army's requirements in Germany. Because of its demand for raw materials, he reported, Berlin would furnish "all the war material we need."[39]

The rapidly emerging identification of military interests with trade policy was strengthened by heightened concern about Brazil's vulnerability in the face of menacing international conditions, particularly in South America. A trip to Rio Grande do Sul at the end of 1934 had left Vargas in agreement with the army general staff, which was a "bit alarmed" by Paraguayan and Argentine machinations. "Our policy has been one of cordial friendship with Argentina and abstention from intervention in the Chaco question," Vargas had remarked to Aranha. "We should maintain it, but we need to take military precautions. . . . We lack, however, almost everything."[40] When General Pessôa accompanied Vargas to Buenos Aires months later, the soon-to-be chief of staff witnessed *in loco* the "superiority" of the Argentine armed forces, noting particularly that they possessed a full group of antiaircraft guns whereas Brazil had none.[41]

The state of the Mato Grosso flotilla and naval arsenal worried naval strategists throughout 1935, and army planners under General Pessôa's direction busied themselves with defense plans for the southern states and Mato Grosso.[42] Detailed surveys of Argentina's military posture by the army general staff and Itamaraty further attest to governmental preoccupation with the perceived imbalance in continental power and with Argentine intentions.[43]

Given this increased anxiety in governmental circles, Brazil's military capacity was a source of even graver discontent than before. The sole part of the army reorganization plan of 1934 that had met with any degree of success was the provision for increased self-sufficiency in the production of small arms and munitions. The army still found itself with relatively few—a total of 160—Krupp 75s of 1898 vintage that lacked recoil cylinders and as a result allowed only a slow rate of fire. Repair shops worked on changing the breechblocks of these cannon and placing the barrel assemblies on spare 1908-model carriages with modern recoil mechanisms, but just two of the renovated batteries would be nearing completion by mid-1936.[44] The military purchasing commission sent to Europe in 1933 had made no important acquisitions, and the defects in personnel and communications persisted—along with the ill humor of the high command.

A special committee set up in August 1935 under General Pessôa to draw up a long-term plan for remodeling the army decided at its first meeting that it was useless to consider enlarging or reorganizing the army until it possessed adequate equipment and supplies.[45] Weeks later Góes Monteiro, no longer minister of war, made public issue of the matter, claiming that the country was "stripped completely" of the means of war. "Our army has no technical equipment of any kind whatsoever, or armament or gear or anything," he groused, adding that "any small country of South America" would have the advantage in a war with Brazil. The new minister, General João Gomes, reprimanded his predecessor, but after circularizing army commanders he was himself obliged to paint for the National Security Council a "very pessimistic" picture of the army's preparedness.[46] General Gomes found graphic confirmation for his report to the Council when, concerned about western border defenses, he was compelled to make the humiliating request that the navy loan him two heavy batteries from the tired battleship *Minas Gerais* in order to bolster Fort Coimbra.[47]

The validity of Brazilian leaders' estimates of the nation's military capabilities could naturally be proven only in combat. It is noteworthy, however, that expert foreign observers agreed with those assessments. German Minister Schmidt-Elskop, after witnessing a military parade in Rio designed to impress visiting Argentine dignitaries with the "power and discipline" of Brazilian troops, wrote in 1933 that the parade produced the "opposite effect" on anyone who had attended Argentine military demonstrations. British embassy observers in both Rio and Buenos Aires made a more empirical comparison of the military strength of the two rivals, concluding that Argentina's navy was "considerably more powerful" and her army "better trained and better equipped than any other army in South America." The American military attaché in 1934 judged coastal defenses at the strategic harbors of Rio and Santos to be "of little use against modern ships," and the following year, when Góes Monteiro publicly disparaged Brazil's combat potential, the attaché advised Washington that the deficiency of Brazilian armaments "is no secret and long has been patent to even casual observers." Comintern analysts also perceived the Brazilian army as inefficient, ill equipped, and thoroughly demoralized, an image that encouraged Communist agents in their belief that Brazil was ripe for revolt.[48]

The Communist-led uprising that began on November 23 indirectly reinforced the linkage between commercial policy and military requirements. The revolt lasted only a few days and was limited to Natal, Recife, and Rio de Janeiro, but it dramatically reinforced the apprehension of government leaders about the state of the armed forces. The threat to national security had now assumed graver proportions, as internal subversion perhaps directed from abroad was added to international instability. In ensuing weeks the government, prodded by the Ministry of War, tightened controls over the political system. Rumors of imminent military dictatorship were rife, and civilian leaders, even if they had not shared the military's fears, could ill afford inaction in updating defense services.[49]

The putsch also contributed to the merger of defense needs and trade policy by placing additional strains on national finances. The federal deficit for 1934 had been over $44 million, and by mid-1935 the government was running around $41 million in the red.[50] The army's "public budget" for 1935 was one-third more than the 1933 allocation had been—in dollar terms it represented an increase from $32.6 million in 1934 to $36.8 million—but this had proven insufficient to meet expenses, and the general staff had even been forced to cancel plans for maneuvers. Pleas for extrabudgetary credits had been firmly resisted by Souza Costa, who had insisted that unless the government undertook "severe" retrenchments the future would bring "grave consequences."[51]

Now, the Communist revolt brought a sudden run on the treasury as police and military expenses shot upward, and requests for emergency funds from the army, navy, Ministry of Justice, and federal police flooded Souza Costa's desk.[52] There were other special expenditures that the administration considered it prudent to endorse. Lamenting that circumstances, "imperious to be sure," had prevented the navy from operating within its regular budget, Souza Costa nonetheless approved and forwarded to Vargas on November 25 a navy request for a supplementary credit of $656,000 (8,000 contos).[53] Both the president and the finance minister deemed it politic to ask the Chamber of Deputies in December for over $13 million (162,000 contos) in order to continue payment for another year of the monthly salary bonus voted for the military the previous May.[54]

All this financial pressure came as the value of Brazil's export surplus was falling to its lowest level in three years. Only days before the uprising, in fact, Vargas had declared himself forced by the "absolute necessity of maintaining rigorous economy" to veto a number of items in the budget voted by the Chamber.[55] It was but natural in such circumstances that the large stocks of compensation marks piling up in the Banco do Brasil as a result of the boom in trade with Germany took on added attractiveness as a possible way out of the dilemma created by military demands and depleted coffers, especially in view of the promises of assistance from Germany.[56] Only a "system of exchanges controlled by special currency," General Pessôa later recalled, would permit the government to make the minimum purchases.[57]

After conferring with Vargas immediately after suppression of the uprising, Macedo Soares told Schmidt-Elskop that obtaining artillery and antiaircraft guns was now of "pressing importance," and he revived his suggestion for a triangular arrangement to include Sweden.[58] The foreign minister perhaps thought that Versailles restrictions would still prevent Krupp from making direct deliveries. But the main reason for his proposal was the fact that the government by this time had committed itself, morally if not contractually, to placement of armaments orders with Bofors. Góes Monteiro had informed a representative of the Swedish firm at the beginning of the year that he had approved the report of the purchasing commission in Europe, that the legislature had revalidated the secret credit, and that he was waiting only for formal terms from Sweden. General Gomes had subsequently reiterated this pledge, and the definitive proposal from Bofors, delivered at the end of August, was under study when the November disorders occurred.[59] But the financial situation and Krupp's reentry into the arms-exporting business during this period did not augur well for Germany's competitor.

With the Reich's rearmament publicly proclaimed, Krupp had moved rapidly in 1935 toward reasserting its former position, and, under pressure from Stockholm, it severed its connections with Bofors.[60] Brazilian overtures late that year met therefore with indications that Krupp itself was eager to fill military contracts,[61] and in December the Brazilian Ministry of War informally sounded Schmidt-Elskop on the possibility. Both the Wilhelmstrasse and the arms manufacturer were keenly interested, the minister learned.[62] Moniz de Aragão confirmed this in January 1936 when he forwarded the original SOINC trade proposal to Rio de Janeiro. He emphasized that it had the approval of Reich authorities and that Brazil could secure warships and armaments in return for the extraquota coffee.[63]

Macedo Soares, knowing in March that there were over 14 million compensation marks in the Banco do Brasil, instructed Moniz de Aragão to determine confidentially what kind of armaments Krupp could supply, "the Ministry of War being disposed to acquire artillery and it being convenient to the Ministry of Finance to harmonize interests with Germany, which would acquire from us coffee, cotton, cacao, tobacco, rubber, and other products . . ." The reply from the envoy in Berlin was that all Brazil's needs could be met and that in return Germany wanted mainly cotton.[64]

In the case of the influential Souza Costa, pragmatism rapidly gained ground on his classical liberal orientation in financial matters. Like Vargas and other civilian leaders, he shared the military's concern about the nation's notoriously inadequate defense capabilities, and he little enjoyed the job of continually having to delay legitimate defense expenditures. By 1936 he had come to see payments for military purchases indirectly in raw materials as the most satisfactory solution to the problem. He was indeed now encouraging negotiations with Rome, because the blocked lire arising from the sale of raw materials were to be applied against the cost of submarines.

German ships did not interest him or Brazilian military chiefs, but cannon did, and at the beginning of April he sought confirmation through Souza Aranha that Berlin would make war matériel available if Brazil acquiesced in SOINC's scheme and reinstated compensation trade in cotton.[65] The confidential explanatory note that Souza Costa then sent to Vargas was striking evidence of the impact of military pressure on the selection of policy alternatives in the trade sphere. Any commercial understanding with Berlin, he recommended, should be "subordinated" to, or made contingent upon, realization of an armaments contract. Although he found bilateralism distasteful in principle, expanded exports to Germany would permit the administration to do something for the army.[66]

Berlin moved quickly to capitalize on the encouraging atmosphere in Rio de Janeiro. The Wilhelmstrasse and the Ministry of Economic Affairs authorized Beutner to wire his partner that Brazil could obtain military equipment "immediately" with the extraquota coffee.[67] Karl Ritter called Moniz de Aragão in to stress the desire of his government to see SOINC transactions carried out. Although Berlin had emphasized railway equipment in connection with the proposal, it had done so, reported the Brazilian envoy, only to avoid a possible leak of information and resultant international "polemic" about Germany. It also wanted to prevent discovery by other South American countries that Brazil was buying a "great quantity" of armaments. The Wilhelmstrasse had advised him, said Moniz de Aragão, that the Reich was "willing and prepared to furnish Brazil with any quantity of land, air, and naval war matériel, including artillery of any caliber."[68]

Brazilian officials shared Berlin's desire to minimize publicity about military contracts. Góes Monteiro's earlier admonition that purchases abroad should be of an "absolutely secret character" was indicative of thinking in army circles.[69] Vargas agreed with this viewpoint. Argen-

tina's military superiority was partially a result of Brazil's "inept lo-
quacity," he had commented to Aranha. "We draw up plans for military preparedness and announce them. With this prior knowledge the
Argentines carry out an off-setting program and we content ourselves
with words," the president observed, adding that, "in order to guarantee a better future," this past error should not be repeated. Souza
Costa also wanted to maintain "maximum reserve" in the negotiations, although his attitude was apparently caused as much by fear of
repercussions in other trading countries as by reasons of security. An
allied motive for the administration's willingness to work through
SOINC, Ritter later explained, was that it would thus obviate the need
for legislative sanction of special credits for the army.[70]

Following conclusion of the gentlemen's agreement in June, the way
seemed clear for negotiation of the armaments order. The first contract, however, was not signed for several months. The uncertainty
prevailing in Europe as a result of the Rhineland crisis and the Spanish
Civil War raised momentary doubts within military circles about placing orders in a continental country that might soon find itself plunged
into war.[71] More importantly, though, Brazilian leaders faced the
ticklish question of what to do about previous pledges to Bofors. The
Swedish firm, after all, had been conducting experiments and tests
for the Brazilian army since 1933, which represented a considerable
investment in time and money. And both General Gomes and his
predecessor had given verbal assurances to Bofors. Committed to compensation trade as a means of securing armaments, Brazilian leaders
thought one solution would be to convince Bofors to accept at least
partial payment in German compensation marks. Souza Costa had, in
fact, just prior to conclusion of the gentlemen's agreement, dusted off
this triangular proposal made earlier by Macedo Soares, but Swedish
authorities balked at the idea. Brazilian army technicians now began
several futile weeks of examining the possibility of combining Bofors
and Krupp matériel.[72]

Brazil's apparent willingness to deal with the Swedish competitor
left Berlin officials "astonished." The recent commercial arrangement
would receive a "severe blow" if Reich firms did not land the contract,
the Ministry of Economic Affairs warned the Auswärtiges Amt.[73]
The Krupp directorate, faced with a now "extremely difficult situation," quickly dispatched Fritz von Bülow to Rio de Janeiro to take
personal charge of the campaign to win the contract.[74] Nephew of
the former imperial chancellor and a man "of high social position,

enjoying great prestige in German industrial circles,"[75] von Bülow arrived in the Brazilian capital late in July. There is little detailed information about his activities. He stayed in an elegant suite at the Copacabana Palace and drew funds from an account opened for him by his employer in the Banco Alemão Transatlântico. The home office covered all overdrafts, and later Brazilian wartime investigators discovered that his expenses were "considerable and by far exceeded the amount necessary for even a life of great luxury." No documents ever came to light showing how the money was spent.[76] The Krupp agent did enlist the services of SOINC, which became a representative of Krupp's interests in Brazil during ensuing years.

Krupp received active support from the Nazi government, which was undertaking intensive preparations for war during the latter part of 1936 and was thus increasingly anxious about dwindling supplies of raw materials. Because of the "direct and unalterable" link between imports and exports, Foreign Minister Konstantin von Neurath at the end of July instructed German diplomats abroad to promote German exports "at every single opportunity." For those missions not directly involved in major political issues, there was, he admonished, "no task more important," since the Reich needed raw materials. Hitler himself drew up a secret memorandum in August announcing that he wanted the economy to be "on a war footing" by 1940. The Reich must use "all means" to secure raw materials and strengthen its armies, for, if it did not, he exclaimed, "Germany will be lost!" Hermann Göring read the Führer's statement to his economic staff in September and gave instructions to proceed as though war were imminent.[77]

Because the sale of armaments was one means of expanding industrial capacity and helping to attain that "war footing," the Brazilian order took on even more attractiveness for German authorities. The Wehrmacht instructed the newly appointed naval attaché for eastern South America to do all he could to promote armaments transactions in Brazil, and both the Ministry of Economic Affairs and the Wilhelmstrasse kept steady diplomatic pressure on the Brazilian government. Karl Ritter of the Wilhelmstrasse also moved to forestall potentially divisive competition between Krupp and arch domestic rival Rheinmetall by persuading the latter to remain out of the Brazilian negotiations in return for a share of the contract, once Krupp landed it.[78]

Schmidt-Elskop, since June an ambassador, worked energetically in Rio de Janeiro on Krupp's behalf, conferring with military and civilian officials, including Vargas. In the main the ambassador and von Bülow concentrated on army spokesmen and Itamaraty, while Souza Aranha lobbied diligently at the Ministry of Finance.[79] Brazil's financial situation was on Krupp's side, and German agents pushed this advantage, offering to accept 80 percent of the payment in compensation marks.[80] This accorded with Souza Costa's thinking, and Macedo Soares had displayed "real enthusiasm" for an agreement with Berlin all along. "Krupp guns were undoubtedly the best available, and the clearing system facilitated a method of payment convenient for Brazil," Schmidt-Elskop recorded the foreign minister as saying. "He would support Krupp in every way and was sure that he would succeed."[81] Macedo Soares exaggerated his influence, but his support was not unimportant and was indicative of civilian conviction regarding armaments and trade.

The problem of General Gomes's reluctance to exclude Bofors was removed with the general's resignation as minister of war on December 3. His departure from office came after weeks of tension between him and other generals, particularly Góes Monteiro, over domestic political questions. The essential issue separating the two military chiefs was the political activity of Flores da Cunha, the caudillesque governor of Rio Grande do Sul and bitter enemy of Góes Monteiro. Flores had national political ambitions, insofar as he at least wanted to determine the selection of Vargas's successor in 1938, and he had broken politically with the president in 1935. Building up a strong state militia force of several thousand men, Flores was openly proclaiming his intention to resist what he claimed were plans by Vargas and sympathetic generals to have the president remain in power after his present term ended. Góes Monteiro was willing to force a military confrontation with the southern governor, not solely for personal reasons but also because he regarded Flores as the embodiment of those baleful regionalist tendencies that Góes believed had impeded national unity throughout Brazilian history. General Gomes, however, was unsympathetic to Góes's admonitions, and, when it became clear that he also faced considerable opposition from other generals and lacked presidential backing as well, Gomes resigned, telling Vargas that he could not be party to efforts to involve the army in politics. Vargas privately informed Aranha that Gomes had become "imbued with the negativistic reservations and mentality of the administration's adversaries." SOINC agents apparently did what they could to encourage the friction between Gomes and his opponents. One agent exaggeratedly claimed credit for the general's removal, saying that he had "applied a bit more oil" on the Krupp bargaining wheel by seeing to it that Vargas learned of Gomes's opposition to his alleged plans to stay in office. "We are indeed sorry," reported the SOINC functionary, "but, under the circumstances, no other way was possible."[82]

Sizing up Gomes's possible replacements, Schmidt-Elskop hoped the choice would be General Eurico Dutra, commander of the First Military Region, whose attitude was known to be favorable to Krupp. Souza Costa advised the German diplomat that Krupp's prospects were now better and promised to see Vargas about the matter.[83] The 18 million compensation marks then sitting in the Banco do Brasil[84] clinched the case for the German firm, as far as the finance minister was concerned. Another propitious development for German interests was fulfillment of Schmidt-Elskop's hopes regarding the new war minister. In a speech delivered when he assumed his new duties on December 9, Dutra pledged himself to energetic efforts on behalf of the armaments program.[85]

The new atmosphere of harmony in Rio de Janeiro in regard to army needs and financial possibilities rapidly revealed itself in the delaying tactics adopted in dealing with Bofors. Dutra indicated a willingness to go ahead with Gomes's commitment, but he told a Bofors agent that he would need time to study the matter.[86] Increasingly confident, Krupp entered into formal agreement with Rheinmetall on December 18 for a fifty-fifty split of the total Brazilian order.[87] Increasingly exasperated, the Bofors negotiator informed Dutra on December 22 that the firm could not maintain past January 7 the prices it had quoted. Days later he packed his suitcases and sailed for home, after learning from Dutra during a farewell visit that Vargas had decided to send the draft of the Bofors contract to the head of the purchasing commission in Europe for study. Objections that the officer in question had already made extensive tests of Bofors equipment and had recommended giving the contract to the Swedish enterprise fell on deaf ears.[88]

General Dutra, prodded by the finance minister, had already decided to initiate his program with Krupp material. An optimistic telegram from Schmidt-Elskop on New Year's Eve advised the Wilhelmstrasse that Dutra had promised von Bülow a contract for cavalry cannon and had held out prospects for larger slices of the overall program, a pledge that Vargas confirmed two weeks later.[89] Resolving the financial aspects of the deal proved relatively easy, and in mid-February a contract for one hundred pieces of light field artillery, valued at some 10 million marks, was signed. Krupp agreed to accept 80 percent of that sum in compensation marks.[90] The new year thus opened on a favorable note for the high command, which had taken the first consequential step toward acquiring the modern equipment it had so long been seeking.

At the same time that they endorsed the government's trade policy as a means of satisfying the need for armaments, military leaders adopted a complementary attitude toward other spheres of economic activity. Indeed, it was only logical that, given military perceptions of international conditions, short-term security considerations would also be the major determinant of the military position on industrialization. Army leaders realized that the day when Brazil would be industrially self-sufficient was in the distant future, and, consequently, when allocating resources they stressed more immediate projects linked to mobilization: fuel and transportation, individual supplies (small arms and clothing), and munitions for heavier armaments purchased abroad.

The National Steel Commission established in the Ministry of War in 1931, which has been cited as evidence of the army's interest in a large-scale steel industry,[91] did study the question, but it decided that a more pressing problem was securing coal supplies. The Commission took the position that a modern steel works would have to await expansion of the internal market and the development of domestic technical skills.[92] Its survey of the steel situation, moreover, was one of *existing* plants in order to determine how they might be integrated into the army's program.[93] The special military mission to Europe in 1933 was sent not so much "to study European steel plants,"[94] as it was, initially, to purchase arms and later to gather information to help in the "creation and development of military industries in our country."[95] Again, it is important to distinguish between a project like the Volta Redonda steel complex and "military industries," by which army leaders meant primarily plants for the production of arms and munitions. Góes Monteiro in 1934, for example, urged upon Vargas both secret purchases of armaments abroad—a requirement he considered to be of "first urgency"—and "industrial mobilization." The army reorganization program that he launched months later showed what the general intended by the latter phrase: expansion of army plants, mainly those producing munitions.[96]

The emphasis on short-term dividends for resource investment should not be construed as a lack of interest in general industrialization or long-range development projects, such as a great steel complex. Unquestionably, military leaders favored these goals, since they would contribute to the "economic independence" that was so often cited within military circles as a desirable goal. It is relatively easy to find articles in service journals extolling, explicitly or implicitly, the advantages of increased steel-making capacity or calling for establishment of new industries based on national raw materials.[97] Privately, too, army chiefs contemplated with longing the day when Brazil would achieve self-sufficiency in armaments production.[98] And Vargas's project late in 1936 for a national survey of industrial capacity and needs, with a view toward expansion of manufacturing, naturally brought expressions of interest from the high command.[99] But the latter's major concern remained matériel deficiencies, and for that reason military leaders gave their most active support to the administration's trade program.

In evaluating the determinants of Brazil's decision to accept bilateral commerce with Germany, it should be emphasized again that the "military factor" was not originally the major one. In 1934 Vargas had responded mainly to the demands of coffee, cotton, and tobacco growers, shippers of meat and hides, and exporters of other primary products. But the discontent expressed publicly and privately by military spokesmen had been an important ingredient of the atmosphere in which policy makers weighed alternatives, and that dissatisfaction, given the opportunities for satisfying military needs that compensation trade seemed to offer, strengthened the resolve of government leaders. The scheme under discussion at that time to link military contracts to commercial pacts is clear evidence of the nascent interdependence of national defense requirements and trade policy. A convenient alliance, in effect, of the export sector, urban consumers interested in cheaper goods, and military planners was being forged.

The delay in signing an armaments contract resulted from both external factors—European turmoil, prior verbal commitments to Bofors, the necessity of caution in negotiations with Germany because of American opposition—and domestic developments, particularly personnel instability at the highest army levels, which hindered completion of rearmament plans.[100] It is clear, however, that by 1936 both military and civilian policy makers had become deeply security conscious, and commercial policy decisions reflected that concern. The negotiations with Rome for submarines and export quotas, and Souza Costa's suggestion in April that Brazil continue to play Berlin's trade game only if an armaments contract were realized, showed how profoundly key administrators were influenced by military arguments. The first Krupp contract directly involved the Ministry of War in the trade issue, and it meant that commercial policy was to a considerable degree now a function of the material needs of the armed forces. Satisfaction of military requirements, in other words, had become a major objective of Brazil's trade program, an objective that took on increasing importance as Brazilian policy makers struggled to promote national interests in the face of mounting international rivalry.

Chapter 5

The Great Powers and the

Brazilian Market (1935–1937)

Germany's aggressive pursuit of raw materials and buyers in South America after 1934 was a source of deep concern to British and American competitors. The governments in London and Washington differed, however, in their assessments of the magnitude—and after 1936 the nature—of the challenge, and this consequently had a differential effect on the relations of each with Berlin. The trade rivalry in Brazil had its major impact on relations between Germany and the United States, since the latter had a vital political stake in the arena of competition. Economic considerations dominated the American attitude toward Germany's inroads in South America until late 1936, when apprehension about the political implications of German commercial success began to grow. Beleaguered Britain, with economic and political unrest at home, the Empire threatened in the Far East, and a resurgent Germany across the Rhine, followed a policy of imperial preference, endeavored to appease Berlin, and abandoned foreign policy initiative elsewhere. As far as Latin America was concerned, the onset of the Depression marked the beginning of a British withdrawal, one expression of which was a decline in British investments in that area by one-half over the next twenty years.[1]

Initially the British were as worried about Brazil's trade discussions with the United States as the latter was about the Brazilian-German talks. "It seems that the father, that is, England, is jealous of the son's prosperity," Vargas aptly put it.[2] The appointment of Gibson, a top-ranking diplomat, as ambassador to Rio de Janeiro had been interpreted by the Foreign Office as evidence that the Americans "mean to develop their opportunities in Brazil,"[3] and the following year British observers feared they had further evidence of such intentions in Vargas's delay in granting a promised contract to a British firm for electrification of the Brazilian Central Railroad. Ambassador Seeds was afraid the contract would prove to be the "last straw" for Washington, which would take steps to stop the diversion of dollars to England, particularly when American exporters were being forced to wait in line for their money. Because of its coffee purchases, Washington, he knew, was in a position to exert forceful pressure on the Vargas government. "The Brazilian gifts of shilly-shally and obstruction may perhaps stave off a decision for some time," he wrote, "and we here can be trusted to enliven as much as may be Brazilian suspicions of falling entirely into American hands. But I fear Oswaldo Aranha is 'for it' when he gets to Washington, if not before."[4]

When Aranha had assumed his new post and begun treaty negotiations with the State Department and the electrification contract remained unapproved, British suspicions seemed confirmed. "The conclusion seems to me difficult to escape," worried the British commercial secretary in Rio, "that the Americans, having adopted the policy of aggressive expansion in South America, and having Aranha in Washington, are about to make a serious attempt to gain some advantage." American companies would in the "corrupt atmosphere" of Washington undoubtedly find support, and the State Department, he pessimistically predicted, would seek preferential treatment for American interests in the projected commercial agreement.[5]

General circumstances were against British supporters within the Vargas administration. Prominent among them was Souza Costa, whose conservatism in financial matters and links to tradition led him to back a strengthening of ties with London during policy debates in the latter part of 1934. Brazil could not think only in terms of foreign trade, he argued, reminding the CFCE that the British were the country's traditional creditors. "If we have to depend upon the United States or on England," he concluded, "it is preferable to depend upon England." Vargas objected that, because of the Empire, Great Britain should actually be considered a competitor in many products. Moreover, the British had given special privileges to Argentina in regard to the frozen meat imports and were causing "difficulties" in Brazil's relations with Italy. "On the other hand, everything," said Vargas, "leads us to draw closer to the United States, a vast market for our products."[6]

Final granting of the electrification contract and, particularly, the rapid development of German-Brazilian trade during the last few months of the year shifted British attention to the new and more serious challenger. London became increasingly uneasy about the gains that the Germans were suddenly making in areas formerly monopolized by United Kingdom suppliers, such as coal exports. By early November the Mines Department was urging that something be done about the "serious disadvantage" at which British firms found themselves compared to German competitors because of the latter's guarantee of exchange. The Board of Trade agreed that clearing practices between Brazil and the Reich were having "a definitely adverse effect" on British trade and assured Mines Department spokesmen that it was already looking into the possibility of adopting "defensive measures."[7]

The Foreign Office informed Seeds on November 16 that export interests were "alarmed" about an alleged agreement between Berlin and Rio de Janeiro that ensured payment for German goods—as compensation in fact did—and instructed him to make "strong representations" if the Banco do Brasil was discriminating in favor of German traders.[8] The substitution of "strong" for "strongest possible" in the final draft of these instructions suggested awareness that Great Britain had to proceed carefully. Brazil could always point to the Ottawa agreements, and, as a Foreign Office official noted, the preferential Roca-Runciman pact with Argentina was an "awkward precedent."[9]

The ambassador's reply was not reassuring. Brazilian officials denied the existence of a clearing agreement with Berlin, he wrote in mid-November, but he correctly suspected "a working arrangement between banks" that in reality was the same thing. Although this situation was damaging to British commerce, Seeds saw no possibility of any effective demarche against a practice he thought the Brazilians were forced to adopt in order to maintain coffee sales to Germany. "If we could protest it would be rather to the Germans than to the Brazilians," agreed a Foreign Office analyst.[10]

British policy makers thus accepted the notion that Brazil was the victim of circumstances, the submissive partner in a match forcibly arranged by Berlin. A second and much more important reason for the caution and moderation that characterized British official policy toward Brazil in trade matters was the general commercial situation between the two countries. As the Board of Trade said, "not only are there no special concessions which we could make in Brazil's favour but it is also the case that we are in a weak position to threaten her." Aside from possible restrictions on imports of Brazilian meat, or higher duties on oranges and bananas, there was nothing to be done. Besides, if Britain adopted "retaliatory or punitive measures," Brazil, the Board thought, would probably suspend debt payments to British creditors.[11] The United Kingdom, moreover, had frozen credits in

Brazil worth an estimated £6 million by the beginning of 1935.[12] Although British officials viewed compensation trade as "blatantly discriminatory," London thus found itself with little ammunition for the commercial battle ahead.[13]

Business circles sought in vain to get strong official support for their efforts against the newly wrought "privileged position" of German exporters in Brazil. In a confidential memorandum to Seeds early in 1935, the British Chamber of Commerce in Rio warned that, under the stimulus of "exchange facilities" arranged between the Banco do Brasil and the Reichsbank, "a general drive" to intensify the importation of German goods was underway. So favorable had conditions suddenly become that importers of German products were scrambling to dispose of merchandise on hand in order to get new supplies, which they could sell "at very low prices" because of discounted compensation marks. "This is especially true as regards the heavy chemicals and drugs trades," read the memorandum, "but we also have proof that we are being ousted by the Germans in many other lines, such as machinery, railway equipment, iron and steel."[14] This appeal was futile, since London had already concluded that "it was no use protesting to the Brazilians, as the privilege is granted not by them but by the Germans, who permit their currency to be sold cheap."[15]

In ensuing months British authorities received "a fair number" of protests about compensation marks in Brazil.[16] Representatives of the Anglo-American business community in Brazil met together in July to discuss the effects of German competition. The British subsequently sent another memorandum to their embassy warning that compensation trade was threatening to swell to "uncontrollable proportions." One result of such trade, they complained, was a reduction in the amount of free currency available to Brazil and a consequent lessening of its ability to finance imports from Britain.[17]

The British trader was left largely to his own devices, however, since London held firm to its policy of reserve. The Foreign Office was reluctant to adopt the complaint of the Chamber of Commerce as its own, and even found it "odd" that British and American businessmen should be making common cause, "particularly in Brazil where American interests have been our principle [sic] rivals in the last few years." Anyway, one official concluded, pressure from the State Department would be "more effective than ours." Indeed, added a Department of Overseas Trade analyst, "the only hope of getting any satisfaction lies in action being taken by the U.S." The Treasury agreed with the hands-nearly-off approach, since "we have no grounds for raising objection to the system however much our traders may dislike it." The two main objections to compensation practices were that the exchange that Brazil earned from sales to the Reich was blocked for payment of imports from that country and that the currency used by the two nations in their commercial dealings sold at a discount. In view of the Roca-Runciman pact with Argentina and the depreciation of the pound, London had no basis for protests, said a Treasury agent.[18] An interdepartmental conference in September flirted with the idea of a Rothschild loan of £1 million to Brazil as a means of "reassuring and pacifying anxious and impatient creditors," but nothing came of it. And it was not until mid-October that the Foreign Office replied to the August report from the Rio embassy about the appeal of the Chamber of Commerce, and then it merely instructed the chargé d'affaires to point out informally to Macedo Soares that German methods were causing "grave anxiety" in British trading circles.[19]

Additional information from Germany later that year reinforced the prevalent Foreign Office view that compensation trade was a passing fancy whose results had been purposefully anticipated in neither Berlin nor Rio. "The Germans have not been attempting, in their trade with Brazil to prove that a snake can continue forever to swallow its own tail," wrote the commercial secretary in Berlin. They had been forced into their present trade policy by financial difficulties, he argued, and had of late "merely seen and accepted the incidental and doubtful advantage that has accrued from it, to wit, the compulsion on Brazil vastly to increase her German imports." London was curiously reassured by this analysis and blindly accepted the argument that German commercial gains in South America were unintentional and ephemeral. "The position seems to be," concluded a Foreign Office expert, "that while there is nothing we can do in the immediate future the system is likely to come to an end in due course."[20] One is tempted to speculate that readiness to accept this view of Germany's trade push in South America was part of the Foreign Office's general attitude of appeasement toward Berlin, symbolized most dramatically in 1935 by the Anglo-German Naval Agreement, which sanctioned expanded German naval construction.

The statistics of British-Brazilian trade for 1935, compared with those for the year preceding Brazil's bilateral union with the Reich, were eloquent testimony to Berlin's success (see table 1). British exports had declined sharply, showing the same rough percentage decrease as the increase in German sales. In 1933, Great Britain had provided Brazil with nearly a fifth of its imports and was its leading European source of imports. That share declined by 10 percent during 1934, and now, after the first full year of compensation trade between Brazil and the Reich, it had fallen to only 12 percent of Brazil's total importation. Germany's share during the same period rose from less than 12 percent to around 20 percent. An authoritative estimate of the sterling loss to United Kingdom merchants was nearly ₤2 million.[21]

Table 1 *Percentage Share of Brazilian Imports and Exports, 1933–1938*

	Imports					
	1933	1934	1935	1936	1937	1938
Germany	11.95	14.02	20.44	23.50	23.88	24.99
Great Britain	19.44	17.14	12.43	11.26	12.09	10.38
United States	21.18	23.67	23.36	22.12	22.99	24.21

	Exports					
	1933	1934	1935	1936	1937	1938
Germany	8.12	13.13	16.51	13.23	17.05	19.06
Great Britain	7.48	12.10	9.26	11.93	9.07	8.77
United States	46.71	39.17	39.44	38.85	36.19	34.32

SOURCE: Brazil, Ministério das Relações Exteriores, *Comércio Exterior do Brasil, 1937–1939*, pp. xiv, xvi, xx, xxii.

The inability of British exporters to compete with German suppliers in the Brazilian market remained in evidence during 1936, as British sales continued on a downward course that by 1938 would reach a level only half that of 1933. Appeals from British traders to the Brazilian government and the Chamber of Commerce in the United Kingdom and warnings in prominent London publications of the "German Trade Push in South America" were of little avail.[22] Direct official backing from British authorities was still an elusive goal. The manager of one firm was told simply that there was "very little" the Foreign Office could do, while a Liverpool company that had suffered losses "difficult to exaggerate" gained from the Board of Trade nothing but an apologetic explanation that German trading policies gave no grounds for diplomatic representations.[23]

It was not that the government was indifferent to the problem. The

question of Nazi influence was in fact the subject of special study by
the Foreign Office early in 1936. The study concluded that Berlin's
major efforts in the region were indeed being directed toward commercial "penetration," and the embassies in Washington, Berlin, and
Latin America were subsequently instructed to "keep a careful watch"
on German activities.[24] Sir Hugh Gurney, Ambassador Seed's replacement in Rio, attentively followed German-Brazilian negotiations
late that spring, correctly fearing that British traders would lose "a
great deal" more business to Germany if an accord were reached.[25]
But watching and mildly expressing concern was as far as London
would allow Gurney to go. After Macedo Soares assured Gurney that
the projected understanding with Berlin would protect Anglo-American interests, one Foreign Office analyst exulted over the fact that the
Brazilian government was "wise enough to check and even reduce"
trade with Germany. Others saw the future more clearly but resigned
themselves to the possibility that compensation trade and export subsidization would eventually prove too costly for Berlin to maintain.[26]

In September and October 1936 the British government paused to
reassess its foreign trade policy. Surveying German rivalry on a worldwide basis, the Department of Overseas Trade judged that it was really
up to the importing nations themselves to remedy the evils of German
practices. The department's only specific suggestion was that British
manufacturers might seek an understanding with their German counterparts. From the standpoint of policy recommendations, another
special Foreign Office memorandum on the "truly remarkable" success of the Nazi trade thrust in South America was likewise negative.
The study reaffirmed British inability to make any official protest,
emphasizing that Berlin's gains in this region were only part of the
general question of German competition around the globe and had to
be viewed in that context. The respective positions of the United Kingdom and Germany in terms of general exportation had not changed
"very greatly" in recent years, and, it was thought, there was always
the hope that the "irresponsible" methods adopted by the Hitler government would soon reveal their disadvantages and the two countries
could reach a mutually satisfactory understanding on trade policy.[27]

London thus opted to remain, officially, near the rear lines of the
commercial battle underway in Brazil. The grave international difficulties elsewhere undoubtedly help explain British reluctance to come
forthrightly to grips with the Germans over trade with South America.
Indeed, that attitude was totally coherent with London's policy toward

Germany in Europe, obviously a more crucial theater of interests. Hitler's illegal reoccupation of the Rhineland the previous March had met with little more than moderate expressions of moral indignation by government spokesmen in London, who were anxious to appease the Nazi leader and therefore did not want to encourage a forceful reaction by the irate French. "I believe that if we assist Germany to escape from encirclement to a position of balance in Europe, there is a good chance of the twenty-five years peace of which Hitler spoke," Lord Lothian, a prominent political figure and later ambassador to Washington (1939–1940), wrote in June, giving voice to sentiment widespread in government circles.[28] The outbreak of civil war in Spain weeks later presented another major political problem, one that threatened to involve the great powers and that was consequently additional cause for avoiding antagonisms in such far-off secondary regions as Brazil.

The British bargaining position in Brazil seemed weak, moreover, and the only thing to do was keep a stiff upper lip as Britain's share of Brazil's total importation continued to decline. Brazil's clear commitment, because of domestic demands, to compensation trade strengthened British reluctance to enter the lists too boldly, and British diplomats began to look increasingly to the United States for initiative and support in the commercial struggle with Germany in Brazil. Only the "strongest pressure" from Washington could induce the Vargas administration to change its policy, but, mused the British chargé in Rio, "Mr. Hull in pursuance of his 'good neighbor' policy is unlikely to take such a step."[29]

Private American interests shared fully the official British desire for more energetic intervention by Washington in the trade dispute. American exporters and cotton producers had been loudly voicing their grievances ever since Berlin's initial overtures to Rio in 1934. Cotton shippers were particularly alarmed at the rapidly expanding cultivation of that product in Brazil: "In fact, one speaks of nothing but Brazil's cotton!" the Brazilian consul in New Orleans had written to Aranha.[30] Roosevelt resisted the arguments of advisers like George Peek that dumping surpluses was the answer to the American producers' plight. Increasing production in places like Brazil and India was a threat, Roosevelt realized, but dumping would mean "starvation" for planters and would, he thought, in no way ensure greater sales or a reduction in the volume of foreign production. "I think that is the thing that ought to be emphasized and emphasized and emphasized," the president publicly declared.[31] To the dismay of American shippers, Brazilian cotton therefore continued to flourish under the protective umbrella of Washington's price-support program. Noting that under the compensation system Germany was increasing not only purchases from Brazil but also its exports to that country, a leading trade journal in 1935 bemoaned that double-edged sword slicing away at American exports: "We lose the cotton market and we lose part of our Brazilian market, too."[32] During 1935 American sales to Germany declined by nearly a half-million bales. The financial loss because of Brazilian competition that year was publicly estimated by the vice-president of the American Manufacturers' Export Association (AMEA) to have been $20 million.[33]

The rapid advances of German manufacturers in the months following the initiation of compensation trade "shell-shocked" some American exporters and their distributors: "I ran into one case in Brazil where a man had a very good American line, and he could talk of nothing but German competition," reported the editor of *American Exporter* after a trip to South America early in 1936.[34] An export manager of a leading drug company visited Rio de Janeiro during the same period, and upon his return he told a business group that the "most striking development" in Brazilian trade over the preceding year had been the "success of the German compensation mark idea." He found it "amazing to see how completely German products have come into almost every class of merchandise."[35]

Throughout 1935 manufacturers had carried their complaints about unfair German competition to the State Department and Brazilian authorities in the United States,[36] and in 1936 these protests gained in strength and volume, became increasingly public, and were sprinkled with words and phrases like *menace, serious handicap, disastrous, unfair,* and *rapidly losing the market.*[37] A Wisconsin producer of electrical appliances found the situation "very disgusting." As soon as Brazil began trading in *Aski* marks, said a company spokesman early in 1936, "our sales dropped overnight and have now dwindled to almost nothing."[38] The AMEA "vigorously" maintained that compensation marks were "unfair" and that Washington should "work diligently" to have them eliminated in Brazil and other Latin American nations.[39] Such currency, railed the president of an export advertising agency who visited Brazil in March 1936, "has played havoc with American and British trade, especially in machinery, electrical supplies and similar lines."[40]

The official organ of the newly created National Foreign Trade Association ran an article in its August issue that included two pages of quotations from exporters who had incurred losses in Latin America because of compensation trade.[41] Other forms of export promotion by Berlin also came in for criticism. At the annual convention of the NFTA in November, a delegate from the National City Bank asserted that "nearly every competitive article" sold to Brazil by the United States, including trucks, tires, bicycles, razor blades, and adding machines, was "suffering" because of German export subsidies.[42]

The observations of a businessman who visited the national fair in São Paulo reflected the impressions and views prevalent in the American exporting community after two years of competition under the New Plan. Noting that the Deutsches Haus was the only sizeable display building, he observed:

Packed solidly with attractive displays of German-made goods *and* eager interested Brazilian citizens (they know how to merchandise, these Germans), it was evident to even a casual observer that the compensation mark idea, agreed though we are that it is not a long-run trade builder, is working NOW.

Add further to the German score: they smother the east coast with frequent broadcasts from a "directed beam" shortwave transmitter in the homeland. . . . Representatives of German exporters likewise blanket the continent. One sees them everywhere.[43]

The American government was likewise seriously apprehensive about German commercial methods and gains in South America. Reflecting upon his service as secretary of commerce during the 1930s, Daniel Roper wrote that the "rise of the totalitarian states with their predilection to barter" had perhaps an "even more destructive effect" on American foreign trade than other factors.[44] Nazi successes in Brazil were particularly discouraging because the United States was by far the largest consumer of coffee and provided the South American country with a substantial commercial balance—over $80 million in 1936, for example.[45]

The enthusiastic optimism of the State Department in 1934 about Brazil's enlistment as a fellow torchbearer had by late 1936 given way to a more realistic appraisal of that country's potential as an ally in the battle against bilateralism. Initially, the State Department, like the Foreign Office, had viewed Brazil as the victim of German coercion.

"Brazil is not responsible for this situation of 'blocked marks' and cannot be charged with discrimination," one Latin American specialist had written early in 1935.[46] Brazil's extension of bilateral dealings to Italy disturbed American officials,[47] but Aranha's candor and completely cooperative attitude allayed anxieties, at least for a while. The resumption of compensation trade with the Reich in mid-1935 after a brief halt dismayed the department; however, the ostensible exclusion of cotton and Souza Costa's assurances that Brazil's basic liberal policy had not changed were balm for Hull's wounds. He therefore decided against any direct protest but merely instructed the Rio embassy to let Itamaraty know of his "uneasiness and fear" over unfair German competition.[48]

Within the embassy opinions differed sharply over the proper response to German advances and Brazil's attitude. Chargé Wesley Frost wanted more forceful action. In Gibson's absence during the latter part of 1935, he pressed Washington for authorization to describe "rather vividly" to Brazilian authorities the unfair damage suffered by the American exporter and to make a "plain intimation" that the United States was pondering "self-protective" measures.[49]

Gibson's special assistant, Xanthaky, was aghast at the "dangerous ideas" of the chargé and fired off an admittedly "somewhat hysterical" report to Gibson in Buenos Aires. "He has already come to the conclusion (and he is as opinionated as hell!)," Xanthaky complained, "that all this business of good friendship with Brazil is bull, that they are constantly proving that they are not our friends, and that we must clamp down on them." Unless the ambassador returned soon, it would be impossible to avert a "head-on collision," Xanthaky feared. "The Lord knows that I have no illusions about the Brazees," he explained, "but I think that they are more like children than like knaves."[50] Xanthaky realized that compensation trade was hurting American interests, but "this is a matter that you can personally persuade the Brazilians to rectify without the necessity of using the big stick," he assured Gibson.[51] For Cordell Hull, who, as Donald Drummond has so aptly observed, was "always inclined to emphasize the verbal aspects of foreign policy" and generally had trouble distinguishing "between words and deeds,"[52] the suggestion of failure implicit in Frost's request was psychologically impossible to accept. He refused to sanction the demarche that the chargé wanted to make and simply told the embassy to keep an eye on Brazil's commercial relations with Germany.[53]

The negotiations between Rio and Berlin in 1936 held the State Department's close attention. Germany's trade with Brazil had "jumped markedly" since 1934, and department planners predicted apprehensively that, if the trend continued, Hull's "whole program will ultimately fall."[54] Heartened by Gibson's reports in May that Brazil intended to restrict bilateralism with the Reich, department analysts initially refused to perceive the subsequent setback inherent in the gentlemen's agreement, and indeed they even outreached themselves to find victory in defeat. Vargas, after all, had not signed a formal treaty, wrote Laurence Duggan, head of the Division of American Republics, so "now Brazil is free to restrain German compensation trade whenever such action appears desirable." Duggan also saw no cause for representations to the Brazilian authorities, since the department "has probably gone as far as it can in making known its position . . ."[55]

Duggan, of course, overlooked the fact that the Brazilian government had been "free" to restrict its bilateral commerce with Germany from the very beginning, and he failed to see the meaning of the gentlemen's agreement. True, he based his opinions on Gibson's optimistic reassurances, but when he made those statements late in June, Duggan had in hand a copy of the private dissenting appraisal by the embassy counselor in Rio, an appraisal that accurately said, in effect, that Gibson had been duped.[56] Duggan rejected this negative feedback and, consciously or unconsciously, made the kind of analysis his superiors wanted to hear.

Even after the true significance of the Rio-Berlin accord sank in, the State Department was in a quandary over what action to take. Other than trying to persuade other countries to follow Washington's lead and seek legal redress in cases of discriminatory treatment, "what else is there to do except forsake this policy for one of compensation and clearing arrangements?" Duggan asked.[57] Department agents in Brazil were pointing out in the latter part of 1936 that only "outside pressure" would lead the government there to restrict trade with the Reich,[58] but there is no evidence that the State Department ever gave serious consideration to applying such pressure.

Indeed, Hull had only recently opposed, vigorously but unsuccessfully, the Treasury Department's proposal to apply, under the Tariff Act of 1930, countervailing duties on imports from Germany because of that country's export subsidization policies. Hull argued that currency manipulation to promote exports was a practice that not only

Germany but also several Latin American states, including Brazil, engaged in; and, furthermore, such manipulation could be considered a form of currency depreciation, a step the United States itself had taken in 1933. A major fear of Hull's was that the move would adversely affect his general trade program by evoking retaliation. "Whenever things go wrong, at the present time the tendency seems to be to hit the other fellow in the nose and we do not think this is the right way to proceed," he pleaded futilely at an interdepartmental meeting on May 29. "We want to work things out in a spirit of fairness and good fellowship."[59]

If to take retaliatory measures against Germany was unwise, in Hull's opinion, to do so against a hemispheric ally was unthinkable. It would have been an open admission of defeat, not only for his trade policy but also for those broader principles of good-neighborliness that guided the State Department's activity in Latin America. The imminence of a Pan-American peace conference scheduled to convene at Roosevelt's request in Buenos Aires that December was an additional factor in Hull's rejection of any thought of coercion to secure his commercial objectives in Brazil.

The previous January, when the president had sounded his Latin American counterparts on the possibility of a conference to improve machinery for keeping the peace in the hemisphere, the immediate thing on his mind had been the bitter and bloody Chaco War between Bolivia and Paraguay, halted by a truce signed in Buenos Aires in June 1935. But Roosevelt also had a skeptical eye on the machinations of the totalitarian states. Germany was openly engaged in an unprecedented military buildup, Italian troops were overrunning Haile Selassie's small African kingdom, and Japan continued its meddling in China.

His decision personally to inaugurate the conference in Buenos Aires—and thereby become the first United States president to set foot on South American soil while still in office—reflected the importance he attached to greater solidarity among American nations and his hope of providing Europe with an object lesson. "That visit will have little practical or immediate effect in Europe," he wrote to Ambassador William Dodd in Berlin, "but at least the force of example will help if the knowledge of it can be spread down to the masses of the people in Germany and Italy." At a November cabinet meeting before he sailed, FDR speculated that, if the nations of the Western Hemisphere could take effective steps at Buenos Aires toward permanent peace and perhaps disarmament, a similar conference in the Pacific might neutralize the Philippines, Hong Kong, the Dutch East Indies, British North Borneo, and other spots.[60]

The Buenos Aires conference in December 1936 gave New Deal diplomats an opportunity to meet personally with Brazilian leaders and endeavor to wean them away from their disturbing liaison with Berlin. Looking ahead to the inter-American gathering, and with pessimistic reports from Brazil in hand, Sumner Welles thought that Hull should discuss with Brazilian officials the "whole vitally important problem" of German competition when he passed through Rio de Janeiro on his way to the Argentine capital. Welles, now under secretary, instructed Feis to have details on hand for briefing Hull on board ship. If American traders were not receiving fair treatment, Gibson was informed, then "candid though entirely friendly" talks must be held with the Brazilians.[61]

If Hull needed particulars, he did not need any reminder of the general predicament. Germany may not have been "straining every tendon" to thwart American commercial objectives in South America, as Hull later exaggeratedly claimed,[62] but the signs and impact of Germany's aggressive interest were clear. Treated royally by his Brazilian hosts, the secretary of state responded to the flattery with homely prose: "Your coffee refreshes and makes fragrant our breakfast table when the morning air is purest," he told guests at a dinner given by Macedo Soares. But more than the aroma of Brazilian coffee was on his mind. He expressed confidence that both countries wanted trade between them to flourish and also desired "at all times treatment as truly advantageous" as either might extend to a third nation.[63] In a typical display of self-deception, Hull told reporters afterward that Rio and Washington had harmonious views on commercial matters, and he praised the Brazilian government for having given "concrete and unequivocal proof" of its adherence to liberal principles by signing a reciprocity accord with the United States.[64] A few days later Roosevelt arrived on a brief visit, during which he discussed privately with Vargas the possibility of financial assistance to Brazil,[65] the one offensive weapon the State Department was beginning to think of using in its trade struggle with Berlin.

Following the meeting in Buenos Aires, where an American-sponsored resolution was adopted that called on the nations of the hemisphere to avoid "so far as possible" tariff barriers and "every other kind of restrictions which directly or indirectly hinder international trade and resulting payments,"[66] Welles and State Department technicians stopped over in Brazil on the way home to take up with Souza Costa the question of Nazi competition and Brazil's plans for monetary stabilization.

By the end of 1936 German rivalry had become a matter of urgent concern. According to a memorandum prepared for Welles's use in Rio de Janeiro, exports from the Reich during the first half of the year amounted to nearly a quarter of Brazil's total importation. They had risen about 30 percent over a corresponding period the previous year, and for the first time Germany had surpassed the United States as the main supplier of goods to the Brazilian market.[67] Welles also received a timely reminder of the disquiet in business circles: at the request of representatives of "important American interests," Thomas of the NFTC cabled him on December 29 from New York expressing the hope that his talks with Brazilian authorities would lead to an improvement in the "onerous" conditions created by German practices.[68]

Souza Costa assured Welles in a memorandum dated December 31—the same day that Schmidt-Elskop wired Berlin that General Dutra had promised a first artillery contract to Krupp—that Brazil did not want any expansion in trade with "compensation" countries. "The *modus vivendi* made with Germany has precisely the objective of preventing normal commercial operations between the two countries from increasing," asserted the finance minister, in bald contradiction to the obvious aims of the June understanding. Furthermore, he continued, Germany had actually not surpassed the United States in exports to Brazil, since the latter's statistics overvalued imports from the Reich. Consular invoices, which served as the basis for official calculations, showed values in reichsmarks, whereas Brazil was really paying in cheaper compensation marks.

These meetings heartened American officials. They responded by encouraging the idea of a gold loan from Washington to permit stabilization of the milreis,[69] and they also publicly expressed their satisfaction. When the CFCE welcomed the visitors in a special session, Welles hailed the close ties between Brazil and the United States. Both countries, he claimed, had "firmly maintained an identical point of view in their commercial policy" and believed that the world would be better off if trade moved according to "free economic considerations." The under secretary, not wanting to let the opportunity pass to score a public mark against the Germans, alluded critically to the foreign policies of the totalitarian states, declaring that Brazil and his country felt neither desire nor need to "subordinate the economic well-being of our peoples to military objectives or to the attainment of any kind of hegemony."[70]

As he sailed for home aboard the *Southern Cross*, Welles sent a message of appreciation to Vargas for his "generous and understanding spirit" during an interview with the American experts. Welles was now "certain" that recent trade problems would be solved in such a way that both trade and the "traditional lasting friendship" between Brazil and the United States would be strengthened.[71] The American diplomat, however, probably had difficulty in freeing his thoughts from the knowledge that, during the conference in Buenos Aires, Berlin had actively striven to protect its economic gains in South America and would undoubtedly continue to do so.[72]

The German government had recognized at the outset of its trade drive in South America that opposition from Washington and London would be inevitable. Even before dispatching the Kiep delegation in 1934, the Wilhelmstrasse had asked Itamaraty to handle the matter "with all possible discretion" so that the talks could be concluded quickly and "without any interference."[73] Brazil's conduct during ensuing negotiations and its reluctance to sign a formal agreement strengthened Berlin's conviction that its rivals, especially the United States, were bearing down on the South American country in order to thwart German aims. The Brazilians had undoubtedly encountered "strong pressure" from the Americans, who, remarked Kiep in March 1935, had done "everything to keep German-Brazilian relations from becoming a danger to the sale of North American cotton." Weeks later he repeated this message in a circular telegram. During his tour he had "repeatedly" run into problems because of "financial and economic pressure" from competitor nations who were now continuing their attack through diplomatic channels and the press.[74] Both the consulate in New York and the embassy warned the Auswärtiges Amt of a lively campaign by American exporters and the press to discredit German trade policies, which seemed to substantiate Kiep's charges.[75]

Reich observers regarded Brazil's momentary stop-and-go attitude toward compensation trade during mid-1935 as largely a result of Anglo-American pressure. Following Rio's proscription of compensation transactions in May, Schmidt-Elskop informed Berlin that Brazilian authorities were "strongly influenced" by the Americans, who naturally saw Germany's shift to Brazilian cotton as "a thorn in the eye." After resumption of compensation in all products but cotton,

Schmidt-Elskop urged his superiors not to restrict coffee imports as a means of forcing Brazil to make concessions on the cotton question, since Brazil had gone as far as it could "vis-à-vis the United States and England without bringing reprisals upon itself."[76]

Reports from Washington likewise pointed to American pressure as the cause of Brazil's attitude and reminded the Wilhelmstrasse of the "strong influence" that the United States, as the major consumer of Brazilian coffee, could exercise on that country's cotton program. Even Aranha contributed to this belief by telling the German embassy counselor that his government had halted transactions in blocked currencies because of Washington's remonstrations. This, in the eyes of the Wilhelmstrasse, confirmed its belief that Brazil's "intransigent" behavior was due "primarily" to American interference.[77]

During negotiations for a modus vivendi in 1936, Berlin took for granted that Washington's influence sparked the criticism in Brazil of compensation trade. The German embassy in Rio de Janeiro and its Brazilian "friends" managed with a press campaign to "strengthen the backbone" of the government. But the disappearance of Gibson's "superior smile" meant that Germany's opponents would neither rest nor spare expense to prevent a definitive treaty from being signed, Schmidt-Elskop cautioned.[78]

About the same time that British and American diplomats in Rio de Janeiro were wishing for strong pressure from the State Department to force Brazil to slow down Germany's commercial advance, Berlin was informing its missions abroad that the United States was making "every effort" to block Germany's progress in South America, where the Reich's goal was to "cultivate and in the long run build up economic relations." In a number of countries on that continent, "and especially during the recent negotiations with Brazil," Washington's obstructionism had been "fairly well resisted," but the Auswärtiges Amt wanted its missions in the area to follow American activities "attentively."[79] The day after dispatch of these instructions, Hjalmar Schacht saw Ambassador William Dodd and "was almost violent" in attacking American policy toward Brazil.[80] The financial wizard was irate about Washington's recent decision to slap countervailing duties on subsidized German exports—"the first check to Germany's career of economic conquest," Secretary of Treasury Henry Morgenthau, Jr., proudly claimed[81]—and he vented his rancor on Hull's policy, "which he said had defeated German trade plans in Brazil."[82]

Roosevelt's call for a Pan-American conference aroused suspicion, and American criticism of the Reich's commercial expansion in South America heightened Berlin's misgivings. Schmidt-Elskop nonetheless was confident that any proposals from the United States at Buenos Aires for economic neutrality or isolation would meet with "strong opposition" on Brazil's part: "The Brazilian government has already shown that it is not disposed to hurt its economic interests by contracting international obligations." Brazil, he thought, would "in no circumstances" let itself become dependent upon the United States by agreeing to embargo shipments of raw materials to warring nations. Any neutrality pact with such a provision would deprive Rio de Janeiro of the "strongest prop" of its policy: "the playing off of North American and European interests against each other." Consequently, he concluded, only "unusually strong pressure" from Washington could bring Brazil to sign such an agreement.[83]

Still uneasy about the perceived thrust of American policy, Berlin instructed the embassy in Buenos Aires to undertake a countercampaign during the gathering. Reports indicated that the United States would seek the isolation of the Western Hemisphere to pave the way for an antitotalitarian front, wrote State Secretary Ernst von Weizsäcker, and a related objective was to block "German and Japanese economic penetration in South America." These aims, he declared, should be resisted, perhaps through delegations from countries interested in "further cooperation" with Europe and in the "struggle against Communism"[84]—criteria that Brazil neatly fitted. Although the results of the Buenos Aires meeting showed that Berlin's perception of American goals there was erroneous, German policy makers did not revise their views, and in the case of Brazil they moved to counteract the visits of Roosevelt, Hull, and Welles by dispatching Gustav Schlotterer, head of the Commercial Section of the Ministry of Economic Affairs, to Rio de Janeiro.

Schlotterer's trip was occasion for considerable fanfare and propagandizing. He visited São Paulo and Rio de Janeiro, spending ten days in the capital. Feted at the Jockey Club, the German expert lauded Brazil's attitude in trade matters as an example for other nations.[85] In a lengthy press interview, he defended compensation trade as the only system possible for Germany. Anglo-American complaints about the cheapened currency were unjustified in view of the devaluation of the pound and dollar. Besides, he continued, policy could not be "dogmatically" formulated. The present arrangement with Brazil satisfied the interests of both nations and the "laws of good sense," which required not what would be "theoretically desirable but what can be achieved in practice." Speaking in French, Schlotterer said that Brazilian leaders had given "a magnificent example of political wisdom and perfect understanding of the world economy when they facilitated the development of this system born of necessity."[86] Coming as they did on the heels of speeches by Welles and Hull extolling Brazil's attitude, these statements were a revealing commentary on the success of Vargas's policy and on American official capacity for ignoring reality.

The interview was republished by various *carioca* newspapers, and eventually it appeared in the press of São Paulo, Santos, Joinville, and other cities. The Deutsche-Brasilianische Handelskammer made several thousand reprints for distribution throughout Brazil.[87] Schlotterer also held conferences with a number of Brazilian officials, a notable omission being Pimentel Brandão, who had become acting foreign minister when Macedo Soares resigned as expected on January 1 to look to his ill-fated and short-lived presidential campaign and who held a "well-known antagonistic attitude" toward bilateralism.[88]

The publicity and promotional activities attendant upon Schlotterer's visit reflected the German perception that it was necessary to counteract what seemed to be a more aggressive campaign by the United States to roll back the Reich's economic push in Latin America. More graphic and explicit evidence of such a definition by Berlin of its position in that region vis-à-vis Washington came days after Schlotterer's departure from Brazil, when Karl Ritter dispatched special instructions on the trade issue to the missions in South America.

Statements by Hull at Buenos Aires and the dissemination of what Ritter called a propaganda article of the Pan American Union prompted this move. Although Hull had not specifically mentioned Germany, it was obvious to Berlin that his criticism of bilateralism was directed against the Reich. Moreover, said Ritter, an article entitled "German Trade Competition in Latin America," which appeared in the October issue of *Commercial Pan America*, gave an intentionally erroneous view of German policy. Author H. G. Smith suggested, for example, that Brazil had hurt its own interests by selling cotton to Germany, since its coffee sales in 1935 had correspondingly dropped. While this was true, it had taken place with the full understanding of the Brazilian government, Ritter explained.

To Berlin these incidents meant that the United States was prosecuting its "trade war" against the Reich in Latin America by means of "political pressure," "false press statements," and "seemingly correct" statistics, tactics that made necessary the "special vigilance and increased resistance of all German authorities." Berlin wanted its diplomats to combat the false American propaganda "with all means and without reserve in all pertinent official and private circles." The main line of argument should be that Germany's present policy was unavoidable in view of the world financial crisis. Because influencing the press was "especially important," the missions were to try to bring local Nazi organizations into the struggle against Yankee propaganda.[89] These instructions provide considerable insight into the psychological ordering of external events by German policy makers in order to justify their own actions. Having launched an aggressive drive to force new markets in South America in 1934, now, three years later, Berlin saw itself forced into "defensive" measures by a ruthless American thrust.

The major battleground was Brazil, where Schmidt-Elskop warned his government to expect "ever sharper and more intensive" attacks by Germany's opponents[90] and requested more funds for his "Gegenangriff."[91] That the Reich intended vigorously to prosecute this counterattack was clear from its decision to send the Wilhelmstrasse's top commercial expert to head the command post in Rio de Janeiro.[92] And things augured well. The armaments contract signed on February 18 with Krupp was a step in the direction Berlin wanted to travel, and, before Schlotterer sailed for Hamburg, Souza Costa had assured him that a larger share of the army's program would go to German manufacturers. Vargas had also added a promise of further orders.[93]

The president's general attitude was eminently gratifying and gave reason for optimism. The embassy in Rio de Janeiro even hoped that the stories of his desire to remain in power were true. For Germany's commercial interests his continuation would be "most advantageous," wrote the chargé, "since he recognizes the value of these economic relations and constantly defends and encourages them despite all difficulties with other countries."[94] As a reward for his tireless efforts to strengthen ties with Germany, Vargas gave Sampaio the legation in Prague. And he would be pleased, Berlin learned, to welcome Karl Ritter as the new German ambassador in Rio de Janeiro.[95]

The expansion of commerce between the two nations since 1934 testified eloquently to Brazil's commitment to cooperation with the Reich. As Moniz de Aragão remarked in the spring of 1937, "Brazil's economic policy has coincided perfectly with the ideas set forth in Germany's 'New Plan' for foreign trade."[96] It was precisely this situation that Washington now made a strong bid to reverse when Souza Costa traveled to Washington on a special mission for high-level discussions of the German trade issue.

Souza Costa's trip grew out of the debate in the spring of 1937 on the question of renewing the German-Brazilian agreement. Within Brazil, opponents worked against the tide trying to block renewal. Partly at the instigation of Bouças, the CFCE called on Souza Costa at the end of February to provide data on the functioning of the compensation arrangement. Bouças charged that Brazil was a victim of what amounted to dumping of German goods, and other members of the Conselho thought that in view of the world situation the government should take precautions.[97] The response to these appeals was the establishment of a special committee to examine the matter.

Itamaraty, with Macedo Soares and Sampaio gone, now opposed compensation, but its influence on the formulation of foreign economic policy had declined along with its interest in the gentlemen's agreement. Pimentel Brandão had slight experience in financial and economic affairs, and as a career diplomat he possessed negligible influence in the Brazilian political arena. He therefore carried "very little weight" with either Souza Costa or Vargas.[98] And the acting foreign minister freely admitted this to British and American allies. "His own Department was, he said, opposed to such renewal," Ambassador Gurney reported, "but it depended less on them than on the Ministry of Finance and the Bank of Brazil." The American chargé on several occasions called the State Department's attention to Pimentel Brandão's lack of authority, and Bouças, too, cautioned that Souza Costa would "have the deciding voice in this question no matter what the attitude of the Foreign Office may be."[99]

Decisive governmental and commercial opinion stood firmly behind continuation of the arrangement with Berlin. Commercial associations from Porto Alegre to Belém wired federal authorities urging a continuation of compensation trade, a display of support that led one ambassador on duty at Itamaraty to privately predict that, "if the present situation continues, in a short while we will be importing everything from Germany!"[100] The conclusion of the CFCE's special study group was likewise an endorsement of the modus vivendi with Berlin, despite an attempt to placate adversaries of the accord with a hollow caveat about a need for further examination. The committee reached the surprising conclusion that "only exceptionally" did German products compete with American, and it rejected a suggested additional duty on imports from the Reich, since cheaper goods were to Brazil's advantage.[101] The committee also reiterated that Brazilian statistics overvalued those imports by about 20 percent, the general discount of the compensation mark.[102]

Pimentel Brandão's repeated statements to the American embassy that he had the backing of Catete were a reflection of Vargas's conciliatory demeanor rather than his position on policy. The president, in fact, supported his finance minister. He called on mutual friends interested in the German market to write Aranha explaining the harm that would result from a cessation of compensation trade, and he himself endeavored to allay Aranha's anxieties by assuring the ambassador he agreed that American objections should be attended to "as far as possible." But, Vargas emphasized, Brazil could not afford to "stop trading" with Germany. Indicative of Vargas's intentions in 1937 was his response to an anxious inquiry from the governor of Paraíba about a rumored ban on cotton sales in blocked currency. Tell the governor to "be calm," that northern interests "will not be hurt," Vargas instructed his secretary.[103]

Authorities in Berlin were generally satisfied—"The agreement has technically, as well as materially, stood the test entirely," was the judgment of an interdepartmental conference early in April[104]—and the Wilhelmstrasse arranged with Moniz de Aragão to begin talks later that month for renewal of the modus vivendi. The major fear of pro-compensation traders in Brazil, it learned from the embassy in Rio de Janeiro, was simply that commerce with the Reich might be restricted because of the compensation marks accumulating in the Banco do Brasil. But this was no problem, pointed out Schmidt-Elskop, since they were earmarked for armaments purchases.[105] SOINC agents in Brazil actively promoted the German cause and claimed credit for at least part of the demonstration of public opinion. They contacted business associations about sending telegrams to the government, conferred with deputies, and prepared materials—probably on compensation transactions between American and German firms—for Souza Costa, all in the hope of countering the "very strong pressure of the North Americans."[106]

German competition had indeed become a matter of "steady concern" to Washington, and throughout the spring of 1937 it pressed its case in Rio de Janeiro.[107] To quash the idea that the United States sanctioned trade with the Reich on the same basis Brazil did—a belief encouraged by Souza Aranha, who reportedly was "bombarding" Souza Costa with newspaper clippings to this effect[108]—the State Department pointed out that private barter or compensation transactions were tolerated only when Berlin allowed no bounties or price discounts on the goods. Furthermore, the American government had levied extra duties on subsidized imports from Germany and forced it to relinquish this practice in commerce with the United States.[109]

What most bothered American interests by this time was export subsidization. Because of the devaluation of the dollar, the State Department had decided that the complaints of exporters about the depreciated blocked marks were unjustified but protests against export bounties were legitimate.[110] Berlin knew that its export promotion devices were spurring its critics on, and months earlier, at the insistence of the Ministry of Economic Affairs, all unapproved press commentaries on the subject had been banned.[111] But during the late spring of 1937 Washington received several reports from Ambassador Dodd in Berlin on Germany's "great efforts" to check American trade with South America, where "the subsidy business still goes on and will be greatly increased." The Brazilian and other Latin American envoys, he told Hull, "shout their agreement with you," but at the same time they admitted their countries accepted subsidized German exports.[112] The professor-turned-diplomat also wrote to Roosevelt and Secretary of Commerce Roper in the same vein. "The subsidies paid for exports have been increased," he informed the president, "and sales to Latin America . . . pressed stronger than ever."[113]

Evaluating policy alternatives, the State Department, supported by the Treasury Department, rejected a suggestion that the Brazilian-American treaty be amended to give "greater protection" to American trade. This, again, would have amounted to an admission that Hull's opponents in 1934 had been right. American exports to Brazil, furthermore, although not as rapidly as had been hoped, were nonetheless rising. Brazil's argument that it had no alternative to bilateral trading methods with the Reich had also not been without some effect, and authoritative opinion within the department viewed the maintenance of the principle of liberal trade through formal declarations a perhaps more realistic objective than forcing the abandonment of the German-Brazilian accord.[114] The Treasury Department agreed that the United States could not ask Brazil to discontinue compensation trade and suggested that "the problem of German advantages in Brazil can be handled most advantageously through informal discussions."[115]

Having accepted the probable inevitability of compensation trade between Brazil and Germany, Washington turned to monetary blandishments in an effort to diminish the effects of German competition. The possibility of a loan for currency stabilization had been broached to Brazilian leaders at the time of the Buenos Aires Conference, and, when presidential hopeful Macedo Soares visited the United States in February 1937 to represent Vargas at Roosevelt's inauguration, Sumner Welles had indicated to him that the United States was willing to grant "on exceptional terms" a $50 million gold loan for Brazil's projected central bank.[116]

A Treasury Department staff report to Secretary Morgenthau delineated Washington's anticipated gains from such assistance: a stronger milreis and thus greater attraction for foreign investors, elimination of current exchange problems, a favorable influencing of Latin American attitudes toward the United States, and a possible beneficial effect on American trade. "Another possibility in the negotiations," suggested the treasury experts, "may be to obtain some concessions from Brazil in return for the loan with respect to trading arrangements with Germany in the use of the ASKI marks." Hull and his aides, they noted, were "eager" to persuade Brazil to do something in that regard.[117]

As the expiration date for the German-Brazilian modus vivendi drew nearer, the State Department redoubled its efforts. In successive meetings with Aranha early in May, Welles, Feis, and Morgenthau urged him to persuade his government to take advantage of the offer. Aranha agreed that the gold would help to solve the "money troubles" with German importers, and he recommended to Rio that technicians be sent to Washington to work out the necessary details.[118] Oddly enough, the department passed up an opportunity for joint representations with the British. The suggestion for common action came from the new American chargé in Rio, Robert Scotten, who was running the embassy while awaiting the arrival of Jefferson Caffery, Gibson's replacement. Ambassador Hugh Gurney was cold to the proposal, since it would be difficult, he thought, to come up with "real evidence" that the modus vivendi had hurt British trade. Exports had fallen, yes, but it could be argued that this was not "exclusively" the result of compensation marks.[119]

London was astonished at Gurney's remarks. Even though "chapter and verse" could not be cited to prove that British losses stemmed from German methods, the evidence seemed clear enough to the Foreign

Office. Brazilian authorities had sought by "ingenious juggling of figures" to convince other nations that the value of German exports to Brazil was not as much as it appeared, but tonnage statistics revealed an "enormous rise" in those sales and an "equally large fall" in British and American exports to Brazil. The idea of collaborating with the Americans was also sound, and the Board of Trade agreed. "It is seldom that we get such an opportunity of useful cooperation with the United States Government," a Foreign Office spokesman reminded Gurney.[120] When the ambassador referred to the conclusions of the recent study of German penetration of Latin America, London explained that, while it had concluded that countries in the region must find their own way out of their difficulties, "there is nothing to prevent us urging them to save themselves, and incidentally us."[121]

That no joint representation was made was not London's fault. The State Department frowned on the idea and wanted, as a matter of policy, to avoid giving the impression that it acted in concert with European powers. And it was no satisfaction to the State Department to see the British willing to associate themselves with the United States in Brazil, when they would not do so in Argentina, where their own position was stronger.[122]

The British embassy therefore limited its action to individual remonstrations. The Foreign Office declined to offer detailed recommendations as to how Brazil could satisfy the conflicting interests of the countries concerned, even though the new director of the CFCE, a former commercial attaché in London, "begged" for such counsel. "I am afraid there is no further advice that we can give the Brazilians," remarked one official. "They must find their own solution for themselves."[123]

The American business community and embassy in Brazil worked overtime trying to convince Souza Costa of the need to revise the arrangement with Berlin. Scotten tirelessly repeated the arguments against bilateralism, and the Chamber of Commerce sent the finance minister a memorandum pleading for Brazil not to "shackle" itself to a country that "in many lines is slowly destroying the trade of Brazil's best customer and staunchest friend."[124] The result of these efforts was a small dividend: Souza Costa on June 3 told Scotten that Brazil would extend the modus vivendi for three months, during which time the whole question would once again be thoroughly studied. But, the finance minister hastened to make clear, this did not represent denunciation of the agreement, since he saw no reason to abandon it.

Pimentel Brandão later listened sympathetically to Scotten, but he again confessed his own helplessness. "There is only one way for the American Government to obtain what they want in Brazil," he candidly explained, "and that is to bring pressure to bear upon our country and to talk in strong terms to the Minister of Finance." The American case was "hopeless," Scotten agreed, unless the State Department followed that advice.[125]

Late that same evening Souza Costa telephoned his ambassador-friend in Washington to report the extension of the German agreement. Aranha's reaction was strong. There was nothing worse than a "policy of subterfuge and inveiglement," he said angrily.[126] Tempers flared momentarily and the two friends had a "heated" exchange, Bouças later learned, with Aranha insisting that something had to be done to eliminate the cause of Washington's grievances.[127] It was difficult, Aranha bluntly stated, for a diplomat to be forced to "humiliate his country, invoking groundless arguments and making ethereal suggestions."[128] The next day Aranha cabled Vargas urging him to send Souza Costa to Washington to discuss the trade question with American authorities—a proposal Vargas accepted—and he later asked Welles to back up his efforts by having Scotten once more speak to the finance minister.[129]

Itamaraty, through the uncoordinated efforts of Pimentel Brandão and Aranha, thus sought to bring into play its only weapon—American pressure—in order to assert itself in government councils. This attempt of opponents of compensation trade to reverse previous trade policy was partially successful in that they gained additional time in which to press their views. But it was clear that the locus of real authority was the Ministry of Finance and that ultimate success or failure would depend on Souza Costa's experience in Washington.

As the director of the nation's finances prepared to leave on his special mission, there was no sign that he would alter his views. On June 10 he urged Schmidt-Elskop not to demand more than the short extension, since it would make things harder for Brazil. He promised that he would see that the present volume of trade between the two countries was maintained, and he said that he was making the "gesture" of going to Washington only to "soothe" the government there, which was "furious" about the extension. When the German diplomat protested Washington's intervention, Souza Costa assured him that he would "calm down the Americans."[130]

Pimentel Brandão saw the finance minister shortly before he left and pleaded with him to consider carefully the political effects of bilateral trade with Germany on relations with the United States. Souza Costa retorted that what mattered to him was the material side of the question. "I wish to repeat," Pimentel Brandão told Scotten after the finance minister's departure, "that I cannot too strongly urge your government to maintain a very firm attitude with this man."[131]

The Brazilian delegation met with a cordial reception in Washington. Because Souza Costa's mission was "of very considerable importance," Welles sent an official from the State Department to meet his plane in Miami and accompany the Brazilian visitors to the national capital. Besides the finance minister, the group consisted of the director of the CFCE, a representative of the Banco do Brasil, and Bouças, who went along as a specialist on the foreign debt. Hull welcomed them in a ceremonial meeting at the State Department on June 19. After Aranha stated that the principal task of the mission was to study and clear up trade problems and then discuss plans for the central bank and the foreign debt question, Hull launched into a long discourse on American commercial policy. He again stressed Brazil's importance to Washington as an example for the other American nations. If Brazil tolerated unfair trading practices, he said, it would create a "dangerous precedent." Encouragement of Europe's egoistic policies by countries in the Western Hemisphere would bring "grave consequences," he admonished his listeners. The Brazilian guests responded with the expressions of support that Hull craved. The "atmosphere of complete harmony of views" between their governments was proof, said Souza Costa, of Brazil's desire to cooperate.[132]

The Brazilians held several sessions with State Department officials in ensuing days. Since Souza Costa emphatically ruled out the possibility of getting Berlin to trade on a "free" basis, the meetings dealt mainly with ways to control compensation. Nothing substantial emerged from these initial talks, as Souza Costa merely agreed to study various possible steps suggested by American technicians, such as setting maximum limits on exports to Germany or getting the Germans to pay partly in free currency and abstain from sending subsidized goods to Brazil.[133] Although the Banco do Brasil representative privately admitted to other members of the delegation that American complaints were justified, Souza Costa steadfastly declined to make any concessions.[134]

Among themselves, State Department experts openly expressed their disenchantment with the negotiations. Herbert Feis was sufficiently disgusted to recommend that the United States abandon its "completely passive" attitude. "I think it grows increasingly plain," he wrote on June 29, "that the Brazilian authorities would like to have us accept some form of arrangement that would seem to be satisfactory on the surface but consistently with which the trade with Germany could be developed just as in the past." Donald Heath of the Division of American Republics shared Feis's pessimism: "More probably, we will merely get an unreliable assurance from Brazil that she will take measures against German compensation and subsidy procedures which she will not carry out and Germany will still feel ill-will toward us for attempting to curb her trade with Brazil."[135]

Heath guessed correctly on both counts. Having failed in its bid to get the negotiations for a renewal of the modus vivendi transferred to Berlin, where American influence would be weaker,[136] the German government was dismayed by its rival's success in arranging for a special mission to visit Washington. While Souza Costa was en route to the United States, the Wilhelmstrasse had expressed its displeasure to Moniz de Aragão and made the customary hints that Brazil's competitors were eager to enjoy the favors that Brazil was treating lightly.[137] Berlin's apprehensions were encouraged by reports from Rio about Anglo-American "interference," and the German embassy in Washington was instructed to follow closely the proceedings there. Shortly before Souza Costa's arrival, Ambassador Hans Dieckhoff talked with Aranha and argued Germany's case. The Brazilian envoy assured Dieckhoff that the Americans had not threatened Brazil, but the Germans were not inclined to accept at face value statements conflicting with their image of Washington's intentions, especially from a man who, in their opinion, had "allowed himself to be taken too much in tow by the North Americans."[138]

Incensed at developments, Reich authorities late in June directly challenged Washington. Hjalmar Schacht opened the attack, on June 27, at the annual congress of the International Chamber of Commerce in Berlin by publicly reprimanding the United States for its attitude toward German-Brazilian relations. Later Schacht spoke to Ambassador Dodd in terms that led Dodd to send Hull a private note of warning: "All that Schacht has said confirms the purpose here: to defeat you."[139] To avoid possibly antagonizing the Brazilians, the Wilhelmstrasse requested that the German press refrain from further comment on German-Brazilian negotiations or on the Souza Costa trip, explaining that "a vigorous struggle between . . . Washington and us for the Brazilian market has broken out."[140] But Washington's sensitivities were not spared.

Under Secretary Hans von Mackensen summoned Dodd and, over the ambassador's denial, insisted that he knew the United States was threatening to stop importing coffee if Brazil continued to deal with Germany. The same day in Washington, Dieckhoff received orders to make a similar protest to the State Department. The German government, he told Welles, was "irritated and annoyed" by the "unwarranted interference" of the United States and the latter's unjustified efforts to "coerce" Brazil into restricting commerce with Germany. Welles vigorously denied that pressure had been applied or threats made against Brazil, and he branded as completely false the notion that there was an official American propaganda campaign to thwart German economic activity in South America. The United States, Welles said "with some emphasis," wanted nothing but "fair play" in international trade.[141]

The clash between the two powers also found echo in Brazil, leading one senator-journalist to assert that "Brazil is joining battle like Spain: what is at stake is the process of trading in compensation currency."[142] Partisans of bilateralism were clearly more active and vocal than opponents. Souza Dantas, now a leading member of the Integralist party, published with SOINC's financial support a long newspaper article on July 1 outlining the "true history" of compensation marks and expounding the advantages of the system. Without explicitly naming the United States, he declared that the origin of the "tempestuous campaign" against Brazil's transactions with the Reich lay in the efforts of "certain commercial and financial imperialisms." The question, he privately explained to Aranha, had been so "poisoned" and he had been attacked "with such brutality" that he had considered it necessary to clarify public opinion. In another article "inspired" by SOINC, a writer in the *Correio da Manhã* on July 3 criticized what he saw as American infringements on Brazil's right to self-determination. "Two things are involved: Brazil's interests and its very dignity," he exclaimed.[143]

The Chamber of Commerce and Industry in Rio, earlier labeled by German diplomats as "friendly toward us,"[144] passed a resolution that day protesting "any interference of foreign authorities in the business affairs of our internal economy, whether this interference be through diplomatic channels or in the character of conversations or agreements with persons" representing the country.[145] The president of the Chamber explained to a reporter that the news from Washington indicated that the State Department was putting pressure on Aranha. Compensation trade, he said, had unquestionably brought "great advantages" to Brazilian exporters, and American "intromission" into Brazil's domestic affairs was understandably causing serious apprehension in German circles.[146]

The American government, despite the misgivings of some State Department officers, showed that the recriminations of its adversaries were unwarranted by stressing the wholesomeness of the carrot rather than the thickness of the stick as its weapon of defense in the commercial fight. Aranha had pointed this out to German diplomats on June 30, and when asked about it by a reporter the next day he again denied that the Americans had in any way menaced Brazil. "I must declare categorically that the United States exercised no pressure on us," he said, "and that we never had a better understanding with the United States than now." Indeed, he privately wrote Vargas, American authorities "want to help, asking only that we 'put on a thicker veil' to hide better the 'nakedness of the truth' from their public opinion."[147]

No matter how the reality of German competition was clothed, American businessmen objected strongly. A vice-president of Westinghouse International complained to Hull that it had lost $500,000 worth of business in Brazil because of German price discounts, and Thomas of the NFTC sent the secretary a six-page letter protesting Brazil's violation of the American treaty.[148] Throughout the month anxious pleas for assistance against German competition reached the State Department, to be answered with the laconic assurance that the department "has been doing and will continue to do all that it properly can to develop American trade in the Brazilian and other markets."[149]

By the middle of July the negotiators concluded their discussion of trade and financial problems. Bouças's talks on the foreign debt produced no meaningful results, since he had perceived early that American cooperation in a general financial reform program for Brazil "depends exclusively" on a satisfactory solution of the trade question.[150] In regard to this aspect of the mission, Souza Costa sent Vargas an exultant cable saying that Brazil had "merely" agreed to the creation of two joint advisory committees, one in New York and the other in Rio de Janeiro, to supervise the operation of the Brazilian-American pact. A written pledge from Aranha that Brazil would "use every effort" to see that imports that competed with American goods were not subsidized rounded out Hull's requirements of Brazil in exchange for a promise to loan Brazil up to $60 million worth of gold, whenever it wanted such assistance, to establish a central bank. These terms, re-marked Aranha, exceeded his expectations, and "good will" was the only explanation, given the "advantages that we are conceding to Germany."[151]

Perhaps most important of all to Hull, whose emphasis on public reaffirmations of harmony and solidarity bespoke considerable internal doubt and anxiety about the effectiveness of his policies, was a joint statement proclaiming anew the support of the two nations for liberal trading practices. The declaration, issued by the secretary and Souza Costa on July 15, reiterated faith in the Brazilian-American treaty and announced that by making "every effort" they would work toward realization of the ideals underlying it. Some "minor complementary measures" had proven necessary to "safeguard its principles and benefits in view of the form of trading pursued by some countries," read the statement, and the two governments would act to protect those advantages "against outside competition that is directly subsidized by governments."[152]

Publicly and privately Aranha extolled Washington's attitude. His government would be "very pleased," he told a reporter, "if all countries treated Brazil on the same friendly terms that the United States has . . . for many years, and now more than ever." To Vargas the ambassador sent word that "we arrived at an understanding on a way to *violate the commercial accord with this country* without disagreeable complaints and protests and without the risk of measures harmful to Brazil's interests in the United States." Aranha could not accept his government's policy as a "useful and constructive one" and had defended it against his better judgment. His letter ended with a plea that Vargas guard against the "Germanic neocolonization" of Brazil that would surely ensue if Brazil delivered itself, "as we are doing, hands and feet to Germanic greed and cupidity."[153]

As Berlin viewed matters, its hold was being threatened by Washington's grip on Brazil's arm, and the Souza Costa mission only embittered the already strained relations between the United States and Germany. On learning of the joint statement, the Wilhelmstrasse quickly sent out circular instructions to the missions in Latin America informing them that one of their "most important trade tasks" was now the *"Abwehrkampf"* against American efforts to force the Reich out of the markets of that area. To protect recent advances there, "this defensive struggle must be taken up with all force," urged Ritter, the author of the instructions. He suggested that German diplomats might profitably exploit the "sensitivity" of the Latin Americans to American encroachments on their sovereignty, and he held out the promise of additional funds for propaganda if needed. In view of the Hull–Souza Costa declaration, it was no longer necessary, he said, for German agents to show "too much restraint" in their endeavors to counteract Washington's drive. Dieckhoff also received orders to inform the State Department that his government regretted the "so unusual and aggressive" interference in Germany's relations with another country and refused responsibility for any "disagreeable" intensification of trade rivalry in Brazil.[154]

Berlin now lifted the ban on press commentaries. On July 21 the official *Deutsche Nachrichtenbüro* released a lengthy critique of American opposition to German methods and its offer of financial assistance to Brazil, branding these developments as a mere "pretext" for dominating the Brazilian market. Playing to the South American audience, the article stressed the advantages Brazil gained from cheaper imports and charged that the United States wanted Brazil to curtail purchases from the Reich in order to compel the latter to turn once again to American producers for cotton supplies.[155] An authoritative German business journal declared that the joint Brazilian-American pronouncement had "moved Brazil to the center of the commercial battle."[156] Dantas's review of compensation trade published in the *Correio da Manhã* now appeared in paraphrased form in leading German newspapers, and Ritter sent the text of the article to the embassies and legations in Latin America for use "in an appropriate way."[157]

With a decree of July 20 naming Ritter ambassador to Brazil, the Reich government served public notice that it was taking the gloves off. The timing of the announcement was obviously not coincidental but rather demonstrated, as Moniz de Aragão pointed out, Germany's desire to shore up its economic ties with Brazil at a time when "certain difficulties" had cropped up.[158] The new American envoy to Brazil, Jefferson Caffery, a career diplomat whose last post had been the Havana embassy, received while still in Washington a personal message from Allan Dawson, until recently attached to the Rio embassy but now consul in Hamburg, warning him that Ritter was "a very shrewd and able man, chosen to push German hopes along commercial lines to the utmost in Brazil." Caffery knew from previous reports that his German counterpart was a "Nazi go-getter," and he expected to "hear a lot from him later on."[159]

Although privately quite skeptical, Caffery announced to reporters on his arrival in Brazil in August that the Souza Costa mission had been "crowned with success," that its effects would "very rapidly" be felt in the commercial sphere.[160] Diplomatic niceties thus led Caffery to reaffirm a view of the results of the mission that was excessively optimistic, although the profundity of the failure of American policy in this episode would become clear only later. That view, which implicitly held that the mission highlighted an effective move by the United States to check German trade advances in Brazil, has nonetheless passed into history as the prevailing one. "Throughout 1936 Secretary Hull had to keep repeating Washington's opposition to Brazilian flirtations with Germany," Lloyd Gardner has written. "Finally Rio cut free from this infatuation in exchange for a sixty-million dollar loan from the United States." John M. Blum, too, interpreted the episode as one that thwarted an alleged Fascist politicoeconomic threat in Brazil: "This [financial] arrangement [of 1937] helped to keep Vargas a Pan-American," he stated, implying that the Brazilian government altered its policy toward Germany.[161]

The fact is that from the American standpoint the mission was a total failure. In the subsequent words of Secretary Morgenthau, "it was purely window dressing and nothing happened."[162] Clearly, the key Brazilian policy makers, Vargas and Souza Costa, in agreeing to the mission had no intention of restricting trade with Germany. That the finance minister was the most influential civilian voice in the cabinet was obvious from the events preceding his mission, and, during his stay in Washington, he and Aranha corresponded directly with Vargas, bypassing Itamaraty completely. The Germans fully understood this power relationship. Souza Costa "has this year been the decisive and authoritative minister in the negotiations and will continue to be," a Wilhelmstrasse official commented on August 10. "Whether or not we reach an understanding will depend primarily on him."[163]

Nothing happened in Washington to change Souza Costa's mind about Brazil's commercial policy. Satisfied with his conduct of the talks, he boasted to a colleague that he had finally "convinced the Americans that Brazil's trade relations with Germany had necessarily to be on a special basis and that there wasn't much Brazil could do to avoid a barter or compensation arrangement with Germany." His colleague, the Brazilian commercial attaché in Berlin who had gone to Washington to assist the delegation, revealed the finance minister's judgment of the results of his mission in a "long and illuminating" conversation with Consul Dawson in Berlin. "This seems to confirm the feeling which I have," Dawson informed Caffery, "and which seemed also to be yours . . . that it would be up to you and your personal suasion to keep Souza Costa to the vague promises he made in Washington."[164]

Subsequent months-long negotiations between Rio de Janeiro and Berlin, on the one hand, and Rio de Janeiro and Washington, on the other, over the question of German subsidies resulted in no meaningful action.[165] Throughout 1937 the Reich continued to subsidize exports to Brazil, a portion of them more than necessary to offset the devaluation of the dollar, and even increased subsidies in 1938.[166] Brazilian authorities also held the exchange value of compensation marks steady while the dollar increased in value, thus widening the discount rate of the marks and encouraging imports from Germany. Three months after Souza Costa left Washington, Caffery was forced to protest this procedure.[167]

When the short-term extension of the modus vivendi expired in September, Brazil and Germany simply renewed it for another three months. "There's no use saying 'I told you so,'" Dawson remarked to Caffery. When the ambassador's "lively exchange of ideas with the Brazilians" failed to produce any agreement on the limitation of compensation trade, Rio de Janeiro and Berlin merely renewed the gentlemen's agreement again, and they periodically did so until the outbreak of war in 1939.[168]

Nor was the loan ever completed. As late as September 1940, State Department officials were commenting on Brazil's failure to request the gold backing for the elusive central bank.[169] Finally, the joint watchdog committees, which were supposed to make certain that commerce between Brazil and the United States proceeded in accordance with the 1935 treaty, never got off the ground. The State Department itself admitted in February 1940 that "after the [American] nominations to the Committees were made [in January 1938], the Department for all practical purposes forgot their existence." In response to a query from Washington, the Rio embassy reported a month later that "the Committee in this country has not been effective because of the lack of cooperation of the Brazilian members and the Brazilian Government . . ."[170]

Two documents written months after Souza Costa's return to Brazil, one a dispatch from Caffery and the other a memorandum by the counselor of the German embassy, neatly summed up the results of the finance minister's special journey. Caffery, writing in February

1938, recalled "that the members of the Brazilian Mission who were in Washington last summer were particularly anxious to ascertain whether retaliatory measures could be expected from the United States in case Brazil continued her compensation mark trade with Germany. As the members of the Mission received the distinct impression that retaliatory measures were not to be expected, they have been since that time impervious to blandishment or argument and have, thus far at any rate, demonstrated only faint interest in the point of view set out in the Department's various telegrams on the subject."[171] Two months later the German *Botschaftsrat* surveyed Germany's position in Brazil vis-à-vis the United States and concluded: "The year 1937 opened the offensive of North American diplomacy against German influence in Brazil. This struggle, despite the negotiations of Finance Minister Souza Costa in Washington, did not lead to favorable results for America. On the contrary," he reported with satisfaction, "German-Brazilian compensation trade continued de facto after the expiration of the [1936] agreement and reached ever larger figures."[172]

From the viewpoint of Rio de Janeiro, the trip of the finance minister was a complete diplomatic success, in that the American government did not adopt any coercive measures against Brazil; the latter was thus left free to continue dealing with the Reich on the existing basis. But, in terms of American anticipations, the mission yielded negative results on every count. Hull had his public statement of solidarity, but this had little practical value in the international competition for the Brazilian market. Washington not only failed to obtain the elimination of objectionable German commercial procedures but also earned the reproaches and hostility of official and private supporters of compensation trade on both sides of the Atlantic.

American-German relations during the early Nazi years had deteriorated rapidly for several reasons: Berlin's anti-Jewish policies, a number of incidents involving physical assault on American citizens in Germany, Nazi activities within the United States, the Reich's failure to clear up its indebtedness to Americans, and a decline in trade relations because of fundamental policy differences.[173] An ingredient in this latter phenomenon was Germany's attention to South American markets, particularly Brazil's. The relative importance of commercial rivalry in South America as a factor in the widening schism between the United States and Germany is, of course, impossible to calculate, but undoubtedly that rivalry gave impetus to their estrangement. The conclusion reached by one German historian of American-

German relations that the trade clash in South America was "of the greatest importance" in promoting the Washington-Berlin schism seems indeed unquestionable.[174]

The European crisis of 1936—the Rhineland, the Spanish Civil War with patent Italo-German involvement—marked a turning point in American perceptions of the Nazi experiment. Heretofore concerned with an economic challenge, American policy makers were increasingly nagged by uneasiness about the military implications of German ambitions, which explains Roosevelt's admonition at Buenos Aires in December 1936 that the Western Hemisphere should bind together for common safety.[175]

In Brazil's case, American concern over German political and ideological penetration was evident, perceptibly if not insistently, during the 1937 negotiations. Herbert Feis, for example, worried about Berlin's throwing "its trade weight in whatever direction it wants either for economic or political purposes." And Bouças, after lengthy sessions with American officials, sensed the new dimension of American policy: "It's Democracy struggling against Fascism!" he told Souza Costa.[176] Although there is no evidence to support the contention that Germany had political ambitions in Brazil or any other country of Latin America, beyond doing what it reasonably could to encourage governments friendly to Berlin, the German government deeply resented Washington's efforts to close hemispheric ranks after 1936. Berlin's reaction to the American-Brazilian discussions in 1937 amply demonstrates its keen desire to counteract Washington's attempt to draw Brazil into a closer alliance.

In retrospect, the Souza Costa mission appears to be a watershed in the clash between the two leading pretenders for Brazil's commercial affections, since it marked the end of what had been essentially an economic struggle. Henceforth, political motives would play an increasing role in the dispute.

Chapter 6

Trade, Armaments, and International Politics (1937–1939)

The period between the proclamation of the Estado Novo and the outbreak of war in Europe saw a sudden shift to the Right in Brazilian politics, a change that seemed at first to portend a reorientation of Brazil's foreign policy. To the surprise of foreign observers, Berlin did not reap major political benefits from the change of regime in Rio de Janeiro. Economically, however, the two countries drew closer together—to the grave anxiety of Washington—as the Reich expanded its vital role as a supplier of goods and armaments to Brazil, and the latter continued to supply the cotton, coffee, and other items that the Hitler government was feverishly stockpiling in anticipation of the war it would launch in September 1939. In the face of the ominous Nazi challenge, the United States concentrated on Brazil in its efforts to close hemispheric ranks.

The dramatic events of November 1937 opened a new chapter in Brazil's political history. The collapse of constitutional government and proclamation of a dictatorship came not unexpectedly to attentive observers of the Brazilian scene. Ever since suppression of the Communist revolt two years earlier, there had been a marked drift to the Right. On the heels of that abortive uprising had come a suspension of constitutional guarantees under a "state of siege" that was periodically renewed until June 1937. The nation had been swept by a wave of anti-Communism, as leftist critics of the regime were subjected to the scrutiny of a National Commission for the Repression of Communism whose most prominent member thought "it is better to make one or more unjust arrests than to permit Brazil to be bloodied again."[1]

The putsch was a godsend to Plinio Salgado's right-wing Integralist party. The Integralists wore green shirts, used stiff-armed salutes, and adopted the sigma as their symbol. Through "nuclei" spread across the country they preached the virtues of God, Country, and Family, and for some time had been warning of Communist subversion. Now, their political and ideological support was more than welcome in the "sanitizing campaign" launched by the government.[2] Integralist themes and slogans were increasingly sounded by high federal officials, including Vargas himself. In at least three major addresses in 1936 the president borrowed the Integralist motto of "Fatherland, family, and religion." "When the highest authority of the Republic speaks like this," cabled one party member, "we Integralists applaud, because it is our language."[3] Salgado's emboldened followers, despite the hostility of state political machines, intensified local electoral campaigning in 1936 and made significant headway for the nation's first really national political movement. By 1937 Salgado was ready to enter the presidential race, as the number of Integralist voters was estimated at perhaps a half-million out of a total electorate of some three million. Salgado could have had no illusions about winning the election. What is likely, in view of the discreet negotiations between him and Catete Palace, is that the Integralist leader wanted to use the party's electoral strength to see that a candidate sympathetic to its civic campaign replaced Vargas.[4]

Many people thought that candidate would be Oswaldo Aranha, on whose behalf relatives and friends had been maneuvering since 1934. Aranha was acceptable to Vargas, the Integralist leaders, and many revolutionaries of 1930. But he was not *persona grata* to the governor of Minas Gerais, because he had in 1933 supported another candidate for the post of federal interventor in that key electoral state; nor was he at all popular in the strategic state of São Paulo, which had been defeated by the revolutionary government in 1932 and whose governor had been president-elect when the Aranha-inspired Revolution had broken out. The governor of Bahia, moreover, opposed the idea of another *gaúcho* in Catete, wanting instead to see a northerner as the "official" candidate. Aranha's only chance therefore was to secure the unconditional support of a united Rio Grande do Sul in the hope that this endorsement would swing the election, and at the end of 1936 he took advantage of the Buenos Aires Peace Conference to return home to mend political fences.[5]

There was, however, to be no reconciling Governor Flores da Cunha with Vargas, and Aranha's candidacy collapsed in the spring of 1937. Embittered by the failure of his weeks-long efforts, the ambassador returned to Washington in April. Another early casualty was Macedo

Soares, who resigned as foreign minister while still in Buenos Aires, immediately after the close of the peace conference. Macedo Soares's entry into the race was a result of an unrealistic assessment of his projection in the national arena and of the possibility of securing Vargas's endorsement. His candidacy therefore never really got off the ground. Outside the state of São Paulo his support was virtually nil, and even within São Paulo his strength was far from decisive, since the governor, Armando Salles de Oliveira, was himself a candidate. After a brief effort, Macedo Soares fell from public view, to be resurrected for a brief period by Vargas in June, when the president offered him the portfolio of Justice.[6]

In mid-1937 the political pot began to boil. The "official" candidate selected at a "convention" in Rio late in May was José Americo de Almeida, a native of the northern state of Paraíba, former minister of transportation and a revolutionary of 1930. José Americo was liked by neither Flores da Cunha, who threw his support to Governor Armando Salles of São Paulo, nor by Vargas, who like other conservatives grew progressively alarmed by Americo's increasingly radical, populist stance during the campaign.[7]

The release by Macedo Soares of numerous political prisoners in June and the end of the state of siege that same month led to open and bitter debate in the press and legislative chambers. Integralist and leftist opponents once again clashed in the streets, oftentimes leaving dead and wounded, as Brazil seemed to be reliving the turbulent early months of 1935. But this time some roles would be reversed. Góes Monteiro, now chief of staff, and backed by Minister of War Dutra, began carefully moving troops and shifting commanders in preparation for taking revenge on Flores da Cunha, who once again was belligerently challenging the federal authorities and decrying an obvious drift toward dictatorship.

The last phase in the drama began on October 1, when the military ministers, seizing upon an alleged Communist plan for a new revolt— the Cohen Plan—pressured the administration into securing declaration of a state of siege. The leading generals in Rio, headed by Dutra and Góes Monteiro, had already committed themselves to a change of regime, and the state of siege was the necessary first step in stifling potential opposition. Integralist leader Salgado, sounded confidentially by Vargas on the possibility of cooperation in a "new order," publicly supported the administration. In turn, the government encouraged Integralist propaganda, which was helping to create a climate propitious for the projected coup d'état, and, in a personal encounter with Salgado, the president even offered him the portfolio of Education after the new regime was launched.

The hour of truth for Flores da Cunha now came, as the government removed supervision of the state of siege in Rio Grande do Sul from his hands and then ordered the integration of the state militia with the federal army. When the militia commander quietly placed his men under the authority of the regional army commander, Flores stood alone. His hasty departure for exile in Uruguay marked the end of his running battle with Góes Monteiro and Vargas, and it removed the major potential military obstacle to execution of the plans for extending Vargas's mandate and decreeing a new constitution. At the end of October a presidential emissary left on a special confidential mission to secure the acquiescence of northern governors in those plans. The parade of thousands of greenshirts through the streets of Rio on November 1 gave, in the eyes of foreign observers, an ominous tinge to events, although the alliance between the government and the party was justifiably more uneasy than it appeared.[8]

Discovery of the plans for a coup led the conspirators to act on November 10. With the military firmly behind him, Vargas dissolved congress, nullified the constitution of 1934, and promulgated a new charter creating the Estado Novo. This constitution greatly strengthened the powers of the executive, lengthening his tenure of office to six years, permitting consecutive terms, and authorizing him to govern by decree. It provided for a national economic council, to be composed of representatives from different agencies of production and having some legislative powers. A congress was to be chosen only after a plebiscite had ratififed the new order, but during the eight remaining years of Vargas's rule the new code was never submitted to a popular vote. Under the state of emergency proclaimed at this time, Vargas ruled by decree. That night he went on the radio to explain his action to the nation. "The constitutional organization of 1934, poured in the classic molds of liberalism and the representative system, revealed lamentable faults," he said. The former charter was "outdated in relation to the spirit of the time . . . and intended for a reality that had ceased to exist."[9]

The abandonment of parliamentary government, the corporative nature of the new system, and Vargas's radio message touched off widespread speculation on the imminence of a full-fledged Fascist state in Brazil. The *New York Times* fretted that Brazil appeared "to have posed the problem of a Fascist government in this hemisphere." It was "a dangerous development and the contagion may spread," warned the *Washington Post*. "The Nazi-Fascist axis has extended to our own Americas," cried a St. Louis daily, and *Newsweek* magazine agreed that "Getulio Vargas Makes Brazil First Fascist State" in the Western Hemisphere. Senator William Borah told newsmen that he believed the new regime had every characteristic of Fascism and that he opposed "contributing in any way to the success of a system that is at war with every principle on which republican government rests."[10]

Rio de Janeiro was quick to deny that the dictatorial move foreshadowed any changes in foreign policy. Pimentel Brandão issued a statement assuring that there would be no such shifts and refuting the rumors of Brazil's imminent adherence to the Anti-Comintern Pact.[11] When Caffery queried him about the implications of the new constitution and a possible increase in Integralist influence, Pimentel Brandão replied that the Integralists were "clowns in the political circus" and that a desire to check the growth of the movement had been a main reason for the coup.[12] Hull informed Caffery of the emphasis being given by the American press to the "Fascist nature of the new set-up" and instructed him to confer privately with Vargas to determine whether there was any basis for the claims of Rome and Berlin that the coup was a sign of sympathy for the Axis. The secretary wanted full information, "specifically with regard to any possible increased influence . . . of the German and Italian governments." He also recommended that American consuls in Brazil be ordered to keep a close watch on developments among the German and Italian colonists. Vargas told Caffery that it was "laughable" to imagine that the totalitarian nations had anything to do with the coup. He said that the new constitution was not Integralist, Nazi, or Fascist and that his government had "absolutely no connection with Rome, Berlin, or Tokyo."[13] Despite these disclaimers, the Estado Novo was a jolt to Washington and remained for some time a source of concern.

Italian and German circles warmly hailed the new order. "*Lo Stato corporativo in Brasile*," exulted a leading Rome daily, while Foreign Minister Galeazzo Ciano called in the Brazilian ambassador and expressed Italy's "sympathy for the policy of Vargas and promised him the support of the Italians in Brazil."[14] The reaction of German authorities was one of "suppressed elation," as American correspondents in Berlin privately termed it.[15] Apprehensive that ebullient press coverage might spur Washington to intervene more energetically in Germany's economic relations with Brazil, the Nazi government ordered the press to be moderate in its commentaries. Vargas, above all, should not be designated as "our man."[16] After talking with a Wilhelmstrasse spokesman, Moniz de Aragão had the "best possible impression" of Germany's attitude. "Partisans as they are of regimes strong and anticommunist in character," he reported, "the attitude of these circles toward the important decisions taken by our government could not be otherwise."[17]

The German embassy in Rio de Janeiro enthusiastically greeted the new political order: "As for the effect of the turn of events on Brazil's relations with Germany," wrote a thoroughly pleased Chargé von Levetzow, "it can neither economically nor politically be an unfavorable one, since the president, who is friendly toward us, remains in power." Although as a matter of principle Vargas believed in "free trade," the chargé continued, "he recognizes Germany's special position and desires the continuation of compensation trade in order to facilitate the sale of Brazilian products." It was therefore unlikely that he would "submit" to American pressure and abandon the arrangement with the Reich.[18]

Neither von Levetzow nor Karl Ritter anticipated the ensuing political conflict with Brazil. There had been signs lately of a local reaction in the southern states to Nazi activities, but the chargé expected no real trouble from the federal authorities.[19] On the eve of his departure for Rio de Janeiro in the latter part of November, Ritter told a correspondent that there were no political differences between the two countries and said he could not imagine any arising in the future.[20] The German diplomats did not have long to wait for proof of their miscalculation.

Scattered throughout the southern states of Paraná, Rio Grande do Sul, and Santa Catharina were approximately 100,000 German immigrants and over 800,000 *teuto-brasileiros*. The colonists and their descendants had retained most of their Old World culture and formed what the Brazilians called "ethnic cysts." In the atmosphere of intense nationalism that witnessed the conception and birth of the Estado Novo, the proselytizing efforts of Nazi agents became increasingly offensive to Brazilian leaders, particularly army planners concerned with internal security, and they determined to force the assimilation of the foreign colonies and bring a halt to the propagandizing of a foreign political party on Brazilian soil. The ban on the NSDAP in April 1938, which followed proscription of domestic political organizations the previous December, and restrictions on the use of German in the private schools converged to give the "Brazilianization" campaign the appearance of a general drive against German cultural and political influence.[21]

Brazil's relations with the Reich reached their lowest point after an Integralist putsch in May 1938. Vargas's break with the greenshirts had been one of the great surprises of the Estado Novo. Following establishment of the dictatorship, Salgado had been informed that his participation in the government was now contingent upon dissolution of the Integralist organization, a step the party directorate resisted. A decree of December 3, clearly aimed at the Integralists, formalized the break. Not only were all political parties forbidden, but also any civic militias and auxiliary organizations. The use of uniforms, banners, and special emblems or insignia was likewise prohibited. Salgado lost control over the party, more militant subordinates asserted themselves, and the result was an attempt in May 1938 to seize the government. In the most dramatic incident of the revolt, Vargas and his family and house attendants stood off a group of insurgents at Guanabara Palace until help arrived. The revolt, a hasty, ill-organized affair, was limited almost exclusively to Rio and was easily suppressed. It was the only internal political challenge that Vargas would face until 1945.[22]

Why did Vargas turn on the Integralists, when he so obviously shared many of their sociopolitical ideas? A conspicuous motive was a desire to remove a potential challenge to his own authority. Despite common belief that the party had the support of the armed forces, senior army officers also favored removal of the party as an organized political force. The party's dedicated supporters in the upper ranks of the officer corps were clearly a minority, and most of them placed unity of the armed forces above the party's survival. Only one general actively participated in the planning of the May 1938 revolt, and plotters with the rank of colonel were noticeably absent.[23]

Considerations of foreign policy, moreover, were probably involved in Vargas's decision to eliminate Integralism as an organized political force. The alarm and consternation with which American opinion had received the Estado Novo—established as it was with the assistance of a Fascist party—combined with American sensitivity about German trade penetration of Brazil, created a potentially serious diplomatic situation. Brazilian policy makers considered the maintenance of strong ties with the United States essential to Brazil's international projection, especially in South America, and one of the advantages Vargas may have seen in checking the party was the reassurance this would give to a crucial diplomatic partner that the Estado Novo was a *Brazilian* phenomenon. The anti-Integralist drive, at any rate, did allay much American anxiety and was interpreted by interested parties as having been intended to do precisely that. Pointing to the prohibition of political organizations in December, the American chargé noted with relief that "it would appear that the danger of the Integralists coming into power has passed." Vargas's move, he suggested to Washington, represented in part a "keen desire" to erase the impression abroad that Brazil was "tending toward the Rome-Berlin axis," a view his German counterpart shared.[24]

American relief over the unexpected break between Vargas and the greenshirts stemmed from the assumption that Integralism and Nazism, or Fascism, were one and the same, and that more than coincidental ties bound the Integralist and Nazi parties. Although Integralism "wears the garments of rabid nationalism," one American journalist typically remarked, "it is in reality a hot-house product of German official intrigue."[25] The Integralists admittedly borrowed a great deal in ideology, tactics, and symbols from similar European movements, and they made the greatest headway in precisely those areas of heavy German settlement: Rio Grande do Sul, Santa Catharina, and Paraná. But, far from welcoming the movement and abetting it, German observers actually feared it, essentially because the party's nationalistic insistence on creating national cultural as well as political unity threatened German cultural interests in Brazil. During 1935–1936, German observers, private and official, sounded a continual cry of alarm over the spread of Integralism.[26]

Their opposition to Integralism notwithstanding, German interests suffered along with the greenshirts in the government's drive against political parties and foreign activities within Brazil. Momentarily convinced that German agents had aided the Integralists in their May 1938 putsch, Brazilian authorities arrested several Reich citizens, a step that prompted sharp criticism of Vargas by the Nazi press. The situation created considerable ill will between the two countries, and the objectionable conduct of Karl Ritter heightened the antagonism. Aranha, who had objected vigorously to the November coup but who was subsequently persuaded to take charge of Itamaraty, could not abide Ritter, and the two had several disagreeable encounters. Relations continued to deteriorate during ensuing months, and finally

Brazil informed Berlin at the end of September that its envoy was *persona non grata*. When the German government retaliated three days later by asking for the recall of Moniz de Aragão, a complete break between Brazil and the Reich seemed imminent.[27]

Rather than an augury of a worsening of the conflict, the forced withdrawal of ambassadors was actually a cathartic, as neither country wanted political strife to impair their valuable economic ties. Brazilian policy makers by 1938 were more certain than ever that the nations of the world were engaged in a "furious economic struggle"—they had proof of this at home—and that such "old" procedures as most-favored-nation treatment were insufficient. "Brazil will perforce have to seek an approximation with those countries with which it has fewer economic incompatibilities," agricultural spokesman Torres Filho reminded government and business leaders in March of that year.[28] Heading the list of such states was, of course, the Third Reich, whose importance in Brazil's foreign trade rose considerably in the immediate prewar years.

During the three-year period 1936–1938, the respective percentages of imports supplied by Germany were 23.50, 23.88, and 24.99, according to official and allegedly slightly inflated statistics. Brazil's principal imports from the Reich by 1938 included coal, chemical and pharmaceutical supplies, cement, iron and steel products, electric motors, appliances, sewing machines, and typewriters. Germany also played an enlarged role in Brazil's export trade: during the biennium 1937–1938 its purchases went up nearly 50 percent over 1936, and in the last year before the war it provided the South American country with over 19 percent of its total revenues from exports.[29]

Germany retained its newly won position as the principal market for Brazilian cotton with purchases of 85,000 tons in 1937 and 82,000 tons in 1938. These represented over 30 percent of Brazil's total cotton sales abroad for the two years. Viewed from Berlin's standpoint, the share of the total volume of the Reich's imports of cotton enjoyed by Brazilian exporters rose from just under 26 percent in 1937 to over 32 percent the next year.[30]

Germany's consumption of Brazilian coffee increased from around 75,000 tons to over 100,000, making it the leading customer after the United States. By the end of 1938 the Reich also ranked second to the latter as a consumer of Brazilian cacao, having bought nine times the amount it had the previous year. As a market for Brazilian hides and skins, Germany ranked first, with purchases equivalent to 34 and 38 percent, respectively, during 1937 and 1938. The Reich took more than 40 percent of Brazil's tobacco exports during these two years, which made it the principal market for this product. Imports of Brazilian woods went up sixfold in 1938, to put Germany in second place behind Argentina as a customer. Although rubber occupied a relatively minor place in Brazil's export trade at this time, it is significant that sales to Germany exceeded those to all other countries combined. Brazilian oranges were another product that the Reich imported in much greater quantities during the biennium: in 1937 purchases were 160,000 cases, and during 1938 consumption was more than 600,000 cases.[31]

The groups in Brazil with a stake in close economic ties with the Reich were therefore numerous and insistent in 1938. From cotton growers in São Paulo and the North to cattle ranchers in Rio Grande do Sul; from tobacco and cacao planters in Bahia and Pernambuco to lumber exporters in Santa Catharina; from rubber-gathering enterprises in the Amazon region to citrus farmers and coffee *fazendeiros* in São Paulo, Paraíba, and Rio de Janeiro—from all these interests came appeals in the latter part of the decade for protection of their German markets.[32]

And, as Hitler's plans for expansion became increasingly discernible, the possibilities of greater sales to the Reich looked more promising than ever.[33] The Reich was now Brazil's leading European market and second only to the United States as an overall trade partner, Moniz de Aragão pointed out in a press interview at the beginning of the year. "Consequently, you understand our strongest interest in expanding still further all our commercial and economic relations with you," he declared. The fact that the trade balance for the first months of the year was registering a deficit of several million pounds also concerned policy makers in Rio de Janeiro—"That is a matter that I keep my eye on always," Souza Costa privately remarked in May—and made them even more anxious to retain existing outlets and avoid surpluses. "In my frequent conversations with the Brazilian authorities regarding the German situation," wrote American Chargé Scotten, "they have frankly admitted their ever present fear of losing the German market for coffee and cotton." With the coming cotton crop expected to be the largest in Brazil's history, "maintenance of the German market is an absolute necessity," one newspaper editorialized.[34]

Early in 1938 discussions also took place in Berlin between Brazilian officials and representatives of German firms on Brazil's plans for a steel industry, a project dear to Vargas's heart. Siemens, Krupp, Demag, and Stahlunion, which had some property rich in iron ore in Brazil and had shipped some sixty thousand tons to Germany the previous year, all expressed an interest in exploiting Brazil's ore reserves and assisting in the establishment of a steel mill. Since coal was a major problem, Siemens suggested the use of hydroelectric power and was informed that Vargas would receive a concrete proposal "with attention and interest." During negotiations for further artillery contracts, Krupp expressed its willingness to assist Brazil, and it subsequently joined Demag and Stahlunion in an informal arrangement to explore the matter further. Although the latter companies balked several weeks later because of the political situation in Brazil,[35] the idea remained alive, especially at Krupp. The possibility of aid from Germany for a project vitally important to Brazilian leaders was an additional recommendation for cautious management of the dispute over the political activities of German agents in Brazil.

Because of the existing and potential importance of Germany for the Brazilian economy, the government in Rio de Janeiro made every effort to keep politics and economics separated in the quarrel with Berlin. Vargas himself, on each occasion that he talked with Ritter that spring, "noticeably" underscored his desire to expand economic relations with the Reich. Aranha, now seeing matters from a different vantage point and deeply concerned about national defense, stressed the importance of commercial ties in his communications with Moniz de Aragão on the subject of Ritter's behavior, and the Brazilian envoy in turn advised the Wilhelmstrasse that his government wanted "very strongly" to see trade between the two nations "thrive" and that it simply believed that Ritter's disagreeable nature made achievement of that goal more difficult. When von Levetzow called at Itamaraty on October 5 to report that Moniz de Aragão was no longer welcome in Berlin, Aranha took the occasion to emphasize once more his interest in commercial ties with Germany. São Paulo authorities also tried to work privately around the political squabble to promote an "intensification" of trade.[36]

Berlin shared this desire to prevent any serious disruption of commerce with Brazil, a source of vital raw materials. Under the stimulus of rearmament and general mobilization for war, Germany's demand for cotton had increased enormously since 1933.[37] The Anschluss with Austria in March 1938 inflated the demand for raw materials and foodstuffs, which could be acquired only through expanded exports, and weeks later the Ministry of Economic Affairs signalled the building up of stocks of raw materials and food supplies as the basic task of trade policy.[38]

Following Brazil's ban on foreign political parties, Ritter cautioned the Auswärtiges Amt against letting political friction affect economic relations. A trade war would bring "perceptible losses" in the Reich's stores of raw materials, he noted, and London and Washington would only step in if Germany withdrew from the Brazilian market. Moniz de Aragão discovered that the Wilhelmstrasse was "very apprehensive" about the trouble in Brazil. Berlin wanted to clear the air right away, he was told, in order to maintain friendly relations, "which it considers necessary and useful, having in mind the great commercial interests at stake."[39]

In the latter part of June the Banco do Brasil found itself with large stocks of compensation marks, a result of heavy German buying. To discourage further sales to the Reich until offsetting imports had been realized, the Banco suspended purchases of the blocked currency. When some German newspapers criticized this move, an alarmed Ministry of Economic Affairs informed the Wilhelmstrasse that it was "absolutely necessary" to make a conciliatory statement to Moniz de Aragão. He should be told that Berlin "in no way whatsoever" wanted to disrupt trade with Brazil. Ministerialdirektor Emil Wiehl, Ritter's replacement in the Auswärtiges Amt, talked with Moniz de Aragão a few days afterward and assured him that the government deplored the press items. At a subsequent departmental meeting it was agreed that the "seriousness" of the raw materials situation made protection of the Brazilian trade imperative.[40]

The withdrawal of ambassadors produced "grave misgivings" in the Ministry of Economic Affairs. Schlotterer reminded a Wilhelmstrasse official that "from an economic point of view Brazil was for us by far the most important country in South America." The Reich now would need another eighty thousand tons of cotton a year to provide for the newly incorporated Sudetenland, and Brazil happened to be "the only supplier that could be considered," because of the shortage of foreign exchange. It was therefore "most important," Schlotterer appealed, "that economic relations not be disturbed through further deterioration in political relations." The Wilhelmstrasse spokesman realized that this argument was a weighty one, since "Brazil's economic significance for us is very great and is constantly increasing."[41]

The Munich episode encouraged a new meeting of commercial minds. If it was clearly only a stopgap measure in the struggle to avoid war, did it not also create commercial opportunities? Before the settlement—but when it was clear that Czechoslovakia would be truncated, only days after Neville Chamberlain's historic trip to Berchtesgaden—the commercial attaché in Paris had written Vargas that "Germany's continental hegemony can now no longer be denied or doubted." Having absorbed Austria and on the verge of gaining the Sudetenland "without a shot, the Reich is increasing its population by thirteen million inhabitants!" he exclaimed. And the implications of the final accord seemed clear—"Is it possible to imagine a greater economic victory for the Reich?" asked the ambassador in London.[42] With Germany apparently destined to control much of Europe, would it not be politically prudent to remain on reasonably good terms with Berlin?

Vargas and his advisers asked the questions and found the answers. To satisfy Germany's greater demand for raw materials arising from its territorial expansion, Aranha and Souza Costa informed von Levetzow in mid-November that they would agree to a 15 percent increase in the cotton quota and a 10 percent hike in all other quotas. Because of American pressure, the chargé reported, the Brazilians preferred the "old tactic of tacit continuation" of the agreement to a public acknowledgment of its extension. Resumption of full transactions in compensation marks by the Banco do Brasil days later—it had earlier renewed purchases of such currency derived from all exports except cotton and cacao—left German authorities, a Brazilian official in Berlin hyperbolized, "pleased, very satisfied, and delighted." An exchange of notes early in December extending the compensation agreement for six months was hailed by von Levetzow as the "most important event" in the perceptible change in Brazil's attitude toward Germany since Ritter's recall.[43]

Although the controlled Brazilian press toned down its criticism of German foreign policy, the Vargas administration refused to make any concessions of substance in its campaign against German cultural and political influence within Brazil, and Berlin declined to force the issue, rejecting all retaliatory measures. One such step, a proposed mass exodus of German settlers from Brazil, met with successful opposition in the Wilhelmstrasse. The head of the American Department argued that "German interest in the smooth-running evolution of German-Brazilian commerce is too great to be interrupted by any kind of political burden." Economic experts in the Auswärtiges Amt concurred. It would be "prejudicial and even dangerous" to attempt to bring such pressure to bear on Rio de Janeiro in the hope of attenuating its nationalistic drive. Germany's need for Brazilian raw materials, especially cotton, was "exceptionally urgent," and any increased friction between the two countries would be welcomed and "most intensively exploited" by the United States.[44]

The fact that trade weighed much more heavily than politics in determining the official German position toward the squabble with Brazil found expression in various ways. The Brazilian Commercial Bureau in Berlin was pressed about the possibility of acquiring raw materials "on a much greater scale," a phrase that the bureau's director used in two letters to Vargas in January 1939. The Auswärtiges Amt, moreover, acted quickly to still impolitic newspaper criticisms that Rio had acted under American influence to hinder compensation trade, and it even apologized to the Brazilian embassy. Fearful of "difficulties for our trade with Brazil," the Wilhelmstrasse also urged German firms to refrain from using "Heil Hitler" on correspondence with parties in Brazil, in order to avoid offending the nationalistic sensibilities of Brazilian postal censors.[45]

The possibility of participating in Vargas's pet project for a steel mill—and thereby enormously increasing the Reich's influence and prestige—contributed to Berlin's acquiescence in the Brazilianization campaign. On learning at the turn of the year of Vargas's "firm intention" to make a reality of this long-time dream, Krupp informed him through Souza Aranha of its "greatest interest" in assisting Brazil. The German firm proposed that Brazil meet a "considerable portion" of the cost of the mill with raw materials, a decided attraction to Brazilian planners. After "numerous" meetings with Souza Aranha, the president allegedly sent word to Krupp that he would "preferably" deal with Germany and that he would make no definite decision without consulting Krupp.[46]

Germany's interest in Brazil was a function of intense preparations for war, and Brazil's interest in the Reich was likewise determined largely by the imminence of the gravest international developments. If Berlin was eager to assure what was one of its major sources of foodstuffs and raw materials, particularly cotton, Rio de Janeiro looked anxiously to Germany as a source of the items it needed for military preparations. For Vargas's counselors, at least his military ones, armaments were even more important than steel.

The economic goal of the Estado Novo was that of the period 1930–1937: economic development, with heavy emphasis on industrialization. The difference was that, with the extinction of congress and suppression of organized parties, politics was virtually eliminated from economic policy decisions. What more than ever determined policy after November 1937 was the assessment of national interests made by Vargas, his closest civilian advisers, and, especially, the army high command upon whose support the regime rested.

The military view of the international environment had changed during 1937–1938 only in the sense that the anxieties that it produced had reached new heights. A key ingredient in the pessimism and concern of Brazilian leaders was the tempo of Argentina's military build-up. Various reports during 1937 from the embassy in Buenos Aires on Argentina's military preparations, coupled with the continuing European crisis, deepened, Góes Monteiro confessed, "in startling fashion" the fears of policy makers in Rio de Janeiro.[47] The Destroyers Episode in August, in which an outcry from Argentina blocked the leasing by Washington of six overage destroyers to Brazil, greatly reinforced Brazilian mistrust of the La Plata adversary. Brazilian officials were incredulous at the opposition. "Fear in any country toward Brazil's actual naval power," Aranha told a reporter, "would be the same as a man armed with a machine gun being afraid of another armed with a simple pocketknife." There were indignant outbursts in the Brazilian press and legislative halls as the country bristled at Argentina's intervention. So alarmed were Brazilian leaders that war with Argentina was now seen as a distinct possibility.[48] The navy quietly took stock of its fuel supplies for the Mato Grosso flotilla and surveyed defense capabilities at its air base in Rio Grande do Sul, while Góes Monteiro sent directives to regional commanders in the South and West on mobilization procedures in the event of a surprise attack.[49] To examine the Argentine situation *in loco*, Góes Monteiro the following spring visited Argentina, where the undisguised "hostility" of the Argentine minister of war deeply impressed him. Upon his return to Brazil the general immediately put his staff to work on guidelines for defense against a sudden attack from the south.[50]

The acquiescence of the great powers in Hitler's program of territorial expansion took on ominous meaning that year and heightened the sense of urgency with which Brazilian planners considered defense needs. On the day after Hitler rode triumphantly into Vienna, a Brazilian colonel opened the new course at the General Staff School with a speech on the need for immediate preparations for war, particularly in view of "certain manifestations in Europe in regard to a new division of South America and, especially, Brazil." The leading military journal, *A Defesa Nacional*, sounded a continual alarm during 1938. "Are we or are we not an independent state?" it asked rhetorically in mid-year. "If so, let us arm ourselves as quickly as possible . . ." In October the journal, in a reminder made ominous by Munich, warned that the world was divided into "colonizing peoples and colonies. Unhappily," wrote an editor, "there is no place for intermediary categories." And, given recent events, he said, Brazil must dedicate itself "body and soul" to military preparations. That same month, days after the ill-fated Munich Conference, General Dutra urged Vargas to organize defenses against air attacks, and naval planners initiated studies for laying mine barriers at Rio de Janeiro and other ports. In a confidential report to Dutra early in 1939, Góes Monteiro once again stressed the disconcerting possibility of an ill-prepared nation finding itself suddenly and unwillingly at war.[51]

The sense of urgency that dominated military perceptions of national security needs explains why the high command did not actively lobby during 1938–1939 on behalf of long-range development projects, such as a major steel complex, but instead campaigned to improve immediate defense capabilities. Military leaders understood the importance of heavy industry, and the army provided technical assistance for steel projects. But, in government thinking, the plans for a major steel complex and those for defense preparations were separate things. Vargas, for example, in his speech proclaiming the Estado Novo, stressed the need to install heavy industry and "also to provide the armed forces with efficient equipment." One staff officer, describing in *A Defesa Nacional* how best to defend the national "homestead," symbolically outlined the military's unavoidable choice between long-range development and short-term security in a world heading for disaster: "Employ the maximum of our resources on the construction of a strong fence of rails and barbed wire, on the purchase of ironwork, crossbars, metal plates for the safety of the doors, and a launch for the steady surveillance of those wanting to cross over from the other side of the river," he admonished. "Once this is done, we can, in the shelter of this defense, plant, raise, and manufacture."[52] Brazil, in other words, had first to obtain the means of combat, in order to give the nation the security necessary for economic development. A steel industry would, of course, contribute to the nation's ability to fend for itself in a turbulent international society, but it would do so only in a general sense—particularly since the future Volta Redonda complex was never intended to produce armaments—and only after years had been spent planning, financing, constructing, and expanding it. Immediate national defense was a different and more pressing concern for military planners, who believed that they were operating on borrowed time.

The officers who participated in steel discussions were consequently not major power holders in the high command. Major Edmundo Macedo Soares e Silva, who played a significant role in helping to clarify technical aspects of the alternative steel plans whose analysis the Vargas government pressed—now that congressional stumbling blocks and political ferment had been eliminated—was an army technician with no political influence. He had, in fact, spent most of the decade in Europe on special commissions. The other military figure usually cited in connection with the steel issue was Colonel João de Mendonça Lima, who had assumed the portfolio of Transportation late in 1937. Prior to entering the cabinet, Mendonça Lima had been director of the government-owned railroad, the Central do Brasil, not a post aspired to by staff officers or the military-politicos. He reached the cabinet because of his experience and administrative skills, and he did not command the kind of personal support within the officer class that a Góes Monteiro did. "A young man who has had no political career, but is regarded as a competent administrator," was how British embassy experts characterized Mendonça Lima in 1938.[53]

As minister, Mendonça Lima's primary interest logically was rolling stock, and that is where the emphasis lay in his proposal for exchanging iron ore for railroad equipment, coal, and a steel mill. During the period of intense debate in government circles on the steel question, Mendonça Lima was stressing to Vargas the "urgent necessity" of acquiring new railroad equipment and underlining the possibility of bartering raw materials for German machines. The fate of Mendonça Lima's iron ore plan demonstrated that policy initiative on the steel issue remained in executive councils.[54] When the proposal was put forth early in 1938, Vargas paid little attention to it, allowing a newly created Technical Council on Economy and Finances, the "voice of private enterprise" in the Estado Novo, to study the various options. The Council rejected the idea of a steel plant dependent upon foreign coal and recommended the separation of iron ore exports from the steel plans. When the CFCE, which followed closely the progress of compensation trade with Germany and undoubtedly thought in terms of facility of payment, revived the idea of trading ore for a steel plant, Vargas again shelved the plan, this time definitively, by sending it to the National Security Council "for further study." The formula finally adopted was the separation of ore exports from steel.[55]

The most influential military figures of the Estado Novo, Minister of War Dutra and Chief of Staff Góes Monteiro, were most actively concerned about armaments and other military supplies. General Dutra, in his annual report to Vargas delivered in May 1938, devoted only two sentences to "our steel problem." Dutra, furthermore, was not talking about a project like Volta Redonda but about improving and utilizing existing steel plants, such as one at Sabará, where tests had led in 1937 to a decision to use locally produced steel for rifle barrels, an achievement that delighted the high command because it reduced dependence upon imported steel. Góes Monteiro was unequivocal in a secret memorandum on defense requirements in January 1939. What the army really needs, he wrote, was "copious" military equipment. The distribution of the army's official share of funds under the five-year Special Plan announced that same month also reflected the short-term orientation of military planners. The funds were to be applied to the "first phase" of the program for "development of our Military Industry," Dutra informed Vargas. Priorities included increased production of cartridges at the Realengo plant and grenades at the War Arsenal in Rio de Janeiro, completion of a gas mask factory, and new machinery for regional army repair shops.[56] The army launched at the same time a program to assist cooperative civilian industries by providing technical assistance and financial support through defense contracts and encouragement of Banco do Brasil loans. The undertakings "of greatest importance for the creation and development of new industries" included contracts with copper and aluminum producers, São Paulo firms producing munitions, nitric acid, and machinery, and orders for steel from the mills at Sabará and Neves.[57]

The indispensable complement of increased production of munitions and light matériel was the acquisition of armaments abroad, a defense measure that had found increasing support among key civilian policy makers. Aranha from Washington in mid-1937 had cautioned Vargas about Argentina's defense expenditures and admonished him that "we must arm ourselves, placing vast orders, cost what it may." During the Destroyers Episode, Souza Costa privately wrote that the proper reply to Argentina would be to build up military capabilities "without advertisement, but with efficiency." The incident, he noted, had "served more than words and arguments to generalize the conviction." Months later Caffery, in assessing Brazil's tenacious adherence to bilateral trade, noted that nobody questioned the wisdom of military purchases. "It is a subject on which there is near unanimity of opinion," he wrote.[58]

Discussions with various foreign manufacturers of artillery about an expanded armaments program were in progress in 1937, but financial conditions kept Krupp in a favored position. Despite a deficit of nearly $30 million by August, the government that year had conceded, in accordance with a secret law of November 1936, hidden credits to the army of over $9 million. In October, Vargas approved a third secret credit of $2.4 million for the purchase of aircraft.[59] With a treasury suffering from chronic anemia, compensation trade at least had the advantage of making it possible for Brazil to meet military demands for equipment, an argument Aranha used with American officials. In August the General Staff forwarded a Krupp bid to Vargas with a favorable evaluation, and overtures for higher quotas for exports of raw materials were subsequently made to Berlin in the hope, the German embassy perceived, of accumulating compensation marks to cover additional arms contracts.[60]

The domestic political crisis culminating in the Estado Novo greatly increased the administration's dependence on the armed forces. Important details of the conspiracy, particularly those involving Vargas and the military plotters, remain obscure, but there is some evidence that the president found himself obliged either to reiterate former pledges or give new guarantees to the army regarding acquisitions of matériel. Aranha, for example, later confided to Ambassador Caffery that a major reason why the army had supported Vargas in 1937 was that he promised to "stop payment on the [foreign] debt and to let them have the money." Vargas, in fact, immediately after the coup decreed suspension of service on the debt, an act that elicited a prompt warning from Caffery about the "most unfortunate" reaction in the United States.[61]

Lending substance to Aranha's assertion are comments by Góes

Monteiro in his confidential annual report for 1937 as army chief of staff. In the document, presented to Dutra early in 1938, Góes Monteiro twice hinted at a political understanding with Catete. The army, he said at one point, "deposits its hopes in the Government's promise" to restore national military power. Later on he expressed confidence that the administration would fulfill the "commitments that it assumed to equip the Armed Forces" with the means necessary to defend the country. After the coup, Vargas's repeated public references to the necessity of providing the military with new equipment were perhaps in part a reflection of a political understanding with the high command.[62] Not that his commitment to heavier military expenditures was solely payment of a political loan: Vargas, like other civilian leaders, shared the military's perception of a threat to national security. But it is unquestionable that his continuation in power depended upon the high command's good will, which in turn would hinge on realization of the armaments program, a task to which the government quickly turned.

Negotiations lasted until March 1938 because of delay caused, on the German side, by short-lived competition between Krupp and Rheinmetall and, on the Brazilian, by Souza Costa's reluctance to sanction the cost of the projected order. With SOINC's assistance, agreement was finally reached on payment terms for a substantially reduced consignment that the finance minister persuaded the army to accept. Krupp gave the Rio de Janeiro government the "option" of paying for three-fourths of the cost—around Ł8 million sterling—in compensation marks that Brazil would earn from extraquota shipments of raw materials to Germany. A fourth of these additional German imports were to consist of coffee, and the remainder of any products needed by the Reich. These terms were the least onerous for the treasury, Souza Costa assured Vargas, given the fact that satisfaction of the army's demand for equipment was "absolutely nondeferrable." The contract signed on March 28 called for delivery over a six-year period of nearly nine hundred pieces of artillery ranging from howitzers to antiaircraft guns, with ample munitions and some transport equipment. General Dutra sent Vargas a confidential note of appreciation the following day, promising in return to circulate a secret document among army officers informing them of the "great favor" Vargas had done them.[63]

In the sale of armaments, Germany had a weapon of decisive significance in its battle with the United States and Great Britain for influence in Brazil, since neither of these two competitors was in a position to participate in Brazil's armaments program. Washington's policy was precisely the opposite of Berlin's; that is, it discouraged private exportation of arms and munitions to Latin America, although it sympathized with the disappointment of its agents at the resultant increment in the "political and commercial prestige of our European rivals." Nevertheless, active efforts to promote private sales, Welles had explained a few months earlier, would "not only be futile so long as we are not disposed to accept payment in kind, but would probably in the end weaken rather than strengthen our prestige throughout the hemisphere." Foreign Office spokesmen were more realistic than their American counterparts, but they were helpless. On learning of the Krupp contracts, the Foreign Office, dismayed at having been treated "shabbily" by Brazil, immediately undertook to devise an offensive policy to counteract the German coup. The War Office, however, reported that it would be impossible for Great Britain to supply any war matériel to Brazil, and the Treasury Office rejected the idea of diplomatic remonstrations. The Foreign Office argued that a protest "in a spirit more of pained surprise than of anger" might lead Rio de Janeiro to reconsider the placing of official orders with German manufacturers when it had suspended service on its foreign debt. The Treasury and private banking circles nonetheless steadfastly opposed the idea. "Of course, I agree with you that the Brazilians are dirty dogs," explained a Treasury spokesman, "but my point is that I do not think it would help the bondholders to tell them so." Ambassador Gurney also recommended against any official demarche, and the matter was dropped, leaving the field to the Germans.[64]

With the Krupp order of March 1938 the alliance between the Brazilian high command and commercial bilateralism was greatly reinforced. The army, wrote Dutra to Vargas, would now receive "what it most needed: the armament with which the country's defenders must wage war." The interest of the Ministry of War in the maintenance of friendly relations with the Reich was accordingly of supreme importance now, as Karl Ritter realized. Brazil would continue compensation trade, he confidently predicted during the height of his dispute with Itamaraty, because it was to Brazil's advantage and "especially" because military leaders supported it "in the interest of rearmament."[65]

Ritter, of course, was right. Financial problems, military weakness, and trade opportunities all combined to act as a constant stimulus to the clearing of the political air. As the level of threat perception rose in 1938, the high command stepped up its pressure on national finances. Five secret decree-laws in 1938 opened new credits for military purchases, and in January 1939 the five-year Special Plan established additional annual credits of over $4 million (80,000 contos) for the armed forces. Moreover, the sum allotted to the Ministry of Finance under the plan—some $14 million (275,000 contos) per year—was actually intended as cover for secret army and navy contracts. With no foreign exchange, there was only one direction to go.[66] Souza Costa endorsed additional contracts complementing the major Krupp order, and General Dutra hailed the renewal of the modus vivendi with its increased quotas as a new opportunity to expand defense purchases.[67]

The arrival in March 1939 of the first consignments of artillery ordered two years earlier greatly enhanced the prestige of German suppliers. The international scene also encouraged conciliatory gestures toward Berlin. Only days before, Hitler had violated the Munich agreement by sending troops to seize what remained of Czechoslovakia, and war obviously was a matter of time. Gratified that Germany was providing sorely needed equipment for national defense, Vargas was anxious to firm up his diplomatic position with the European power. On March 24, after inspecting the new artillery, he made a short speech to the assembled military leaders in which he declared the bankruptcy of the old foundations of social and political organization. "Nations are seeking new forms of equilibrium," he asserted with calculated ambiguity, "and the great national coalitions are expelling from their midst all forces of dissension and negativism." Brazil was dedicated to continental defense, said Vargas, but this did not spell hostility toward any country that respected Brazilian sovereignty and laws. His opportunism was obvious. "This appears to be just another way of saying that Brazil should not place all of her eggs in one basket until she is definitely obliged to commit herself in the event of a world war," Caffery wryly observed, "and in this manner squeeze the maximum out of the United States on the one hand and the Fascist powers on the other."[68]

The desire to protect Brazil's interests in both camps prompted General Dutra a few weeks later to send Vargas a lengthy memorandum on foreign policy. The general had recently been in contact with Souza Costa about the possibility of placing further contracts with Germany, now that compensation trade was flowing relatively smoothly again, and he wanted nothing to interfere with the supply of European armaments. Political and economic cooperation with the United States was fine, as long as it did not impede trade with "European nations— our principal markets for war matériel," Dutra admonished. Vargas had no disagreement with the point of view of his military counselors. His notation on Dutra's memorandum called for neutrality in any European war, "examination" of any offers of aid from the United States, and maintenance of full ties with third countries, provided they respected Brazil's sovereignty.[69]

The climate for normalization of diplomatic ties had been forming since the end of 1938, and the keen interest of Rio de Janeiro in obtaining armaments hastened that process. Once Berlin accepted the necessity of acquiescing in Brazil's nationalist campaign, resolution of political differences was relatively easy. In June 1939 announcement was made that Freitas-Valle, Aranha's cousin who had served with him in Washington, had been appointed ambassador to Germany, while Berlin had designated Kurt Prüfer to take charge of the German embassy in Rio de Janeiro. Three weeks later the National Security Council debated the wisdom and feasibility of further exchanges of coffee and cotton for German military hardware. Both Aranha and Dutra argued in favor of gambling on German manufacturers rather than American. The foreign minister believed that, even if war should break out, a way might be found to get compensating shipments of raw materials through the inevitable Allied blockade. Dutra rightly insisted that only Germany could provide certain vital complementary equipment for the artillery already contracted, and he gained a seven-to-four vote in favor of his stand. Over the next few weeks the Ministry of War closed additional contracts with German firms, headed by Krupp, for artillery transport equipment. The cost of this supplementary program was $1.7 million, 85 percent of which was to be paid in compensation marks.[70]

Krupp thus landed its third important armaments contract from Brazil in thirty months. According to company representatives, that contract had been obtained in the face of "very strong American competition."[71] If they were referring to active American competition for the Brazilian armaments orders, then they were probably endeavoring to embellish their achievement for the benefit of Nazi leaders. The Krupp spokesmen were faithfully reporting the facts, however, if they were alluding to widespread concern in the United States about German influence in Brazil and to Washington's recent attempts to draw Brazil more firmly into an informal alliance with the United States.

Washington had watched in dismay and alarm as the European crisis reached increasingly acute levels, and by 1938 it was wondering to what extent South America entered into the calculations of Nazi strategists. Brazil in particular was a question mark as the year opened. All the assurances from Rio de Janeiro had not removed the uneasiness about the seemingly fascistic Estado Novo, which posed for American policy makers a potentially serious problem. The State Department worried that a totalitarian form of government in one country might spread "like a disease" and disrupt the hemispheric solidarity "so painstakingly cultivated" in recent years. Furthermore, the appearance of even a "superficial" totalitarianism might prepare the way for the "economic and political penetration of South America which seems to be one of the aims of Fascist Italy and Nazi Germany."[72] Vargas's nationalistic attack on German influence within Brazil was therefore received with understandable relief and satisfaction in Washington, especially since efforts to persuade him to restrict commerce with Germany had been so unsuccessful.

Throughout the early months of 1938 American publicists and businessmen maintained their vigil against German competition. "Reich's Trade Hold Tightens in Brazil" was the heading of an article in the *New York Times* by a correspondent in Rio de Janeiro; it warned of "an aggressive German commercial drive carried on with the direct aid of the Reich and on the ground here by the best economic and diplomatic talent Germany has to offer." The Axis nations were doing their utmost to win Brazil over, but their sights were not solely on that country, the *Times* editorialized in February. "They extend throughout most of South and Central America and Mexico." Washington was aware of this "threat," yet it remained curiously passive, "apparently" banking on the Good Neighbor policy to protect American interests. "It is doubtful, however, whether this admirable course is in itself sufficient to counterbalance the pervasive and damaging propaganda of the fascist Powers," the *Times* concluded.[73]

Caffery's fruitless and frustrating conversations with Brazilian officials about German subsidies and compensation marks—matters "outstandingly important" to Washington, he admonished Aranha— brought home to him the need for more vigorous action if anything substantial were to be accomplished. The ambassador constantly remonstrated with Brazilian authorities, made press statements implicitly exhorting the Brazilians to join wholeheartedly in Washington's trade program, and sent documents on German competition to Bouças in the hope that he might be able to help, all in vain. There was really only one way to make the point. If the United States adopted "retaliatory measures envisaging definite economic pressure," he suggested in May, "Brazil would change her policy overnight."[74]

But the State Department, despite its preoccupation with Nazi trade gains in Brazil and the rest of Latin America—report in detail on the subject, Welles instructed the missions there in January 1938—allowed the initiative to remain in German hands, holding firmly to its policy of not using material pressure on Rio de Janeiro. Department spokesmen persisted in their reluctance to admit defeat and continued to see achievement in rhetoric. Reading over reports from Caffery on promises made by Brazilian officials, Duggan concluded that the ambassador had mistakenly "minimized" Brazilian efforts to restrict compensation trade. Agreeing, Hull and Welles "assumed" that Brazil was making "earnest efforts" to eliminate unfair competition, and they declined to endorse Caffery's recommendation that pressure be applied. When Scotten visited Washington in mid-1938, he conferred with Welles and left convinced that Caffery had things "sized up exactly right. I do not see the slightest chance of expecting any pressure," he glumly informed the ambassador.[75]

The State Department did move haltingly toward a change in its stand on armaments sales, which were giving Berlin a decided advantage in South America. If private transactions seemed ill advised, perhaps the government itself could enter the business by selling surplus matériel? It would require a revision of existing regulations that banned such official transactions, but the situation seemed to require action. "German and Italian activities in South America are especially pronounced at the present time," read a memorandum sent to the War and Navy departments, "and those two European Governments are endeavoring, with some success, to exert an increased political and commercial influence through their various military and naval missions." After studying the matter, the army recommended that the government push private sales instead. The State Department, however, was unwilling to reverse its policy and encourage transactions over which it would have little control, and nothing immediate came of the talks.[76]

The department was also unwilling as yet to follow the treasury in using United States gold reserves on a large scale as a weapon against Axis influence. Secretary Morgenthau had for some time been mulling over this possibility. One month after Vargas proclaimed the Estado Novo, the secretary had remarked to his staff that economic problems seemed to be pushing Latin American nations into the arms of the Axis. On June 7, 1938, with the headlines of the Integralist putsch and alleged German involvement still fresh in his mind, Morgenthau urged Roosevelt to seek legislative authorization to extend financial aid to Latin American governments "by reason of a violation or threatened violation of the Monroe Doctrine, or by reason of a disturbance or threatened disturbance of the peace of nations of the Western Hemisphere." After conferring with Welles, the president expressed skepticism, fearing that "it would be greatly misunderstood down there and be regarded as a resumption of dollar diplomacy."[77]

In ensuing weeks, as increased German pressure on Czechoslovakia showed that the Anschluss with Austria in March was not the last step in Hitler's expansionist program, and as the State Department's policy of moralistic admonitions to Brazil about German trade competition continued to yield embarrassing results, opinion within the department began to change. The fact that Washington itself had decided to retreat a bit from its previous stand on "unliberal" trading methods by inaugurating a wheat-subsidy program encouraged a reassessment of the department's attitude toward German rivalry. "It has become increasingly clear," wrote the head of the Trade Agreements Division late in August, "that however much the Brazilians may wish to take a stiff position against the Germans in order to please us, they are under the practical economic necessity of carrying on trade with Germany on terms that cannot be determined by Brazil alone." In view of the wheat-subsidy plan, he saw "a very real danger" in continuing to press Brazil about German methods, a judgment in which other department officials concurred. Idealism would have to make concessions to realism; other means would have to be found to check the Reich's trade advance in Brazil. With the statistics of Brazil's commerce with a Germany bent on conquest showing a steady rise, the use of America's wealth to bolster hemispheric defenses against perceived totalitarian inroads looked a great deal less like dollar diplomacy and more like a positive and necessary step to defend the hemisphere. It was necessary, urged Secretary of Commerce Roper, for the United States to be more "aggressively alert."[78]

The Munich crisis late in September and Germany's absorption of the Sudetenland promised to be a turning point in American policy toward the German trade challenge. Washington's anxieties deepened markedly in the face of Hitler's latest triumph, and Roosevelt privately expressed apprehension about the "unfortunate fact that the fuss and pushing and guns on the other side are coming closer to our country all the time."[79] What was next? he wondered. Perhaps Trinidad and Martinique? Before that happened, he vowed to Secretary of Interior Harold Ickes, the American fleet would seize the islands. To the nation Roosevelt revealed his evaluation of Munich by announcing an increase of $300 million in defense spending.[80]

Throughout ensuing weeks the question of Axis competition in South America occupied public attention. Elder statesman Bernard Baruch, a friend and sometime Roosevelt adviser, returned from Europe mincing no words: "The natural course is for the aggressor nations to seek penetration into this hemisphere, and with their usual thoroughness they have been doing it for some time." Arthur Krock cautioned readers of the *New York Times* that South America, a "target of steady propaganda for the fascist ideologies," was "ripe for infiltration, first at the expense of our commerce southward," ideas echoed by Warren Pierson, director of the Export-Import Bank, in a special article for the *Times* after a two-month tour of South America. "Today the challenge is being thrown down in every Latin American country," and, warned Pierson, "commercial penetration is frequently followed by political domination." German rivalry in South America was naturally a major theme of discussion at the annual convention of the National Foreign Trade Council, which opened in New York on October 31. Delegates warned of "intensified competition from the totalitarian states, not only in trade, but in the field of ideas," and others called for a vigorous commercial offensive to offset the Nazi trade thrust. "We cannot sit by complacently and expect by conversation, the passing of laws and regulations, or by exhorting each other, that we are going to get anywhere in South America," one banking representative told a sympathetic audience.[81]

Morgenthau watched the latest triumph of German diplomacy with dismay, and he now seized upon the changing mood in the United States to revive his earlier recommendation that American gold be used to bolster Latin American resistance to Axis blandishments. If aid were not extended, he pleaded in a message to Roosevelt on October 17, the Latin American countries would become a "helpless field for political and economic exploitation by the aggressor nations." The secretary and his staff were not interested in short-run solutions. They envisioned not only gold loans for currency stabilization and credits to clear up commercial arrears, but also long-term development loans aimed at a basic restructuring of national economies. A primary objective of such assistance would be to "encourage the growth of democratic institutions in Latin America and to check the incursion of political and commercial practices inimical to the peace, ideals and economic interests of the United States."[82]

This scheme, a forerunner of postwar foreign aid programs, would not be a revival of dollar diplomacy, Morgenthau explained in another memorandum to Roosevelt on November 7, since the loans would be government-to-government and the recipient nation would thus be free from the "unfortunate tactics" of private creditors. Indeed, the program would actually promote good-neighborliness, he argued, since the purpose of the financial aid would be "really to help Latin American countries and thereby help this country, rather than to help this country at the expense of Latin American countries."[83]

Rather than approaching the matter on a Pan-American basis, Morgenthau recommended to Hull that bilateral negotiations be held "on specific problems, specific situations, and between specific Treasuries." The place to start, he said, was Brazil, a country that for a number of reasons presented both an opportunity and a challenge. It had vast economic potential, yet it lacked capital and it was plagued by perennial financial instability. Furthermore, he reminded Roosevelt, "the presence of large German, Italian and Japanese minorities makes Brazil especially vulnerable to anti-democratic movements."[84]

Generalized anxiety about alleged Axis political designs in South America now brought support for Morgenthau's ideas from other governmental agencies. Early in November, Warren Pierson of the Export-Import Bank met with Pimentel Brandão, who had traded places with Aranha the previous spring, and stressed to him that, if Brazil could find a way to restore the confidence of American investors, "there was no limit to what might be done toward the strengthening of her domestic economy." Settlement of the debt question would be a giant stride toward an economic alliance between the two nations, said Pierson, who was "extraordinarily" insistent on bringing Brazil firmly into the American camp. Another major obstacle was Brazil's commercial relations with Germany. "According to him, it's impossible for us to continue to say one thing and do another . . . ,"

Pimentel Brandão informed Aranha. Sumner Welles reinforced Pierson's bid days later when he told the Brazilian envoy that the United States wanted to adopt "a policy of absolute financial and military solidarity" with Brazil and urged that Rio act to placate disgruntled American creditors. Pimentel Brandão was delighted with this attention. As a strong advocate of a total alliance with the United States, he regretted his government's trade policy. A few weeks earlier he had written to Vargas outlining Brazil's possibilities in the United States. The only hurdles, he had told Vargas, were the debt question and "our commercial practices with Germany, which are manifestly contrary to the treaty commitments we undertook with this country and which we have always professed to recognize and respect." The overtures now from Pierson and Welles seemed to strengthen his argument. "Our time has come," he somewhat dramatically suggested to Aranha. "We have to decide: the United States or Germany."[85]

Policy makers in Rio de Janeiro, however, did not share this restricted view of the options available to Brazil. Why sever or even relax commercial ties with Germany? How else could Brazil secure armaments? Berlin, after all, was delivering while Washington made promises. If the economic partnership with Berlin continued, would Washington retaliate? Hardly, Brazilian leaders told themselves. Everything indicated that the Americans were more eager than ever to accommodate Brazil, and their pronounced uneasiness about alleged German political objectives in South America even gave Brazil new leverage.[86] It was "obvious" to Vargas that the United States had to view its security requirements as embracing the whole hemisphere, and if it failed to respond to a challenge it would find itself in the same position as those European powers that had recently "abandoned their smaller allies, thus losing them and at the same time losing whatever credibility and prestige they still enjoyed."[87]

Confident that it could continue to trade with Germany without any reprisals—indeed, that trade seemed to make the Americans even more eager to accommodate Brazil—the Vargas government not only restored but expanded compensation transactions. At the same time, Brazilian leaders skillfully encouraged Washington's fears in an effort to obtain economic and military concessions. Aranha had written Welles after Pierson's visit, probing an old wound by reminding him that the Germans were offering lower prices and better credit terms. Late the following month, when Assistant Secretary of State Breckinridge Long visited Brazil as Roosevelt's personal representative to inaugurate the Munson Line's "Good Neighbor fleet" servicing the east coast of South America, the Brazilian government turned up a "dangerous" plot, allegedly originating with Hitler himself, to convert Brazil, Uruguay, and Argentina into Nazi-dominated states. The "very defense of the continent and its institutions is at stake . . . ," Aranha warned in a letter to Hull that Long carried back to Washington. The foreign minister revealed the aim of this ploy in a subsequent letter to Welles. If Brazil would get military and naval aid, he said, it could "easily and victoriously" meet any Axis challenge. "To arm Brazil is to prepare the defense of half of South America and enhance the security of the other half," he declared.[88]

The signals produced the intended reaction by leaving Washington authorities "deeply preoccupied" with the question of German activities in Brazil.[89] On November 14, two days before the news of the alleged Nazi plot reached Washington, a "momentous" meeting on national defense had taken place at the White House. Roosevelt's concern for the security of the hemisphere was manifest. For the first time since the days of the Holy Alliance, he told his civilian and military advisers, the United States was confronted with the "possibility of an attack on the Atlantic side in both the Northern and Southern Hemispheres."[90] And now the suspicion of German intentions in Brazil was seemingly vindicated.

On receiving Aranha's letter, Welles first made certain that Roosevelt agreed that a projected joint resolution authorizing the War Department to sell matériel to Latin American governments would take care of Brazil's request for military aid. He then assured Aranha in reply that the United States wanted to assist Brazil "in every effective way possible." On the economic front Morgenthau moved forward with the blessings of both the White House and the State Department. Through the Brazilian financial attaché he sent a message to Souza Costa—a message he "insisted very emphatically . . . was of exceptional importance"—saying that Washington was "keenly" anxious to help Brazil with its financial and economic difficulties. The secretary later repeated to Pimentel Brandão that the United States wanted to cooperate "on any commercial, economic or financial plane." All that was necessary was to know Brazil's needs, said Morgenthau, since the White House had said "by all means go ahead."[91]

At the end of November, as they made ready to renew the modus vivendi with Berlin, Brazilian officials replied to the overtures from Washington. Souza Costa indicated that long-term credits would be desirable, especially to acquire railroad equipment. Brazil also owed $3.5 million in overdue commercial payments and could use a loan to clear these up. While recognizing the need for a settlement of the foreign debt, Souza Costa said that this would have to wait until commercial arrears had been paid and other measures taken to stimulate exports. Both he and Aranha brandished again their most effective weapon: European competition. Some of the credit proposals were "really interesting," Aranha informed Pimentel Brandão in a letter that the ambassador subsequently read to Welles. In an obvious maneuver to better terms from Washington, Souza Costa told Morgenthau that credit offers from Europe, "mainly German," were only for six years.[92]

The Lima Conference, a regularly scheduled inter-American gathering, temporarily delayed the American-Brazilian negotiations, but its results also heightened Washington's desire to reach a special understanding with Rio. The conference opened on December 9. Hull personally headed the American delegation, and Aranha prevailed on his old friend Melo Franco to represent Brazil. The secretary of state was now convinced that "the danger to the Western Hemisphere was real and imminent." The Axis threat indeed lay at the heart of the debates, and, according to Hull, Berlin actively strove to counter the American thrust. "The Germans sought in every way to cast the shadow of the Axis over the conference and to intimate to the delegations that they had better take account of the new forces in Europe and Asia," he later wrote.[93]

As the delegates gathered in the Peruvian capital, American observers kept the challenge of German economic penetration of Latin America before the public. Gaining markets in that region, one publicist claimed, was "a matter of life and death" to Berlin, which was engaged in a "desperate drive" to achieve its aims.[94] *Time* magazine spoke of Germany's lead in its "seesaw race" with the United States for the Brazilian market, and the Inter-American Center of George Washington University sponsored a three-day forum to debate the question "Can the United States Retain Latin American Trade and Cultural Relations Against German, Italian and Japanese Competitors?" In his major address at Lima, Hull spoke eloquently of the military and political threat that certain aggressive nations posed to all countries—"Their ominous shadow [even] falls athwart our own Hemisphere"—and then reminded his audience that there were other kinds of dangers and that it was necessary to keep up the struggle against the "artificial channels of narrow bilateralism or exclusive regionalism." In private conversations he also remonstrated with Latin American delegates about compensation trade with the Reich.[95]

The results of the conference were not what Hull had hoped for, as once again Argentina blocked a strong resolution on continental solidarity. With Melo Franco's help, he finally got Buenos Aires to agree to a diluted statement pledging consultation in case the "peace, security, or territorial integrity" of an American nation was threatened in any way. But Argentina secured the loophole that would permit her to follow an independent course vis-à-vis the conflicting blocs: "It is understood that the Governments of the American Republics will act independently in their individual capacity, recognizing fully their juridical equality as sovereign states," read one paragraph in the Declaration of Lima.[96]

Although Washington officially hailed the Lima meeting as a milestone in hemispheric relations, privately there was substantial disappointment within government circles, and, before Hull even got back to Washington, Roosevelt authorized Welles to telephone Aranha and sound him on the possibility of his coming to the United States for special negotiations on military and economic cooperation between the two countries. When Vargas approved the idea, Roosevelt sent an official invitation that was promptly accepted.[97]

By early 1939 American perceptions of South American nations, particularly Brazil, as victims of, and vulnerable to, Axis economic and political pressure had hardened into conviction. Within the State Department the concern was general. Josephus Daniels, ambassador to Mexico, found Hull in mid-January "in a more pessimistic mood about Pan America than I had expected after his public report of the Lima Conference. He thinks Germany is trying to get footholds there by barter transactions and otherwise." J. Pierrepont Moffat, chief of the European Division, foresaw trade rivalry in South America "fought not only with increasing intensity, but with illegitimate methods," and he also feared greater meddling by the Reich in the internal politics of countries in that region.[98]

Breckinridge Long's visit to Brazil months before and Aranha's startling revelation of the alleged Nazi conspiracy led him to serious thinking about the United States position in South America, and in January 1939 he tried unsuccessfully to sell the government on a scheme to set up a special federal corporation to buy up Latin American surpluses and then resell them. This plan, he said, "has the definite purpose to free certain of the South American republics from the strangling effects of both the totalitarian states and to diminish the influence of those states in the internal affairs of our natural political friends." But Welles and Feis objected to the proposal and it was abandoned. The under secretary preferred to await the results of discussions with Aranha, hoping that they would produce a program for assistance to Brazil that could serve as a model for aid to other countries.[99] The next twelve months, he remarked to Morgenthau, would be the most significant "in the history of the State Department, and the Treasury, as far as South America goes."[100]

Treasury experts, of course, agreed that Brazil was a crucial test case, indeed was the "key to the American system." Roosevelt, too, was sharply aware of Brazil's strategic importance and the possibility of German-fomented political turmoil in that country. Only days after inviting Aranha to Washington, he discussed the international situation with his long-time friend Ambassador Daniels and indicated "that the first danger to us would come from Brazil." Suggestive of influential opinion in congressional spheres was a speech by Key Pittman, chairman of the Senate Foreign Relations Committee, a short while after Aranha's arrival. Addressing the National Radio Forum, Pittman declared that "these dictatorial powers are through every means, monetary, financial and political, preparing for the domination of Latin America."[101]

A propitious atmosphere thus seemingly awaited Aranha, as he sailed for the United States on January 29, accompanied by his *chefe de gabinete* Dantas, who once again was working for the Banco do Brasil, and two other officials. During the voyage the delegation discussed projects and negotiating strategy. They were well aware that Axis interest in Brazil was their trump card. One memorandum drawn up for delivery to the Americans stated that assistance for Brazil's development, particularly in the areas of steel and transportation, had been offered "on several occasions by the totalitarian countries—Germany, Italy, and Japan—whose need for raw materials is urgent." If American cooperation was not forthcoming, then Brazil would be "forced to accept that of some other industrial power. The expansion of our commerce with Germany in recent years," read the memorandum, "is but a sign of Brazil's need to supply itself economically, paying for its equipment with the only money that it possesses—raw materials."[102]

As the *Nieuw Amsterdam* approached New York, Aranha finished a

lengthy letter to Vargas outlining his expectations. They were high because the international climate appeared to favor Brazilian interests
more than ever. "Everything indicates that the American government,
because of the situation in Europe and Asia, has now become convinced," he wrote, "that it must drop that puritan policy of 'good-
neighborliness' in favor of the creation in America of markets and
great, strong natural allies, especially since if it doesn't do it, other
nations will try to." If things went according to plan, he jokingly
exaggerated, "you run the risk of drowning with your government in
a fountain of gold and achievements."[103]

The reception in Washington seemed to confirm his forecast. It was
the "friendliest possible," he wired Vargas. Brazil had an "open field
for great possibilities" in all areas. "One senses in everything and
everybody the desire to please us, to show how earnest this country
is in wanting to collaborate with us," another member of the delegation informed the president.[104]

Aranha displayed his ace on every occasion. At his first press conference, on February 9, he spoke of international conditions and the
German colonists in Brazil and affirmed that "all friendly people have
to fear Germany."[105] Brazil was ready to side with the United States,
but "suppose a country in South America should be attacked. Are
you sure the American people would favor the United States going to
that country's assistance?" he asked with a mischievous grin.[106] In his
initial meeting with Welles and Morgenthau he stressed the effectiveness of German competition in the Brazilian market and "constantly
referred to what the Germans were willing to do." A week later, in
a speech to the National Press Club, he again raised the specter of Axis
advances. "We must realize that we are in a world of forces which are
trying to subjugate each other, and that America offers the only ex-
panse of fertile land still unexploited and having an abundance of
natural resources . . .," he declared, going on to chide his audience because American participation in Brazil's development was of "insig-
nificant proportions when compared with that of other countries."
Morgenthau the next day complimented him on "an awfully good
speech." "The Nazis will not like it much," replied Aranha. "And they
had their people there," Morgenthau observed. "I guess they know
where you stand."[107]

Such good will had to be rewarded—in America's own interest.
"Brazil has been within an ace of jumping clear away from us within
the last two or three years," one Treasury Department official thought,

while within the State Department there was concern that Aranha's "bluntly written" memorandum was a warning of precisely that possibility.[108] Morgenthau agreed, and the memory of the 1937 failure still nettled him. "I mean I went all through that with Brazil last time and spent weeks and weeks, and it was purely window dressing and nothing happened," he complained. Morgenthau suggested, in addition to aid in clearing up Brazil's back payments to American exporters and possible backing for a central bank, the establishment of a United States–Brazilian Development Corporation to be funded in part by the Treasury Department and in part by American banks and private citizens from both countries. Morgenthau wanted to act quickly so Aranha "could show the folks back home that his mission was meeting with considerable success." Welles was "simply delighted" with the idea, and Aranha saw it as a possible avenue to steel and petroleum industries for Brazil. But Vargas was cautious. It was "more complex" than the other projects, he said, and would require careful study.[109]

The German trade problem was not forgotten. Indeed, it was much on the minds of Hull's tireless adversaries. The United States had made reciprocal agreements in good faith, groused one congressional critic, but the behavior of some signatories reminded him of those "old first Mondays in which all the horse traders came to the swapping place and . . . profited on an unlearned and unsuspecting buyer." Sure, the Axis rivals were making "tremendous inroads" in South America and the United States was "sore about it," but what could be done? one senator wondered.[110] The American negotiators did not push the issue as vigorously as they had in previous years, and they contented themselves with the hope that an Export-Import credit for Brazil would help the American exporter in his rivalry with German merchants. State Department experts also got the Brazilian negotiators to agree that the Banco do Brasil would try to control more tightly all transactions in compensation marks, to avoid accumulating surpluses of such currency.[111]

Military assistance was of paramount importance to Rio de Janeiro, and the first item on the agenda that Hull had suggested for the talks with Aranha was cooperation in Brazil's defense program. Roosevelt was anxious to promote a military understanding with Brazil, and he pressed Aranha for an exchange of visits by the Brazilian and American army chiefs of staff, Góes Monteiro and George Marshall, to discuss defense needs and forms of cooperation. Brazilian military leaders were skeptical and wanted to wait until Aranha's mission was completed to see what practical results it yielded. Vargas sought more information on the military purpose of the proposal, or "does the visit have purely political aims?" he asked. Aranha acknowledged that Washington was motivated by political considerations, but he also stressed the potential military benefits of personal contact between army leaders of both nations.[112]

Armaments were what really interested Brazilian leaders. Before Aranha left for the United States, army leaders had outlined general matériel requirements for him, and in Washington he met with repeated assurances that the United States would provide the equipment Brazil desired.[113] But words were the only thing Roosevelt could give at the moment. Providing arms depended on congressional approval of a bill, introduced in the House early in March, authorizing the War Department to sell surplus arms at cost. It rapidly became clear to Brazilian leaders that Washington could not make good on its promises. Indeed, during Marshall's visit to Brazil in May and June, the American military attaché was reduced to expressing to Góes Monteiro his hope that the Brazilian army would be able to take delivery of the German artillery according to schedule.[114]

After all the fanfare, the results of Aranha's trip seemed meager. Washington's hands were legally tied as far as military equipment was concerned. Welles tried to get the Treasury Department to issue a statement flatly guaranteeing a gold loan for the elusive central bank, since otherwise "the whole thing blows up and is a complete flop and failure."[115] But Rio de Janeiro had no specific plans for setting up a central bank in the foreseeable future, and Morgenthau did not see how he could commit resources to an undefined project. The promise of future assistance in the undertaking was therefore only more window dressing until Brazil took the initiative.

Because of congressional limitations on the lending power of the Export-Import Bank, Aranha carried home a letter from Hull saying only that the Bank had "agreed to consider" a long-term loan to Brazil to finance the acquisition of "economic equipment" from American suppliers. Vargas was not overly enthusiastic about the joint development corporation, so that scheme bore no fruit. The only concrete, immediate aid the mission obtained was a short-term credit of some $20 million to settle commercial arrears with American shippers. In return, Aranha promised that exchange controls would be abandoned for commercial transactions and that Brazil would resume payment on the dollar debt beginning July 1.[116]

On the way home aboard the S.S. *Argentina*, Aranha telegraphed
Hull that the negotiations signaled "a new era of closer collaboration"
that would create "a safer, happier and stronger continent," but in-
wardly he was doubtless deeply chagrined. The glowing reports he
had sent Vargas! We will get at least $100 million, he had predicted.
"The whole country is following with interest the progress of your
mission to the United States," had been the reply from Catete. And
now he was returning home with promises and what Morgenthau
would subsequently dismiss as "mere pin money," and even that
destined for goods Brazil had already received. Welles drafted a letter
to Roosevelt "frankly" pointing out that Aranha was dissatisfied, but
that, because of restrictions on Export-Import capital, "we are doing
as much as we can." On second thought Welles decided not to send
the letter.[117]

The domestic storm was already breaking before Aranha reached
Rio de Janeiro. When the results of the mission became public, the
response in Brazil was "disappointment, especially in military circles."
Summing up widespread sentiment, the influential *Correio da Manhã*
noted that "today we have a very real commercial relationship with
certain European countries, and we cannot abandon it in exchange for
vague promises."[118] The exchange director of the Banco do Brasil immediately resigned in protest of Aranha's pledges on exchange controls and compensation trade.[119]

Vargas wired the White House his appreciation for the "courtesies
and hospitality" shown his foreign minister, but the generals had
hoped for more tangible benefits. According to Caffery, they "bitterly
attacked" Aranha for promising to resume service on the dollar debt.
The new ambassador in Washington, Carlos Martins, who had gone
from Tokyo to Brussels and in the spring of 1939 switched posts with
Pimentel Brandão, cautioned Welles that the army's disgruntlement
was "particularly strong, and even vocal," because it wanted any spare
foreign exchange to be spent on military supplies rather than on the
debt. In Aranha's talks in Washington the smallest sum mentioned
for debt service had been $9 million, but Vargas, under strong pressure
from the army, agreed reluctantly to put up a token payment of only
$1 million on July 1—a "regrettably and decidedly inadequate" step,
groused Hull. ". . . I have to be practical," Aranha explained to Caffery, "and they should realize that it was only by threatening to
resign that I got the million dollars for you."[120]

The foreign minister was so upset about the reaction at home that he suffered a "near breakdown" and went into seclusion for a month at a health spa in Minas Gerais, privately attributing the "atmosphere of suspicion and backbiting" that enveloped his mission to an "organized and intelligent German campaign within the armed forces."[121]

The public reaction in the United States to the Aranha mission tended to be favorable. Many newspapers emphasized a German danger and praised the administration's efforts to check the Reich's penetration of Brazil. "Germany has started an economic war on us," said a West Coast daily, but the Aranha negotiations should thwart Berlin's attempt to make "Brazil a western outpost of Nazi expansion."[122] In Washington, however, there was pervasive discontent over the mission. The administration's opponents complained because too much had been done for a country that, in the view of one senator, "having had many, many millions of dollars from our country, will pay nothing, promise everything and do nothing." He also pointed an accusing finger at Brazil's "double dealing" in playing the United States off against Germany. A colleague concurred: " . . . in my opinion Mr. Aranha, of Brazil, gave this country the finest dry cleaning it has ever experienced." Instead of Washington's seeking the good will of the Brazilians, he fumed, "they should be endeavoring to curry favor with us."[123] Irate bondholders wrote the State Department criticizing the "sucker policy" of lending Brazil money, arguing that, if the administration was going to put dollars into the hands of American exporters, it should also pay bondholders. One chemical firm publicly bemoaned German "depredations" on American business with South America and then protested privately to the State Department about Rio de Janeiro's "increased indulgence" in bilateral dealings with the Reich. "In other words, our economic help to Brazil is being dissipated by Brazil's giving economic help to Germany," wrote an angry company spokesman.[124]

Within the State and Treasury departments there was also embarrassment because too little had been accomplished and apprehension that Aranha's pledges might not be fulfilled. "There is no need to emphasize that if the Brazilian authorities do not act to carry out these agreements," Feis remarked, "it will be a great setback to the whole of our Latin American relations." A State Department assessment in July of the results of the talks noted that to date the "direct benefits" to Brazil had been "small," as the $20 million had been spent and no other funds had been made available. The fault, however, lay not entirely with the United States. Brazil had taken no initiative in submitting a long-range development program or in creating a central bank.[125]

Morgenthau was disgruntled because "mere pin money" had been loaned to Rio de Janeiro, and he told Drew Pearson, a pal of Aranha, that he was "particularly distressed" about the foreign minister's position within the cabinet. "I talked to the president about it this morning," he informed his staff at the end of July. "I said, 'You know, Mr. President, we are right where we were in Brazil and one of these days they will come running to you after some Latin American country has done some big deal with some fascist country. The State Department will say, "For God's sake, save us!" I think it is unfortunate that we have to wait for that to happen.'"[126]

The Fascist country on Morgenthau's mind had watched with concern and indignation the efforts made by Washington over the past two years to forge a Pan-American front against the Axis. In assessing its difficulties with Brazil, Berlin saw the hand of the State Department everywhere and regarded American pressure as the major obstacle to its economic program for that country. The Destroyers Episode late in 1937, coming as it did on the heels of the Souza Costa mission, had been to German observers dramatic confirmation of their evaluation of American policy as one based on the premise that German advances in Brazil had to be rolled back at all costs.

A letter that Hull sent privately to several congressmen soliciting approval of the leasing proposal, which the State Department broadened to include any American state, mentioned that the Brazilian government had recently notified Washington of its growing concern about certain trends in international politics. "The desire on the part of some nations for access to raw materials, and the forceful action taken by those nations to consummate these desires," said Hull, "has made Brazil, a country of vast territory and relatively small population, particularly apprehensive."[127] Release of this letter by the chairman of the Senate Committee on Naval Affairs touched off the public furor that led to the abandonment of the proposal.

German agents were incensed at what they rightly perceived as a critical allusion to the Reich and its allies. "To the American government any means appears suitable to discredit Germany in Brazil and thereby force back German competition to America's benefit," grumbled the chargé in Washington. The naval attaché for Brazil and Argentina thought the incident showed "how intensive the economic and political pressure must be" that the United States was bringing to bear on Brazil. The German press ridiculed the idea of a Teutonic menace in South America. "Everyone knows that Germany pursues solely legitimate economic aims on the American continent," declared the official organ of the Wilhelmstrasse, "and that its efforts are aimed at living in profitable and trusting relationships with all countries of South America."[128]

Having attributed blame for the episode to American desire to weaken Germany's position in South America, Berlin wanted to avoid giving offense to Brazil, and it readily complied with von Levetzow's appeal not to permit the press to use such words as *colony* or *protectorate* when referring to Brazil's relationship with the United States. The chargé feared that such labels would irritate Brazilian authorities and provide fuel for the attacks of Germany's "economic opponents."[129] If he perceived "no cause for excessive optimism" about the outcome of the alleged American campaign to drive Germany out of the Brazilian market, he detected "really less grounds for pessimism." Even if Itamaraty did want to follow Washington's lead, Souza Costa and Vargas would probably be able to assert themselves for continued cooperation with the Reich. But, von Levetzow warned, the United States would undoubtedly proceed with its "struggle for the Brazilian market."[130]

The difficulties that cropped up in commercial relations with Brazil during 1938—and indeed the Brazilianization campaign—seemed to confirm von Levetzow's warning.[131] The temporary cessation of trade in July led one Berlin newspaper to wonder how far the Banco do Brasil's action had been "inspired by friends of the Brazilian economy on Wall Street." Writing in October, von Levetzow cautioned Berlin that Washington was spending "great sums" on political and economic propaganda against the Reich. Warren Pierson's recent visit to South America in September had been, said the chargé, an "additional thrust forward in the American struggle to make Brazil, like South America in general, into a North American sphere of influence."[132] Baruch's public warnings in October about the German threat touched off violent criticism in the German press. In a more restrained statement, the official *Deutsche Diplomatische-Politische Korrespondenz* labeled them part of Washington's "systematic campaign" to check Germany's economic advance in South America.[133] To gather information on "attacks against us by the United States" was a chief objective of the private economic mission to South America carried out at this time by Count Adolf Mecklenburg, a mission given strong diplomatic support by the Auswärtiges Amt.[134]

The Lima Conference occasioned further severe criticism of American "imperialistic" intentions. Before the conference opened, the *Korrespondenz* accused the United States of stirring up "instincts of hatred" throughout the hemisphere "in order to make a military and ideological Monroe Doctrine palatable to the twenty-one states assembled at Lima." The Latin American nations, it warned, "will indeed soon have to ask themselves who is actually the master in Brazil and the other states . . ." On the other hand, "German endeavors in the economic field in the New World are free of any aggressiveness and tutelage."[135]

The Wilhelmstrasse and the Ministry of Economic Affairs laid plans during the period of the conference to provide special funds for propaganda in the "most important South American countries, especially in Brazil." German cotton importers promised to contribute the money, which would be placed at the disposal of the embassies in Rio de Janeiro, Buenos Aires, and Santiago on a 3:2:1 ratio for payment of fees to local editors and journalists, "primarily for the dissemination of German economic news." A portion of the funds was allotted for Lisbon representatives of the "large Brazilian newspapers" to ensure publication in Portuguese of Berlin-sponsored articles on Germany.[136] The Führer himself felt compelled to rebuke Washington for its attitude toward the Reich's commercial policies. "The question, for instance, whether Germany maintains economic relations and does business with the countries of South and Central America concerns nobody but them and ourselves," he angrily declared in a speech at the end of January 1939.[137]

During Aranha's mission to Washington, the attitude of German authorities was one of cordial restraint, unlike their reaction to Souza Costa's similar trip in 1937. Privately, German observers were uneasy about Aranha's journey—this "countermove by the Americans against German trade successes" was decidedly unfavorable for the Reich, said von Levetzow[138]—but the government ordered the press not to editorialize on Aranha's journey.[139]

Ironically, the Germans were perhaps the only ones pleased with the outcome of the talks. The special effort made by Brazilian authorities to allay Berlin's apprehension was a sign that there would be no change in Brazil's policy. Von Levetzow received assurances from Itamaraty that Aranha would resist any attempt by the United States to undermine compensation trade, and Souza Costa emphasized this in two interviews with the German chargé while Aranha was still in Washington. The finance minister indicated that the mission had been a "failure" and laid most of the blame at Washington's door. As for a trade treaty with Germany, which had been discussed recently, Souza Costa preferred the present informal arrangement, since it "would give the North Americans fewer possibilities of interfering." Chargé Thomsen in Washington also learned from an unreliable "reliable" source that the Americans had demanded that Vargas reestablish a democratic form of government and guarantee that he would not imitate the Mexican government, which had expropriated American-owned oil companies in Mexico a year before, and nationalize any American enterprises in Brazil. Vargas, the German envoy was pleased to report, rejected these demands.[140]

Summing up Berlin's impressions of the mission, a Wilhelmstrasse analyst noted that no concrete political or military agreements had resulted and that Rio de Janeiro had exploited Washington's eagerness for closer cooperation in order to get commercial and financial aid without any substantial concessions of its own. "Obviously President Vargas has completely by design left the door open for friendly cooperation with Germany," he concluded.[141]

Berlin had not been idle in promoting such cooperation following Washington's demarche. One of the first steps it took after announcement of Roosevelt's invitation to Aranha was to invite Góes Monteiro to attend Wehrmacht maneuvers, a move von Levetzow had been recommending for weeks because the Brazilian chief of staff was a "decisive factor not only in the area of political relations but also for the development of economic interchange." The Wilhelmstrasse also invited Souza Costa to visit Germany, and it sought to counter Washington's assistance to Brazil with blandishments of its own.[142] Inform Brazilian authorities that "as always" German firms were able and willing to extend handsome credit terms to Brazilian importers, von Levetzow was instructed. Stress our interest in delivering railroad supplies, industrial equipment, and war matériel, said the Wilhelmstrasse. While moving cautiously toward a political rapprochement with Brazil, Berlin also worried about its general position in South America, and two days before Aranha left Washington it decided to send two Wilhelmstrasse trade experts to the region to study ways of making "a more vigorous defense against the offensive measures directed toward us by the North Americans."[143]

In Brazil, the Reich really had small cause for concern. Trade, and especially the overriding significance that armaments had for Brazilian policy makers, ensured Germany great influence in Rio de Janeiro. Once concessions were made to Brazilian nationalism, Berlin had no great difficulty in clearing the political air. A few days after announcement of the decision to exchange ambassadors, Reichsminister of Economic Affairs Walther Funk publicly lauded the "thorough appreciation" that the Vargas government had shown for the Nazi commercial program,[144] and of course that "appreciation" deepened as a result of the complementary armaments contracts signed a few weeks later. On August 12, Freitas-Valle boarded ship for Europe, carrying instructions to promote the "best relations" with Berlin and to remind German authorities of Brazil's "collaboration" by placing armaments orders with Reich firms.[145]

The rapidly deteriorating international conditions augured ill for Brazil's plans for expanded commerce with Germany. The world, noted Góes Monteiro in August, was "openly and feverishly" girding for the conflict.[146] Berlin and Rome had signed their "Pact of Steel" late in May, and, by the beginning of August, Germany was moving cautiously toward the negotiations with Russia that would lead to the nonaggression pact that stunned a frightened world.

As Freitas-Valle sailed for Europe, a German agent also departed on a special, confidential mission bearing the code name "Operation Himmler." The consequences of that mission would seriously hamper Brazilian plans for arming itself with Berlin's aid. They would also lead to the goal—a cessation of Brazil's compensation trade with Germany —that the State Department's policy of appealing to idealism and making pious admonitions had been unable to achieve. The agent was an S.S. officer named Alfred Naujocks. His destination was Gleiwitz, on the Polish border. His assignment was to await a signal from Berlin to lead a group of S.S. men dressed in Polish army uniforms in a fake attack on the radio station in Gleiwitz, thus providing Hitler with a pretext for adding Poland to his list of conquests. At eight o'clock on the evening of August 31, as Freitas-Valle made preparations to pre-

sent his credentials to von Ribbentrop and Hitler the next day, Naujocks, following orders received at noon, completed his mission.[147]
Some nine hours later, at daybreak, troops and planes of the Third
Reich crossed the Polish frontier. Three days later Great Britain and
France responded to Hitler's challenge with declarations of war. Soon
afterward London announced the blockade that would halt trade between Brazil and Germany.

Chapter 7

Epilog: Brazil and the

Great Powers at War

The impact of the coming of war on the rivalry among Germany, Great Britain, and the United States for the Brazilian market was profound. Because of the British blockade, Germany's trade with Brazil and other South American neutrals dwindled to virtually nothing overnight. "A ship here and there detouring over little-used sea lanes to its destination; another slipping along the coast from temporary refuge in an unscheduled port en route" were all that remained of the hundreds of vessels that not long before had briskly plied the Atlantic between Germany and South America.[1] The statistics of Brazil's cotton sales to the Reich dramatically reflected the effects of war: German purchases during the first six months of 1940 were only 3,000 tons, compared with over 53,000 for the same period in 1939. Axis domination by July 1940 of the whole European continent west of Russia, with the exception of Switzerland and the Iberian Peninsula, forced London to extend its blockade, and German trade with Brazil became fond memory for compensation dealers who had benefited from the prewar boom. "What the commercial policy of the United States failed to achieve with its relentless opposition to the expansion of our compensation trade," one Rio daily aptly remarked, "the war brutally realized from one moment to the next."[2]

Flushed with victory after having overrun Denmark, Norway, the Low Countries, and France in only ten weeks and anticipating an early triumph over Great Britain, Berlin authorities did endeavor in mid-June 1940 to salvage Germany's prewar position in Brazilian commerce by promising to purchase "fairly large amounts" of various Brazilian products once the war had ended. The quid pro quo would be an assurance that "no substantial change is made in the present state of Brazil's neutrality."[3] Faced with a bid from a previously excellent trading partner and one now the master of continental Europe, Vargas prudently cultivated German good will. On June 21 he invited Ambassador Prüfer to a private talk and told the German envoy that "he very much regretted the deterioration in economic relations with Germany, which had been caused by the war and in the continuation of which he saw Brazil's salvation." Vargas suggested that the two countries begin negotiations for commercial exchanges, and, for Prüfer's benefit and to convince Berlin of his responsiveness, Vargas took care to express "personal sympathy for the authoritarian states." The Auswärtiges Amt was delighted with Vargas's attitude and instructed the ambassador to inform the Brazilian leader that Germany was "especially willing" to assist him in his development plans. "The Reich Government sees therein a broad and lasting field for cooperation to the advantage of both countries," read the telegram that Prüfer received.[4]

As representatives of the American governments prepared to gather at Havana for an emergency consultative meeting called by Washington to consider the problem of French possessions in the Western Hemisphere, Berlin moved to strengthen Vargas's resolve not to become involved in any anti-German policies. Assuming that he was "anxious to have an impressive proposal from us before the Havana Conference," the Auswärtiges Amt sent word to Vargas on July 10 that Germany would purchase after the war 300 million reichsmarks' worth of Brazilian exports per year, a startling jump from the annual average of 170 million in the immediate prewar years. The increase would cover, said Berlin, future armaments contracts, railroad equipment, and even a steel mill.[5]

Nothing came of this gambit, however, since Germany's failure to move quickly and successfully against England encouraged greater caution on the part of Brazilian authorities. In September 1940, as the Battle of Britain raged, Ambassador Prüfer pointed bluntly to the obvious: Brazil's responsiveness to Germany's commercial overtures would depend entirely on the course of the war.[6] By the beginning of 1942, with the United States at war and Brazil's diplomatic relations with Germany severed, the Third Reich was out of the arena. Brazil's entry into the war in August 1942, following German submarine attacks on Brazilian merchant vessels, was, insofar as it implied cessation of financial and commercial relations, merely recognition of the existing state of affairs.

The elimination of Germany seemingly left the Brazilian market for the British and Americans to dispute. The British, nonetheless, were not as formidable an opponent as the Germans had been (see table 2). London's attitude toward American and German competition in

Table 2 *Percentage Share of Brazilian Imports and Exports, 1940–1942*

	Imports		
	1940	1941	1942
United States	51.0	60.3	53.3
Germany	1.8	1.8	0.0
Great Britain	9.5	5.7	5.8
Argentina	10.8	11.3	16.9

	Exports		
	1940	1941	1942
United States	43.0	57.0	45.6
Germany	2.2	1.2	0.0
Great Britain	17.3	12.2	16.4
Argentina	7.2	9.2	13.2

SOURCE: CFCE, *Dez Anos de Atividade*, pp. 252, 255, 262–263, 271–272.

Brazil and the rest of Latin America had come increasingly to be determined by two novel realities: the political indispensability of maintaining Washington's good will, and inability to do anything about that competition anyway. Great Britain had consequently fought a "rearguard action" in South America during the middle and late 1930s, hoping to defend its own interests behind the shield of the Good Neighbor policy.[7] Writing in September 1938, one Foreign Office expert had succinctly expressed London's volte-face since the beginning of the decade: Given the increase in Axis activity in South America, he said, Britain welcomed the fact that the influence of the United States in that region was "happily enormous." Washington's drive as war approached to forge a Pan-American front had London's endorsement, since, as the Foreign Office noted on the eve of the Lima Conference, this would "only be to our advantage in so far as it may result in an organized attempt to arrest the forward movement of the totalitarian states in the American Hemisphere." For this same reason, London was pleased with Washington's initiative in inviting Aranha to Washington for bilateral talks.[8]

The policy of the United States was nevertheless a mixed blessing, and many British observers wondered if the United States, in combatting German influence in Brazil, might not also eliminate British influence.[9] While Washington acted, complained the London *Financial News* in March 1939, the talk of Great Britain's launching a trade drive in Brazil "reminds us of a slow-motion picture of a car on a wintry morn." Weeks later the *Financial News* was more explicit: ". . . the real sufferer from a concentrated U.S. trade drive in Latin America is bound to be Great Britain." A prominent representative of London bankers and long-time resident in Brazil sharply expressed the resentment of London's apparent passivity felt by British financial and commercial interests. "What are we, the British, doing? Nothing!" he railed. "Just sitting back with inertia allowing our prestige and past performance in all affairs here to fade away."[10]

Germany's absence from the Brazilian market after war spread across Europe did not redound as much to Great Britain's benefit as might have been expected, since the war prevented Great Britain from asserting herself. Engaged in a life-or-death struggle, the island nation strained its resources to the near breaking point, as its industry geared for the production of war items rather than consumer goods. British purchases and shipping therefore had to be concentrated on only absolutely essential items. The Foreign Office worried in the early months of the war about the long-range effects of Britain's wartime retreat from Brazil and the rest of South America: "We may well wake up to find our whole position in South America so seriously affected by this concatenation of circumstances that it will never recover," one official gloomily noted.[11]

But, since Brazil was "near the bottom of the list" in terms of its political importance to the United Kingdom, other influential agencies, such as the Board of Trade and Ministry of Economic Warfare, were little disposed to seek political favors by making economic concessions that might disadvantageously burden the nation. The Foreign Office's reminder in January 1940 that Brazil was "larger and perhaps potentially more important than any other country in South America" simply could not arrest the impositions of international circumstances.[12] Because of the increased wartime demand in many lines, British imports from Brazil rose to approximately 15 percent of Brazil's total exportation during the triennium 1940–1942, while exports to Brazil declined to 7 percent of its total imports. Reflecting the general tightening of the national economic belt, British nominal capital invested in Brazil began a descent from £163 million in 1939 to half that amount in the immediate postwar years.[13]

London authorities little relished the idea of taking a permanent back seat to the United States in South America, although for reasons of high policy there was no serious thought of a confrontation on the issue, and by late 1942 government councils were turning attention to ways of placing bets on future trade dividends in South America. There seemed to be hope, since London perceived in Latin American countries "a distinct tendency to look to friendship with the United Kingdom to save them from too close an embrace with, and possibly, if remotely, some measure of absorption by, the United States." The policy most likely to succeed seemed to be that of the "honest broker," which meant that "it would be our task to reassure the Latin American countries that an increase of United States influence will not imply monopoly and domination, if only because we are the friends and associates of both parties; and to reconcile the United States to the retention by us of a 'special' position in what they regard as primarily an American sphere of influence by helping them to secure the willing co-operation of the American republics."[14] London spent the rest of the war trying to devise means of implementing that policy, for it was clear that there was no hope of ever challenging the United States for economic supremacy in South America, especially in Brazil. ". . . American influence in Brazil . . . is so preponderant," the British embassies in Washington and Rio were agreed, "that there can be no fear of rivalry from Great Britain, much as the Brazilians may seek to hold out this bogy in order to extract further rewards."[15]

The war, by closing the major European markets, had indeed forced Brazil to look to the Western Hemisphere for commercial interchange. The European conflict seemed to offer an excellent opportunity to expand sales of manufactured goods, and Vargas, in accordance with his long-time dream of making Brazil the industrial entrepôt for South America, dispatched a special trade mission to several neighboring countries in the fall of 1940 to explore market possibilities for light manufactured goods. The results of the mission were uneven, but a further step had been made toward Vargas's goal.[16] The effect of the war on trade with some countries, notably Argentina, was dramatic, in absolute terms. Prior to the war Argentina had taken less than 5 percent of Brazil's exports, but by 1942 that percentage had doubled and by 1943 it had risen to over 13 percent of the total. Argentina's sales to Brazil increased from 12 to 17 percent of Brazil's total imports during the period 1938–1943.

In the main, it was the United States that made the greatest gains in the Brazilian market as a result of the war. The possibilities were obvious, of course, and once the conflict began Roosevelt immediately instructed the Department of Commerce to "make particularly earnest efforts to hold the Latin America trade that would be diverted to us from the belligerent nations."[17] Private business eagerly turned southward now that European markets were shut off. "Chicago industries are preparing for an invasion of the Latin American market on a scale never before attempted . . . ," a regional newspaper announced in December 1939.[18] In Brazil's case, the American share of the import market rose from 24 percent in 1938 to an average of 55 percent for the first three full years of war, a level more or less steadily maintained for the rest of the war. Largely for political reasons, the United States undertook, through a series of special agreements, to cushion Brazilian producers against the shock of losing European outlets, and, for military reasons, it very early in the war began stockpiling strategic raw materials produced by Brazil. The result of all this was a marked increase in American absorption of Brazil's total exportation. In 1938 the United States had purchased about one-third of Brazil's exports; during the period 1940–1942 it bought over 48 percent. In other words, nearly half of Brazil's overseas sales and over half of its purchases were made in the United States.

The war also resulted in American official participation in the development of Brazil's steel industry. Although Vargas had encouraged Krupp's interest in the Volta Redonda project, he clearly preferred to deal with the United States, mainly, perhaps, because a war would not cut off deliveries of equipment and capital. But Krupp's interest gave Brazilian negotiators great bargaining leverage, and they constantly held the German challenge before American eyes. Aranha in mid-1939 had taken care to inform Caffery of the "flattering offer" made by Krupp; and Vargas at the end of the year informed Ambassador Martins in Washington that he would consider Krupp's bid only "if the project should prove unfeasible in that country," a warning obviously intended for transmission to American authorities. When American steel companies, led by United States Steel, decided after lengthy studies not to invest in the Volta Redonda scheme, Vargas stepped up the pressure on the Washington government. Unsheathing his most effective weapon, he wired Martins in January 1940 of his desire to negotiate first with the United States. "If we find no support there, however, we will examine the other possibilities [that] are appearing." The circumstances were favorable and Vargas intended to force Washington's hand. "The United States has a plethora of money and demonstrates good will toward us," he remarked in a letter to Martins the following month. "We need to take advantage of that special situation, and to that end I am counting on your best interest." Martins, in his talks with State Department officials, duly "insinuated confidentially" that German firms were eagerly seeking the steel contract, and this pressure, coupled with press reports on German interest in Volta Redonda, left American officials in a state of "poorly concealed agitation."[19] With Sumner Welles in Europe on a special mission aimed at weaning Italy away from its alliance with the Reich and delaying Hitler's anticipated spring offensive, a mission to which Aranha gave diplomatic support,[20] definitive action from the State Department on the Brazilian steel question was impossible to obtain. After Welles's return, the department began marshalling support for aid to Brazil. In a conference with Roosevelt, Welles, and Jesse Jones of the Export-Import Bank, on April 10, Martins received assurances that the American government would do what it could to assist Brazil.[21]

The end of the "Phony War" in Europe that month shattered any remaining illusions that Hitler could be stopped without total war. Germany's conquest of Denmark and Norway in April; Holland, Luxemburg, and Belgium in May; and France in June left only Britain standing between the Nazi military hordes and Western Hemisphere defenses. The resultant anxiety in the United States about German activities in South America, particularly Brazil, was "great and insatiable," in the words of a Brazilian official on special assignment in New York. Martins early in July urged Vargas to send steel technicians to Washington "as soon as possible, while the American government, worried about the possible economic activity of Germany in South America, is eager to meet our wishes."[22] Ominous reports from Caffery that month heightened Washington's concern. Krupp agents were "working hard and with some success" to land the steel contract, offering "extremely advantageous terms," he warned on July 8. A week later he told the State Department that there were only two factors that might help to stem German penetration of Brazil, the "desire of the Brazilian military" for armaments and the "desire of President Vargas" to acquire financing for the steel project:

. . . if the Brazilian military authorities cannot purchase arms on credit in the United States they will purchase them on long-term credit or accept them as a gift from the Germans. This will eventually be followed by German dominance in the Army and elsewhere. . . . If President Vargas cannot obtain the desired steel plant financing in the United States, he will accept it from Krupp. . . . If the Germans furnish the arms and finance the steel project, or if they do either of those things, it is idle for us to hope to maintain our present position in Brazil. . . . The time has come when we must decide whether keeping Brazil out of the German orbit is worth taking these risks . . . or not.[23]

Caffery's argument impressed the State Department. The steel project was of "utmost importance," Welles agreed. In a letter to the Federal Loan Administration, he warned that American failure to help Brazil would mean that "Germany's predominance in Brazilian economic and military life would thereby be assured for many years."[24] It took a few weeks to iron out details, and then on September 26 an agreement was signed providing for a loan of $20 million for a future steel complex at Volta Redonda.[25] Vargas's long-time goal was now in sight.

If Washington could put up the funds for a development project, it unfortunately could not provide the arms that Brazilian military leaders desperately wanted, and that failure constituted the chief impediment to the wholehearted cooperation that the United States sought from Brazil during the years of neutrality. Faced with deficient supplies of its own and trying to become the "arsenal of democracy" from which the Allies could draw support, the United States could not divert matériel to Brazil. The only armaments supplied by Washington before January 1942 were ninety-nine surplus 6-inch mobile guns that, as the official American history of the subject confesses, "added nothing to the defenses of Brazil, since the Brazilians were not able to get any ammunition for them in the United States or to manufacture it themselves." Under the Lend-Lease program inaugurated early in 1941 Brazil hoped to get up-to-date matériel, but before Pearl Harbor it received "only a few searchlights and a token shipment of automotive equipment and light tanks." Furthermore, despite a great deal of talk in Washington about supplying aircraft to Brazil, the only planes sent before 1942 were three primary trainers.[26]

Privately, Brazilian leaders were highly exasperated by American failure to supply armaments. Returning from a trip to Washington in

October 1940, Góes Monteiro glumly and irritably informed Dutra that "in a few words" he could sum up the results of his attempt to get aid in the "life or death" matter of national defense: little practical progress along the "trail of promises" from Washington since the Aranha mission early the previous year. The minister of war was profoundly disgruntled and complained to Vargas that the United States was offering a "pseudosolution of vague promises, delayed in time, imprecise in quantity and quality, and still subordinated to criteria of priorities that for certain will only redound to our disadvantage." The government, said Dutra, must therefore "with all perseverance" continue its efforts to secure the matériel already ordered from Germany.[27]

This possibility played a vital part in Vargas's tenacious adherence to neutrality in 1940 and his efforts to keep open all channels of communication to Berlin. The German government immediately after the onset of hostilities in Europe had agreed to continue shipments, and early in 1940 the British allowed the last consignment of the Krupp artillery ordered in 1937 to pass through the blockade, since payment had been made before the war.[28] Securing the equipment ordered in 1938 and 1939, however, proved to be a more formidable task. Ultimately only a portion of that matériel ever reached Brazil, and that after a bitter diplomatic squabble with London at the end of 1940. Ironically, it was the American government that smoothed this quarrel over and persuaded the British to allow a major shipment to cross the Atlantic to Brazil. Unable itself to supply the weaponry Brazil needed, Washington was willing to assist Brazil in receiving the armaments whose original purchase via compensation it had opposed.[29]

American intervention in the matter of the Krupp armaments helped to attenuate the resentment in Brazilian military circles over their inability to get modern equipment from the United States itself, and the preponderant role of American capital in Brazil's major development project, combined with American domination of Brazilian foreign trade, ensured a generally cooperative attitude on Brazil's part in hemispheric defense. The Vargas government supported the United States vis-à-vis other Latin American nations in various matters, and during the period of neutrality it moved, albeit at times grudgingly, toward cooperation in other politico-military spheres, such as the elimination of Axis-controlled airlines in Brazil and the leasing of air bases to the United States. Following Pearl Harbor, Vargas unhesitatingly declared Brazil's solidarity with Washington, and at the Rio de Janeiro Conference in January 1942 he announced a severance of relations with the Axis powers. Seven months later Brazil entered the war, and it ultimately became the only Latin American nation to send combat troops to the European theater.[30]

If the Second World War forged the kind of close economic relationship with Brazil that Washington had sought since 1933, that relationship then was unavoidable and, to an extent, artificial. One of the costs to the United States—a cost, to be sure, that brought political and military advantages—was the transformation of Brazil, through specialized training of Brazilian officers and the supply of vast amounts of matériel during 1942–1945, into the major military power of South America. That price Washington had not wanted to pay during the prewar decade, and largely for that reason Brazil had steadfastly refused to abandon its bilateral trade with Germany.

Brazilian military leaders were not representatives of a powerful country who formulated demands on governmental resources in an environment of stability and peace. On the contrary, they were agents of a weak nation in a time of widespread international turmoil. A serious war was fought on Brazil's very borders between 1932 and 1935, and an uneasy truce between the belligerents endured until 1938. Argentina's foreign policy and military buildup throughout the decade was, in Brazilian eyes, a further ominous sign. In 1937 and 1938 the high command seriously feared an Argentine attack. Developments abroad in Ethiopia, Spain, Austria, and Czechoslovakia confirmed the conclusion that Brazil must arm as quickly as it could.

Army planners naturally favored industrialization, but the immediacy of the perceived threat to national security led them to give priority, when lobbying for financial resources, not to long-range development projects, but to production of munitions and small arms and to encouragement of private industries that could manufacture items needed by the armed forces. This policy was continued as war spread across the globe, and by early 1943 it was thought to have yielded the "best of fruits." But, since the primordial concern of the high command was still armaments, and neither any existing civilian industry nor the Volta Redonda plant abuilding could produce armaments, the War Ministry in 1943 was strongly attracted to the possibility of acquiring, through Lend-Lease, complete plant equipment in the United States and producing its own automatic weapons, artillery, and even tanks. Washington's desire to bolster hemispheric defense seemed to

present "a very rare opportunity" to move toward the "complete outfitting of national industry for the production of all war matériel."[31]
Vargas naturally approved the idea and the War Ministry, in response
to a gambit from the United States, decided in mid-1944 to gradually
substitute American for existing Brazilian equipment, provided it
could be manufactured in Brazil.[32] These plans were still under discussion when the war ended.

Throughout the post-1930 period military leaders had expressed
their discontent over matériel inadequacies through consistent and increasingly insistent pressure for funds. The social cost of military expenditures is impossible to assess, since such outlays may have
averted costlier sacrifices, however unlikely an attack on Brazil may
seem in retrospect. Be that as it may, the fact is that a great deal of
money was spent on the armed forces. The combined "official" annual
budgets of the army and navy rose from less than $28 million in 1931
to over $52 million by 1939, and they increased even more during the
war period. Public statistics, furthermore, do not reveal the whole
story, since numerous secret laws and decrees provided the armed
forces with supplementary credits.[33] This financial pressure was
exerted on a government that annually operated in the red, and it
heightened—in the latter 1930s—at a time when Vargas "urgently"
wanted to carry out his steel plans but financing was "still the major
obstacle to overcome."[34] Seen from this perspective, it could even be
argued that the overall effect of military lobbying was to delay the
establishment of Brazil's large-scale steel industry—a project that was
part of the high command's more general and much less urgent vision
of Brazil as an industrial power.

Under the impact of international turbulence, with a relatively
strong and potentially aggressive neighbor on the southern flank, the
high command gave top priority throughout the post-1930 period to
purchases of armaments abroad. The opportunity that compensation
trade offered for acquiring those armaments was a factor of paramount
importance in Brazil's tenacious adherence to bilateralism.

Military leaders, of course, were not the only group interested in
the government's commercial policy. The German trade issue in the
1930s engendered considerable debate within Brazilian government
circles, in the press and legislative chambers, and between business
and commercial associations. Despite the arguments of contemporary
opponents of compensation trade, Brazil on the whole benefited from
the system. German demand for raw materials stimulated a diversifi-

cation of Brazilian exports that relieved somewhat the overwhelming dependence upon coffee. Local economy in many areas was sustained by sales to the Reich. Not only did the country acquire manufactured goods at prices often considerably lower than those of similar products from the United States or Great Britain, but it also was able to dispose of raw materials and foodstuffs for which no other market was available, as had been the case of the millions of sacks of coffee burned to support prices. There was unquestionably substantial merit to the "better blocked currency than ashes" argument.[35]

Agricultural and commercial groups played a significant role in policy formulation, serving as sources of information on local and regional conditions and needs, and as vehicles for feeding back to federal authorities the effects of policy maneuvers. The influence of such groups was naturally most effective and most in evidence during the period 1934–1936, when the commitment of the central government to bilateralism with Germany was being solidified. The apparent decline of active lobbying by associational interests more or less coincided with the demise of the Conselho Federal de Comércio Exterior as an influential component of the decision-making unit. Initially the CFCE filled major functions in gathering and assessing data. The meetings of that body during the early months of its existence were the scene of the most significant debates on policy alternatives, its members had access to full information on negotiations with Berlin and Washington, and its resolutions had the force of policy. Information leaks, combined with an increasing desire for secrecy because of the nature of the understanding with Germany and because of the projected use of compensation marks for armaments, brought a rapid decline in the influence of the CFCE on policy decisions. It received no confidential information on the progress of talks with the Germans in 1936, and during the final stages of those negotiations in late May and early June the CFCE did not discuss the impending modus vivendi.[36]

Itamaraty's influence in comparison with other ministries—where matters of trade and finance were concerned—had never been strong, in contrast to the impact of the State Department on American foreign economic policy. Finding it impossible to get any "real action" from Itamaraty, Gibson early in 1934 began "peddling our business around town in complete disregard of all the official proprieties, but considerably to the advancement of our interests."[37] Itamaraty at that time was under the interim leadership of a career diplomat lacking in personal authority. When Macedo Soares took over the portfolio of

Foreign Affairs, Itamaraty's influence in government councils increased a little, but it never rivaled that of the Ministry of Finance. Vargas had considerable disdain for the average diplomat, who he said was "ignorant of the country's most elementary interests." He wanted to substitute "capable and efficient" men for those "bureaucrats given to promenading."[38] Pimentel Brandão and other officials often complained of executive interference in internal matters at Itamaraty, which reflects a lack of authority on the part of its directors.[39] The bitter dispute between Itamaraty and its key embassy during 1934–1936 undoubtedly contributed to the low esteem that Itamaraty enjoyed in other executive departments. Aranha himself had little use for regular diplomatic channels and preferred direct communication with Vargas or Souza Costa to discuss or clarify issues. The tendency on Aranha's part to circumvent Itamaraty became, of course, more pronounced as friction between him and Macedo Soares grew.

The SOINC negotiations that were largely responsible for the gentlemen's agreement of 1936 were conducted mainly outside official channels, chiefly through Souza Aranha and Souza Costa. If Itamaraty was a full party to the arrangements, it is difficult to escape the impression that this was only because Macedo Soares endorsed the policy of compensation with Germany. The trade discussions of 1937 and the Souza Costa mission revealed fully Itamaraty's lack of institutional authority. Souza Costa and Aranha kept in direct contact with Catete, and Pimentel Brandão was informed only of the results. Clearly, what ultimately determined the relative influence of Itamaraty directors were political power and personal relationship with Vargas. Aranha acknowledged this after becoming foreign minister, when he indicated that his role in the cabinet stemmed more from his personal standing than from his official position.[40]

Aranha's attitude toward compensation trade changed markedly after he returned to Brazil and took charge of Itamaraty. During his three years in Washington he had consistently opposed his government's policy, fearing that it would adversely affect the Rio-Washington axis that he considered essential to Brazilian security and development. His admonitions in this regard rapidly lost their effect, simply because Washington never retaliated as he constantly predicted it would. Once in Brazil, however, where he could see the issue from another vantage point, Aranha supported bilateralism. More than anything else, it was because compensation trade was the most advantageous and effective way to acquire armaments that Aranha, long a champion of national preparedness, modified his stance. The intimate linkage between armaments and trade policy was, of course, a major factor in the narrowing of the decision-making unit to essentially Vargas, Souza Costa, and the army high command.

Vargas was the supreme broker in the trade issue, always seeking to reconcile conflicting interests and find a compromise formula. Preferring to deal with his advisers individually rather than as a group, Vargas cared little for decision making by council, although he was not above allowing responsibility for decisions to be shared as insurance against adverse public reactions to those decisions. A supreme judge of men, Vargas typically allowed subordinates sufficient latitude to defend their positions against contrary opinion, and, in Rooseveltian fashion, he oftentimes had contending parties believing that he agreed with each or all of them. After the air had been cleared and the issues stripped of ambiguities and personality investments, he would resolve matters. Yet his decisions frequently were themselves ambiguous and were decisions not to make final decisions. The informal banking arrangement with Germany in 1934 and the gentlemen's agreement of 1936 were expressions of his refusal to commit himself definitively to a course of action that a formal treaty would have signified.

In the face of conflicting external pressures, Vargas sanctioned a treaty commitment to a "liberal" trade policy and then, to satisfy national interests, sought a *jeito* of circumventing that obligation. If this required subterfuge and calculated misleading of one or both major trade partners, Brazilian leaders were nonetheless willing to make that investment of a potential loss in international respectability because of the urgent demands of commercial groups and the armed forces. An opportunist *par excellence*, Vargas played the great powers off against each other, utilizing pressure or alleged pressure from one as a lever to pry concessions from the other. The view of Brazil as a helpless victim of German commercial aggressiveness simply does not stand up against the evidence. Rio met Berlin at least halfway, and it welcomed compensation as a way out of several muddles.

Cordell Hull's trade program, it has been suggested, made a "great contribution" to the development of a broad reciprocity in inter-American relations, a practice meaning that, "if the United States did certain things desired by Latin American states, these states would respond by doing other things desired by Washington."[41] In his memoirs the secretary of state made the same claim, positing a causal relationship between his trade agreements in the 1930s and subsequent wartime cooperation. "The political line-up followed the economic line-up," he succinctly put it.[42]

Argentina, of course, was a glaring and important exception. That country's foreign policy had traditionally been oriented toward Europe, and open clashes between Argentines and Americans had enlivened many Pan-American conferences, particularly those of the 1930s. Hull failed to get the Buenos Aires government to sign a reciprocal agreement, although trade relations with Argentina, "the foremost American exponent of bilateralism," had reached a "highly critical stage" by 1939. Negotiations throughout that year were fruitless, and four months after the outbreak of war the two governments issued a joint statement announcing the termination of the talks because of their inability to reach an understanding.[43]

Since 1933 the Roosevelt administration had also made a strenuous effort to win the political good will of Argentina. At Buenos Aires in 1936 and Lima in 1938 Washington adjusted its goals to meet strong objections from Buenos Aires. In 1936 Hull actively supported Foreign Minister Saavedra Lamas for the Nobel Peace Prize, which he won.[44] And the administration backed off from its plans to lease outdated destroyers to Brazil in 1937 because of Argentine opposition that threatened to disrupt hemispheric "unity." Argentina's well-known record after the fall of France was the bitter fruit yielded by this appeasement of Buenos Aires in prewar years.

Most writers concede that Argentina was a bad penny—indeed, the exception that proved the rule. But what about Brazil, the "traditional" ally, the first nation to sign a reciprocal trade agreement and enlist in Hull's "crusade for economic sanity"?[45] Insofar as his program was aimed at countering bilateral trading practices, the example of Brazil points up the need for a revision of prevailing notions about the effectiveness of Good Neighbor diplomacy. For in Brazil, a country Hull regarded as crucial to his plans, American policy met with a resounding rebuff.

Vargas and his counselors made a shrewd reading of the international political system during the 1930s. After a period of hesitant starts during which they took the measure of the larger powers, Brazilian leaders realized that systemic conditions would allow them to maintain Washington's political support while pursuing a goal seemingly incompatible with that support: the expansion of trade with Nazi Germany. And they pursued that goal resolutely.

Previous writers have stated or implied that Brazil ended its compensation arrangement with Berlin in 1936 or 1937. The fact is that the only effective check to Brazil's bilateral dealings with the Reich was the British blockade. Washington's good-neighborliness and restraint in the commercial sphere did not evoke reciprocity; on the contrary, they encouraged what amounted to de facto neutralism toward the trade struggle between the United States and Germany. The restrictions that Rio de Janeiro occasionally placed on compensation transactions in 1938 and 1939 resulted from an assessment of Brazil's interests in the face of grave developments in Europe, rather than from a desire to compensate Washington for its benevolent attitude.

In reality, when it perceived its interests as different from Washington's, as in trade matters, Rio de Janeiro followed essentially the same independent policy as Buenos Aires. The difference seems to be that Brazil publicly and privately at every turn assured the United States of its solidarity, whereas Argentina seemed to take pride in open confrontations with Washington. Once Brazilian policy makers learned how prized the rhetoric of good-neighborliness was in Washington, they skillfully used their protestations in conjunction with hints about what Berlin was doing, or was willing to do, for Brazil in order to ward off American pressure or secure further concessions from the United States.

The Good Neighbor policy was probably the most potent weapon in Brazil's diplomatic arsenal, as Brazilian officials masterfully exploited Washington's unwillingness to adopt sanctions against Brazil for infringements of the American-Brazilian treaty and its readiness to be satisfied with rhetoric in pursuing its commercial aims. Jefferson Caffery was undoubtedly correct in 1938 when he argued that Brazil would quickly change its policy if the United States adopted a "hard" line. Washington could have frozen Brazilian commercial balances in the United States and used them to pay American exporters, or it could have levied countervailing duties on Brazilian coffee, arguing that Vargas's coffee price-support program amounted to an export subsidy. But maintenance of a façade of hemispheric unity on commercial and political questions was a matter of overriding importance to the State Department, and it preferred to allow violations of the treaty rather than make a public confession of failure and disunity by retaliating.

Washington was encouraged to lay the big stick aside by the fact that American exports to Brazil increased from a yearly average of $41 million during 1931–1935 to an average of around $68 million for the triennium 1936–1938, while imports from Brazil rose only slightly from averages of $102 million to $117 million for those periods.[46] Concern about German political influence in Brazil after 1937—a largely misplaced concern, since Berlin subordinated political considerations to economic relations—greatly reinforced American desire to accommodate Vargas.

Brazil's reaction to the Hull trade program, an integral part of the Good Neighbor policy, raises questions about Rio's motivation for political cooperation with the United States in the 1930s, notably in the Chaco negotiations and during the inter-American conferences at Buenos Aires and Lima. Was this cooperation a result of a desire to reciprocate Washington's good will or a function of national interest? Did Brazil play the role of mediator between the Argentines and Americans at those conferences out of devotion to principles and ideals of Pan-American fraternity; or was it because Brazil's patent military inferiority and its deep suspicion of Argentine intentions made preservation of at least outwardly cordial relations with that country a political necessity? When Aranha expressed apprehension that Washington's efforts to build a "continental good neighborhood" would place Brazil "on an equal footing" with other Latin American nations,[47] was he expressing a concern common to other Brazilian leaders? If so, it would appear that the leveling effects of the Good Neighbor policy clashed with what Brazilian policy makers perceived as their interests. How was Washington's appeasement of Buenos Aires received in Rio de Janeiro? Did such things as the Destroyers Episode preserve continental unity or encourage as much neutralism as the overwhelming American economic and military hegemony would permit? Was subsequent wartime cooperation between Brazil and the United States a dividend paid on the Good Neighbor policy or a result of the fact that the war destroyed Brazil's trade with continental Europe and forced Brazil into even greater dependence on the American market? Only further research will answer these questions, but their asking is compelled by the story of Brazil's opportunistic response to the prewar economic rivalry of the great powers, a response grounded in a cold, realistic assessment of national interests.

Notes

Abbreviations Used

(For full descriptions, see Bibliography.)

AAA   Archiv des Auswärtigen Amts

AHI   Arquivo Histórico do Itamaraty

AM   Arquivo da Marinha

CFCE   Conselho Federal de Comércio Exterior (and Records of)

DGFP   U.S. Department of State, *Documents on German Foreign Policy, 1918–1945*

DOT   Department of Overseas Trade

EME   Estado-Maior do Exército (and Records of)

EMA   Estado-Maior da Armada

FDRL   Franklin D. Roosevelt Library

FR   U.S. Department of State, *Foreign Relations of the United States*

MRE   Ministério das Relações Exteriores

NFTC   National Foreign Trade Council

NSDAP   Microfilmed records of the National Socialist German Labor
        Party

PR   Coleção Presidência da República

RFO   Records of the British Foreign Office

RGFM   Microfilmed Records of the German Foreign Ministry

RWM   Reichswirtschaftsministerium

SD   Files of the U.S. State Department

WD   Files of the U.S. War Department

NOTE: Brazilian personalities are identified in the text as they are
        usually known to the Brazilian public. Full family names are
        indicated in the notes.

Introduction

1. Standard works on British activity in Brazil during the nineteenth and
early twentieth centuries are Alan K. Manchester, *British Pre-eminence in Brazil*, and Richard Graham, *Britain and the Onset of Modernization in Brazil*. The
figures on investments are taken from J. Fred Rippy, *British Investments in
Latin America, 1822–1949*, p. 150.
2. Gerhard Brunn, *Deutschland und Brasilien*, pp. 9, 120, 232–252.
3. E. Bradford Burns, *The Unwritten Alliance*, p. 63.
4. Lawrence F. Hill, *Diplomatic Relations between the United States and Brazil*,
p. 294.

5. Victor Valla, *Os Estados Unidos e a Influência Estrangeira na Economia Brasileira*, p. 47.
6. Ibid.
7. Ibid., p. 95.
8. Ibid., pp. 92, 94; Rippy, *British Investments in Latin America*, p. 150.

1. Brazil's View of the World Crisis

1. Felix Pacheco to Afrânio de Melo Franco, January 20, 1929, Afrânio de Melo Franco Papers (henceforth Melo Franco Papers), *arcaz* I-36, *gaveta* 5 (henceforth I-36/5). All translations are mine.
2. Robert M. Levine, *The Vargas Regime*, pp. 16–17, has an interesting description of Brazilian social conditions during the 1930s. For the statistical information, see Anníbal V. Villela and Wilson Suzigan, *Política do governo e crescimento da economia brasileira, 1889–1945*, pp. 258, 393, 406; Ministério da Guerra, *Relatório . . . 1940*, pp. 43–44. Kenneth Boulding argues convincingly that a foreign policy elite's "map image" is an important determinant of foreign policy attitudes ("National Images and International Systems," *Journal of Conflict Resolution* 3 [June 1959]: 124). For the military image of Brazil's geopolitical situation, see, for example, EME, *Relatório . . . 1933*, p. 9, and *Relatório . . . 1938* (typewritten).
3. Villela and Suzigan, *Política do governo*, p. 70.
4. On politics during the 1930s, see John W. F. Dulles, *Vargas of Brazil*, pp. 83–197; Levine, *Vargas Regime*; Thomas E. Skidmore, *Politics in Brazil, 1930–1964*, chap. 1, and "Failure in Brazil: From Popular Front to Armed Revolt," *Journal of Contemporary History* 5 (1970): 137–157; Stanley E. Hilton, "*Ação Integralista Brasileira*: Fascism in Brazil, 1932–1938," *Luso-Brazilian Review* 9 (December 1972): 3–29.
5. Carlos Martins Pereira de Sousa to Melo Franco, June 11, 1932, and May 30, 1933, Melo Franco Papers, I-36/29; Mario de Pimentel Brandão to ex-Foreign Minister Otávio Mangabeira, April 4, 1933, Otávio Mangabeira Papers (henceforth Mangabeira Papers); *Jornal do Brasil* (Rio), May 21, 1933; Pedro A. de Góes Monteiro to Getúlio Vargas, n.d. [January 4, 1934], Getúlio Vargas Papers (henceforth Vargas Papers); Oswaldo Aranha to Vargas, September 7, 1934, Vargas Papers.
6. Commercial attaché João Pinto da Silva (Madrid) to Mangabeira, April 12, 1934, Mangabeira Papers; Adalberto Guerra-Duval (Berlin) to Melo Franco, January 11, 1933, Melo Franco Papers, I-36/36; Caio de Melo Franco (London) to Melo Franco, February 10, 1934, Melo Franco Papers I-36/5; Afrânio de Melo Franco Filho (Paris) to Melo Franco, April 13, 1935, Melo Franco Papers

I-36/21; Chargé Antonio Camilo de Oliveira (Paris) to MRE, April 23, 1935, AHI 405/2/10.

7. João Carlos Muniz (Geneva) to Aranha, August 13, 1935, Oswaldo Aranha Papers (henceforth Aranha Papers); EME, Boletim Especial de Informações, September 1935, maço 25.771, AHI; Aranha to Vargas, December 3, 1935, Aranha Papers.

8. Dispatches and telegrams to MRE from the legation/embassy (Berlin), 1934–1937, AHI 397/3/7–397/3/11, 397/4/10.

9. Min. José J. Moniz de Aragão (Berlin) to MRE, March 9, 1936, AHI 397/3/9; Austregesilo de Athayde, "Revelação dos tempos novos," Diário da Noite (Rio), March 11, 1936; Gen. Miguel de Castro Ayres, O Exército que eu vi, pp. 31–32; Adm. Henrique Guilhem to Aranha, April 1, 1936, Aranha Papers; Min. da Guerra, Relatório . . . 1936, pp. 6–7.

10. Letters to Hildebrando Acioly (MRE) from Camilo de Oliveira (Paris), May 14, 1936, and Renato de Almeida (Geneva), September 24, 1936, Hildebrando Acioly Papers (henceforth Acioly Papers); Melo Franco Filho (Paris) to Melo Franco, December 9, 1936, Melo Franco Papers, I-36/7; letters to José Carlos de Macedo Soares (MRE) from Moniz de Aragão (Berlin), July 7, 1936, and Guerra-Duval (Rome), June 17, 1936, José Carlos de Macedo Soares Papers (henceforth Macedo Soares Papers); Luis Simões Lopes (Naples) to Vargas, November 21, 1936, PR, lata 28, processo 21379 (henceforth 28/21379).

11. Camilo de Oliveira to Acioly, August 31, 1936, Acioly Papers; Renato de Almeida to Macedo Soares, October 24, 1936, Macedo Soares Papers; Simões Lopes to Vargas, October 24, 1936, PR 28/20870; R. Ribeiro Couto (Le Havre) to Melo Franco, December 4, 1936, Melo Franco Papers, I-35/23.

12. Amb. José P. de Rodrigues Alves (Buenos Aires) to Macedo Soares, October 24, 1936, Macedo Soares Papers. For military uneasiness over South American turmoil, see Min. da Guerra Espírito Santo Cardoso to Aranha, December 12, 1932, Aranha Papers; EME, Relatório . . . 1933, pp. 9–10; Gen. Almerio de Moutra to EME, February 23, 1933, PR 1/MRE folder.

13. Gen. Pantaleão da Silva Pessôa to Vargas, February 7, 1934, Vargas Papers; EME, Relatório . . . 1936, p. 14.

14. Pres. Sèc. Luis Vergara (for Vargas) to Orlando Leite Ribeiro (Buenos Aires), March 12, 1935, PR 17/1805.

15. Góes Monteiro to Aranha, February 2, 1934, PR 11/40.627; report by Gen. Constancio Cavalcante, n.d. [December 1934], Pantaleão da Silva Pessôa Papers (henceforth Pessôa Papers); Vargas to Aranha, December 24, 1934, Vargas Papers; memo by Com. Renato Guillobel, n.d. [November 1936], Macedo Soares Papers.

16. Gustavo Capanema to Afonso Arinos de Melo Franco, March 14, 1934, Afonso Arinos de Melo Franco Papers (henceforth A. A. Melo Franco Papers);

Gen. Eurico Dutra to EME, November 3, 1934, AHI 425/2/9; Mario Pinto Serva, "A posição internacional do Brasil," *Diário de São Paulo*, November 28, 1934.

17. Delegação do Brasil à Conferência do Desarmamento, Acta da primeira reunião, February 2, 1934, Macedo Soares Papers; Min. da Marinha, *Relatório* . . . *1932*, pp. 12–13; Valentim Bouças to Aranha, July 12, 1932, Valentim Bouças Papers (henceforth Bouças Papers).

18. Aranha, speech of May 24, 1934, *Brazilian Business* 14 (June 1934): 166; Capt. César da Fonseca, "Defeza Nacional," *O Jornal*, September 24, 1934; Min. da Guerra [Góes Monteiro], *Relatório* . . . *1935*, p. 5.

19. MRE memo ("O Brasil e o Conflicto Italo-Ethiope"), May 1936, Macedo Soares Papers; Melo Franco Filho to Melo Franco, March 11, 1936, Melo Franco Papers.

20. Renato de Almeida (Geneva) to Acioly, September 24, 1936, Acioly Papers; Moniz de Aragão to MRE, January 27, 1937, AHI 397/3/12.

21. Vargas, speech of January 2, 1930, Getúlio Vargas, *A Nova Política do Brasil*, I, 40; MRE [Melo Franco], *Relatório* . . . *1931*, I, xiv; Bouças to Aranha, May 30, 1934, Bouças Papers; CFCE, Acta da 14ª Sessão [November 5, 1934], PR 19/3946; H. Pinheiro de Vasconcellos (Brussels) to Macedo Soares, January 27, 1935, Macedo Soares Papers; CFCE, 32ª Sessão [March 25, 1935], PR 18/2635; memo by Artur Torres Filho, April 5, 1935, CFCE, *lata* 20, *processo* 318 (henceforth 20/318). For similar commentaries, see Azevedo Amaral, *O Brasil na Crise Actual*, p. 113; Vargas, message to Congress, May 3, 1935, Câmara dos Deputados, *Annaes 1935*, I, 58; Macedo Soares, speech of March 4, 1936, *Correio da Manhã*, March 5, 1936.

22. Martins to Vargas, January 15, 1935, PR 17/1732.

23. Martins to Melo Franco, June 11, 1932, Melo Franco Papers, I-36/29; Martins to Macedo Soares, September 16, 1934, Macedo Soares Papers; Martins to MRE, October 5, 1934, AHI 407/3/5; Martins to Vargas, December 21, 1934, PR 17/1234; Amb. Pedro Leão Velloso to Acioly, July 31, 1936, Acioly Papers.

24. Gilberto Amado to Vargas, December 27, 1933, *maço* 9399, AHI; Vargas to Aranha, June 17, 1937, Aranha Papers. On the perceived Argentine interest in Bolivian oil, see, for example, Brazilian minister (La Paz) to MRE, February 28, September 3, 1931, AHI 401/5/16, 402/1/1; Leite Ribeiro (Buenos Aires) to Melo Franco, January 24, 1934, Melo Franco Papers, I-36/7; Rodrigues Alves (Santiago) to MRE, March 11, 1934, PR I/MRE folder; MRE circular, August 22, 1934, AHI, Circulares; EME memo, March 1935, AHI.

25. Aranha to Vargas, July 1, 1935, Aranha Papers; Melo Franco to Melo Franco Filho, September 7, 1935, A. A. Melo Franco Papers; João Alberto Lins de Barros to Vargas, February 25, 1936, PR 25/12226.

26. Min. da Guerra to MRE, September 4, 1932, AHI 425/2/5; EME to Min. da Guerra, November 1, 1932, AHI 425/2/6; EME to MRE, December 11, 1932, AHI 425/4/L2.

27. EME, *Relatório* . . . *1933*, p. 9; Pessôa to Vargas, n.d. (November 26–27, 1934), PR 8/Pessôa folder; Góes Monteiro to Macedo Soares, January 26, 1935, AHI 425/2/10.

28. Pessôa, undated memo [draft of speech?], [1934], Pessôa Papers; Gustavo Barroso, *Brasil*, p. 115; *A Pátria* (Rio), July 5, 1935.

29. Memo by Torres Filho, April 15, 1935, CFCE 15/189-1; Aranha to Vargas, June 18, 1935, Aranha Papers; editorial, "A Industrialização da África e a Economia Brasileira," *O Jornal*, July 31, 1935; memo by J. M. Lacerda, August 1, 1935, CFCE 24/395-v. 2/1; Benedicto Silva, "O café brasileiro e a ameaça crescente da concorrência," *Revista do Departamento Nacional do Café* 3 (January 1936): 21–26; memo by Bouças, April 26, 1937, CFCE 34/544.

30. EME, Boletim Especial de Informações, September 1935, *maço* 25.771, AHI; EME, *Relatório* . . . *1936*, p. 12; Gen. Waldomiro Lima, lecture to Escola do Estado-Maior, June 12, 1937, *O Jornal*, June 13, 1937; Góes Monteiro, speech, July 2, 1937, *A Pátria*, July 3, 1937; EME [Góes Monteiro], *Relatório* . . . *1938*.

31. Brazilian minister (Bern) to MRE, September 17, 1935, Macedo Soares Papers; João Alberto to Vargas, February 25, 1936, PR 25/12226; Macedo Soares to Aranha, April 2, 1936, AHI 408/3/L3; Aranha to Vargas, September 15, 1936, Vargas Papers; Acioly to Aranha, October 26, 1937, Aranha Papers; statements by Roberto Simonsen, CFCE, 170[a] Sessão [October 13, 1937], PR 34/33502.

32. Memo ("A Situação de Defeza Naval do Brasil em face da Argentina e do Chile") by Adm. C. de Sousa e Silva, January 7, 1931, Melo Franco Papers, I-36/34; unsigned memo ("Situação Internacional do Brasil—Sua Defeza Militar"), n.d. [1932–1933], Pessôa Papers; Rodrigues Alves to MRE, March 28, 1934, AHI 406/4/12; Paulo Hasslocher to Vargas, October 9, 1934, Vargas Papers; Aranha to Vargas, January 15, 1935, Aranha Papers; MRE memo, October 1936, Macedo Soares Papers; EME [Góes Monteiro], *Relatório* . . . *1938*.

33. Warren K. Dean, *The Industrialization of São Paulo, 1880–1945*, pp. 181–233; John D. Wirth, *The Politics of Brazilian Development, 1930–1954*, pp. 1–6, 67, 89–117. For similar argument that Vargas was not interested in developing manufactures, see Robert Daland, *Brazilian Planning*, p. 22, and Hélio Jaguaribe, *Economic and Political Development*, pp. 142-144.

34. Vargas, speeches of January 15, 1935, and February 23, 1931, *Nova Política*, I, 39, 97, 100.

35. Memoranda by Bouças, January 15, 1935, CFCE 8/57; April 26, 1937, CFCE 34/544.

36. Aranha to Vargas, July 1, 1935, Aranha Papers; memo by Lacerda, August 1, 1935, CFCE 24/395-v. 2; memo by Torres Filho, April 5, 1935, CFCE 20/318.

37. Interview with Pessôa, April 12, 1971; Edward J. Rogers, "Brazilian Success Story: The Volta Redonda Iron and Steel Project," *Journal of Inter-American Studies* 10 (October 1968): 639.

38. Carlos M. Peláez, "Itabira Iron and the Export of Brazil's Iron Ore," *Revista Brasileira de Economia* 24 (October–December 1970): 166–167.

39. Interview with Pessôa, April 12, 1971. On Farquhar, see Charles A. Gauld, *The Last Titan*.

40. Wirth, *Politics of Brazilian Development*, pp. 80–85.

41. Stanley J. Stein, *The Brazilian Cotton Manufacture*, pp. 140–153; Min. of Labor, Industry, and Commerce Lindolfo Collor to Vargas, September [?], 1931, volume: Presidência da República, Documentos de Terceiros, AHI.

42. Centro de Indústrias (São Paulo) to Collor, May 16, 1931, Lindolfo Collor Papers (henceforth Collor Papers).

43. Villela and Suzigan, *Política do governo*, p. 324; State Dept. to International Register Co., January 10, 1934, SD 832.5151/239; DOT, *Economic Conditions in Brazil . . . 1936*, p. 2.

44. Carlos M. Peláez, *História da Industrialização Brasileira*, pp. 202–207; *Brazilian Business* 14 (April 1934): 119; federal interventor (Pará) to Vargas, July 7, 1933, PR 3/folder: Interventor no Pará; Hoelzel & Cia. (Rio Grande do Sul) to Vargas, December 12, 1933, PR 6/folder: Hoelzel & Cia.; Vargas to federal interventor (Pará), July 8, 1933, PR 3/folder: Interventor no Pará.

45. Lily-Tulip Cup Corp. to State Dept., April 25, 1934, SD 632.113/35; DOT, *Economic Conditions in Brazil . . . 1932*, pp. 38–39.

46. Quoted in memo by Lenhoff Brito, May 18, 1936, CFCE 24/395.

47. *Brazilian Business* 14 (July 1934): 204; Henri von Deursen, "L'émancipation industrielle du Brésil: Caractères et développement de l'industrie dans l'état de Sao-Paulo," *Revue Economique Internationale* 26 (August 1934): 312; Confederação Industrial do Brasil to Artur Souza Costa, August 24, 1934, volume: Diversos no Interior, Documentos de Terceiros, Oficios, 1931–1946, AHI.

48. Vargas, speech of October 3, 1931, *Nova Política*, I, 163; Min. da Fazenda memo, September 18, 1934, volume: Diversos no Interior, Documentos de Terceiros, Oficios, AHI; Federação das Indústrias do Estado de São Paulo, *A situação econômica da América Latina*, Quadros 26–28, n.p.

49. Charles W. Anderson, *Politics and Economic Change in Latin America*, pp. 163, 175; Vargas, speech of January 2, 1930, *Nova Política*, I, 22–28.

50. The literature on the subject is voluminous. See, for example, Fritz Machlup, *Education and Economic Growth*; Alexander L. Peaslee, "Education's

236 Notes to Pages 21–22

Role in Development," *Economic Development and Cultural Change* 17 (April 1969): 293–318; C. Arnold Anderson and Mary J. Bowman, eds., *Education and Economic Development*. For specific discussion of Latin America, see Thomas J. La Belle, ed., *Education and Development*. Students of African development find a "positive relationship" between the level of education and entrepreneurial success (E. Wayne Nafziger, "The Relationship between Education and Entrepreneurship in Nigeria," *Journal of Developing Areas* 4 [April 1970]: 349–360).

51. Vargas, *Nova Política*, I, 40; *O Jornal*, September 1, 1931; José Honório Rodrigues, *The Brazilians*, p. 135; Capanema, speech, *Jornal do Commércio*, January 8, 1940; Robert J. Havighurst and J. R. Moreira, *Society and Education in Brazil*, p. 187.

52. Hirosê Pimpão, *Getúlio Vargas e o direito trabalhista*, pp. 65–85. The concept of human capital was not new (B. F. Kiker, "The Historical Roots of the Concept of Human Capital," *Journal of Political Economy* 74 [October 1966]: 481–499). For contemporary statements on the importance of human capital, see T. W. Schultz, "Investment in Human Capital," *American Economic Review* 51 (March 1961): 1–17, and Ronald A. Wykstra, "Economic Development and Human Capital Formation," *Journal of Developing Areas* 3 (July 1969): 527–538. Continuing Brazilian interest in the problem of human resources is reflected in José Francisco de Camargo, "Recursos Humanos e Desenvolvimento," *Problemas Brasileiros* 7 (April 1969): 22–27.

53. Vargas, *Nova Política*, I, 28, III, 132; Costa Leite and Lyra Madeira, "Salário Mínimo," *Boletim do Ministério de Trabalho, Indústria e Comércio* 1 (September 1934): 242; Vargas, *Nova Política*, V, 304.

54. Cf. Dean, *Industrialization of São Paulo*, p. 184. The general dimensions of the flight to more urbanized regions are sketched in José Francisco Camargo, *Exodo Rural no Brasil*, pp. 104–105, 123, and Villela and Suzigan, *Política do governo*, pp. 282–284.

55. Philip M. Hauser, "Cultural and Personal Obstacles to Economic Development in the Less Developed Areas," *Human Organization* 18 (Summer 1959): 80; Gideon Sjoberg, "Rural-Urban Balance and Models of Economic Development," in *Social Structure and Mobility in Economic Development*, ed. Neil J. Smelser and Seymour M. Lipset, p. 252. Brazilian analysts remain concerned with the problem. See Eugenio Gudin, "O problema nacional da urbanização e as deseconomias de escala," *O Globo* (Rio), April 22, 1974; Felipe Nery Moschini, "Exodo e Urbanização," *Problemas Brasileiros* 9 (March 1972): 21–38; Roberto C. Cesar, "As migrações internas," *O Estado de São Paulo*, October 18, 1970. For a case study of the phenomenon in Andean America, see René Vandendries, "Internal Migration and Economic Development in Peru," in *Latin American Modernization Problems*, ed. Robert E. Scott, pp. 193–208.

56. Min. of Labor Pedro Salgado Filho to Maurício Joppert, September 5,

Notes to Pages 22–27 **237**

1934, Pedro Salgado Filho Papers (henceforth Salgado Filho Papers). For the impact of the rural exodus on the economy of the interior, see federal interventor (Ceará) to Vargas, April 26, 1932, PR 2-A/folder: Interventor no Ceará.
57. Charles W. Anderson, *Politics and Economic Change in Latin America*, p. 87; Roberto de Oliveira Campos, "A Retrospect over Brazilian Development Plans," in *The Economy of Brazil*, ed. Howard Ellis, p. 317. Cf. Joseph Grunwald, "Some Reflections on Latin American Industrialization Policy," *Journal of Political Economy* 78 (supplement to July–August 1970): 843; Manning Nash, "Social Prerequisites to Economic Growth in Latin America and Southeast Asia," *Economic Development and Cultural Change* 12 (April 1964): 225–242. For further comparative insights, see Edwin Dean, "Noneconomic Barriers to Effective Planning in Nigeria, 1962–1966," *Economic Development and Cultural Change* 19 (July 1971): 560–579.
58. Vargas, speech of January 2, 1931, *Nova Política*, I, 86. The data on administrative turnover are taken from Alzira Vargas do Amaral Peixoto, *Getúlio Vargas, meu Pai*, pp. 267–285.
59. Luis Simões Lopes to Vargas, July 28, 1938, PR 44/17174.
60. Lawrence S. Graham, *Civil Service Reform in Brazil*, p. 26. Francis Lampert agrees that, although the reform movement did not achieve all its goals, the changes made in 1936 constituted "one of the major revolutions in thinking about the civil service in Brazil" ("Trends in Administrative Reform in Brazil," *Journal of Latin American Studies* 1[November 1969]: 173).
61. Min. da Fazenda, Comissão de Estudos Financeiros e Econômicos, *Finanças dos Estados do Brasil*, p. 2; director, Dept. Nacional de Estatística to Aranha, February 10, 1932, Aranha Papers; Bouças to Aranha, February 23, 1933, Aranha Papers; director, Dept. Nacional de Estatística to Aranha, June 8, 1934, Aranha Papers; U.S. commercial attaché (Rio) to Dept. of Commerce, September 18, 1934, container 1497, Files of the U.S. Dept. of Commerce (RG 151); U.S. Amb. Jefferson Caffery (Rio) to State Dept., September 22, 1938, SD 810.5562/191.
62. Vargas, speech of May 30, 1938, *Nova Política*, V, 227; Benedicto Silva, "A cooperação inter-administrativa na estatística brasileira," pp. 312, 316–317; Salgado Filho to Gov. J. F. Flores da Cunha (Rio Grande do Sul), December 14, 1932, Salgado Filho Papers.
63. Silva, "A cooperação inter-administrativa na estatística basileira," *Boletim do Ministério de Trabalho, Industria e Comércio* 3 (February 1937): 319–321; Macedo Soares (Instituto Brasileiro de Geografia e Estatística) to João Alberto (Comissão de Defesa da Economia Nacional), October 19, 1940, CFCE 81/1060.
64. Vargas, *Nova Política*, I, 38; Vargas to Alcides Etchegoyen, February 3, 1932, Vargas Papers; Vargas, speech of November 15, 1933, *Nova Política*, III, 85; Villela and Suzigan, *Política do governo*, p. 406; statements by minister of Agriculture, *Correio da Manhã* (Rio), July 3, 1935.
65. British Amb. William Seeds (Rio) to Foreign Office, February 20, 1932,

RFO 371, doc. A1497/575/6; DOT, *Economic Conditions in Brazil . . . 1935*, p. 4; director, Dept. Nacional de Estatística, to Aranha, [April] 12, 1934, Aranha Papers; Vargas to Aranha, October 1, 1934, Aranha Papers.

66. Villela and Suzigan, *Política do governo*, pp. 214, 367.

67. Nathaniel Leff, "Long-Term Brazilian Economic Development," *Journal of Economic History* 29 (September 1969): 474.

68. Vargas, *Nova Política*, I, 97–98; Brazilian minister (La Paz) to MRE, various reports, 1931, AHI 401/5/16; MRE memo, December 14, 1933, *maço* 32.796, AHI.

69. Arthur G. Bastos, Relatório político sobre o Paraguay, October 10, 1934, Macedo Soares Papers; Brazilian minister (La Paz) to Sec. Gen. Pimentel Brandão (MRE), January 17, 1935, AHI, Questão do Chaco, vol. I; EME, memo, March 12, 1935, AHI; Aranha to Macedo Soares, May 14, 1935, Aranha Papers; memo by Macedo Soares, October 1, 1935, PR 21/6884; MRE memo, October 10, 1935, Macedo Soares Papers.

70. MRE to Brazilian embassy (Buenos Aires), June 11, 1931, AHI 400/3/6; Vargas to Aranha, July 27, 1935, Aranha Papers; memo by Bouças, January 15, 1935, CFCE 8/57; Torres Filho (Asunción) to Macedo Soares, October 12, 1935, Macedo Soares Papers; statements by Euvaldo Lodi, CFCE, 119ª Sessão [November 4, 1936], PR 28/20869.

71. Memo by Torres Filho, April 5, 1935, CFCE 20/318; Peláez, *História da Industrialização Brasileira*, pp. 154, 200; Vargas, speech of September 7, 1936, *Nova Política*, IV, 182.

72. Executive director, CFCE, circular, November 16, 1936, CFCE 26/426-v. 2.

73. The documents relating to the survey are in CFCE 26/426.

74. Cf. Dean, *Industrialization of São Paulo*, pp. 185, 196.

75. See Bruce F. Johnston and John W. Mellor, "The Role of Agriculture in Economic Development," *American Economic Review* 51 (September 1961): 566–593, for a critique of the "false dichotomy of agricultural vs. industrial development." For area studies of the contribution of agriculture to general development, see Kazushi Ohkawa and Henry Rosovsky, "The Role of Agriculture in Modern Japanese Economic Development," *Economic Development and Cultural Change* 9 (October 1960): 43–68; Richard W. Parks, "The Role of Agriculture in Mexican Economic Development," *Inter-American Economic Affairs* 18 (Summer 1964): 3–28; and John Macrae, "The Relationship between Agricultural and Industrial Growth, with Special Reference to the Development of the Punjab Economy from 1950 to 1965," *Journal of Development Studies* 7 (July 1971): 397–422.

76. Roberto Simonsen, *As Crises no Brasil*, p. 4.

77. Dean, *Industrialization of São Paulo*, pp. 181, 194.

78. Vargas, speech of July 22, 1938, *Nova Política*, V, 291; José Maria Whitaker to Aranha, August 31, 1931, Aranha Papers.

79. Peláez, *História da Industrialização Brasileira*, pp. 154, 200.

80. Melo Franco to Aranha, February 22, 1935, Aranha Papers; Vargas to Aranha, October 16, 1934, ibid.; Aranha to Macedo Soares, May 14, 1935, ibid.

81. Vargas, message to Congress, May 3, 1935, Câmara dos Deputados, *Annaes, 1935*, I, 58.

82. Roberto Simonsen, *Aspects of National Political Economy*, p. 62; Macedo Soares to Aranha, July 24, 1935, AHI 408/3/4.

83. MRE memo, n.d. [August 1935], PR 25/12529; *A Nação*, March 10, 1936; Ribeiro Couto (Le Havre) to Melo Franco, December 4, 1936, Melo Franco Papers, I-35/23; Francisco d'Alamo Lousada (Bern) to Vargas, November 27, 1937, PR 36/172; EME memo, September 21, 1939, EME; EME[Góes Monteiro], *Relatório . . . 1939* (typewritten).

84. *Correio de Manhã*, December 5, 1930; Melo Franco to Elias Besseb, April 27, 1931, maço 9.739, AHI; *A Federação* (Porto Alegre), April 12, 1934; CFCE, 10ª Sessão[October 8, 1934], PR 19/3945.

85. Melo Franco to Pimentel Brandão, March 23, 1932, Melo Franco Papers, I-36/17; Afonso Arinos de Melo Franco, *Estadista da República*, III, 1378–1379.

86. Melo Franco to Macedo Soares, February 7, 1935, Macedo Soares Papers; Vargas, speeches of February 23, July 5, 1931, *Nova Política*, I, 98, 135–136.

87. Memo by Joaquim Eulalio de Nascimento e Silva, April 25, 1933, maço 7.100, AHI.

88. Memo by Amb. J. F. de Assis Brasil, May 23, 1933, ibid.

89. Regis de Oliveira, report, November 1933, AHI 403/2/13.

90. *Times* (London), July 28, 1933.

91. *A Nação* (Rio), September 14, 1933; *Folha da Manhã* (São Paulo), July 29, 1933; Nascimento e Silva, interview, *A Noite*, August 29, 1933.

92. Feliks Gross, *Foreign Policy Analysis*, p. 119; Richard C. Snyder et al., *Foreign Policy Decision Making*, p. 156.

93. Karl Deutsch et al., *France, Germany and the Western Alliance*, p. 6.

94. Rodrigues, *Brazilians*, p. 46; Sérgio Buarque de Holanda, *Raízes do Brasil*, p. 150; Anthony Leeds, "Brazilian Careers and Social Structure," *American Anthropologist* 66 (December 1964): 133.

95. Quoted in Alberto Rangel, *No rolar do tempo*, p. 19.

96. John F. Santos, "A Psychologist Reflects on Brazil and Brazilians," in *New Perspectives of Brazil*, ed. Eric N. Baklanoff, p. 236.

97. Clodomir Viana Moog, *Bandeirantes and Pioneers*, p. 223.

98. Richard M. Morse, "Language as a Key to Latin American Historiography," in *Latin American History*, ed. Howard F. Cline, p. 664.

99. João Cruz Costa, *A History of Ideas in Brazil*, p. 274.

100. Charles Wagley, *An Introduction to Brazil*, pp. 126–127, discusses present-day value conflicts of the Brazilian middle class.

101. Quoted in Rangel, *No rolar do tempo*, p. 22.

102. U.S. consul general (Rio) to State Dept., January 12, 1933, SD

832.5151/117; Seeds to Foreign Office, June 5, 1934, RFO 371, doc. A5053/310/6; British chargé (Rio) to Foreign Office, August 19, 1935, Board of Trade Records, class 11, piece no. 345; Amb. Karl Ritter (Rio) to Auswärtiges Amt, April 28, 1938, RGFM, roll 1913, serial 3954, frame E054436 (henceforth 1913: 3954/E054436).
    103. Albert O. Hirschman, *Journeys toward Progress*, pp. 228–229.

2. Between Washington and Berlin (1934)

1. Arthur Schweitzer, *Big Business in the Third Reich*, p. 414.
2. Guerra-Duval to Melo Franco, June 16, 1933, Melo Franco Papers, I-36/36.
3. Douglas Miller, *Via Diplomatic Pouch*, pp. 191–192.
4. C. W. Guillebaud, *The Economic Recovery of Germany from 1933 to the Incorporation of Austria in March 1938*, p. 62.
5. George Messersmith (Berlin) to William Dodd, April 3, 1934, R. Walton Moore Papers, Box 5, FDRL.
6. Reichsbank Directorate to RWM, June 18, 1934, *DGFP, Series C*, III, 48–50.
7. Circular of the Auswärtiges Amt, August 20, 1934, *DGFP, C*, III, 347.
8. Hans Kroll, *Lebenserinnerungen eines Botschafters*, pp. 76, 82–83.
9. Circular of Auswärtiges Amt, June 28, 1934, *DGFP, C*, III, 33–35.
10. H. Kroll, *Lebenserinnerungen*, p. 76.
11. Miller, *Diplomatic Pouch*, pp. 189–197; Hjalmar Schacht, *76 Jahre Meines Lebens*, p. 415; RWM memo ("Bisheriges Ergebnis der Massnahmen zur Forderung der deutschen Ausfuhr"), June 5, 1936, Bundesarchiv, file R7VI, folder 615 (henceforth R7VI/615), Koblenz.
12. Aski is derived from *Ausländer Sonderkonto für Inlandszahlungen* ("Foreigner's special account for domestic payments").
13. Circular of Auswärtiges Amt, August 17, 1936, RGFM, 68:74/54134–135. Unless otherwise indicated, the microfilm cited is T-120.
14. *Anglo-Brazilian Chronicle* (Rio), June 19, 1936.
15. Auswärtiges Amt memo, May 3, 1935, *DGFP, C*, IV, 121–122.
16. Gerhard Kroll, *Von der Weltwirtschaftskrise zur Staatskonjunktur*, p. 492.
17. Schweitzer, *Big Business*, p. 446.
18. For German economic interest in Brazil prior to 1930, see Mark Neven du Mont, "A cooperação do trabalho alemão na indústria brasileira," in *O Brasil e a Allemanha 1822–1922*, ed. Alfred Funke, pp. 149–156; Carl Cornelius, *Die Deutschen in brasilianischen Wirtschaftsleben*; and, especially, Gerhard Brunn, *Deutschland und Brasilien*.
19. G. Flaschbart, "O commercio teuto-brasileiro, 1822–1922," in *Brasil e a Allemanha*, p. 82.
20. Gilberto Amado, *Depois da Política*, p. 80.

21. M. Stemmler, "Der Luftverkehr nach Südamerika im Dienste des Aussenhandels," *Der Deutsche im Auslande* 7 (July 1934): 150.

22. Unsigned memo ("Propaganda do Brasil no Exterior"), n.d. [1934], Macedo Soares Papers.

23. Associação Commercial (Rio), *Boletim Semanal*, July 9, 1937, p. 1938.

24. Bouças to Hull, March 25, 1935, SD 611.3231/949; Daniel Roper, *Fifty Years of Public Life*, p. 343.

25. Memo by Otto Kiep ("Erfahrungen der Handelsdelegation"), June 12, 1935, RGFM 3008:6483/485862. For similar reasoning see [?] von Protsch, "Deutschbrasilianische Schulen und Deutsche Gesandtschaft," *Mitteilungsblatt der NSDAP Ortsgruppe Rio de Janeiro* 6 (November 1932): 17; unsigned memo ("Das Deutschtum im Ausland als Stütze der deutschen Aussenhandelsinteressen"), n.d. [late 1937], NSDAP 613:831/5405517 (microcopy T-81); Auswärtiges Amt to various departments, September 1933, Auswärtiges Amt, Abteilung III, Politik 25, Akten betreffend Deutschtum in Brasilien . . . , Band 3, AAA.

26. Various documents, Bundesarchiv R7VI/202(2); U.S. consul (Porto Alegre) to State Dept., July 13, 1939, SD 632.6215/3.

27. German consul (Curitiba) to Auswärtiges Amt, Abt. III, Pol. 25, Akten betr. Deutschtum in Brasilien . . . , Band 3, AAA; Carlos Gomes de Oliveira to Vargas, September 4, 1936, PR 27/18370.

28. The British embassy once suggested with undisguised disgruntlement that Germany enjoyed another advantage that other powers did not, namely, that "in Brazilian eyes, she has no bondholders to be stigmatised as Shylocks or public utility companies to be fleeced as extortioners" (British embassy [Rio], Annual Report, 1933, RFO, class 371, doc. A2865/2865/6).

29. Pres. da República, circular 363, June 1933, PR 5/folder: Circulares expedidas pela Secretaria.

30. John Wirth, *The Politics of Brazilian Development, 1930–1954*, p. 10.

31. Numerous letters to State Dept., January–February 1934, SD 832.5151/223, 228, 242, 257, 270, 272, 276.

32. J. A. Kulenkampff to Artur Souza Costa, November 18, 1935, RGFM 4465:K913/226350.

33. Francisco de Sousa Neto to Virgílio de Melo Franco, March 19, 1934, Virgílio de Melo Franco Papers (henceforth V. Melo Franco Papers).

34. U.S. Tariff Commission, *Economic Controls and Commercial Policy in Brazil*, p. 15. The state of Piauí, for example, depended upon such levies for around 40 percent of its income. Assoc. Commercial de Parnaíba to Dir. da Fazenda (Piuaí), October 26, 1931, Aranha Papers.

35. Commercial attaché (Berlin) to A. Melo Franco, March 23, 1933, Melo Franco Papers, I-36/5; Min. da Fazenda, *Commércio Exterior do Brasil 1931–1935*, p. 18.

36. Raul Gomes to A. Melo Franco, April 16, 1933, Melo Franco Papers, I-36/26; commercial attaché (Berlin) to A. Melo Franco, June 15, 1933, ibid, I-36/5.

37. H. G. Smith, "German Trade Competition in Latin America," *Commercial Pan America* 53 (October 1936): 10.

38. Circular of Auswärtiges Amt, June 18, 1934, *DGFP, C,* III, 34–35; Brazilian chargé (Berlin) to MRE, June 18, 1934, AHI 397/4/10; German legation (Rio) to MRE, June 20, 1934, AHI 419/2/20.

39. Handelspolitischer Ausschuss Protokoll, May 24, 1934, RGFM 2612: 5650/H003887.

40. H. Kroll, *Lebenserinnerungen,* p. 73.

41. Handelspolitischer Ausschuss Protokoll, June 27, 1934, RGFM 2612: 5650/H003904, pp. 906–907; Ritter to various missions in South America, June 11, 1934, RGFM 3400: 8731/609965.

42. Ritter to various missions in South America, June 11, 1934, RGFM 3400:8731/609967; German legation (Rio) to MRE, June 13, 1934, AHI 419/2/20.

43. German legation (Rio) to MRE, June 25, 1934, AHI 419/2/20.

44. Kiep to Ritter, July 24, 1934, RGFM 3008:6483/485927.

45. Ibid.

46. CFCE, 3ª Sessão[August 20, 1934], PR 32/485927.

47. Aranha to Vargas, n.d. [1934], Vargas Papers; unsigned memo ("Propaganda do Brasil no Exterior"), n.d. [1934], Macedo Soares Papers.

48. Macedo Soares to Vargas, February 25, 1935, Macedo Soares Papers; Amb. Seeds to Foreign Office, December 27, 1934, RFO 420, doc. 47.

49. Hélio Silva, *1931: Os Tenentes no Poder,* p. 250.

50. Nathaniel Leff's discussion of the sources of the *técnicos'* influence, although referring essentially to the post–World War II period, is relevant to Dantas's case. See his *Economic Policy-Making and Development in Brazil, 1947–1964,* pp. 148–152.

51. British commercial sec't. (Rio) to DOT, November 14, 1934, RFO 371, doc. A9558/7738/6.

52. Dantas et al. to CFCE, August 10, 1934, CFCE 70/979.

53. Quoted in Carolina Nabuco, *A vida de Virgílio de Melo Franco,* p. 17.

54. Souza Costa to Vargas, June 3, 1937, PR 31/27869.

55. Vargas to Aranha, October 1, 1934, Aranha Papers.

56. Vargas to Aranha, January 11, 1935, Souza Costa to Aranha, November 8, 1934, ibid.; CFCE, 2ª Sessão[August 13, 1934], PR 32/29515.

57. CFCE, 3ª Sessão, PR 32/29463; 4ª Sessão[August 27, 1934], PR 32/29467.

58. Dantas to Câmara de Comércio de Acôrdos (CFCE), August 31, 1934, CFCE 4/3; CFCE, 5ª Sessão[September 3, 1934], PR 32/29466.

59. The act was an amendment to the Smoot-Hawley Act permitting

executive discretion in adjusting tariff rates as much as 50 percent (Cordell Hull, *Memoirs*, I, 357–359).

60. Franklin D. Roosevelt to Hull, November 19, 1934, Edgar B. Nixon, ed., *Franklin D. Roosevelt and Foreign Affairs*, II, 274; Hull, *Memoirs*, I, 370.

61. Lloyd C. Gardner, *Economic Aspects of New Deal Diplomacy*, pp. 41–44.

62. Sec't., International Apple Assoc., to State Dept., March 2, 1934, SD 832.5151/306; Ad. Auriema, Inc., to State Dept., April 17, 1934, SD 832.5151/341. For letters on the projected Brazilian treaty, see letters to Hull or State Dept. from Merchants' Assoc. of New York, January 25, 1934, SD 832.5151/270; American Exporters' and Importers' Assoc., January 25, 1934, SD 832.5151/272; Newark Chamber of Commerce, January 31, 1934, SD 832.5151/276; Baltimore Assoc. of Commerce, February 6, 1934, SD 832.5151/280; St. Louis Chamber of Commerce, February 9, 1934 SD 832.5151/320; American Chamber of Commerce for Brazil, July 13, 1934, SD 832.5151/401.

63. Acting sec't. of state to Roosevelt, June 27, 1933; Roosevelt to acting sec't. of state, June 29, 1933, *FR, 1933*, V, 61.

64. U.S. consul general (Rio) to State Dept., March 15, 1934, and Hugh Gibson to Edwin Wilson (State Dept.), April 13, 1934, SD 832.5151/339½.

65. Gibson to Wesley Frost, September 24, 1935, and Joseph Grew, March 28, 1934, Hugh Gibson Papers (henceforth Gibson Papers), Box 46.

66. Gibson to Ray C. Cox, May 2, 1934, ibid., Box 45.

67. Gibson to J. Phillip Groves, September 25, 1933, ibid., Box 46.

68. Cover note to dispatch from Seeds, February 21, 1934, RFO 371, doc. A1492/310/6; Seeds to Robert Craigie (Foreign Office), June 5, 1934, RFO 371, doc. A5053/310/6.

69. Aranha and Dantas to John Williams, July 23, 1934, SD 810.5151/Williams Mission/44; Aranha to MRE, October 4, 1934, AHI 408/1/4.

70. Gibson to Sumner Welles, September 5, 1934, Gibson Papers, Box 48.

71. Gibson to Roosevelt, September 4, 1934, Roosevelt Papers, OF 405; memo by British commercial sec't. (Rio), n.d. (sent to Foreign Office on September 19, 1934), RFO 371, doc. A7671/310/6.

72. Aranha to Vargas, November 2, 1934, Aranha Papers. For other examples of his impressions of the United States, see his letters to Souza Costa (September 18, 1934), Vargas (October 10, 1934), and Bouças (October 24, 1934), ibid.

73. Chairman, Brazil Committee, American Exporters & Importers Assoc., to State Dept., September 4, 1934, SD 832.5151/423; memo by Feis, September 14, 1934, SD 832.5151/430.

74. Memo by W. Manning and Donald Heath, September 27, 1934, SD 832.5151/444.

75. Aranha to MRE, October 1, 2, 5, 6, 1934, AHI 408/3/8; State Dept. memo,

October 8, 1934, SD 632.6231/14; Heath to Feis, October 11, 1934, SD 611.3231/659.

76. Aranha to MRE, October 5, 1934, AHI 408/3/8; Paulo Hasslocher to Vargas, October 9, 1934, and Aranha to Vargas, October 10, 1934, Vargas Papers.

77. *Brazilian Business* 14 (April 1934): 114–115; Sebastião Sampaio to Vargas, January 14, 1938, PR 37/2612; Kiep to Auswärtiges Amt, October 11, 1934, RGFM 4463:K906/224813. On Sampaio's desire for promotion, see his letter to Vargas, April 12, 1934, Vargas Papers.

78. Gibson to Welles, August 4, 1936, Gibson Papers, Box 48; remarks by Sampaio, CFCE, 10ᵃ Sessão [October 8, 1934], PR 19/3945.

79. Bouças to Aranha, October 5, 1934, Aranha Papers.

80. The "Macedo Soares" folder in PR 9 has pertinent material on Macedo Soares's efforts to unify *paulista* dissidents and restore amicable relations with the federal authorities.

81. Foreign Office memo, February 13, 1935, RFO, doc. A1388/1388/6; Afonso Arinos de Melo Franco to Melo Franco, May 28, 1932, Melo Franco Papers, I-36/14; Gibson to Welles, October 2, 1934, Gibson Papers, Box 48.

82. CFCE, 10ᵃ Sessão, PR 19/3945.

83. MRE to Aranha, October 12, 1934, AHI 408/3/12. Sampaio told the CFCE on October 15 that Dantas had collaborated in drafting the communication (CFCE, 11ᵃ Sessão, PR 19/3945).

84. Kiep to Auswärtiges Amt, October 11, 1934, RGFM 4463:K906/224810–813.

85. Kiep to Auswärtiges Amt, October 20, 1934, RGFM 4463:K906/224825–826.

86. CFCE, 12ᵃ Sessão, PR 19/3945.

87. Ibid.

88. Aranha to MRE, October 25, 1934, AHI 408/3/8; Aranha to Vargas, October 10, 1934, Vargas Papers; Aranha to MRE, October 16, 1934, AHI 408/3/8.

89. Welles to Gibson, October 19, 1934, Gibson Papers, Box 48; Welles to Asst: Pres. Sec't. Marvin H. McIntyre, October 26, 1934, Nixon, *Roosevelt and Foreign Affairs*, II, 244; Peek to Francis Sayre, October 19, 1934, Roosevelt Papers, OF 11, Brazil 1933–1939.

90. Aranha to MRE, October 26, 1934, AHI 408/3/12; Hasslocher to Vargas, October 27, 1934, PR 14/49244.

91. Welles to Aranha, October 30, *FR, 1934*, IV, 551; Aranha to Macedo Soares, October 30, 1934, Aranha Papers.

92. Vargas to Aranha, October 30, 1934, Aranha Papers; Sampaio to Vargas, October 28, 1934, PR 14/49190.

93. Handelspolitischer Ausschuss Protokoll, October 15, 1934, RGFM 2612:

5650/H003960; Auswärtiges Amt to Kiep, October 16, 1934, RGFM 4463:K906/ 224819; Ministry of Food and Agriculture to Auswärtiges Amt, October 27, 1934, RGFM 4463:K906/224832; RWM to Auswärtiges Amt, October 27, 1934, RGFM 4463:K906/224835; Ritter to Kiep, October 29, 1934, RGFM 4463:K906/ 224842–843; Kiep to Auswärtiges Amt, November 7, 1934, RGFM 4463:K906/ 224921; Auswärtiges Amt memo ("Kommentar zum deutschbrasilianischen vertraulichen Notenwechsel . . ."), n.d., RGFM 4463:K906/224938.

94. For the texts of the notes, see RGFM 4463:K906/224932–941. The note of acknowledgment from Sampaio and Dantas is on frames 224963–964.

95. Kiep to Auswärtiges Amt, November 7, 1934, RGFM 4463:K906/224922–925. On the trade delegation's trip to Argentina, see Arnold Ebel, *Das Dritte Reich und Argentinien*, pp. 102–109.

96. CFCE, 4ª Sessão, PR 32/29467; Vargas to Aranha, October 30, 1934, Aranha Papers.

97. For a stimulating discussion of power relationships and the role of sanctions, see Peter Bachrach and Morton S. Baratz, "Decisions and Nondecisions: An Analytical Framework," *American Political Science Review* 57 (September 1963): 632–642.

98. Kiep to Auswärtiges Amt, November 7, 1934, RGFM 4463:K906/224923.

99. Dantas et al. to CFCE, August 10, 1934, CFCE 70/979.

100. Macedo Soares to Aranha, November 23, 1934, Aranha Papers.

101. Gibson to State Dept., August 21, 1933, *FR, 1933*, V, 18–19.

102. MRE to Cyro Freitas-Valle, August 28, 1934, AHI 408/3/12; Freitas-Valle to MRE, August 29, 1934, AHI 408/3/8; CFCE, 5ª Sessão, PR 32/29466.

103. Bouças to Vargas, March 7, 1934, PR 12/41860; Aranha to MRE, November 1, 1934, AHI 408/3/8; Aranha to Vargas, November 2, 1934, Aranha Papers; MRE to Aranha, October 12, 1934, AHI 408/3/12.

104. CFCE, 14ª Sessão, PR 32/29467; 5ª Sessão, 32/29466; MRE to Aranha, October 6, 1934, AHI 408/3/12.

105. Sampaio to Vargas, November 4, 1934, PR 14/49141.

106. MRE to Aranha, November 1, 1934, AHI 408/3/12; Aranha to MRE, November 12, 1934, AHI 408/3/8.

107. Kiep to Auswärtiges Amt, October 20, 1934, RGFM 4463:K906/224825–826; Vargas to Aranha, October 30, 1934, Aranha Papers; Góes Monteiro to Vargas, November 8, 1934, PR 15/49820.

108. Kiep to Auswärtiges Amt, November 7, 1934, RGFM 4463:K906/224923.

109. CFCE, 11ª Sessão, 12ª Sessão, PR 19/3945.

110. CFCE, 4ª Sessão, PR 32/29467; 16ª Sessão [November 19, 1934], PR 16/24; Juracy Magalhães to Vargas, November 8, 1934, PR 14/49283; Sindicato dos Invernistas (Barretos, São Paulo) to Vargas, October 26, 1934, PR 14/48763.

111. Vorstand des Gesamtverbandes der deutschen Baumwollspinnereien,

Präsidium der Vereinigung des Baumwollgrosshandels, and Präsidium der Bremer Baumwollbörse to Hitler, et al., May 28, 1934, Bundesarchiv, R43 II/313.

112. Alfred Rosenberg, *Das politische Tagebuch Alfred Rosenbergs aus den Jahren 1934/35 und 1939/40*, p. 27.

113. Otto Behr & Co. to Brazilian chargé (Berlin), June 29, 1934 (copy), and G. Gaelzer Netto (Berlin) to Min. de Trabalho, July 2, 1934, Bouças Papers. Behr & Co. reiterated the offer in September (CFCE 6/29).

114. Memo by representative of Min. de Trabalho, August 27, 1934, and memo by Torres Filho and Clovis Ribeiro, n.d. [August 1934], CFCE 4/10.

115. Statements by Macedo Soares, *Correio da Manhã*, August 16, 1934; speech by Cincinato Braga, October 26, 1934, Câmara dos Deputados, *Annaes 1934*, VI, 261; Raul Fernandes to Aranha, November 9, 1934, Aranha Papers.

116. Commercial sec't. (Rio) to DOT, November 14, 1934, RFO 371. doc. A9558/7738/6; Souza Costa to Aranha, December 14, 1934, Aranha Papers.

117. Souza Costa to Vargas, November 29, 1934, Vargas Papers.

118. British Amb. Seeds (Rio), Annual Report, 1934, RFO 371, doc. A4406/4406/6.

119. Kiep to Auswärtiges Amt, November 7, 1934, RGFM 4463:K906/224926.

120. *DGFP, C*, III, 511.

121. CFCE, 3ᵃ Sessão, PR 32/29463.

122. Sampaio to sec't. gen. (MRE), June 15, 1934, Diversos do Ministério, Serviços Econômicos e Commerciaes, AHI.

123. Reich Min. of Food and Agriculture to Auswärtiges Amt, October 27, 1934, and RWM to Auswärtiges Amt, October 27, 1934, RGFM 4463:K906/224832, 224835.

124. MRE to Aranha, October 4, 1934, AHI 408/3/12.

125. Dantas et al. to CFCE, August 10, 1934, CFCE 70/979; CFCE, 12ᵃ Sessão, PR 19/3945.

126. CFCE, 10ᵃ Sessão, PR 19/3945; 4ᵃ Sessão, PR 32/29467; 14ᵃ Sessão, PR 19/3946; 15ᵃ Sessão [November 12, 1934], PR 16/24.

127. Kiep to Auswärtiges Amt, November 7, 1934, RGFM 4463:K906/224922–925. On the influence of an organization's "climate of opinion" on decision making, see Joseph de Rivera, *The Psychological Dimension of Foreign Policy*, p. 70.

128. CFCE, 4ᵃ Sessão, PR 32/29467; 12ᵃ Sessão, PR 19/3945; Ronald de Carvalho (for Vargas) to Hasslocher, November 12, 1934, PR 14/49244.

129. Lester Grinspoon's observations on the psychological interplay between leader and subordinate in a decision-making situation are suggestive in this regard. See his "Interpersonal Constraints and the Decision-Maker," in *International Conflict and Behavioral Science*, ed. Roger D. Fisher, pp. 242–243.

130. Gibson to Bouças, November 13, 1933, Bouças Papers; Gibson to J. Reuben Clark, June 1934, Gibson Papers, Box 45.

131. Gibson to Welles, January 16, 1936, Gibson Papers, Box 48.

132. H. G. Brock to Aranha, June 8, 1936 (copy), Bouças Papers.

133. Gibson to Welles, January 16, 1936, Gibson Papers, Box 48.

134. Bouças to Aranha, October 26, 1934, Aranha Papers; Gibson to Welles, January 16, 1936, Gibson Papers, Box 48.

135. Bouças to Gibson, June 4, 1936, Bouças Papers; Bouças to Aranha, October 5, 1934, Aranha Papers.

136. Bouças to Aranha, October 26, 1934, Aranha Papers.

137. CFCE, 10ª Sessão, PR 19/3945.

138. Vargas to Aranha, October 30, 1934, Aranha Papers.

139. Bouças to Aranha, October 26, 1934, ibid.

3. Between Washington and Berlin (1935–1936)

1. Alton Frye, *Nazi Germany and the American Hemisphere*, p. 75.

2. Aranha to Vargas, January 15, 1935, Vargas Papers; Aranha to MRE, November 12, 1934, AHI 408/3/8; Muniz to Aranha, November 14, 1934, AHI 408/1/4; Aranha to MRE, November 12, 1934, AHI 408/3/8; Muniz to Aranha, November 14, 1934, and Freitas-Valle to Aranha, November 13, 1934, AHI 408/1/4.

3. Memo by Welles, November 15, 1934, SD 724.3415/4337½; CFCE, 15ª Sessão, PR 16/24.

4. Macedo Soares to Aranha, November 23, 1934, Aranha Papers.

5. MRE to Aranha, December 1, 1934, AHI 408/12.

6. Aranha to Macedo Soares, January 18, 1935, Aranha Papers.

7. Freitas-Valle to MRE, August 9, 1934, AHI 408/3/8; George Peek to Welles, November 23, 1934, SD 611.3231/718; memo by Sayre, November 23, 1934, and Peek to McIntyre, December 10, 1934, Roosevelt Papers, OF 11, Brazil 1933–1939.

8. Aranha to MRE, December 6, 1934, AHI 408/3/8; memo by Feis, December 6, 1934, *FR, 1934*, IV, 568–569.

9. Muniz to Aranha, December 14, 1934, AHI 408/1/4; Souza Costa to Aranha, December 14, 1934, Aranha Papers.

10. Cordell Hull, *Memoirs*, I, 373–374; William Phillips to Hull, December 13, 1934, Cordell Hull Papers (henceforth Hull Papers), container 37, folder 81 (henceforth 37/81).

11. Hull, *Memoirs*, I, 373.

12. Aranha to MRE, December 15, 1934, AHI 408/3/8.

13. Vargas to Aranha, October 16, 1934, Aranha Papers; Macedo Soares to Aranha, November 27, 1934, ibid.; Aranha to Macedo Soares, October 30, 1934, ibid.

14. Aranha to Macedo Soares, October 30, 1934, ibid.; Aranha to Vargas, November 13, 1934, ibid.; Souza Costa to Aranha, December 14, 1934, ibid.; Souza Costa to Vargas, November 29, 1934, Vargas Papers.

15. MRE memo, March 28, 1935, PR 17/2231; Aranha to MRE, February 13, 1935, AHI 408/1/5.

16. MRE to Aranha, December 24, 1934, AHI 408/3/12. See also MRE (for Souza Costa) to Aranha, January 2, 1935, AHI 408/3/13.

17. Aranha to MRE, January 12, 1935, AHI 408/3/8.

18. Aranha to Vargas, n.d. [January 9, 1935], and January 15, 1935, Vargas Papers; Aranha to MRE, January 9, 1935, AHI 408/3/8.

19. Aranha to Melo Franco, January 13, 1935, Aranha Papers.

20. MRE to Aranha, January 9, 1935, AHI 408/3/4; Aranha to Vargas, January 9, 1935, Vargas Papers; State Dept. memo, January 30, 1935, *FR, 1935*, IV, 338–339; Souza Costa to Vargas, January 29, 1935, Vargas Papers.

21. Souza Costa et al. to Vargas, March 19, 1935, PR 69/1585.

22. Ibid.

23. Ibid.

24. Souza Costa to Vargas, February 2, 1935, PR 16/381; *New York Herald Tribune*, February 3, 1935; *New York Times*, February 3, 1935.

25. Aranha to Hull, February 2, 1935, *FR, 1935*, IV, 340–341.

26. Aranha to MRE, February 13, 1935, Aranha Papers.

27. Aranha to Macedo Soares, February 12, 1935, Macedo Soares Papers.

28. Aranha to A. Melo Franco, January 13, 1935, Aranha Papers.

29. Aranha to Rubens Rosa, February 18, 1935, ibid.; Aranha to Vargas, February 27, 1935, Vargas Papers.

30. MRE memo, March 28, 1935, PR 17/2231.

31. Vargas to Poder Legislativo, April 20, 1935, PR 18/2901; MRE to Aranha, April 20, 1935, AHI 408/3/12; *Correio da Manhã*, April 24, 1935.

32. U.S. Chargé George Gordon (Rio) to State Dept., May 31, 1935, SD 611.3231/964.

33. Gordon to State Dept., June 6, 1935, *FR, 1935*, IV, 301–303; memo by Lodi, June 24, 1935, CFCE 24/395-v.1; Bouças to Aranha, June 14, 1935, Aranha Papers.

34. "Proteccionismo norte-americano," *Diário da Noite*, June 4, 1935.

35. "A América Latina e a crise econômica," ibid., June 5, 1935.

36. "O tratado de commércio brasileiro-norte-americano," ibid., June 7, 1935.

37. "A importação de productos norte-americanos," ibid., June 8, 1935.

38. MRE memo, n.d. [June–July 1935], Aranha Papers.

39. Bouças to Aranha, June 28, 1935, ibid.

40. "O tratado de commércio brasileiro-norte-americano," *Correio da Manhã*, June 25, 1935; Bouças to Aranha, June 28, 1935, Aranha Papers. For other articles by Bouças, see "A fallência do proteccionismo brasileiro: Novos rumos da nossa política tarifaria," *O Jornal*, June 28, 1935; "Tratado commercial norte-americano—o Brasil: Colônia ou nação?" *O Jornal*, July 6, 1935; "Tratado commercial norte-americano—Deve o Brasil praticar uma política 'de avestruz'?" *O Jornal*, July 7, 1935.

41. Bouças to Aranha, June 14, 1935, Aranha Papers; Gordon to State Dept., June 29, 1935, *FR, 1935*, IV, 304–305.

42. Aranha to Souza Costa, June 18, 1935, Aranha Papers.

43. See Irving L. Janis, "Decisional Conflicts: A Theoretical Analysis," *Journal of Conflict Resolution* 3 (March 1959): 6–27, for convincing suggestions on the sources of decisional conflict and the decision maker's behavior when he is confronted with "negative feedback."

44. Aranha to MRE, June 13, 1935, AHI 408/3/8; *Congressional Record*, 74th Cong., 1st. sess. vol. 79, part 2, p. 1473.

45. Hull to Gordon, May 28, 1935, *FR, 1935*, IV, 300; Aranha to MRE, July 3, 1935, AHI 408/3/8; MRE to Aranha, July 4, 1935, AHI 408/3/8; Gordon to State Dept., August 3, 1935, *FR, 1935*, IV, 307.

46. Aranha to Vargas, July 9, 17, 23, 1935, to Souza Costa, July 22, 1935, and to Bouças, July 29, 1935, Aranha Papers.

47. Gibson to Hull, August 23, 1935, *FR, 1935*, IV, 309.

48. Gibson to Allan Dawson, September 4, 1935, Gibson Papers, Box 45.

49. Gibson to Hull, August 23, 1935, *FR, 1935*, IV, 309–310; Gibson to Dawson, September 4, 1935, Gibson Papers, Box 45.

50. Hull to Gibson, August 26, 1935; memo by Wilson, August 21, 1935; memo by Hull, August 27, 1935, *FR, 1935*, IV, 311, 308, 314.

51. Freitas-Valle to MRE, August 27, 1935, AHI 408/3/8; Freitas-Valle to Acioly, September 10, 1935, Acioly Papers.

52. Gibson to Dawson, September 4, 1935, Gibson Papers, Box 45.

53. Gibson to Hull, August 27, 1935, *FR, 1935*, IV, 313.

54. Gibson to Hull, September 20, 1935, Hull Papers, 38/85.

55. Gibson to Hull, August 27, 1935, *FR, 1935*, IV, 315.

56. Gibson to Hull, September 20, 1935, *FR, 1935*, IV, 315–316.

57. Câmara dos Deputados, *Annaes 1935*, XV, 528; XVI, 132, 144.

58. Gibson to Hull, September 13, 1935, Hull Papers, 38/85.

59. Gibson to Hull, September 20, 1935, ibid.

60. Hull to Gibson, October 4, 1935, ibid.

61. E. P. Thomas to Welles, August 26, 1935, SD 611.3231/1002.

62. Foreign Traders' Assoc. of Philadelphia to Roosevelt, September 30, 1935, SD 611.3231/1035; Sargent & Co. (New York) to State Dept., September

27, 1935, SD 611.3231/1027; Durwyllan Co. (Paterson, N.J.) to State Dept., September 27, 1935, SD 611.3231/1028; Roller Bearing Co. of America (Trenton) to Hull, September 30, 1935, SD 611.3231/1045.

63. U.S. consul general (São Paulo) to State Dept., October 2, 1935, SD 611.3231/1055.

64. Aranha to Bouças, October 21, 1935, Aranha Papers; Theodore Xanthaky to Gibson, November 1, 1935, Gibson Papers, Box 47.

65. Ritter to Kiep, January 23, 1935, RGFM 3008:6484/485913.

66. H. Kroll, *Lebenserinnerungen*, pp. 74, 85.

67. Ibid., p. 76.

68. Reichsstelle für den Aussenhandel to Aussenhandesstellen, April 3, 1935, Bundesarchiv R7 VI/201(1).

69. Reichskanzlei to the state sec't., November 19, 1935, Bundesarchiv R43 II/323; Deutsch-Brasilianische Handelskammer, *Bericht über das Jahr 1935*, p. 41; *Frankfurter Zeitung*, June 11, 1936, p. 6.

70. Brazil, Instituto Nacional de Estatística, *Anuário Estatístico do Brasil 1937*, p. 306.

71. U.S. consul (São Paulo) to State Dept., November 28, 1936, SD 632. 6217/19.

72. German consul (São Paulo) to Firma August Schwer Soehne (Villingen), July 8, 1935, Bundesarchiv, R7 VI/202(1).

73. CFCE, 27ª Sessão [February 11, 1935], PR 17/1406.

74. See the notes from German legation, February 21, April 4 and 9, 1935, AHI 420/1/1.

75. Memo by director of Exchange Dept., Banco do Brasil, March 9, 1935, CFCE 12/123.

76. Flores da Cunha to Vargas, February 25, 1935, PR 16/754, and March 25, 1935, PR 16/1103. For the reaction of commercial interests, see Assoc. Commercial (Porto Alegre) to Vargas, February 23, 1935, PR 16/740; Sindicato Arrozeiro to CFCE, April 6, 1935, PR 17/1512; Quarto Congresso de Assoc. Comerciais do Rio Grande do Sul to Vargas, April 30, 1935, PR 17/1512.

77. In a letter to Aranha on May 10, 1935 (Aranha Papers), Vargas complained that the Germans were reexporting Brazilian products, thus securing foreign exchange that could have gone to Brazil. On the growing dependence of cotton producers on the German market, see the memo of May 7, 1935, by representatives of São Paulo Centro dos Exportadores de Algodão and Bolsa de Mercadorias (São Paulo) (CFCE 17/42).

78. Kulenkampff (Rio) to Kiep, May 9, 1935, RGFM 4463:K906/225119.

79. Assoc. Comercial (Belém) to CFCE, May 18, 1935, CFCE 12/122-v. 4; Câmara dos Deputados, *Annaes, 1935*, IV, 91; Magalhães to Vargas, June 13, 1935, PR 17/1794; Assoc. Comercial (Santos) to CFCE, June 18, 1935, CFCE 16/240.

80. American embassy (Rio) to State Dept., May 17, 1935, SD 832.5151/630;

Auswärtiges Amt to German legation (Rio), May 14, 1935, RGFM 4463:K906/ 225114; Auswärtiges Amt memo, May 14, 1935, RGFM 4463:K906/225115; Artur Schmidt-Elskop to Auswärtiges Amt, June 5, 1935, RGFM 4463:K906/ 225170.

81. Schmidt-Elskop to Auswärtiges Amt, May 15, 1935 (with marginal notation), RGFM 4463:K906/225129.

82. Memo by Dr. E. von Bodenhausen (São Paulo), November 4, 1935 (sent to Auswärtiges Amt on November 26, 1935, by Werberate der Deutschen Wirtschaft), Auswärtiges Amt, Abt. III, Akten betr. Deutschtum in Brasilien . . . , Band 4, AAA.

83. Kulenkampff to Kiep, May 14, 1935, RGFM 4463:K906/225144; Gastão Vidigal to Macedo Soares, May 15, 1935, Macedo Soares Papers.

84. Schmidt-Elskop to Auswärtiges Amt, June 13, 1935, RGFM 4463:K906/ 225171.

85. CFCE, 44ª Sessão [June 17, 1935], PR 19/4845.

86. Assoc. Comercial (João Pessôa) to Vargas, June 19, 1935, PR 17/1844; Centro dos Exportadores (Fortaleza) to Vargas, June 22, 1935, PR 17/1869; Assoc. Comercial (Recife) to CFCE, June 23, 1935, CFCE 2/20; Gov. Alvaro Maia (Amazonas) to CFCE, June 18, 1935, CFCE 2/20; *Diário do Poder Legislativo*, July 5, 1935, pp. 2000–2001.

87. Unsigned memo ("Reunião realizada . . . no dia 10 de Julho de 1935, com os representantes dos productores de algodão"), CFCE 17/242.

88. Alan C. Tod (Liverpool) to George Villiers (Bearing Bros.), February 11, 1935, Board of Trade Records, II/345.

89. *O Observador Econômico e Financeiro*, (Rio) 1 (June 1936): 18.

90. Henry Mann to Joseph Flack, December 20, 1934, William E. Dodd Papers, General Correspondence, 1935.

91. NFTC, *Official Report . . . 1935*, p. 351.

92. John R. Huber, "The Effects of German Clearing Agreements and Import Restrictions on Cotton, 1934–1939," *Southern Economic Journal* 6 (April 1940): 420.

93. British commercial sec't. (Rio) to DOT, July 15, 1935, RFO 371, doc. A7126/1279/6.

94. H. G. Smith, "Cotton Trends in Latin America," *Commercial Pan America* 56 (January 1937): 2; memo ("Periplo do Algodão Brasileiro") by Aloysio de Magalhães, September 17, 1936, Macedo Soares Papers; Huber, "German Clearing Agreements," p. 473.

95. José Acioly to Hildebrando Acioly, July 20, 1935, Acioly Papers.

96. German consul (Bahia) to Auswärtiges Amt, September 23, 1936, RGFM 2974:6466/483156.

97. Report to CFCE by representatives of northern cotton producers, July 6, 1935, CFCE 17/242.

98. Memo ("A Exportação de Algodão do Norte e os Marcos Compensa-

dos") by Torres Filho, January 13, 1936, CFCE 21/334; Sen. E. Velozo Borges (Paraiba) to Vargas, November 3, 1935, PR 22/7905.

99. Memo ("Pontos de vista dos algodoeiros de São Paulo relativos à exportação do algodão") by Centro dos Exportadores and Bolsa de Mercadorias (São Paulo), May 7, 1935, CFCE 17/42.

100. Centro dos Exportadores de Algodão (São Paulo) to CFCE, May 17, 1935, CFCE 12/122-v.4.

101. Auswärtiges Amt to Schmidt-Elskop, May 10, 1935, RGFM 4463:K906/ 225/111.

102. Memo ("Gegenwärtiger Stand und Zukunftsaussichten der deutschen Handelsbeziehungen mit Südamerika") by Kroll, June 12, 1935, RGFM 3008:6483/485784–786; Hans-Jürgen Schröder, Deutschland und die Vereinigten Staaten, 1933–1939, p. 229.

103. Ritter to Schmidt-Elskop, June 19, 1935, and Schmidt-Elskop to Auswärtiges Amt, June 20, 1935, RGFM 4463:K906/225173–175.

104. RWM to Auswärtiges Amt, June 29, 1935, RGFM 4463:K906/225177.

105. Centro dos Agricultores (Santos) to Min. of Agriculture, June 30, 1935, CFCE 20/17; N. V. Bananen Import Maatschappij (Amsterdam) to Brazilian legation (Berlin), July 17, 1935, CFCE 20/17; J. Magalhães to Vargas, July 25, 1935, PR 20/5528.

106. Schmidt-Elskop to Auswärtiges Amt, July 6, 1935, RGFM 4463:K906/ 225184; unsigned memo ("Reunião . . . no dia 10 de Julho de 1935 . . ."), CFCE 17/242; Schmidt-Elskop to Auswärtiges Amt, July 18, 1935, RGFM 4463:K906/225195; memo by Kulenkampff, November 18, 1935, RGFM 4465: K913/226355.

107. Auswärtiges Amt to Schmidt-Elskop, October 12, 1935, RGFM 4465: K913/226326–327.

108. Kiep to Schmidt-Elskop, March 12, 1935, RGFM 4463:K906/225049; Schmidt-Elskop to Auswärtiges Amt, May 15, June 5, July 18, 1935, RGFM 4463:K906/225141, 225170, 225197; German embassy (Washington) to Auswärtiges Amt, June 7, 1935, RGFM 6:AHAI6/00925; German embassy (Washington) to Auswärtiges Amt, October 8, 1935, RGFM 3381:8597/603730–731.

109. Memo by Kroll, July 23, 1935, RGFM 2643:5654/H005931.

110. Unsigned memo ("Intercambio com a Allemanha"), n.d. [February 1936], Macedo Soares Papers; O Observador Econômico e Financeiro 1 (June 1936): 18.

111. Centro dos Exportadores de Algodão (São Paulo) to CFCE, July 15, 1935, CFCE 2/20; Orlando de Almeida Prado to Macedo Soares, October 7, 1935, Macedo Soares Papers; CFCE, 100ª Sessão [September 9, 1936], PR 27/18503.

112. Assoc. Comercial (João Pessôa) to Vargas, June 19, 1935, PR 17/1844;

Velozo Borges to Vargas, November 3, 1935, PR 22/7905; memo by Torres Filho, January 13, 1936, and José Pereira Lyra et al. to CFCE, February 21, 1936, CFCE 21/334.

113. Kulenkampff to Auswärtiges Amt, November 20, 1935, RGFM 4465: K913/226345.

114. Schmidt-Elskop to Auswärtiges Amt, October 30, 1935, RGFM 4465: K913/226331; Kulenkampff to Auswärtiges Amt, November 20, 1935, RGFM 4465:K913/226341–342.

115. Memoranda by Kulenkampff, March 16, May 8, 1935, RGFM 4463: K906/225055, 225124–125.

116. Schmidt-Elskop to Auswärtiges Amt, September 28, 1935, RGFM 2643: 5654/H005930; Auswärtiges Amt to Schmidt-Elskop, October 3, 1935, RGFM 2643:5654/H005928; Bouças to Aranha, October 11, 1935, Aranha Papers; MRE to Aranha, October 14, 1935, AHI 408/3/13.

117. Deutsch-Amerikanische Baumwoll-Import G.m.b.H. (Bremen) to P. Salgado & Cia., December 17, 1935, CFCE 21/334.

118. Memo by Kulenkampff, November 18, 1935, and report to Auswärtiges Amt, November 20, 1935, RGFM 4465:K913/226356, 226347.

119. CFCE, 68ª Sessão, November 25, 1935, PR 23/8715; Brazilian chargé (Berlin) to MRE, December 9, 1935, AHI 397/4/10.

120. Kulenkampff to Auswärtiges Amt, November 20, 1935, RGFM 4465: K913/226348.

121. Macedo Soares to Schmidt-Elskop, November 24, 1935, AHI 420/1/2.

122. Hans Dieckhoff to state sec't., June 20, 1935, RGFM 3008:6483/485852–853; Brazilian chargé (Berlin) to MRE, October 11, 1935, AHI 397/4/10.

123. Interview with J. J. Moniz de Aragão, Rio de Janeiro, March 13, 1967.

124. Moniz de Aragão to MRE, January 29, 1936, AHI 397/3/9.

125. Sampaio to João [?], January 3, 1936, V. Melo Franco Papers; Sampaio to Macedo Soares, July 3, 1936, Macedo Soares Papers.

126. Schmidt-Elskop to Kulenkampff, July 2, 1935, RGFM 4463:K906/ 225187–188.

127. Interview with Mário Simonsen, Rio de Janeiro, May 20, 1967.

128. Kulenkampff to Auswärtiges Amt, November 20, 1935, RGFM 4465: K913/226340.

129. Humberto Arruda to Vargas, July 7, 1939, CFCE 68/961-1.

130. Auswärtiges Amt to Ritter, January 19, 1935 (with enclosures), RGFM 4465:K913/226287–297; memo by Kroll, June 20, 1935, RGFM 2643:5653/ H005939–941; Ritter to RWM et al., July 9, 1935, RGFM 4463:K906/225186; Kulenkampff to Auswärtiges Amt, November 20, 1935, RGFM 4465:K913/ 226340–341, –349.

131. Moniz de Aragão to MRE, January 10, 1936, and RWM to Wilhelm

Beutner, February 18, 1936 (copy to MRE by Moniz de Aragão, March 2, 1936), AHI 397/3/9.

132. Instituto Bahiano do Fumo to J. Magalhães, October 15, 1935, and February 19, 1936, CFCE 22/354.

133. Assoc. Citrícola de São Paulo to CFCE, February 3, 1936, CFCE 22/350; Assoc. Comercial (Joinville) to CFCE, February 17, 1936, and governor of Santa Catharina to CFCE, February 26, 1936, CFCE 21/333.

134. Memo by Torres Filho, January 13, 1936, CFCE 21/334.

135. See, for example, PR 19/4120–4123, 4133, 4136, 4175, 4178, 4182, 4238.

136. Telegrams to CFCE from Assoc. Comercial (João Pessôa), February 17, 1936, Assoc. Comercial (Fortaleza), January 23, 1936, Centro dos Exportadores de Ceará, January 23, 1936, CFCE 21/334.

137. Menezes Pimentel to Waldemar Falcão, January 20, 1936, to CFCE, January 20, 1936, CFCE 21/334; to Vargas, January 20, 1936, PR 19/4238.

138. Various congressmen to Vargas, February 14, 1936, CFCE 21/334.

139. CFCE, 80ᵃ Sessão, PR 24/11338; 83a Sessão, PR 25/11908.

140. Memo by Torres Filho, March 18, 1936, CFCE 21/334; Pereira Lyra to CFCE, April 1, 1936, CFCE 21/334; Souza Aranha to Beutner, April 8, 1936, RGFM 4465:K913/226377.

141. Moniz de Aragão to MRE, February 12, 1936, AHI 397/3/9.

142. Memo by Ritter, February 13, 1936, RGFM 4463:K906/225208; Schröder, *Deutschland und die Vereinigten Staaten*, p. 250.

143. Moniz de Aragão to MRE, March 10, 1936, AHI 297/4/10.

144. Souza Costa to Vargas, n.d. [April 2, 1936], PR 52/1667; CFCE to Vargas, April 16, 1936, CFCE 21/334; Souza Aranha to Beutner, April 16, 1936, RGFM 4465:K913/226375.

145. Memo of conference (Auswärtiges Amt, et al.), May 6, 1936, RGFM 4463:K906/225292–293; Auswärtiges Amt to Brazilian legation, May 8, 1936, RGFM 2643:5653/H005891–892; MRE to Moniz de Aragão, May 14, 1936, AHI 397/4/13; Moniz de Aragão to Auswärtiges Amt, May 16, 1936, AHI 397/3/10.

146. Quoted in Souza Aranha to Aranha, July 16, 1936, Aranha Papers.

147. Xanthaky to Gibson, November 9, 1935, Gibson Papers, Box 47.

148. Gibson to Welles, December 30, 1935, ibid., Box 48.

149. Gibson to Welles, February 20, 1936, ibid.

150. Gibson to Hull, April 20 and May 7, 1936, *FR, 1936*, V, 248–249, 250–252.

151. Gaelzer-Netto to Vargas, May 18, 1936, PR 26/14514.

152. Moniz de Aragão to Ritter, May 25, 1936, and Ritter to Moniz de Aragão, May 26, 1936, AHI 397/3/10.

153. Handelspolitischer Ausschuss Protokoll, May 25, 1936, RGFM 2612: 5650/H004083; MRE to Moniz de Aragão, May 23, 1936, AHI 397/4/13.

154. Gibson to Hull, May 25, 1936, *FR, 1936*, V, 252.

155. Hull to Gibson, May 26, 1936, *FR, 1936*, V, 253–254; Aranha to Vargas, May 27, 1936, Aranha Papers.

156. Gibson to Hull, May 27, 1936, *FR, 1936*, V, 254.

157. Gibson to Hull, May 28, 1936, *FR, 1936*, V, 255.

158. MRE to Moniz de Aragão, May 29, 1936, AHI 397/4/13; Souza Aranha to Beutner, May 30, 1936, RGFM 3006:6467/484074.

159. Gibson to Hull, May 30, 1936 (two telegrams), *FR, 1936*, V, 256–257.

160. Gibson to Hull, June 1, 1936, *FR, 1936*, V, 261–263.

161. Amb. Hugh Gurney to J. M. Troutbeck (Foreign Office), June 2, 1936, RFO 371, doc. A5145/1807/6.

162. Welles to Gibson, June 1, 1936, *FR, 1936*, V, 259–261; Aranha to Vargas, n.d. [June 1, 1936], Vargas Papers; Aranha to MRE, June 1, 1936, AHI 408/3/8.

163. MRE to Moniz de Aragão, June 1, 2, 1936, AHI 408/3/8.

164. Moniz de Aragão to MRE, June 2, 1936, AHI 397/4/10.

165. Moniz de Aragão to MRE, June 1, 1936, AHI 397/4/10.

166. Bouças to Aranha, June 11, 1936, Aranha Papers; Gibson to Hull, June 3, 1936, *FR, 1936*, V, 263–264.

167. MRE to Moniz de Aragão, June 5, 1936, AHI 397/4/13.

168. For the texts, see Moniz de Aragão to MRE, June 8, 1936, AHI 397/3/10; RGFM 3008:6492/486123–135; Gibson to Hull, June 6, 1936 (two telegrams), *FR, 1936*, V, 264–266.

169. Gibson to Hull, June 6, 1936, and Phillips (for Hull) to Gibson, June 9, 1936, *FR, 1936*, V, 267, 268–269.

170. *Correio da Manhã*, June 7, 1936.

171. *Diário Carioca*, June 7, 1936.

172. *Diário de Notícias*, June 10, 1936; *Correio da Manhã*, June 10, 1936; *O Estado de São Paulo*, June 13, 1936.

173. Various telegrams mentioned or quoted in *O Estado de São Paulo*, June 14, 17, 1936; *Correio da Manhã*, June 11, 12, 17, 1936.

174. For example, Sindicato da Lavoura de Campinas to Vargas, May 5, 1936, PR 19/5068.

175. CFCE, 80ª Sessão, PR 24/11338.

176. *Folha da Manhã*, June 9, 1936; *Diário de Notícias*, June 11, 1936, reprinted in *Correio da Manhã*, June 14, 1936.

177. Ritter to Souza Aranha, July 2, 1936, RGFM 2974:6466/483053; Reichskanzlei to state sec't., June 23, 1936, Bundesarchiv R 43 II/323.

178. Moniz de Aragão to MRE, June 19, 1936, AHI 397/3/10; *Frankfurter Zeitung*, June 18, 1936.

179. Bestellungen aus der Pressekonferenz vom 9. Juni 1936, Anweisung nr. 530, Sammlung Brammer, Bundesarchiv ZSg. 101/7; Reichsstelle für den Aussenhandel to Aussenhandelsstellen, June 18, 1936, R7 VI/198(1); Abt. Aussen-

handel, Wirtschaftsgruppe GrossEin-u. Ausfuhrhandel to Aussenhandel-sabteilungen der Bezirksgruppen der WiGEA et al., June 22, 1936, R7 VI/198(1).

180. Gibson to Hull, June 10, 1936, FR, 1936, V, 269; counselor of embassy (Rio) to W. Manning, June 11, 1936, quoted in Manning to Lawrence Duggan, June 20, 1936, SD 632.6231/100. The vice-consul at Rio also filed a report on June 11 saying that, although it might appear that failure to sign a formal treaty meant a defeat for Germany, in reality it did not, since "no official action has been taken to eliminate compensation trade on the basis that it has been in effect during the past two years" (SD 632.6231/78).

181. Schmidt-Elskop to Auswärtiges Amt, June 17, 1936, RGFM 2974:6446/483014.

182. Bouças to Aranha, June 18, 1936, Aranha Papers.

183. Bouças to Aranha, June 25, 1936, ibid.; CFCE, 99ª Sessão, PR 26/16132; O Observador Econômico e Financeiro 1 (July 1936): 18.

184. Aranha to Bouças, July 1, 1936, Aranha Papers.

185. Aranha to MRE, June 19, 1936, AHI 408/3/8; MRE to Aranha, June 26, 1936, AHI 408/3/4.

186. Aranha to Vargas, July 14, 1936, Aranha Papers.

187. A revealing example of the secrecy surrounding those credits had occurred months earlier. In December 1935, four days after Schmidt-Elskop presented a note to Macedo Soares pointing out that they amounted to nearly £1 million sterling, Ambassador Gurney sent a dispatch to London mentioning a recent conversation with the foreign minister in which the latter "confirmed my impression that Germany has never had any appreciable frozen credits in Brazil" (Schmidt-Elskop to Macedo Soares, December 2, 1935, AHI 420/1/2; Gurney to Foreign Office, December 6, 1935, RFO 371, doc. A10849/1279/6).

188. Aranha to Vargas, July 21, 1936, Vargas Papers; Aranha to MRE, July 21, 1936, AHI 408/3/8; MRE (for Souza Costa) to Aranha, July 23, 1936, AHI 408/3/13; Vargas to Aranha, July 24, 1936, Vargas Papers.

189. Welles to Gibson, July 24, 1936, FR, 1936, V, 278.

190. Welles to Gibson, July 25, 1936, Gibson Papers, Box 48.

191. Gibson to Welles, August 4, 1936, ibid.

192. Gibson to Welles, July 25, 1936, SD 632.6531/31.

193. Memo by Gibson, July 29, 1936, Gibson Papers, Box 48.

194. German chargé (Rio) to Auswärtiges Amt, July 11, 1936, RGFM 3006: 6467/484146.

195. Memo by Gibson, July 29, 1936, Gibson Papers, Box 48.

196. Gibson to Welles, August 4, 1936, ibid.

197. Bouças to Aranha, June 11, 1936, Aranha Papers.

198. German chargé (Rio) to Auswärtiges Amt, July 9, 1936, RGFM 2974: 6466/483068–069.

199. *A Nota*, August 11, 12, 1936.

200. Schmidt-Elskop to Auswärtiges Amt, August 13, 1936, RGFM 2974: 6466/483098–099.

201. Ritter to Schmidt-Elskop, August 24, 1936, RGFM 2974:6466/483115; memo by Ritter, October 15, 1936, RGFM 235:254/165477.

202. *O Observador Econômico e Financeiro* 1 (August 1936): 14117.

203. Min. da Fazenda, *Commércio Exterior do Brasil 1936–1940*, pp. 16–17.

204. Estado do Rio Grande do Sul, *Annaes da Assembléa Legislativa* [. . .] *1937*, I, 107; U.S. vice-consul (Porto Alegre) to State Dept., April 29, 1939, SD 632.6215/2.

205. Câmara dos Deputados, *Annaes 1936*, III, 378–379; Moniz de Aragão to MRE, June 16, 1936, AHI 397/4/10.

206. Various telegrams, August 1936, CFCE 21/334-v.3.

207. Sampaio to Vargas, September 30, 1936, and CFCE to Banco do Brasil, October 8, 1936, CFCE 21/334-v.3.

208. Gibson to Hull, June 6, 1936, *FR, 1936*, V, 264–266.

209. John D. Wirth, *The Politics of Brazilian Development, 1930–1954*, pp. 54–57.

4. Military Influence on Economic Policy (1934–1937)

1. John J. Johnson, "The Latin American Military as a Politically Competing Group in Transitional Society," in *The Role of The Military in Underdeveloped Countries*, ed. John J. Johnson, p. 121.

2. John D. Wirth, *The Politics of Brazilian Development, 1930–1954*, pp. 8, 52–54, 61, 65.

3. Four letters from Capt. J. Faustino (Rio) to Gen. Bertholdo Klinger during August–September 1931 (Bertholdo Klinger Papers; henceforth Klinger Papers) shed revealing light on the reaction of anti-*tenentista* officers to the confusion of post-October politics. Indispensable accounts by officers involved in the major politico-military events of the 1930s are Lourival Coutinho, *O General Góes Depõe*; Bertholdo Klinger, *Parada e Desfile de uma Vida Militar*; and Pantaleão da Silva Pessôa, *Reminiscências e Imposições de uma Vida*, pp. 82–257.

4. Unsigned memo with notation "Trabalho feito por ordem do General [Alvaro] Mariante," n.d. [1932], Aranha Papers.

5. Maj. L. Nery to V. Melo Franco, August 21, 1932, V. Melo Franco Papers.

6. Góes Monteiro to Vargas, August 14, 1932, Vargas Papers. See also Góes Monteiro, Boletim no. 16, September 7, 1932, Melo Franco Papers, I-36/15.

7. Gen. Espírito Santo Cardoso to Aranha, December 12, 1932, Aranha Papers.

8. Góes Monteiro to Vargas, February 7, 1933, Vargas Papers; *O Jornal*, November 5, 1933.

9. Gen. Manoel Rabello to Min. da Guerra, May 6, 1933, PR 8/Rabello folder; Rabello to Vargas, n.d. [1943–1944], EME (copy in V. Melo Franco Papers).

10. Gen. Manoel Daltro Filho (São Paulo) to Góes Monteiro, February 17 and June 6, 1933, Pessôa Papers; Gen. Pedro Cavalcanti to Vargas, March 24, 1934, PR 11/42.223; Cavalcanti to Góes Monteiro, April 19, 1934, PR 11/42878; Pessôa Memoirs (Mss.), Pessôa Papers.

11. Capt. João P. Machado to Aranha, December 15, 1935, Aranha Papers.

12. Memo ("A Situação de Defeza Naval do Brasil em face da Argentina e do Chile") by Adm. C. de Sousa e Silva, January 7, 1931, Melo Franco Papers, I-36/34; Gen. A. Tasso Fragoso to Min. da Guerra, October 29, 1931, and chief, EMA to Min. da Marinha, October 29, 1931, Macedo Soares Papers.

13. Chief, Div. de Operações (EMA) to Capt. E. Ferraz e Castro, January 5, 1932, Macedo Soares Papers; Min. da Marinha, *Relatório . . . 1932*, pp. 12–13; chief, EMA to commander in chief of squadron, October 25, 1935, EMA, Operações, 1935, AM; chief, Div. de Produção do Arsenal to diretor industrial, October 31, 1935, EMA, Operações, 1935, AM.

14. Machado to Aranha, December 15, 1935, Aranha Papers.

15. Getúlio Vargas, *A Nova Política do Brasil*, I, 29–32, 85; Min. da Marinha, *Relatório . . . 1934*, p. 14.

16. Interview with Pessôa, March 14, 1968; Vargas to Góes Monteiro, August 16, 1932, Vargas Papers; Aranha to Vargas, March 25, 1933, Vargas Papers.

17. Gen. Augusto Espírito Santo Cardoso to Aranha, December 12, 1932, and Aranha to Cardoso, May 29, 1933, Aranha Papers.

18. Góes Monteiro to Vargas, January 4, 18, 1934, Vargas Papers; *Jornal do Commércio*, January 20, 1934.

19. Góes Monteiro to Aranha, February 2, 1934, PR 11/40.627.

20. Min. da Fazenda memo, March 16, 1934, PR 1/Fazenda folder.

21. Aranha to Vargas, May 18, June 5, 20, 30, 1934, Aranha Papers.

22. Góes Monteiro to Vargas, July 14, 1934, and Aranha to Góes Monteiro, July 19, 1934, ibid. According to Aranha, Fazenda would deliver funds within ninety days of requisition. Amounts were not to exceed $420,000 during any one month and could not be utilized in payment of salaries.

23. Pessôa, *Reminiscências*, p. 159.

24. Memo by Pessôa, n.d. [July 1934], Pessôa Papers.

25. *Revista Militar e Naval* 4 (June 1934): 1; Góes Monteiro to Vargas, August

1, 1934, PR 17/1556; Protógenes Guimarães to Vargas, October 1934, PR 2/ Marinha folder.

26. Gibson to Joseph C. Greene (State Dept.), July 13, 1934, Gibson Papers, Box 46; British chargé (Rio) to Foreign Office, October 29, 1934, RFO 371, doc. A9061/979/6.

27. Min. da Marinha, Commissão Consultiva do Programma Naval, Relatório Geral [typed], 3° vol., III^a parte, pp. 324–325, AM; memo by British commercial sec't. (Rio), October 12, 1934, RFO 371, doc. A8837/979/6.

28. MRE to Aranha, December 24, 1934, AHI 408/3/12; MRE memo, December 26, 1934, PR 16/191.

29. CFCE, 22ª Sessão [January 7, 1935], PR 19/3947; British commercial sec't. (Rio) to DOT, January 30, 1935, RFO 371, doc. A1240/267/6 (and cover notes).

30. José Roberto de Macedo Soares to Macedo Soares, March 1, 1935, Macedo Soares Papers.

31. CFCE, 36ª Sessão, PR 18/3359; Armstrong-Vickers agent (Rio) to DOT, October 3, 1935, RFO 371, doc. A8875/267/6.

32. Gibson to State Dept., July 17, 1936, *FR, 1936*, V, 273–274; Min. da Fazenda memo, November 26, 1936, PR 29/23694; Italian chargé (Rio) to Macedo Soares, October 21, 1936, AHI 421/3/5.

33. Auswärtiges Amt memo, June 6, 1934, RGFM 8707:3397/608488.

34. Kiep to Auswärtiges Amt, October 11, November 7, 1934, RGFM 4463: K906/224811, 224926; Schmidt-Elskop to Auswärtiges Amt, January 14, February 5, 1935, 4465:K913/226276, 226317–318, 226320.

35. Friedrich Krupp A.G. to Auswärtiges Amt, memo ("Stellungnahme . . . zur Ausschreibung des brasilianischen Kriegsministerium vom 13.12.1937"), January 7, 1938, RGFM 229:326/194559–560 (henceforth Krupp memo).

36. Interview with Pessôa, March 9, 1968; unsigned memo ("Memorial sobre a questão da Artilharia Bofors") to Vargas, January 6, 1937, Aranha Papers (henceforth Bofors memo); Maj. Henrique Holl (Brussels) to Pessôa, September 14, 1934, Pessôa Papers.

37. RWM to Auswärtiges Amt, January 16, 1935, RGFM 4465:K913/226279; Auswärtiges Amt to Schmidt-Elskop, January 15, 18, 1935, ibid., 226277, 2226280; Auswärtiges Amt memo, January 18, 1935, ibid., 226283.

38. Memo by Kroll, June 20, 1935, RGFM 2643:5653/H005940.

39. Gaelzer-Netto to Pessôa, October 2, 1935, Pessôa Papers.

40. Vargas to Aranha, December 24, 1934, Vargas Papers.

41. Interview with Pessôa, February 17, 1968; Pessôa to author, December 26, 1968.

42. Chief of EMA to Guilhem, February 20 and October 26, 1935, EMA, Div. de Operações, 1935, AM.

43. Unsigned memo ("Material do Exército Argentino conforme os dados da 2ª Seção [EME] em 1935"), Pessôa Papers; MRE memo, n.d. [September–October 1935], Macedo Soares Papers.

44. U.S. military attaché (Rio) to War Dept., January 18, 1935, May 14, 1936, WD, 165, files 2667-K-3/6, 2659-4, 2724-K-5/3.

45. Unsigned memo ("1ª Reunião da commissão . . . August 22, 1935"), Pessôa Papers.

46. *Diário da Noite*, September 17, 1935; interview with Pessôa, March 9, 1968; Coutinho, *General Góes Depõe*, p. 268.

47. Gomes to Guilhem, n.d. (copy to Vargas, October 2, 1935), PR 21/6883.

48. Schmidt-Elskop to Auswärtiges Amt, October 13, 1933, Auswärtiges Amt, Pol. 3, Argentinien-Brasilien, AAA; British embassy (Rio), Annual Report, 1935, RFO 371, doc. A3819/327/2; British embassy (Buenos Aires), Annual Report, 1936, RFO 371, doc. A1665/1665/2; U.S. military attaché (Rio) to War Dept., April 23, 1934, October 4, 1935, WD, files 2667-K-3, 2006-141/1; Thomas E. Skidmore, "Failure in Brazil: From Popular Front to Armed Revolt," *Journal of Contemporary History* 5 (1970): 148–149.

49. On the Communist putsch and its aftermath, see Robert M. Levine, *The Vargas Regime*, pp. 100–137.

50. Souza Costa to Vargas, August 12, 1935, PR 18/3615.

51. U.S. military attaché (Rio) to War Dept., March 17, 1936, WD, file 2006–142/4; EME, *Relatório . . . 1935*, p. 15; Souza Costa to Vargas, August 12, 1935, PR 18/3615.

52. Souza Costa to Vargas, November 28, December [?], 1935, PR 22/8437, and December [?], 1935, PR 23/8907; Guilhem to Vargas, December [?], 1935, PR 23/9198; Souza Costa to Vargas, January 14, 22, February 3, March 31, 1936, PR, Fazenda, Informações, 1936, v. 1.

53. Souza Costa to Vargas, November 25, 1935, PR 22/8465.

54. Souza Costa to Vargas, n.d., and Vargas to Câmara dos Deputados, December 2, 1935, PR 22/8532.

55. Fazenda memo, February 11, 1936, PR 25/13321; Vargas to Câmara dos Deputados, November 13, 1935, *Correio da Manhã*, November 15, 1935.

56. Gen. J. Castro Júnoir to Gomes, n.d. [February/March 1937], in Gomes, "Negociatas no Ministério da Guerra," *O Jornal*, March 5, 1937.

57. Pessôa to author, December 26, 1968.

58. Schmidt-Elskop to Auswärtiges Amt, November 27, 1935, RGFM 2643: 5653/H005920.

59. Bofors memo.

60. Krupp memo.

61. General Pessôa remarked in a note to Vargas on October 30 that "there is talk again of the possibility of the House of Krupp's establishing an [arms]

factory in Brazil." The chief of staff thought the government should "act resolutely, giving all facilities" (Vargas Papers).

62. Memo by Schmidt-Elskop, n.d. [October 1936], RGFM 3006:6467/484165.

63. Moniz de Aragão to MRE, January 10, February 12, 1936, AHI 397/3/9.

64. MRE to Moniz de Aragão, March 27, 1936, AHI 397/4/13; Moniz de Aragão to MRE, March 30, 1936, AHI 397/4/10.

65. Souza Aranha to Beutner, April 1, 1936, RGFM 4465:K913/226366, 226366 370.

66. Souza Costa to Vargas, [April 2, 1936], PR 52/1667.

67. Beutner to Souza Aranha, April 6, 1936, RGFM 4465:K913/226372.

68. Moniz de Aragão to MRE, April 18, 1936, AHI 397/4/10.

69. Góes Monteiro to Vargas, January 4, 1934, Vargas Papers.

70. Vargas to Aranha, December 24, 1934, ibid.; Souza Costa to Vargas, [April 2, 1936], PR 52/1667; Ritter to Schmidt-Elskop, August 24, 1936, RGFM 2974:6466/483116.

71. Miguel de Castro Ayres, *O Exército que eu vi (memórias)*, pp. 31–32.

72. Krupp memo; Bofors memo.

73. RWM to Auswärtiges Amt, July 7, 1936, and Auswärtiges Amt to German chargé (Rio), July 9, 1936, RGFM 3006:6467/484099–100, 484102–103.

74. Krupp memo.

75. Moniz de Aragão to MRE, July 17, 1936, AHI 397/4/10.

76. V. Melo Franco to Souza Costa, February 22, 1943, V. Melo Franco Papers. Vargas appointed V. Melo Franco interventor in the Banco Alemão Transatlântico following Brazil's entry into the war in August 1942.

77. Circular of the foreign minister, July 30, 1936, *DGFP*, C, V, 842; Wilhelm Treue, "Hitlers Denkschrift zum Vierjahresplan 1936," *Vierteljahreshefte für Zeitgeschichte*, April 1955, pp. 205–210; E. M. Robertson, *Hitler's Pre-War Policy and Military Plans, 1933–1939*, pp. 87–88.

78. Memoranda by Ritter, October 14, 1936, RGFM 3008:6483/485770, and October 28, 1936, 3006:6467/484177–178; Gustav Schlotterer to Moniz de Aragão, September 29, 1936 (sent to MRE same date), AHI 397/3/10.

79. Memo by Schmidt-Elskop, October 8, 1936, RGFM 3006:6467/484165–170; Schmidt-Elskop to Auswärtiges Amt, October 15, 1936, RGFM 3006:6467/484174.

80. Memo by Schmidt-Elskop, October 8, 1936, RGFM 3006:6467/484177–178; memo (with enclosure) from German embassy, November 11, 1936, PR 28/20647.

81. Schmidt-Elskop to Auswärtiges Amt, August 6, 1936, *DGFP*, C, V, 883.

82. Gomes to Vargas, December 3, 1936, Vargas to Aranha, December 8, 1936, Vargas Papers; Harold Fehrmann (Rio) to Beutner, December 3, 1936,

RGFM 3006:6467/484208–209. On the political dispute between Flores da Cunha and the central government, see Carlos E. Cortes, "The Role of Rio Grande do Sul in Brazilian Politics, 1930–1967," pp. 95–103.

83. Schmidt-Elskop to Auswärtiges Amt, December 5, 1936, RGFM 3006: 6467/484200.

84. CFCE, 127ª Sessão [December 28, 1936], PR 29/22454.

85. O Jornal, December 10, 1936.

86. Bofors memo.

87. Rheinmetall-Börsig A.G. to Ritter, January 4, 1937, RGFM 3006:6467/ 484212–214.

88. Bofors memo.

89. Schmidt-Elskop to Auswärtiges Amt, December 31, 1936, January 15, 1937, RGFM 229:326/194480, 194483.

90. Schmidt-Elskop to Auswärtiges Amt, February 22, 1937, RGFM 3006: 6467/484277.

91. Wirth, Brazilian Development, p. 84.

92. Carlos M. Peláez, "Itabira Iron and the Export of Brazil's Iron Ore," Revista Brasileira de Economia 24 (October–December 1970): 166–167.

93. Memo ("Preferências pelas manufaturas nacionais nas aquisições dos Ministérios da Guerra e da Marinha") by Col. Silvio Raulino de Oliveira, July 5, 1940, CFCE 81/1060.

94. Wirth, Brazilian Development, p. 84.

95. Min. da Guerra to MRE, May 24, 1933, AHI 425/2/7.

96. Góes Monteiro to Vargas, January 1934, Vargas Papers; U.S. military attaché (Rio) to War Dept., June 2, 1936, file 2724-K-5/3, RG 165.

97. For example, Revista Militar e Naval 2 (January 1932): 2; 3 (January 1933): 19; 3 (June 1933): 7; 3 (August 1933): 7–8.

98. Góes Monteiro to Vargas, January 1934, and Pessôa to Vargas, October 30, 1935, Vargas Papers.

99. Góes Monteiro to CFCE, October 7, 1937, CFCE 26/426.

100. Between 1934 and 1937 Brazil had three ministers of war and four army chiefs of staff.

5. The Great Powers and the Brazilian Market (1935–1937)

1. J. Fred Rippy, British Investments in Latin America, 1822–1949, 75–85.

2. Vargas to Aranha, October 16, 1934, Aranha Papers.

3. Foreign Office Minute, February 21, 1934, RFO 371, doc. A1492/310/6.

4. Seeds to Craigie, June 5, 1934, RFO 371, doc. A5053/310/6.

5. Memo by commercial sec't. (Rio), n.d. (to Foreign Office, September 19, 1934), RFO 371, doc. A7671/310/6.

6. CFCE, 4ª Sessão, PR 32/29467.

7. H. W. Cole (Mines Dept.) to A. E. Overton (Board of Trade), November 9, 1934, RFO 371, doc. A9080/7738/6.

8. Foreign Office to Seeds, November 16, 1934, RFO 371, doc. A9113/7738/6.

9. Foreign Office to A. R. Fraser (Board of Trade), November 21, 1934, RFO 371, doc. A9558/7738/6. The essence of the Roca-Runciman agreement of May 1933 was a pledge by Great Britain to maintain the quotas for imports of Argentine chilled beef stipulated by the Ottawa accords of 1932. In return, the Argentine government promised to apply the sterling it earned from sales to Britain to the "thawing" of frozen British accounts in Argentina and, also, to extend preferential tariff treatment to British exports (Peter H. Smith, *Politics and Beef in Argentina*, pp. 143–145).

10. Seeds to Foreign Office, November 21, 1934, cover note by Broad, November 26, 1934, RFO 371, doc. A9279/7738/6.

11. Board of Trade to Foreign Office, January 10, 1935, RFO 371, doc. A502/173/6.

12. Minutes of Meeting at Board of Trade, February 18, 1935, Board of Trade Records, 11/345.

13. Memo by commercial sec't. (Rio), February 8, 1935, RFO 371, doc. 1256/173/6.

14. British Chamber of Commerce for Brazil to Seeds, January 28, 1935, RFO 371, doc. A1279/1279/6.

15. Cover note by Foreign Office official, RFO 371, doc. A1279/1279/6.

16. DOT to Foreign Office, May 2, 1935, RFO 371, doc. A4144/1279/6.

17. British Chamber of Commerce for Brazil to British embassy, August 8, 1935, RFO 371, doc. A7182/1279/6.

18. Minute by Broad, August 19, 1935, RFO 371, doc. A7182/1279/6; DOT to Broad, August 30, 1935, RFO 371, doc. A7677/1279/6; S. D. Whaley (Treasury) to Broad, September 3, 1935, RFO 371, doc. A7762/1279/6.

19. Confidential Minutes of Interdepartmental Meeting, September 18, 1935, Board of Trade Records, 11/392, file 37/3800; Foreign Office to British embassy (Rio), October 14, 1935, RFO 371, doc. A8559/1279/6.

20. Memo by commercial sec't. (Berlin), December 7, 1935, with Foreign Office cover note, RFO 371, doc. A10498/1279/6.

21. British embassy (Rio) to Foreign Office, August 3, 1936, RFO 371, doc. A6782/1659/6.

22. British Chamber of Commerce for Brazil to Sampaio, January 25, 1936 (to Foreign Office, February 14, 1936), RFO 371, doc. A1807/1807/6; British Chamber of Commerce (São Paulo), circular, March 5, 1936, RFO 371, doc.

A3107/1807/6; *London Financial News*, April 6, 1936. For similar public comment, see *Economist*, May 30, 1936.

23. Evans, Lescher & Well, Ltd., to Board of Trade, July 8, 1936, and Board of Trade to Evans, Lescher & Well, July 24, 1936, RFO 371, doc. A6722/1807/6.

24. Foreign Office, memorandum respecting German influence in Latin America, January 23, 1936, and Foreign Office circular, February 28, 1936, RFO 371, doc. A111/1111/51.

25. Gurney to Troutbeck, June 2, 1936, RFO 371, doc. A5145/1807/6.

26. Gurney to Foreign Office, June 9, 1936, RFO 371, doc. A5255/1807/6; Foreign Office cover note (to memo by commercial sec't. [Rio], June 20, 1936), RFO 371, doc. A5453/1807/6; Foreign Office cover notes (to dispatch from British embassy [Rio], June 16, 1936), RFO 371, doc. A5168/1807/6.

27. Foreign Office memo, October 20, 1936, RFO 371, doc. A8325/1111/51.

28. Lord Lothian to Anthony Eden, June 3, 1936, in Martin Gilbert and Richard Gott, *The Appeasers*, p. 27.

29. British chargé (Rio) to Foreign Office, September 10, 1936, RFO 371, doc. A7342/1807/6.

30. Jaime de Brito to Aranha, December 29, 1934, Aranha Papers.

31. Edgar Nixon, ed., *Franklin D. Roosevelt and Foreign Affairs*, II, 283–286.

32. *Export Trade and Shipper*, December 9, 1935, p. 6.

33. NFTC, *Official Report . . . 1935*, p. 351; Francis T. Cole, "Review of 1935 American Trade," *Overseas Trader* 2 (April 1936): 111.

34. *American Exporter* 118 (May 1936): 28.

35. Joseph D. Bohan, speech to Export Managers Club of New York, May 12, 1936, *Export Trade and Shipper*, May 25, 1936, pp. 4–5.

36. Report ("Escriptório Commercial do Brasil em New York no anno de 1936") by Rafael Corrêa to Min. of Labor, Macedo Soares Papers; Aranha to Vargas, April 17, 1935, and April 22, 1936, to Macedo Soares, May 14, 1935, Aranha Papers.

37. Vice-pres., AMEA, to State Dept., April 8, 1936, SD 632.6217/14; Thomas (NFTC) to Feis, May 26, 1936, SD 632.6231/45, and Hull, May 26, 1936, SD 832.5151/837; U.S. consul general (São Paulo) to Hull, June 2, 1936, SD 632.6231/76; vice-pres., Goodyear Tire & Rubber Export Co., to Hull, July 16, 1936, SD 632.6231/105; *Brazilian Business* 16 (June 1936): 237; "Compensation Marks in Foreign Trade," *Overseas Trader* 2 (June 1936): 175; U.S. vice-consul (São Paulo) to State Dept., November 28, 1936, SD 632.6217/19.

38. Export manager, John Oster Mfg. Co., to editor, *Export Trade and Shipper*, January 13, 1936, p. 13.

39. Harry Tipper, "Report on General Activities of AMEA for the Year 1935," *Overseas Trader* 2 (January 1936): 8.

40. R. C. Lebret, "Business Is Good in South America and Getting Better," *Export Trade and Shipper*, July 13, 1936, pp. 3–4.

41. "Aski Marks Damaging Exports," *Overseas Trader* 2 (August 1936): 250–251.

42. NFTC, *Official Report . . . 1936*, pp. 559–560.

43. Henry L. Metz, "Growing Up Now," *Overseas Trader* 3 (April 1937): 8.

44. Daniel Roper, *Fifty Years in Public Life*, p. 343.

45. State Dept., Division of American Republics, Confidential Book File, Latin American Political and Economic Résumés, I, 5, RG 159, National Archives.

46. Memo by Heath, January 15, 1935, and U.S. consul general (Rio) to State Dept., December 27, 1934, SD 832.5151/483.

47. Amb. Breckinridge Long (Rome) to Roper, March 8, 1935, Roosevelt Papers, OF 3, Box 11.

48. Hull to U.S. embassy (Rio), June 21, 1935, *FR, 1935*, IV, 378–379.

49. U.S. embassy (Rio) to Hull, October 25, 1935, SD 611.3231/1060.

50. Xanthaky to Gibson, October 26, 1935, Gibson Papers, Box 47.

51. Xanthaky to Gibson, October 30, 1935, ibid.

52. Donald F. Drummond, "Cordell Hull," in *An Uncertain Condition*, ed. Norman A. Graebner, p. 194.

53. Hull to U.S. embassy (Rio), December 4, 1935, SD 832.5151/771A.

54. Memo by Feis, May 1, 1936, SD 632.6231/48.

55. Memo by Duggan, June 29, 1936, SD Office of American Republics, General Memoranda, Brazil, Vol. 1.

56. Manning to Duggan, June 20, 1936, SD 632.6231/100.

57. Memo by Duggan, July 8, 1936, SD 632.6231/94.

58. U.S. consul general (Rio) to Hull, September 14, 1936, SD 632.6217/17.

59. Quoted in John M. Blum, *From the Morgenthau Diaries: Years of Crisis*, p. 153.

60. Roosevelt to William Dodd, November 9, 1936, Dodd Papers, General Correspondence; Harold L. Ickes, *The Secret Diary of Harold L. Ickes*, II, 7.

61. Welles to Harry McBride, November 4, 1936, SD 632.6231/134½; Sayre to Gibson, November 18, 1936, SD 632.6231/132.

62. Cordell Hull, *Memoirs*, I, 496.

63. Speech by Hull, November 17, 1936, SD 710 Peace/951.

64. *Correio da Manhã*, November 20, 1936.

65. Henry Morgenthau, Jr., Diaries, Book 68, p. 97, Henry Morgenthau, Jr., Papers, FDRL (henceforth Morgenthau Papers).

66. Inter-American Conference for the Maintenance of Peace . . . , *Proceedings*, p. 514.

67. Memo by L. Stinebower, December [?], 1936, SD 632.6231/208.

68. Thomas to Welles, December 29, 1936, SD 632.6217/21.

69. Memoranda by Souza Costa, December 31, 1936, Vargas Papers.

70. *Gazeta de Notícias* (Rio), January 1, 1937.

71. Welles to Vargas, January 1, 1937, PR 22/7798.

72. Amb. Dodd (Berlin) to Sayre, January 22, 1937, Dodd Papers, General Correspondence, 1937-R; Martha Dodd and William E. Dodd, Jr., eds., *Ambassador Dodd's Diary, 1933–1938*, p. 344.

73. German legation (Rio) to MRE, June 13, 1934, AHI 419/2/20.

74. Kiep to Schmidt-Elskop, March 12, 1935, RGFM 4463:K906/225049; Auswärtiges Amt (Kiep) to various missions, May 4, 1935, RGFM 6:00923.

75. German consul general (New York) to Auswärtiges Amt, July 5, 1935, RGFM 6:AHAI6/00895–897; Botschaftsrat Rudolf Leitner (Washington) to Auswärtiges Amt official (Berlin), June 7, 1935, RGFM 6:AHAI6/00925.

76. Schmidt-Elskop to Auswärtiges Amt, May 15, June 5, July 18, 1935, RGFM 4463:K906/225141, 225170, 225197.

77. German embassy (Washington) to Auswärtiges Amt, June 7, 1935, RGFM 6/00925. For identification of Aranha as the "well-informed Brazilian party," see the embassy memo of June 17 and letter to Berlin, June 21, 1935, RGFM 6/00918–919; Auswärtiges Amt to German embassy (Washington), June 18, 1935, RGFM 6/00901.

78. Schmidt-Elskop to Auswärtiges Amt, June 17, 1936, RGFM 2974:6466/483014.

79. Circular of Auswärtiges Amt, August 17, 1936, RGFM 68:74/54145.

80. Dodd to Hull, August 18, 1936, *FR, 1936*, II, 250.

81. Blum, *Morgenthau Diaries: Years of Crisis*, p. 154.

82. *Dodd's Diary*, p. 344.

83. Schmidt-Elskop to Auswärtiges Amt, November 25, 1936, RGFM 3009: 6483/486679–680.

84. Ernst von Weizsäcker to German embassy (Buenos Aires), November 30, 1936, RGFM 3009:6483/486693; *Berliner Börsen-Zeitung*, December 1, 1936; *Deutsche Allgemeine Zeitung*, December 2, 1936; *New York Herald Tribune*, December 8, 1936.

85. *Correio da Manhã*, February 2, 1937.

86. *Gazeta de Notícias*, February 11, 1937.

87. Schmidt-Elskop to Auswärtiges Amt, February 17, March 25, 1937, RGFM 2972:6464/482703–705, 482707.

88. Chargé Robert Scotten (Rio) to Hull, February 11, 1937, SD 632.6231/145.

89. Auswärtiges Amt (Ritter) to missions in South America, February 15, 1937, RGFM 3008:6483/485724–731.

90. Schmidt-Elskop to Auswärtiges Amt, February 17, 1937, RGFM 2972: 6464/482705.

91. Schmidt-Elskop to Auswärtiges Amt, March 3, 1937, RGFM 3008:6494/486214.

92. Moniz de Aragão to MRE, April 14, 1937, AHI 397/4/10.

93. Schmidt-Elskop to Auswärtiges Amt, January 29, 1937, RGFM 3006: 6467/484264.
94. Chargé Werner von Levetzow (Rio) to Auswärtiges Amt, March 4, 1937, RGFM 3009:6496/486444.
95. Moniz de Aragão to Konstantin von Neurath, April 28, 1937, AHI 397/3/12.
96. Moniz de Aragão to MRE, April 24, 1937, AHI 397/3/12.
97. CFCE, 135ª Sessão [February 23, 1937], PR 30/24292.
98. Scotten to State Dept., September 2, 1937, SD 832.00/1049.
99. Gurney to Foreign Office, May 15, 1937, RFO 371, doc. A4007/316/6; Scotten to State Dept., June 1, 1937, FR, 1937, V, 327.
100. Various telegrams to Vargas, June 21–28, 1937, PR 23/9429, 9464–65, 9482, 9489; to CFCE, June 5–28, 1937, CFCE 36/575; Abelardo Roças to Aranha, July 7, 1937, Aranha Papers.
101. Relatório da Commissão Encarregada do Estudo do Modus-Vivendi Commercial com a Allemanha, June 4, 1937, CFCE 70/979.
102. J. Barbosa Carneiro to CFCE, June 13, 1937, CFCE 36/575.
103. Flodoardo da Silva to Aranha, June 13, 1937, and Vargas to Aranha, June 17, 1937, Aranha Papers; A. Figueiredo to Vargas (with marginal notation by Vargas), June 21, 1937, PR 23/9429.
104. Memo on interdepartmental meeting, Berlin, April 3, 1937, RGFM 2974:6466/483219.
105. Ritter to Schmidt-Elskop, April 3, 1937, RGFM 235:254/165443; Schmidt-Elskop to Auswärtiges Amt, April 1, 1937, RGFM 2972:6464/482707.
106. Fehrmann to Beutner, June 19, 1937, RGFM 2975:6467/483489–490.
107. Memo by Feis, May 10, 1937, SD 632.6231/158.
108. Scotten to Hull, April 23, 1937, FR, 1937, V, 321.
109. Memo by Feis, May 10, 1937, SD 632.6231/158; Hull to Scotten, May 12, 1937, FR, 1937, V, 324.
110. Memo by Heath, April 27, 1937, SD 632.6231/171.
111. Bestellungen aus der Pressekonferenz vom 12 Okt. 1936, Sammlung Brammer, Bundesarchiv ZSg. 101/8.
112. Dodd to Hull, May 27, 1937, Hull Papers, 41/99.
113. Dodd to Roosevelt, June 12, 1937, Roosevelt Papers, PSF Box 6; Dodd to Roper, June 11, 1937, Dodd Papers, Personal Correspondence, 1937-R.
114. H. D. White (Treasury) to H. C. Hawkins (State Dept.), June 8, 1937, SD 611.3231/1172; memo by Heath, April 27, 1937, SD 632.6231/171.
115. White to Hawkins, June 8, 1937, SD 611.3231/1172.
116. Macedo Soares to Vargas, February 17, 1937, Macedo Soares Papers.
117. Treasury staff report, May 11, 1937, Morgenthau Diaries, 68:150–155, Morgenthau Papers.
118. Aranha to Vargas, May 3, 21, 1937, Aranha Papers; Treasury memo,

May 12, 1937, Morgenthau Diaries, 68:100, Morgenthau Papers; Aranha to MRE, May 12, 1937, AHI 408/3/9.

119. Gurney to Troutbeck, April 29, 1937, RFO 371, doc. A3352/316/6.

120. Troutbeck to I. M. Forsyth (Board of Trade), May 11, 1937, RFO 371, doc. A3352/316/6; Forsyth to Troutbeck, May 22, 1937, and Troutbeck to Gurney, May 26, 1937, RFO 371, doc. A3659/316/6.

121. Gurney to Foreign Office, May 10, 1937, and Foreign Office cover note, RFO 371, doc. A3741/316/6.

122. Memo by Duggan, June 2, 1937, SD 632.6231/165½.

123. Gurney to Troutbeck, June 11, 1937, RFO 371, doc. A4385/316/6; Foreign Office to Gurney, June 9, 1937, RFO 371, doc. A3956/316/6; Foreign Office cover note (to Gurney letter, June 11, 1937), RFO 371, doc. A4385/316/6.

124. American Chamber of Commerce for Brazil to Souza Costa, June [2–3], 1937, SD 632.6231/175.

125. Scotten to State Dept., June 4, 1937, FR, 1937, V, 327–328; June 5, 1937, SD 632.6231/173.

126. Aranha to Vargas (letter), June 4, 1937, Aranha Papers.

127. Scotten to Hull, June 4, 1937, FR, 1937, V, 329.

128. Aranha to Vargas, June 4, 1937, Aranha Papers.

129. Memo by Welles, June 4, 1937, FR, 1937, V, 330; Aranha to Vargas, June 4, 1937, Aranha Papers.

130. Memo by Schmidt-Elskop, June 10, 1937, RGFM 2974:6466/483376; Schmidt-Elskop to Auswärtiges Amt, June 8, 1937, RGFM 2974:6466/483324–325.

131. Memo by Scotten, June 10, 1937, SD 632.6231/177.

132. Welles to Protocol Division, June 11, 1937, SD 632.6231/184; memo by Bouças, June 19, 1937, Aranha Papers.

133. State Dept. memoranda, June 24, 26, 1937, SD 632.6231/186, 189; Souza Costa to Vargas, June 24, 1937, Vargas Papers.

134. Memo by A. de Lima Campos, June 22, 1937, Aranha Papers.

135. Feis to Hull, June 28, 1937, SD 632.6231/196; memo by Feis, June 29, 1937, SD 632.6231/202; Heath to Duggan, July 2, 1937, SD 632.6231/275.

136. MRE to Moniz de Aragão, June 2, 1937, AHI 397/4/13.

137. Moniz de Aragão to MRE, June 12, 1937, AHI 397/4/10.

138. Memo by Schmidt-Elskop, June 10, 1937, RGFM 2974:6466/483373–375; Dieckhoff to Auswärtiges Amt, June 15, 1937, RGFM 2975:6467/483403; Reichsstelle für den Aussenhandel to Auswärtiges Amt, June 21, 1937, RGFM 2974:6466/483348, 483350.

139. Tipper, "Germany," pp. 16–17; Dodd to Hull, July 3, 1937, Hull Papers, 41/99-A.

140. Vertraulicher Informationsbericht Nr. 14, June 30, 1937, Sammlung

Brammer, Bundesarchiv ZSg. 101/46.

141. Dodd to Hull, July 1, 1937, SD 632.6231/203; Auswärtiges Amt memo, June 30, 1937, RGFM 235:254/165374; Auswärtiges Amt to Dieckhoff, June 29, 1937, RGFM 2975:6467/483447; memo by Welles, June 30, 1937, SD 632.6231/ 203; Dieckhoff to Auswärtiges, Amt, June 30, 1937, RGFM 235:254/165381.

142. [?] Costa Rêgo, "Nova Hespanha," *Correio da Manhã*, July 4, 1937.

143. Marcos de Souza Dantas, "História Verdadeira dos 'Marcos de Compensação,'" ibid., July 1, 1937; Dantas to Aranha, July 1, 1937, Aranha Papers; *Correio da Manhã*, July 3, 1937; Beutner to Auswärtiges Amt, July 12, 1937, RGFM 2975:6466/483697.

144. German legation (Rio) to Auswärtiges Amt, April 18, 1936, RGFM 4465:K913/226390.

145. *A Nação*, July 4, 1937.

146. Ibid.

147. Aranha to MRE, June 30, 1937, AHI 408/3/8; *Correio da Manhã*, July 2, 1937; Aranha to Vargas, July 3, 1937, Aranha Papers.

148. Vice-pres., Westinghouse Electric Internatl. Co., to Hull, July 1, 1937, SD 632.6217/29; Thomas to Hull, July 6, 1937, SD 632.6231/192.

149. For example, Merchants' Assoc. of New York to Hull, July 16, 1937, SD 632.6217/31; Ruemelin Manuf. Co. to Hull, July 26, 1937, SD 632.6231/218; White Motor Co. to Hull, July 27, 1937, SD 632.6231/219. As an example of the State Dept. response, see State Dept. to Westinghouse Electric International Co., July 15, 1937, SD 632.6217/29.

150. Bouças to Souza Costa, June 29, 1937, Aranha Papers.

151. Souza Costa to Vargas, July 7, 1937, Vargas Papers; Aranha to Hull, July 14, 1937, *FR, 1937*, V, 335; Aranha to Vargas, July 14, 1937, Aranha Papers.

152. *Washington Post*, July 16, 1937.

153. *O Jornal*, July 21, 1937; Aranha to Vargas, July 30, 1937, Aranha Papers.

154. Ritter to missions in Latin America, July 17, 1937, RGFM 2975:6467/ 483560–561, 483566–568; von Weizsäcker to Dieckhoff, July 22, 1937, RGFM 261:320/193065–066.

155. *Deutsche Allgemeine Zeitung* (Berlin), July 21, 1937; *Der Angriff* (Berlin), July 21, 1937, *Frankfurter Zeitung*, July 21, 1937.

156. *Wochenbericht des Instituts für Konjunkturforschung*, July 28, 1937, 167.

157. *Frankfurter Zeitung*, July 22, 1937; Ritter to missions in Latin America, August 9, 1937, RGFM 2975:6467/483896.

158. Moniz de Aragão to MRE, July 22, 1937, AHI 397/3/13.

159. Dawson to Caffery, September 4, 1937, and Caffery to Dawson, September 14, 1937, Jefferson Caffery Papers (henceforth Caffery Papers).

160. *O Jornal*, August 13, 1937.

161. Lloyd C. Gardner, *Economic Aspects of New Deal Diplomacy*, p. 59; Blum, *Morgenthau Diaries: Years of Crisis*, p. 493.

162. Memo of conversation, February 10, 1939, Morgenthau Diaries, 207: 219, Morgenthau Papers.

163. Auswärtiges Amt memo, August 10, 1937, RGFM 235:254/165327.

164. Dawson to Caffery, September 4, 1937, Caffery Papers.

165. See *FR, 1937*, V, 337–349; Auswärtiges Amt to German embassy (Rio), November 25, 1937, RGFM 235:254/165253–254; *FR, 1938*, V, 383–392.

166. Memo by Walter Becker (Auswärtiges Amt), October 6, 1938, RGFM 222:231/154976–977.

167. Caffery to Pimentel Brandão, October 14, 1937, AHI 420/5/15.

168. Dawson to Caffery, October 18, 1937, and Caffery to Dawson, November 8, 1937, Caffery Papers; memo by O. Fernandes Mello, September 18, 1939, CFCE 70/979.

169. Adolf Berle to Morgenthau, September 10, 1940, Morgenthau Diaries, 306:270–271, Morgenthau Papers.

170. State Dept. Memoranda, February 1, March 18, 1940, SD, Office of American Republics, Brazil, III.

171. Caffery to Hull, February 25, 1938, *FR, 1938*, V, 383.

172. Memo by German embassy counselor (Rio), April [?], 1938, RGFM 1913:3954/054428.

173. Gerhard Weinberg, *The Foreign Policy of Hitler's Germany*, pp. 133–158.

174. Schröder, *Deutschland und die Vereinigten Staaten*, p. 261.

175. Arnold A. Offner, *American Appeasement*, p. 168.

176. Feis to Hull, June 28, 1937, SD 632.6231/196; Bouças to Souza Costa, June 29, 1937, Aranha Papers.

6. Trade, Armaments, and International Politics (1937–1939)

1. Quoted in Robert M. Levine, *The Vargas Regime*, p. 126.

2. The phrase is Vargas's. Letter to Aranha, December 14, 1935, Vargas Papers.

3. Getúlio Vargas, *A Nova Política do Brasil*, IV, 145, 155–156, 184–185; Francisco da Silva Piragibe to Vargas, September 10, 1936, PR 21/6511.

4. Relations between the Integralist party and the central government are explored in Stanley E. Hilton, "*Ação Integralista Brasileira*: Fascism in Brazil 1932–1938," *Luso-Brazilian Review* 9 (December 1972): 14–29.

5. For an anti-Vargas interpretation of Aranha's political mission, see Carlos E. Cortes, "The Role of Rio Grande do Sul in Brazilian Politics, 1930–1967," pp. 111–115.

6. Vargas to Aranha, June 17, 1937, Aranha Papers.

7. Levine, *Vargas Regime*, pp. 140–141.

8. Ibid., pp. 143–148; Cortes, "Rio Grande do Sul," pp. 115–132; John W. F. Dulles, *Vargas of Brazil*, pp. 160–168.

9. Getúlio Vargas, *Ideário Político*, p. 75.

10. *New York Times*, November 11, 1937; *Washington Post*, November 12, 1937; *St. Louis Globe-Democrat*, November 12, 1937; *Newsweek*, November 22, 1937.

11. *Washington Post*, November 11, 1937.

12. Caffery to Hull, November 10, 1937, *FR, 1937*, V, 313.

13. Hull to Caffery, November 12, 1937, and Caffery to Hull, *FR, 1937*, V, 313–315.

14. *Il Giornale d'Italia*, November 13, 1937; Galeazzo Ciano, *Ciano's Diary, 1937–1938*, p. 31.

15. Dodd to State Dept., November 12, 1937, SD 832.00/1086.

16. Bestellungen aus der Pressekonferenz, November 11–12, 1937, Sammlung Brammer, Bundesarchiv ZSg. 101/10.

17. Moniz de Aragão to MRE, November 18, 1937, AHI 397/3/14.

18. Von Levetzow to Auswärtiges Amt, November 16, 1937, RGFM 3155: 6939/518365(2)–365(3).

19. Ibid.

20. Moniz de Aragão to MRE, November 29, 1937, AHI 397/3/14.

21. Alton Frye, *Nazi Germany and the American Hemisphere, 1933–1941*, pp. 102–109; Frank D. McCann, "Vargas and the Destruction of the Brazilian Integralista and Nazi Parties," *The Americas* 26 (July 1969): 15–34; Käte Harms-Baltzer, *Die Nationalisierung der deutschen Einwanderer*, pp. 42–63.

22. Levine, *Vargas Regime*, pp. 159–166; Hélio Silva, *1938: Terrorismo em Campo Verde*, pp. 65–262.

23. Hilton, "*Ação Integralista Brasileira*: Fascism in Brazil," pp. 27–29.

24. Scotten to State Dept., December 6, 1937, SD 832.00/1135; von Levetzow to Auswärtiges Amt, December 7, 1937, RGFM 3155:6939/518387.

25. Nathaniel Weyl, "Swastika over Brazil," *Nation*, November 13, 1937, pp. 528–529.

26. Hilton, "*Ação Integralista Brasileira*: Fascism in Brazil," pp. 10–14.

27. Harms-Baltzer, *Die Nationalisierung der deutschen Einwanderer*, pp. 63–105.

28. Statements by Torres Filho, CFCE, Ata da Sessão de Instalação, February 3, 1938, PR 37/3993.

29. Min. da Fazenda, *Commércio Exterior . . . 1936–1940*, pp. 16–17.

30. John R. Huber, "The Effects of German Clearing Agreements and Import Restrictions on Cotton, 1934–1939," *Southern Economic Journal* 6 (April 1940): 420.

31. U.S. Dept. of Commerce, Bureau of Foreign and Domestic Commerce, *Citrus Fruits: World Production and Trade*, p. 26.

32. For example, telegrams to CFCE from Comissão Propagadora Comercial de Bahia, August 5, 1937; Assoc. Citrícola de São Paulo, August 25, 1937; Assoc. Comercial de Joinville, August 17, 1937; Assoc. Comercial de Amazonas, January 13, 1938; Sindicato Patronal dos Madeireios (Curitiba), February 16, 1938, CFCE 36/575.

33. Gaelzer-Netto to Vargas, January 26, 1938, PR 33/32723.

34. *Berliner Tageblatt*, January 4, 1938; Conselho Técnico de Economia e Finanças, minutes, May 27, 1938, PR 67/32733; Scotten to State Dept., April 20, 1938, SD 632.6231/306; *A Nação*, June 14, 1938.

35. Capt. J. P. Machado (Berlin) to Vargas, February 23, 1938, PR 38/5312; John D. Wirth, *The Politics of Brazilian Development, 1930–1954*, pp. 97–98.

36. Ritter to Auswärtiges Amt, June 15, 1938, RGFM 3092:6966/519473–474; Aranha to Moniz de Aragão, June 28, 1938, AHI 397/4/9; Auswärtiges Amt memo, September 30, 1938, *DGFP, D*, V, 872; von Levetzow to Auswärtiges Amt, October 5, 1938, RGFM 3092:6966/519638; Dr. Mário Cardim (Berlin) to Ibero-Amerikanisches Institut, December 1, 1938, Bundesarchiv R40/242.

37. Reichskanzlei to state sec't. September 4, 1937, Bundesarchiv, R43II/323.

38. RWM to Hauptabteilungsleiter I und II, March 22, 1938, and RWM memo, April 11, 1938, ibid., R7VI/505.

39. Ritter to Auswärtiges Amt, April 28, 1938, RGFM 1913:3954/E054438; Moniz de Aragão to MRE, May 16, 1938, AHI 397/4/11.

40. RWM to Auswärtiges Amt, July 16, 1938, RGFM 1624:3252/E000408; memo by Emil Wiehl, July 21, 1938, RGFM 222:231/154937; Moniz de Aragão to MRE, July 21, 1938, AHI 397/4/11; Wiehl to Ritter, July 23, 1938, RGFM 222:231/154940.

41. Auswärtiges Amt memo, October 4, 1938, *DGFP,D*, V, 874–875.

42. João Pinto da Silva to Vargas, September 21, 1938, PR 46/21579; Regis de Oliveira to Aranha, October 7, 1938, Aranha Papers.

43. Von Levetzow to Auswärtiges Amt, November 14, 22, 1938, RGFM 222:231/154992, 154996; Gaelzer-Netto to Vargas, November 30, 1938, PR 49/28095; Aranha to von Levetzow, December 1, 1938, RGFM 3008:6492/486142–143; von Levetzow to Aranha, December 5, 1938, AHI 420/1/6.

44. Memo by R. Freytag, January 4, 1939, and Becker to Freytag, January 6, 1939, RGFM 3967:3828/E043880, E043882.

45. Gaelzer-Netto to Vargas, January 11, 1939 (copy), Bouças Papers, and January 18, 1939, PR 53/2539; Brazilian chargé (Berlin) to MRE, January 10, 12, 1939, AHI 297/411; Becker to Reichsstelle für den Aussenhandel, March 16, 1939, Bundesarchiv R40/215.

46. Krupp to Schlotterer, June 30, 1939, RGFM 3374:8615/604192–195.

47. Chargé Oswaldo Furst (Buenos Aires) to Acioly, April 2, 8, and May 3, 1937, Acioly Papers; EME, *Relatório . . . 1937*, p. 4.

48. *Diário Carioca*, August 12, 1937; Acioly to Aranha, October 26, 1937, Aranha Papers. For a general discussion of the Destroyers Episode, see Bryce Wood, "External Restraints on the Good Neighbor Policy," *Inter-American Economic Affairs* 16 (Autumn 1962): 3–24.

49. Chief, 2ª Seção, EMA, to chief, EMA, November 24, December 22, 1937, EMA, Informações (EM-2), 1937, AM; EME, *Relatório . . . 1937*, pp. 4, 10.

50. Lourival Coutinho, ed., *O General Góes Depõe*, pp. 340–341.

51. "Abertura das aulas da Escola de Estado Maior," *A Defesa Nacional* 25 (May 1938): 482–484; "O Presidente da República e as Forças Armadas,"ibid., 25 (June 1938): 602; editorial, ibid., 25 (October 1938): 410–411; Dutra to Vargas, October[?], 1938, PR 47/24378; chief, 2ª Seção, EMA, to chief, EMA, December 31, 1938, EMA, Informações (EM-2), 1938, AM; EME, *Relatório . . . 1938*.

52. Vargas, *Nova Política*, V, 28; Miguel de Castro Ayres, "O Brasil e Sua Defesa," *A Defesa Nacional* 25 (October 1938): 571.

53. British embassy (Rio) to Foreign Office, January 1, 1938, RFO 371, doc. A744/744/6. Vargas made certain that interested parties understood where authority lay in connection with steel policy. Informed by an officer serving with the Berlin embassy that a German firm had expressed a willingness to help set up a mill "in accordance with the program of Col. Mendonça Lima," an indignant Vargas promptly set the record straight. "Reply that the steel problem is the government's problem and not Col. Mendonça Lima's," read his terse instructions to his personal secretary, instructions that Vargas would hardly have issued had Mendonça Lima been a major power holder within the high command (Capt. Machado to Vargas, February 23, 1938, with attached note by Vargas, PR 38/5312).

54. João de Mendonça Lima to Vargas, October 3, 1938, CFCE 56/807.

55. Wirth, *Politics of Brazilian Development*, pp. 96–104. Vargas objected to Mendonça Lima's project because, probably, it did not go far enough in the direction of the "complete economic independence" that he, Vargas, had recently proclaimed as his goal. The proposal included an exchange of iron ore for coal, and Vargas as early as 1930 had come out strongly against dependence upon foreign coal, which he considered costly and unwise from the standpoint of national security. He promised to promote "systematic utilization" of national coal and later acted on his words. In 1931 he issued a decree requiring coal importers to mix domestic with foreign coal in a 1:10 ratio, a blend he raised to 1:5 in 1937. Only after "exhaustive" laboratory tests in 1940–1941 showed that, although satisfactory coke for the projected steel mill could be made from Santa Catharina coal, it would be much more economical to mix Brazilian and American coals, did Vargas accept this unavoidably limited vic-

tory (Vargas, *Nova Política*, I, 38; V, 219); Edward J. Rogers, "Brazilian Success Story: The Volta Redonda Iron and Steel Project," *Journal of Inter-American Studies* 10 (October 1968): 639–641.

56. Min. da Guerra, *Relatório . . . 1938*, p. 72; *Relatório . . . 1940*, p. 15; Dutra to Vargas, n.d. [January–February, 1939], PR 54/4344.

57. Memo ("Preferências pelas manufaturas nacionais nas aquisições dos Ministérios da Guerra e da Marinha") by Col. Sílvio Raulino de Oliveira, July 5, 1940, CFCE 81/1060.

58. Aranha to Vargas, June 4, 1937, and Souza Costa to Aranha. August 18, 1937, Aranha Papers; Caffery to Hull, May 6, 1938, *FR, 1938*, V, 346–347.

59. Souza Costa to Vargas, July [?], and August [?], 1937, PR Fazenda, Informações, vol. 3. The third secret credit that year was established by decree no. 1268 of October 16 (Souza Costa to Vargas, May [?], 1939, Informações, vol. 8).

60. Memo by Feis, June 29, 1937, SD 632.6231/202; Souza Aranha to Aranha, August 7, 1937, Aranha Papers; von Levetzow to Auswärtiges Amt, October 2, 1937, RGFM 3185:7077/526837.

61. Caffery to State Dept., June 30, 1939, SD 832.51/1494; Caffery to Pimentel Brandão, November 12, 1937, AHI 420/5/5.

62. EME, *Relatório . . . 1937*, pp. 39, 41; Vargas, *Nova Política*, V, 28, 127–128, 173.

63. Ritter to Auswärtiges Amt, March 30, 1938, RGFM 3185:7077/526837; Souza Costa to Vargas, March 16, 1938, and Dutra to Vargas, March 29, 1938, Vargas Papers. For details of the contract, see V. de Melo Franco to Souza Costa, February 22, 1943, V. Melo Franco Papers. V. de Melo Franco was federal interventor in the Banco Alemão Transatlântico during the war.

64. Welles to missions in Latin America, December 17, 1937, SD 810.24/11; War Office to Foreign Office, June 2, 1938, RFO 371, doc. A4371/4176/6; Foreign Office memo, July 15, 1938, RFO 371, doc. A5304/4176/6; Foreign Office to Treasury Office, July 21, 1938, RFO 371, doc. A5304/4176/6; Treasury Office to Foreign Office, August 2, 1938, RFO 371, doc. A6040/4176/6; Gurney to Foreign Office, August 29, 1938, RFO 371, doc. A7113/4176/6.

65. Dutra to Vargas, March 29, 1938, Vargas Papers; Ritter to Auswärtiges Amt, June 15, 1938, RGFM 3092:6966/519473–474.

66. Souza Costa to Vargas, October 11, 1939, PR, Fazenda, Informações, 1939, vol. 9.

67. Dutra to MRE, November 18, 1938, AHI 425/3/6.

68. Vargas, *Nova Política*, VI, 192; Caffery to Hull, April 22, 1939, SD 832.00/1255.

69. Dutra to Souza Costa, April 20, 1939, and Dutra to Vargas, May 5, 1939 (with notation by Vargas), EME.

70. Ata da Quarta Sessão do Conselho de Segurança Nacional [July 4, 1939], EME; Krupp to RWM, August 4, 1939, RGFM 267:346/200692.

71. Krupp to RWM, August 4, 1939, RGFM 267:346/200692.

72. State Dept. memo, February 1938, SD F.W.810.00F/32.

73. *New York Times*, January 26, February 5, 1938. For similar evidence of American concern about Axis activities in South America, see *Washington Evening Star*, January 30, 1938; *Overseas Trader* 4 (February 1938): 21–22; Thomas (NFTC) to Aranha, March 30, 1938, and Thomas to Pimentel Brandão, June 10, 1938, Aranha Papers.

74. Caffery to Aranha, April 4, 1938, AHI 420/5/5; Scotten to Bouças, January 14, 1938, Bouças Papers; memo on Caffery press interview, March 31, 1938, Caffery Papers; Caffery to State Dept., May 6, 1938, *FR, 1938*, V, 346–347.

75. Welles to missions in Latin America, January 8, 1938, SD 610.6231/64A; Duggan to Welles, March 3, 1938, SD, Office of American Republics, Brazil, II; Welles (for Hull) to Caffery, June 2, 1938, *FR, 1938*, V, 348; Scotten to Caffery, June 9, 1938, Caffery Papers.

76. State Dept. memo, March 21, 1938, SD 810.20/62; Stetson Conn and Byron Fairchild, *The Framework of Hemisphere Defense*, pp. 173–174.

77. Treasury memo, December 11, 1937, Morgenthau Diaries, 101:266, Morgenthau Papers; Morgenthau to Roosevelt, June 7, 1938, ibid., 168:203C–203D; Roosevelt to Welles, June 8, 1938, Roosevelt Papers, OF 21, Treasury Dept., 1938; Roosevelt to Morgenthau, June 10, 1938, Morgenthau Diaries, 168:203B, Morgenthau Papers.

78. State Dept. memoranda, August 20, 31, 1938, SD 632.6231/332,338; Roper to Roosevelt, September 1, 1938, Roosevelt Papers, PSF, Box 18.

79. Quoted in James M. Burns, *Roosevelt, The Lion and the Fox*, p. 388.

80. Harold L. Ickes, *The Secret Diary of Harold L. Ickes*, II, 484; Robert A. Divine, *The Illusion of Neutrality*, p. 231.

81. *New York Times*, October 16, 1938; Arthur Krock in *New York Times*, October 16, 1938; Warren Pierson, "Europe Threatens Trade in Americas," *New York Times*, October 30, 1938; NFTC, *Official Report . . . 1938*, pp. 68, 367, 369.

82. Morgenthau to Roosevelt, October 17, 1938, Roosevelt Papers, PSF, Morgenthau, 1938; Treasury staff memo, November 3, 1938, Morgenthau Diaries, 168:203H, Morgenthau Papers.

83. Morgenthau to Roosevelt, November 7, 1938, Morgenthau Diaries, 168:203L, Morgenthau Papers.

84. Morgenthau to Hull, November 1, 1938, SD 710.H Agenda/151; Morgenthau to Roosevelt, November 7, 1938, Morgenthau Diaries, 168:2031–203P, Morgenthau Papers.

85. Warren Pierson to Welles, November 9, 1938, SD 811.503132/24; Pimentel Brandão to Aranha, November 7, 1938, Aranha Papers; Pimentel Brandão to Vargas, September 14, 1938, Vargas Papers; Pimentel Brandão to Aranha, November 8, 1938, Aranha Papers.
86. Álvaro Teixeira Soares (Washington) to Aranha, October 18, 1938, Aranha Papers.
87. Vergara (for Vargas) to Pimentel Brandão, November 16, 1938, PR 48/26159.
88. Aranha to Welles, September 14, 1938, Aranha to Hull, November 3, 1938, and Aranha to Welles, November 8, 1938, Aranha Papers. An English translation of the last letter is annexed to Welles to Roosevelt, November 17, 1938, Roosevelt Papers, PSF, Box 29, Welles, 1938.
89. Welles to Aranha, November 29, 1938, Aranha Papers.
90. John M. Blum, *From the Morgenthau Diaries: Years of Urgency, 1938–1941*, p. 48.
91. Welles to Roosevelt, November 17, 1938, Roosevelt Papers, PSF, Box 29, Welles, 1938; Welles to Aranha, November 29, 1938, Aranha Papers; Financial Attaché Eurico Penteado (Washington) to Aranha, November 23, 25, 1938, Aranha Papers; Pimentel Brandão to Aranha, November 29, 1938, AHI 408/3/9; memo of conversation, November 29, 1938, Morgenthau Diaries, 207:18, Morgenthau Papers.
92. Souza Costa to Morgenthau, December 2, 1938, Morgenthau Diaries, 207:22–27, Morgenthau Papers; Aranha to Pimentel Brandão, November 29, 1938, Aranha Papers; Pimentel Brandão to Aranha, December 27, 1938, AHI 408/3/9.
93. Cordell Hull, *Memoirs*, I, 601–602.
94. T. R. Ybarra, "Door Open to U.S. in Latin America," *New York Times*, December 8, 1938. Cf. Joseph N. Baird, "The Trade Menace: How the Fascist Nations Hurt Us," *Washington Post*, December 4, 1938; Peter Kehss, "The Trade Putsch: Our Imperilled Latin-American Markets," *Washington Post*, December 18, 1938.
95. *Time*, December 12, 1938, p. 12; *Washington Post*, December 12, 1938; Hull, speech of December 10, 1938, State Dept. Press Release 594, SD 710.H/298; unsigned memo, December 13, 1938, Hull Papers.
96. Hull, *Memoirs*, I, 605–608.
97. Aranha to Vargas, March 27, 1939, Aranha Papers (folder: Missão Oswaldo Aranha); Welles to Scotten, January 9, 1939, *FR, 1939*, V, 348.
98. Quoted in Carroll Kilpatrick, ed., *Roosevelt and Daniels*, p. 183; J. Pierrepont Moffat Diary, July 24, 1939, J. Pierrepont Moffat Papers.
99. Breckinridge Long Diary, January 4, 6, 17, 25–26, 1939, Breckinridge Long Papers.
100. Quoted in Blum, *Morgenthau Diaries: Years of Urgency*, p. 51.
101. Treasury memo, February 1939, Morgenthau Diaries, 208:108, Morgen-

thau Papers; Kilpatrick, *Roosevelt and Daniels*, p. 182; Key Pittman, speech of February 20, 1939, *Congressional Record*, 76th Cong., 1st sess., vol. 84, pt. 2, p. 1398.

102. Unsigned memo ("Aparelhamento Ecônomico do Brasil"), n.d. [February 1939], Aranha Papers (folder: Missão Oswaldo Aranha).

103. Aranha to Vargas, February 9, 1939, Aranha Papers.

104. Aranha to Vargas, February 14, 1939, and Simões Lopes to Vargas, n.d., Vargas Papers.

105. *New York Times*, February 10, 1939.

106. *Washington Post*, February 10, 1939.

107. Memo of staff conversation, February 11, 1939, Morgenthau Diaries, 207:242, Morgenthau Papers; Aranha, speech of February 16, 1939, Aranha Papers; memo of conversation, February 17, 1939, Morgenthau Diaries, 208:4, Morgenthau Papers.

108. Memo of conversation, February 10, 1939, Morgenthau Diaries, 207:228, Morgenthau Papers; Ellis Briggs to Welles, February 14, 1939, SD, Office of American Republics, Brazil, II.

109. Morgenthau Diaries, February 10–12, 1939, 207:219, 233, 247, Morgenthau Papers; Aranha to Vargas, February 11, 1939, and Vargas to Aranha, February 24, 1939, Vargas Papers.

110. *Congressional Record*, 76th Cong., 1st sess., vol. 84, pt. 2, pp. 1398, 1683.

111. Ibid., p. 1697; Morgenthau Diaries, 208:282–284, Morgenthau Papers.

112. Aranha to Vargas, February 18, 21, 1939, and Vargas to Aranha, February 20, 1939, Vargas Papers; Coutinho, *General Góes Depõe*, pp. 357–358.

113. EME memo, January 21, 1939, EME; Aranha to Vargas, February 14, 1939, Vargas Papers.

114. Góes Monteiro to Dutra, June 10, 1939, EME.

115. Memo of conversation, March 8, 1939, Morgenthau Diaries, 208:286, Morgenthau Papers.

116. Hull to Aranha, March 9, 1939, and Aranha to Hull, March 8, 1939, *FR, 1939*, V, 352–353, 354.

117. Aranha to Hull, March 13, 1939, SD 033.3211 Aranha, Oswaldo/46; Aranha to Vargas, February 18, 1939, and Vargas to Aranha, February 24, 1939, Vargas Papers; Welles to Roosevelt (draft letter marked "not sent"), March 7, 1939, SD 832.51/1406½.

118. Caffery to Hull, April 22, 1939, SD 832.00/1255; *Correio da Manhã*, April 9, 1939, quoted in Dulles, *Vargas of Brazil*, p. 203.

119. Memo by Feis, March 22, 1939, SD 832.51/1446.

120. Vargas to Roosevelt, March 15, 1939, Roosevelt Papers, OF 11, Brazil 1933–1939; Caffery to State Dept., June 10, 1939, *FR, 1939*, V, 357; memo by Welles, July 5, 1939, SD 832; Caffery to State Dept., July 1, 1939, SD 832.51/1496.

121. Caffery to Hull, June 10, 1939, *FR, 1939*, V, 357; Aranha to J. Baptista

Lusardo, May 24, 1939, Aranha Papers.

122. *San Francisco Chronicle*, March 16, 1939. For similar comment, see *San Francisco Examiner*, March 10, 1939, *Chicago Daily Tribune*, March 10, 1939, and *Philadelphia Inquirer*, March 23, 1939.

123. *Congressional Record*, 76th Cong., 1st sess., vol. 84, pt. 3, pp. 2633–2634.

124. Letters to Berle, June 25–26, 1939, Hull Papers, 44/117; export manager, Omega Chemical Co. to editor, *Overseas Trader* 5 (April 1939): 4; Omega Chemical Co. to Berle, July 11, 1939, SD 832.5151/1419.

125. Memo by Feis, March 22, 1939, SD 832.51/1446; State Dept. memo, July 6, 1939, 832.51/1508½.

126. Drew Pearson to Aranha, July 14, 1939, Aranha Papers; memo of staff conversation, July 26, 1939, Morgenthau Diaries, p. 205, Morgenthau Papers.

127. Hull to Pittman, August 5, 1937, *FR, 1937*, V, 149.

128. German chargé (Washington) to Auswärtiges Amt, August 10, 1937, RGFM 3009:6495/486339; German naval attaché (Buenos Aires-Rio) to Naval Ministry, August 10, 1937, RGFM 3229:7788/559168; *Deutsche Diplomatisch-Politische Korrespondenz*, August 12, 1937.

129. Bestellungen aus der Pressekonferenz, August 16, 1937, Sammlung Brammer, Bundesarchiv ZSg. 101/10; von Levetzow to Auswärtiges Amt, August 14, 1937, RGFM 3009:6495/486295.

130. Von Levetzow to Auswärtiges Amt, August 19, 1937, RGFM 3009:6495/486294–295.

131. *Berliner Börsen-Zeitung*, May 4, 13, 1938; memo by Wiehl, June 18, 1938, RGFM 235:254/157012–014; U.S. embassy (Berlin) to State Dept., June 23, 1938, SD 632.6231/329; *Berliner Tageblatt*, July 6, 1938.

132. *Deutsche Allgemeine Zeitung*, July 14, 1938; von Levetzow to Auswärtiges Amt, October 18, 1938, RGFM 1624:3252/E000421–424.

133. Quoted in Otto Tolischus, "Reich Impressed By U.S. Arms Plan," *New York Times*, October 16, 1938.

134. Auswärtiges Amt to Missions in Latin America, October 4, 1938, RGFM 222:231/154964.

135. *Deutsche Diplomatisch-Politische Korrespondenz*, November 26, 1938.

136. Auswärtiges Amt memo, January 7, 1939, RGFM 222:231/155012–013.

137. Quoted in *New York Times*, January 31, 1939.

138. Von Levetzow to Auswärtiges Amt, January 17, 1939, RGFM 1624:3252/E000471.

139. Brazilian chargé (Berlin) to MRE, January 23, 1939, AHI 297/4/11.

140. Von Levetzow to Auswärtiges Amt, February 12, 1939, RGFM 235:254/157045; Chargé Hans Thomsen (Washington) to Auswärtiges Amt, February 21, 28, 1939, RGFM 235:254/157047, 157050; von Levetzow to Auswärtiges Amt, March 7, 1939, RGFM 1624:3252/E000475.

141. Memo by Becker, March 11, 1939, RGFM 222:231/155029–031.

142. Von Levetzow to Auswärtiges Amt, March 7, 1939, RGFM 1624:3252/
E000475; Wiehl to von Levetzow, March 28, 1939, RGFM 1624:3252/E000477.
143. Wiehl to von Levetzow, March 2, 1939, RGFM 222:231/155025–027;
Handelspolitischer Ausschuss Protokol, March 8, 1939, RGFM 3008:6483/
485701.
144. *Berliner Börsen-Zeitung*, June 16, 1939.
145. Aranha to Freitas-Valle, August 9, 1939, AHI 397/4/9.
146. Góes Monteiro to Dutra, August 11, 1939, EME.
147. Interview with Freitas-Valle, July 12, 1966; William L. Shirer, *The Rise
and Fall of the Third Reich*, pp. 519, 595.

7. Epilog: Brazil and the Great Powers at War

1. Lew B. Clark, "One Year of War, and United States Trade with Latin
America," *Foreign Commerce Weekly*, October 12, 1940, p. 47.
2. *Jornal do Commércio*, July 27, June 14, 1940.
3. Auswärtiges Amt to Prüfer, June 19, 1940, *DGFP, D*, IX, 630.
4. Prüfer to Auswärtiges Amt, June 21, 1940, *DGFP, D*, IX, 659; Auswärtiges
Amt (Ritter) to Prüfer, June 27, 1940, *DGFP, D*, X, 41.
5. Auswärtiges Amt to Prüfer, July 10, 1940, *DGFP, D*, X, 177–178.
6. Prüfer to Auswärtiges Amt, September 9, 1940, *DGFP, D*, X, 426 n.
7. Foreign Office minute, May 12, 1939, RFO 371, doc. A3181/539/6.
8. Foreign Office minute, September 23, 1938, RFO 371, doc. A7280/310/51;
Foreign Office to Gurney, January 19, 1939, RFO 371, doc. A447/447/6.
9. *Financial Times* (London), January 17, 1939.
10. *Financial News* (London), March 13, April 26, 1939; H. J. Lynch (Rio) to
N. M. Rothschild & Sons, May 19, 1939, RFO 371, doc. A3790/539/6.
11. Foreign Office to Board of Trade, November 15, 1939, RFO 371, doc.
A7933/3956/51.
12. Board of Trade to Foreign Office, December 18, 1939, RFO 371, doc.
A8930/539/6; Foreign Office memo, n.d. [January 8, 1940], RFO 371, doc.
A8177/18/51.
13. George Wythe, *Brazil: An Expanding Economy*, p. 314; J. Fred Rippy,
British Investments in Latin America, 1822–1949, p. 191.
14. Foreign Office memo, February 26, 1943, RFO 371, doc. A2230/348/51.
15. British embassy (Washington) to Foreign Office, October 22, 1943, RFO
371, doc. A10016/281/51.
16. CFCE, minutes, June 17, 1940, CFCE 150; head, Brazilian Economic
Mission, to Vargas, November 16, 1940, CFCE 91/1123.

17. Under sec't. of commerce to Roosevelt, November 27, 1939, Roosevelt Papers, PSF, Box 18, Commerce Dept.

18. *Chicago Tribune*, December 10, 1939.

19. Caffery to State Dept., May 17, 1939, SD 832.51/1463; Vargas to Martins, December 1, 1939, January 18, February 15, 1940, and Martins to Vargas, March 1, 1940, Vargas Papers.

20. Stanley E. Hilton, "The Welles Mission to Europe, February–March 1940: Illusion or Realism?" *Journal of American History* 58 (June 1971): 93–120.

21. Martins to Vargas, April 10, 1940, Vargas Papers.

22. Major Napoleão Alencastro Guimarães (New York) to Vargas, July 1, 1940, and Martins to Vargas, July 2, 1940, Vargas Papers.

23. Caffery to Hull, July 8, 16, 1940, *FR, 1940*, V, 608, 49–50.

24. Welles to federal loan administrator, August 7, 1940, *FR, 1940*, V, 609.

25. Hull to Caffery, September 25, 1940, *FR, 1940*, V, 612–613.

26. Stetson Conn and Byron Fairchild, *The Framework of Hemisphere Defense*, pp. 268, 302.

27. Góes Monteiro to Dutra, November 13, 1940, and Dutra to Vargas, November 20, 1940, EME.

28. Min. da Guerra, *Relatório . . . 1939*, p. 5.

29. V. Melo Franco to Souza Costa, February 22, 1943, V. Melo Franco Papers.

30. For a brief survey of Brazilian-American relations during the war, see John W. F. Dulles, *Vargas of Brazil*, pp. 206–244. A more detailed study is Frank D. McCann, *The Brazilian-American Alliance, 1937–1945*.

31. Gen. Firmo Freire to Vargas, February 27, 1943, PR 148/6615.

32. Freire to Vargas, July 20, 1944, PR 197/25284.

33. The law of November 1936, for example, provided an annual credit for the army of 1.5 million contos for ten years (Souza Costa to Vargas, secret memo no. 1124, August 1937, PR, Min. da Fazenda, Informações, 1937, vol.4). For official budget data, see League of Nations, *Armaments Year-Book 1936*, p. 110, and *1939/40*, p. 44. Calculation of actual military expenditures is virtually impossible without access to records of the Tribunal de Contas (author's conversation, June 18, 1969, with Rubens Rosa, former minister of the Tribunal and Aranha's *chefe de gabinete* during his tenure as minister of Finance, 1931–1933). In regard to the problem of determining real military budgets and the application of funds, the American military attaché once remarked that "manipulating allotments within the War Ministry, and every other executive department, is an elastic process with few restraints." He aptly noted, also, that "extraordinary allotments and secret funds also complicate the situation" (report to War Dept., January 10, 1938 WD file 2006–150/4).

34. Vergara (for Vargas) to Pimentel Brandão, November 16, 1938, PR 48/26159. For budget deficits during 1931–1945, see Anníbal V. Villela and Wilson Suzigan, *Política do governo e crescimento da economia brasileira, 1889–1945*, p. 57.

35. The phrase is Souza Aranha's. See his letter to Aranha, June 11, 1936, Aranha Papers.

36. CFCE, 94ª Sessão [May 18, 1936]; 95ª Sessão [May 25, 1936]; 96ª Sessão [June 1, 1936], PR 26/14832, 14830, 14828.

37. Gibson to State Dept., January 24, 1934, SD 832.00/876.

38. Vargas to Aranha, October 16, 1934, Aranha Papers.

39. A. Melo Franco to C. Melo Franco, April 19, October 11, 1935, V. Melo Franco Papers.

40. "A minha colaboração é mais pessoal do que funcional" (letter to Pimentel Brandão, November 29, 1938, Aranha Papers).

41. Bryce Wood, *The Making of the Good Neighbor Policy*, pp. 286–287.

42. Cordell Hull, *Memoirs*, I, 497.

43. State Dept. memo, February 18, 1939, *FR, 1939*, V, 228.

44. Hull, *Memoirs*, I, 497.

45. The phrase is Hull's (ibid., chapter 37).

46. Wythe, *Brazil: An Expanding Economy*, p. 313.

47. Aranha to Vargas, March 6, 1935, Aranha Papers.

Bibliography

Unpublished Sources

PRIVATE COLLECTIONS

Acioly, Hildebrando. Papers. Rio de Janeiro.
Aranha, Oswaldo. Papers. Rio de Janeiro.
Bouças, Valentim, Papers. Rio de Janeiro.
Collor, Lindolfo. Papers. Rio de Janeiro.
Klinger, Bertholdo. Papers. Rio de Janeiro.
Mangabeira, Otávio. Papers. Rio de Janeiro.
Melo Franco, Afonso Arinos de. Papers. Rio de Janeiro.
Melo Franco, Virgílio de. Papers. Rio de Janeiro.
Melo Franco Filho, Afrânio de. Papers. Rio de Janeiro.
Pessôa, Pantaleão da Silva. Papers. Rio de Janeiro.
Vargas, Getúlio. Papers. Rio de Janeiro.

OFFICIAL (PUBLIC) ARCHIVES

Archiv des Auswärtigen Amts. Bonn.
Arquivo da Marinha. Ministério da Marinha, Rio de Janeiro.
Arquivo do Conselho Federal de Comércio Exterior. Arquivo Nacional, Rio de Janeiro.
Arquivo do Estado-Maior do Exército. Ministério da Guerra, Rio de Janeiro.
Arquivo Histórico do Itamaraty. Palácio Itamaraty, Rio de Janeiro.
Board of Trade Records. Public Records Office, London.
Bundesarchiv. Koblenz.
Caffery, Jefferson. Papers. Southwestern Archive and Manuscripts Collection, University of Southwestern Louisiana, Lafayette, Louisiana.
Dodd, William E. Papers. Manuscript Division, Library of Congress, Washington, D.C.
Foreign Office. Records. Public Records Office, London.
German Foreign Ministry. Microfilmed Records. National Archives, Washington, D.C.
Gibson, Hugh. Papers. Hoover Institute, Stanford University, Stanford, California.

Hull, Cordell. Papers. Manuscript Division, Library of Congress, Washington, D.C.

Long, Breckinridge. Papers. Manuscript Division, Library of Congress, Washington, D.C.

Macedo Soares, José Carlos de. Coleção. Instituto Histórico e Geográfico Brasileiro, Rio de Janeiro.

Melo Franco, Afrânio de. Coleção. Seção de Manuscritos, Biblioteca Nacional, Rio de Janeiro.

Moffat, J. Pierrepont. Papers. Houghton Library, Harvard Library, Cambridge, Massachusetts.

Moore, R. Walton. Papers. Franklin D. Roosevelt Library, Hyde Park, New York.

Morgenthau, Henry J., Jr. Papers. Franklin D. Roosevelt Library, Hyde Park, New York.

Nazi Party. Microfilmed Records. National Archives, Washington, D.C.

Presidência da República. Coleção. Arquivo Nacional, Rio de Janeiro.

Roosevelt, Franklin D. Papers. Franklin D. Roosevelt Library, Hyde Park, New York.

Salgado Filho, Pedro. Coleção. Arquivo Nacional, Rio de Janeiro.

United States. Department of Commerce Files, Record Group 151. National Archives, Washington, D.C.

————. Department of State Files, Record Group 59. National Archives, Washington, D.C.

————. Department of War Files, Record Group 169. National Archives, Washington, D.C.

Published Sources

BOOKS AND ARTICLES

Amado, Gilberto. *Depois da Política*. Rio de Janeiro: Editôra José Olympio, 1960.

Amaral, Antônio José Azevedo. *O Brasil na Crise Actual*. Rio de Janeiro: Companha Editôra Nacional, 1934.

Anderson, C. Arnold, and Mary J. Bowman, eds. *Education and Economic Development*. Chicago: Aldine Publishing Co., 1965.

Anderson, Charles W. *Politics and Economic Change in Latin America*. Princeton: Van Nostrand, 1967.

Associação Commercial do Rio de Janeiro. *Boletim*, July 9, 1937.

Assumpção, Antonio G. "A obra revolucionária na atividade industrial paulista." *O Jornal* (Rio), May 2, 1935.

Bachrach, Peter, and Morton S. Baratz. "Decisions and Nondecisions: An

Analytical Framework." *American Political Science Review* 57 (September 1963), 632–642.

Baer, Werner. *Industrialization and Economic Development in Brazil.* Homewood, Ill.: Irwin, 1965.

Barroso, Gustavo. *Brasil: Colônia de Banqueiros.* 6th ed. Rio de Janeiro: Civilização Brasileira, 1937.

Blum, John M. *From the Morgenthau Diaries: Years of Crisis, 1928–1938.* Boston: Houghton Mifflin, 1959.

———. *From the Morgenthau Diaries: Years of Urgency, 1938–1941.* Boston: Houghton Mifflin, 1965.

Boulding, Kenneth E. "National Images and International Systems." *Journal of Conflict Resolution* 3 (June 1959): 120–131.

Brazil. Câmara dos Deputados. *Annaes.* 1935–1936. 55 vols. Rio de Janeiro: Imprensa Nacional, 1936–1937.

———. Conselho Federal de Comércio Exterior. *Dez Anos de Atividade.* Rio de Janeiro: Imprensa Nacional, 1944.

———. Estado de Rio Grande do Sul. *Annaes da Assembléa Legislativa . . . 1937.* 5 vols. Porto Alegre, 1937.

———. Estado-Maior do Exército. *Relatório.* 1933, 1935–1939. 6 vols. Rio de Janeiro, 1934–1940. [The volumes for 1938–1939 are typewritten. The others were published by the Imprensa Militar and were not intended for public distribution.]

———. Instituto Nacional de Estatística. *Anuario Estatístico do Brasil.* 1937, 1939–1940, 1941–1945. 3 vols. Rio de Janeiro: Imprensa Nacional, 1937–1946.

———. Ministério da Fazenda. Comisso de Estudos Financeiros e Econômicos dos Estados e Municipios. *Finanças dos Estados do Brasil, Volume I.* 3d ed. Rio de Janeiro: Imprensa Nacional, 1935.

———. ———. Serviço de Estatística Econômica e Financeira. *Comércio Exterior do Brasil.* 1931–1935, 1936–1940. 2 vols. Rio de Janeiro: Imprensa Nacional, 1936–1941.

———. Ministério da Guerra. *Relatório.* 1935–1940. 6 vols. Rio de Janeiro: Imprensa Militar, 1935–1940.

———. Ministério da Marinha. *Relatório.* 1932, 1934. 2 vols. Rio de Janeiro, 1932, 1934.

———. Ministério das Relações Exteriores. *Comércio Exterior do Brasil, 1937–1939.* Rio de Janeiro: Ministério das Relações Exteriores, Serviço de Publicações, 1940.

———. ———. *Relatório . . . 1931.* 2 vols. Rio de Janeiro: Ministério das Relações Exteriores, Serviço de Publicações, 1934.

Brunn, Gerhard. *Deutschland und Brasilien, 1880–1914.* Cologne: Böhlau, 1971.

Bullock, Alan. *Hitler: A Study in Tyranny.* Rev. ed. New York: Harcourt, Brace, 1956.

Burns, E. Bradford. *The Unwritten Alliance: Rio-Branco and Brazilian-American Relations*. New York: Columbia University Press, 1966.

Burns, James M. *Roosevelt: The Lion and the Fox*. New York: Harcourt, Brace, 1956.

Camargo, José Francisco. *Êxodo Rural no Brasil*. Rio de Janeiro, 1960.

———. "Recursos Humanos e Desenvolvimento." *Problemas Brasileiros* 7 (April 1969): 22–27.

Campos, Roberto de Oliveira. "A Retrospect over Brazilian Development Plans." In *The Economy of Brazil*, edited by Howard Ellis, pp. 317–344. Berkeley: University of California Press, 1969.

Castro Ayres, Miguel de. "O Brasil e Sua Defesa." *A Defesa Nacional* 25 (October 1938): 565–573.

———. *O Exército que eu vi (memórias)*. Rio de Janeiro: A. Coelho Branco, 1965.

Cesar, Roberto C. "As migrações internas." *O Estado de São Paulo*, October 18, 1970.

Ciano, Galeazzo. *Ciano's Diary, 1937–1938*. Translated by Andrea Mayor. London: Methuen, 1952.

Clark, Lew B. "One Year of War, and United States Trade with Latin America." *Foreign Commerce Weekly*, October 12, 1940, pp. 47–48, 50.

Cline, Howard, ed. *Latin American History: Essays on Its Study and Teaching*. 2 vols. Austin: University of Texas Press, 1967.

Cole, Francis T. "Review of 1935 American Trade." *Overseas Trader* 2 (April 1936): 107–118.

Conn, Stetson, and Byron Fairchild. *The Framework of Hemisphere Defense*. Washington, D.C.: Department of the Army, 1960.

Cornelius, Carl. *Die Deutschen im brasilianischen Wirtschaftsleben*. Stuttgart: Ausland und Heimat Verlagsaktiengesellschaft, 1929.

Cortes, Carlos E. "The Role of Rio Grande do Sul in Brazilian Politics, 1930–1967." Ph.D. dissertation, University of New Mexico, 1969.

Costa, João Cruz. *A History of Ideas in Brazil*. Translated by Suzette Macedo. Berkeley: University of California Press, 1964.

Coutinho, Lourival, ed. *O General Góes Depõe . . .* Rio de Janeiro: A. Coelho Branco, 1958.

Daland, Robert. *Brazilian Planning: Development Politics and Administration*. Chapel Hill: University of North Carolina Press, 1967.

Dantas, Marcos Souza. "História Verdadeira dos 'Marcos de Compensação'" *Correio da Manhã* (Rio), July 1, 1937.

Dean, Edwin. "Noneconomic Barriers to Effective Planning in Nigeria, 1962–1966." *Economic Development and Cultural Change* 19 (July 1971): 560–579.

Dean, Warren K. *The Industrialization of São Paulo, 1880–1945*. Austin: University of Texas Press, 1969.

Deursen, Henri von. "L'émancipation industrielle du Brésil: Caractères et développement de l'industrie dans l'état de Sao-Paulo." *Revue Economique Internationale* 26 (August 1934): 275–336.

Deutsch, Karl W., ed. *France, Germany and the Western Alliance: A Study of Elite Attitudes on European Integration and World Politics*. New York: Scribner, 1967.

Deutsch-Brasilianische Handelskammer. *Bericht über das Jahr 1935*. Rio de Janeiro, 1936.

Divine, Robert A. *The Illusion of Neutrality*. Chicago: University of Chicago Press, 1962.

Dodd, Martha, and William E. Dodd, Jr., eds. *Ambassador Dodd's Diary, 1933–1938*. London: V. Gollancz, 1952.

Drummond, Donald F. "Cordell Hull." In *An Uncertain Tradition: American Secretaries of State in the Twentieth Century*, edited by Norman A. Graebner, pp. 184–209. New York: McGraw-Hill, 1961.

Dulles, John W. F. *Vargas of Brazil: A Political Biography*. Austin: University of Texas Press, 1967.

Ebel, Arnold. *Das Dritte Reich und Argentinien*. Cologne: Böhlau, 1971.

Ellis, Howard, ed. *The Economy of Brazil*. Berkeley: University of California Press, 1969.

Federação das Indústrias do Estado de São Paulo. *A situação econômica da América Latina e suas possibilidades em face do Plano Marshall*. São Paulo, 1948.

Flaschbart, G. "O commercio teuto-brasileiro, 1822–1922." In *O Brasil e a Allemanha, 1822–1922*, edited by Alfred Funke, pp. 73–84. Berlin: Editora Internacional, 1923.

Frye, Alton. *Nazi Germany and the American Hemisphere, 1933–1941*. New Haven: Yale University Press, 1967.

Funke, Alfred, ed. *O Brasil e a Allemanha, 1822–1922*. Berlin: Editora Internacional, 1923.

Gardner, Lloyd C. *Economic Aspects of New Deal Diplomacy*. Madison: University of Wisconsin Press, 1964.

Gauld, Charles A. *The Last Titan: Percival Farquhar*. Palo Alto: Stanford University Press, 1968.

Gilbert, Martin, and Richard Gott. *The Appeasers*. London: Weidenfeld, 1963.

Graham, Lawrence. *Civil Service Reform in Brazil*. Austin: University of Texas Press, 1968.

Graham, Richard. *Britain and the Onset of Modernization in Brazil*. New York: Cambridge University Press, 1972.

Great Britain. Department of Overseas Trade. *Economic Conditions in Brazil*. 1932, 1935–1936. 3 vols. London: His Majesty's Stationery Office, 1933, 1935–1936.

———. ———. *Economic Conditions in Germany to March 1936* . . . London: His Majesty's Stationery Office, 1936.

Grinspoon, Lester. "Inter-Personal Constraints and the Decision-Maker." In

International Conflict and Behavioral Science, edited by Roger D. Fisher, pp. 238–247. New York: Basic Books, 1964.

Gross, Feliks. *Foreign Policy Analysis.* New York: Philosophical Library, 1954.

Grunwald, Joseph. "Some Reflections on Latin American Industrialization Policy." *Journal of Political Economy* 78 (supplement to July–August 1970): 826–856.

Gudin, Eugenio. "O problema nacional da urbanização e as deseconomias de escala." *O Globo* (Rio), April 22, 1974.

Guillebaud, C. W. *The Economic Recovery of Germany from 1933 to the Incorporation of Austria in March 1938.* London: Macmillan & Co., 1939.

Harms-Baltzer, Käte. *Die Nationalisierung der deutschen Einwanderer und ihrer Nachkommen in Brasilien als Problem der deutsch-brasilianischen Beziehungen, 1930–1938.* Berlin: Colloquium Verlag, 1970.

Hauser, Philip M. "Cultural and Personal Obstacles to Economic Development in the Less Developed Areas." *Human Organization* 18 (Summer 1959): 78–84.

Havighurst, Robert J., and J. R. Moreira. *Society and Education in Brazil.* Pittsburgh: University of Pittsburgh Press, 1965.

Higgins, Benjamin. *Economic Development: Problems, Principles and Policies.* Rev. ed. New York: W. W. Norton, 1968.

Hill, Lawrence F. *Diplomatic Relations between the United States and Brazil.* Durham: Duke University Press, 1932.

Hilton, Stanley E. "*Ação Integralista Brasileira*: Fascism in Brazil, 1932–1938." *Luso-Brazilian Review* 9 (December 1972): 3–29.

———. "Military Influence on Brazilian Economic Policy, 1930–1945: A Different View." *Hispanic American Historical Review* 53 (February 1973): 71–94.

———. "The Welles Mission to Europe, February–March 1940: Illusion or Realism?" *Journal of American History* 58 (June 1971): 93–120.

Hirschman, Albert O. *Journeys toward Progress: Studies of Economic Policy-Making in Latin America.* New York: Greenwood Press, 1963.

Holanda, Sergio Buarque de. *Raizes do Brasil.* Rio de Janeiro: José Olympio, 1936.

Huber, John R. "The Effects of German Clearing Agreements and Import Restrictions on Cotton, 1934–1939." *Southern Economic Journal* 6 (April 1940): 419–439.

Hull, Cordell. *Memoirs.* 2 vols. New York: Macmillan Co., 1948.

Ickes, Harold L. *The Secret Diary of Harold L. Ickes.* 3 vols. New York: Simon and Schuster, 1953–1954.

Inter-American Conference for the Maintenance of Peace. *Proceedings.* Buenos Aires: Imprensa del Congreso Nacional, 1937.

International Military Tribunal. *Trials of War Criminals before the Nuremberg Military Tribunals . . . Vol. XII.* Washington, D.C.: Government Printing Office, 1951.

Jaguaribe, Helio. *Economic and Political Development: A Theoretical Approach and a Brazilian Case Study.* Cambridge, Mass.: Harvard University Press, 1968.

Janis, Irving L. "Decisional Conflicts: A Theoretical Analysis." *Journal of Conflict Resolution* 3 (March 1959): 6–27.

Johnson, Franklin. "Brazil." *American Exporter* 118 (February 1936): 15–19, 58, 60.

Johnson, John J., ed. *The Role of the Military in Underdeveloped Countries.* Princeton: Princeton University Press, 1962.

Johnston, Bruce F., and John W. Mellor. "The Role of Agriculture in Economic Development." *American Economic Review* 51 (September 1961): 566–593.

Kiker, B. F. "The Historical Roots of the Concept of Human Capital." *Journal of Political Economy* 74 (October 1966): 481–499.

Kilpatrick, Carroll, ed. *Roosevelt and Daniels: A Friendship in Politics.* Chapel Hill: University of North Carolina Press, 1952.

Klinger, Bertholdo. *Parada e Desfile de Uma Vida Militar.* Rio de Janeiro: Emprêsa Gráfica "O Cruzeiro," 1958.

Kroll, Gerhard. *Von der Weltwirtschaftskrise zur Staatskonjunktur.* Berlin: Duncker und Humboldt, 1958.

Kroll, Hans. *Lebenserinnerungen eines Botschafters.* Berlin: Kiepenheuer und Witsch, 1967.

La Belle, Thomas J., ed. *Education and Economic Development: Latin America and the Caribbean.* Los Angeles: Latin American Center, University of California, 1972.

Lampert, Francis. "Trends in Administrative Reform in Brazil." *Journal of Latin American Studies* 1 (November 1969): 167–188.

League of Nations. *Armaments Year-Book.* 1936, 1939–1940. 2 vols. Geneva, 1936, 1940.

Lebret, R. C. "Business is Good in South America and Getting Better." *Export Trade and Shipper,* July 13, 1936, pp. 3–4.

Leeds, Anthony. "Brazilian Careers and Social Structure: An Evolutionary Model and Case History." *American Anthropologist* 66 (December 1964): 1321–1347.

Leff, Nathaniel. *Economic Policy-Making and Development in Brazil, 1947–1964.* New York: Wiley, 1968.

——. "Long-Term Brazilian Economic Development." *Journal of Economic History* 29 (September 1969): 473–493.

Leite, [?] Costa, and [?] Lyra Madeira. "Salário Mínimo." *Boletim do Ministério de Trabalho, Indústria e Comércio* 1 (September 1934): 237–243.

Levine, Robert M. *The Vargas Regime: The Critical Years, 1934–1938.* New York: Columbia University Press, 1970.

McCann, Frank D. "Brazil and the United States and the Coming of World War II." Ph.D. dissertation, Indiana University, 1967.

————. *The Brazilian-American Alliance, 1937–1945*. Princeton: Princeton University Press, 1973.

————. "Vargas and the Destruction of the Brazilian Integralista and Nazi Parties." *The Americas* 26 (July 1969): 15–34.

Macedo Soares, José Carlos de. *Discursos*. Rio de Janeiro: Editôra José Olympio, 1937.

Machlup, Fritz. *Education and Economic Growth*. Lincoln: University of Nebraska Press, 1970.

Macrae, John. "The Relationship between Agricultural and Industrial Growth, with Special Reference to the Development of the Punjab Economy from 1950 to 1965." *Journal of Development Studies* 7 (July 1971): 397–422.

Manchester, Alan K. *British Preëminence in Brazil: Its Rise and Decline*. Chapel Hill: University of North Carolina Press, 1933.

Melo Franco, Afonso Arinos de. *Um Estadista da República*. 3 vols. Rio de Janeiro: José Olympio, 1955.

Metz, Henry L. "Growing Up Now." *Overseas Trader* 3 (April 1937): 8–10.

Miller, Douglas. *Via Diplomatic Pouch*. New York: Didier, 1944.

Moog, Clodomir Viana. *Bandeirantes and Pioneers*. Translated by L. L. Barrett. New York: G. Braziller, 1964.

Morse, Richard M. "Language as a Key to Latin American Historiography." In *Latin American History: Essays on Its Study and Teaching*, edited by Howard F. Cline, pp. 656–668. 2 vols. Austin: University of Texas Press, 1967.

Moschini, Felipe Nery. "Éxodo e Urbanização." *Problemas Brasileiros* 9 (March 1972): 21–38.

Nabuco, Carolina. *A vida de Virgílio de Melo Franco*. Rio de Janeiro: José Olympio, 1962.

Nafziger, E. Wayne. "The Relationship between Education and Entrepreneurship in Nigeria." *Journal of Developing Areas* 4 (April 1970): 349–360.

Nash, Manning. "Social Prerequisites to Economic Growth in Latin America and Southeast Asia." *Economic Development and Cultural Change* 12 (April 1964): 225–242.

National Foreign Trade Council. *Official Report . . . 1934–1938*. 5 vols. New York: National Foreign Trade Council, 1935–1939.

Neven du Mont, Mark. "A cooperação do trabalho alemão na indústria brasileira." In *O Brasil e a Allemanha, 1822–1922*, edited by Alfred Funke, pp. 149–156. Berlin :Editora Internacional, 1923.

Nixon, Edgar, ed. *Franklin D. Roosevelt and Foreign Affairs*. 3 vols. Cambridge, Mass.: Harvard University Press, 1969.

Offner, Arnold A. *American Appeasement: United States Foreign Policy and Germany, 1933–1938*. Cambridge, Mass.: Harvard University Press, 1969.

Ohkawa, Kazushi, and Henry Rosovsky. "The Role of Agriculture in Modern Japanese Economic Development." *Economic Development and Cultural Change* 9 (October 1960): 43–68.

Parks, Richard W. "The Role of Agriculture in Mexican Economic Development." *Inter-American Economic Affairs* 18 (Summer 1964): 3–28.

Peaslee, Alexander L. "Education's Role in Development." *Economic Development and Cultural Change* 17 (April 1969): 293–318.

Peixoto, Alzira Vargas do Amaral. *Getúlio Vargas, meu Pai*. Porto Alegre: Editora Globo, 1960.

Peláez, Carlos M. *História da Industrialização Brasileira*. Rio de Janeiro: APEC, 1972.

———. "Itabira Iron and the Export of Brazil's Iron Ore." *Revista Brasileira de Economia* 24 (October–December 1970): 157–174.

Pessôa, Pantaleão da Silva. *Reminiscências e Imposições de uma Vida*. Rio de Janeiro: Privately published, 1972.

Pimpão, Hirosê. *Getúlio Vargas e o direito social trabalhista*. Rio de Janeiro: Gráfica Guarany, 1942.

Pisani, Salvatore. *Lo Stato di San Paolo nel Cinquantenario dell' Immigrazione*. São Paulo: Typografia Napoli, 1937.

Protsch, [?] von. "Deutschbrasilianische Schulen und Deutsche Gesandtschaft." *Mitteilungsblatt der NSDAP Ortsgruppe Rio de Janeiro* 6 (November 1932): 17–18.

Rangel, Alberto. *No rolar do tempo (opiniões e testemunhos respigados no archivo do Orsay-Paris)*. Rio de Janeiro: José Olympio, 1937.

Rippy, J. Fred. *British Investments in Latin America, 1822–1949*. Minneapolis: University of Minnesota Press, 1959.

Rivera, Joseph de. *The Psychological Dimension of Foreign Policy*. Columbus, O.: C. E. Merrill, 1968.

Robertson, E. M. *Hitler's Pre-War Policy and Military Plans, 1933–1939*. New York: Citadel Press, 1967.

Rodrigues, José Honório. *The Brazilians: Their Character and Aspirations*. Translated by Ralph E. Dimick. Austin: University of Texas Press, 1967.

Rogers, Edward J. "Brazilian Success Story: The Volta Redonda Iron and Steel Project." *Journal of Inter-American Studies* 10 (October 1968): 637–652.

Roper, Daniel. *Fifty Years of Public Life*. Durham: Duke University Press, 1941.

Rosenberg, Alfred. *Das politische Tagebuch Alfred Rosenbergs aus den Jahren 1934/35 und 1939/40*. Edited by Hans-Günther Seraphim. Göttingen: Musterschmidt-Verlag, 1956.

Santos, John F. "A Psychologist Reflects on Brazil and Brazilians." In *New Perspectives of Brazil*, edited by Eric N. Baklanoff, pp. 233–263. Nashville: Vanderbilt University Press, 1966.

Schacht, Hjalmar. *76 Jahre meines Lebens*. Bad Wörishofen: Kindler und Schiermeyer, 1953.

Schröder, Hans-Jürgen. *Deutschland und die Vereinigten Staaten, 1933–1939*. Wiesbaden: F. Steiner, 1970.

Schultz, T. W. "Investment in Human Capital." *American Economic Review* 51 (March 1961): 1–17.

Schweitzer, Arthur. *Big Business in the Third Reich*. Bloomington: Indiana University Press, 1964.

Scott, Robert E., ed. *Latin American Modernization Problems*. Urbana: University of Illinois Press, 1973.

Shirer, William L. *The Rise and Fall of the Third Reich*. New York: Simon and Schuster, 1960.

Silva, Benedicto. "O café brasileiro e a ameaça crescente da concorrência." *Revista do Departamento Nacional do Café* 3 (January 1936): 21–26.

———. "A cooperação inter-administrativa na estatística brasileira." *Boletim do Ministério de Trabalho, Indústria e Commércio* 3 (February 1937): 309–322.

Silva, Hélio. *1931: Os Tenentes no Poder*. Rio de Janeiro: Civilização Brasileira, 1966.

———. *1938: Terrorismo em Campo Verde*. Rio de Janeiro: Civilização Brasileira, 1971.

Simonsen, Roberto. *As Crises no Brasil*. São Paulo: São Paulo Editôra, 1930.

———. *Aspects of National Political Economy*. São Paulo, 1935.

Sjoberg, Gideon. "Rural-Urban Balance and Models of Economic Development." In *Social Structure and Mobility in Economic Development*, edited by Neil J. Smelser and Seymour M. Lipset, pp. 235–261. Chicago: Aldine Publishing Co., 1966.

Skidmore, Thomas E. "Failure in Brazil: From Popular Front to Armed Revolt." *Journal of Contemporary History* 5 (1970): 137–157.

———. *Politics in Brazil, 1930–1964: An Experiment in Democracy*. New York: Oxford University Press, 1967.

Smelser, Neil J., and Seymour M. Lipset, eds. *Social Structure and Mobility in Economic Development*. Chicago: Aldine Publishing Co., 1966.

Smith, H. G. "Cotton Trends in Latin America." *Commercial Pan America*, no. 56 (January 1937), pp. 1–17.

———. "German Trade Competition in Latin America." *Commercial Pan America*, no. 53 (October 1936), pp. 1–12.

Smith, Peter H. *Politics and Beef in Argentina*. New York: Columbia University Press, 1969.

Snyder, Richard, ed. *Foreign Policy Decision Making*. New York: Free Press of Glencoe, 1962.

Stein, Stanley J. *The Brazilian Cotton Manufacture: Textile Enterprise in an Underdeveloped Area, 1850–1950*. Cambridge, Mass.: Harvard University Press, 1957.

Stemmler, M. "Der Luftverkehr nach Südamerika im Dienste des Aussenhandels." *Der Deutsche im Auslande* 7, no. 22 (July 1934): 150.

Tipper, Harry. "Germany." *Overseas Trader* 3 (August 1937): 16–18.

————. "Report on General Activities of AMEA for the Year 1935." *Overseas Trader* 2 (January 1936):8–10.

Treue, Wilhelm. "Hitlers Denkschrift zum Vierjahresplan 1936." *Vierteljahreshefte für Zeitgeschichte* 2 (April 1955): 184–210.

United States. Department of Commerce. Bureau of Foreign and Domestic Commerce. *Citrus Fruits: World Production and Trade*. Washington, D.C.: Government Printing Office, 1940.

————. Department of State. *Documents on German Foreign Policy, 1918–1945, Series C, The Third Reich: First Phase*. 5 vols. Washington, D.C.: Government Printing Office, 1957–1966.

————. ————. *Documents on German Foreign Policy, 1918–1945, Series D, 1937–1941*. 13 vols. Washington, D.C.: Government Printing Office, 1957–1964.

————. ————. *Foreign Relations of the United States, 1933–1940*. 39 vols. Washington, D.C.: Government Printing Office, 1950–1961.

————. Tariff Commission. *Economic Controls and Commercial Policy in Brazil*. Washington, D.C.: Government Printing Office, 1945.

Valla, Victor. *Os Estados Unidos e a Influência Estrangeira na Economia Brasileira: Um Período de Transição, 1904–1928*. São Paulo, 1972.

Vandendries, René. "Internal Migration and Economic Development in Peru." In *Latin American Modernization Problems*, edited by Robert E. Scott, pp. 193–208. Urbana: University of Illinois Press, 1973.

Vargas, Getúlio. *Ideário Político*. Edited by Raul Guastini. São Paulo, 1943.

————. *A Nova Política do Brasil*. 11 vols. Rio de Janeiro: Editôra José Olympio, 1938–1947.

Vergara, Luiz. *Fui Secretário de Getúlio Vargas: Memórias dos anos 1926–1954*. Porto Alegre: Editôra Globo, 1960.

Villela, Anníbal V., and Wilson Suzigan. *Política do governo e crescimento da economia brasileira, 1889–1945*. Rio de Janeiro: INPES, 1973.

Wagley, Charles. *An Introduction to Brazil*. New York: Columbia University Press, 1963.

Weinberg, Gerhard L. *The Foreign Policy of Hitler's Germany*. Chicago: University of Chicago Press, 1970.

Weyl, Nathaniel. "Swastika over Brazil." *The Nation*, November 13, 1937, pp. 528–530.

Wirth, John D. *The Politics of Brazilian Development, 1930–1954*. Palo Alto: Stanford University Press, 1969.

Wood, Bryce. "External Restraints on the Good Neighbor Policy." *Inter-American Economic Affairs* 16 (Autumn 1962):3–24.

————. *The Making of the Good Neighbor Policy*. New York: Columbia University Press, 1961.

Wykstra, Ronald A. "Economic Development and Human Capital Formation." *Journal of Developing Areas* 3 (July 1969): 527–538.

Wythe, George. *Brazil: An Expanding Economy*. New York: Twentieth Century Fund, 1949.

NEWSPAPERS AND JOURNALS

American Anthropologist
American Economic Review
American Exporter
American Political Science Review
Americas
Anglo-Brazilian Chronicle (Rio)
Der Angriff (Berlin)
Berliner Börsen-Zeitung
Berliner Tageblatt
Boletim do Ministério de Trabalho, Indústria e Comércio
Boston Post
Brazilian Business
Chicago Daily Tribune
Commercial Pan America
Correio da Manhã (Rio)
A Defesa Nacional
Deutsche Allgemeine Zeitung (Berlin)
Deutsche Diplomatisch-Politische Korrespondenz (Berlin)
Der Deutsche im Auslande
Diário Carioca (Rio)
Diário da Noite (Rio)
Diário de Notícias (Rio)
Diário de São Paulo
Economic Development and Cultural Change
Economist (London)
O Estado de São Paulo
Export Trade and Shipper
A Federação (Porto Alegre)
Financial News (London)
Financial Times (London)
Folha da Manhã (São Paulo)
Foreign Commerce Weekly
Frankfurter Zeitung
Gazeta de Notícias (Rio)
Il Giornale d'Italia (Rome)
O Globo (Rio)
Herald Tribune (New York)
Hispanic American Historical Review

Human Organization
Inter-American Economic Affairs
O Jornal (Rio)
Jornal do Brasil (Rio)
Jornal do Commércio (Rio)
Journal of American History
Journal of Contemporary History
Journal of Conflict Resolution
Journal of Developing Areas
Journal of Development Studies
Journal of Economic History
Journal of Inter-American Studies
Journal of Latin American Studies
Journal of Political Economy
Il Lavoro Fascista (Rome)
Luso-Brazilian Review
Mitteilungsblatt der NSDAP Ortsgruppe Rio de Janeiro
A Nação (Rio)
Nation
Newsweek
New York Times
A Noite (Rio)
A Nota (Rio)
O Observador Econômico e Financeiro
Overseas Trader
A Pátria (Rio)
Philadelphia Enquirer
Problemas Brasileiros
Revista Brasileira de Economia
Revista do Departamento Nacional do Café
Revista Militar e Naval
Revue Economique Internationale
San Francisco Chronicle
San Francisco Examiner
Saint Louis Globe-Democrat
Southern Economic Journal
Tea and Coffee Trade Journal
Times (London)
Washington Evening Star
Washington Post
Wochenbericht des Instituts für Konjunkturforschung

Index